6

ESTHER: THE AUTOBIOGRAPHY

Esther Rantzen is a household name, thanks to her tireless charity work and 21 years spent presenting *That's Life!* Her humour and energy shone through the programme as she exposed corporate wrongdoings, and played host to a dog that could growl 'sausages'. From there Esther set up ChildLine, the trail-blazing children's charity. Her meteoric rise to become one of the most powerful women in television has paved the way for other women within the profession. *Esther—The Autobiography* is a candid and fascinating account of her life, loves and passions. Esther reveals her pain as her family struggled to cope with serious illnesses and shares her joy at her fulfilling marriage with broadcaster Desmond Wilcox. Here, for the first time, Esther tells us about her life in front of and behind the camera.

ESTHER: THE AUTOBIOGRAPHY

Esther Rantzen

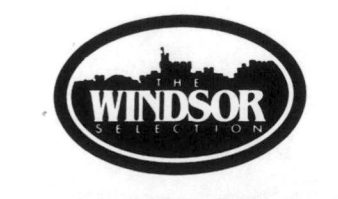

CHIVERS PRESS
BATH

First published 2001
by
BBC Worldwide
This Large Print edition published by
Chivers Press
by arrangement with
BBC Worldwide Limited
2001

ISBN 0 7540 1634 X

British Library Cataloguing in Publication Data available

Printed and bound in Great Britain by
BOOKCRAFT, Midsomer Norton, Somerset

For Desmond

CONTENTS

PREFACE

*For the triumph of evil, it is only necessary
that good men do nothing.*
EDMUND BURKE

Writing this book has been an adventure for me. 'If only . . .' may be the two most pointless words in the English language, but I couldn't resist them when I started to look back over my life.

If only I had known what lay in store, that the dreams I never dared dream really would come true, how much anxiety I could have saved myself. I never thought anyone could possibly fall in love with the dumpy, over-exuberant brunette I was. But Desmond did. I had no idea that a spinster of thirty-seven could still have three gorgeous children, but somehow it happened. I would never have believed that someone so clumsy, with such peculiar teeth and such a vulgar predilection for puns could possibly have a career on television, but I have. And most wondrous of all, though I hoped, I never dared expect that Emily, my oldest daughter, would battle successfully against the paralyzing illness that assailed her, until she finally got out of her wheelchair and walked.

So let me draw a moral from the life you are about to read about. Beware Rantzen's Rule: *If you want something enough, you will get it. But you will get it so long after you've given up hope that you won't remember why you wanted it.*

I longed for a job that would totally absorb me, that I would think about day and night, and that would run me ragged. I got it. I wanted a family I would love and live for, and I have one. But there is a price to pay for both. Sometimes the job shakes me, like a bull-dog shaking a rag doll. Sometimes my family breaks my heart, as, for instance, when Desmond died while I was writing this book. Only the memory of his constant encouragement forced me to finish it, as I remembered him urging me to 'push through the pain.'

In this I have been wonderfully helped and encouraged. The list is too long for me to encompass in this brief preface. But I must thank first of all my family—my late father Harry, my mother Katherine and my sister Priscilla, my children, Emily, Rebecca and Joshua, and my extended family of aunts, uncles and cousins.

In the world of broadcasting I must thank the BBC, who trained me and gave me extraordinary challenges and opportunities. They commissioned this book, and I must especially thank Nick Brett, Sally Potter, Helena Caldon, Linda Blakemore, Miriam Hyman and Barbara Nash who gave me confidence and spurred me on.

My friends Bryher, (the last, and one of the best Editors of *That's Life!*) and Paul Scudamore, Shaun and Camilla Woodward, Patsy Newey, Richard Woolfe, Adrian Mills, Lynda Wood and a secret society called the Hamsters have all given me love, laughter and many hours of happiness.

Sue Santaub and Claire Skinner are the props without whom my life would have collapsed into a tangle long ago, and in thanking them, I also thank Julia Marshall, Jan Booth, and generations of wonderful assistants who preceded them. Jan Kennedy, Luigi Bonomi and Alex Armitage have represented me over the years, sighing patiently when I have yet again put my foot firmly into my mouth. Every programme I have worked on, both in the BBC and Meridian Broadcasting had teams of people whose company I enjoyed, and whose skills I depended upon.

Then there are the charities. I cannot describe how much I have learned from the dedicated staff of so many different organisations, whose work has displayed incredible commitment. I would especially like to thank the ChildLine team. We have weathered many storms together, and the fact that we have now counselled well over one million children is directly attributable to their skill. On behalf of those desperate children who had nowhere else to turn, I must thank them.

I began this preface with my favourite quotation from Edmund Burke. I was brought up during the Second World War, when evil triumphed over so many countries in the world. But there were good men and women who took action to defeat it. Thank God for them.

So here goes—what follows is a story which reveals almost all my warts, though I do admit to the occasional fig-leaf to protect the innocent. You will pick your way, as I did, between rows and prat-falls, but I hope you find as much to amuse you as I did at the time.

Finally I must express my gratitude to all the viewers who watched the programmes, (and who let me know what they thought of them, often very bluntly), to the readers who have bought this book, and most of all, to the millions of generous people who have supported ChildLine over the years. Thank you.

CHAPTER ONE

ANOTHER AGE

Nobody told my mother the facts of life. That is, nobody until her older sister married, and discovered them from her bridegroom on their wedding night. My Aunt Nancy, a steady, warm woman who was one of my closest friends, told me that looking back she cannot now understand why none of the four sisters guessed how human beings reproduce. But I understand.

My mother and her sisters belonged to a world which today would seem prim and repressed, and where rules were unquestioned. It was a matter of good manners and propriety. I grew up with stories of that land 'before the war' throughout my own wartime childhood. Now I know there was wickedness, too, 'before the war', and decadence in the roaring twenties, and even sex. The depression created extreme poverty across the country. But the respectable middle classes were, for the most part, cushioned from all that.

What my mother described to me with wistful nostalgia was safe and comfortable. Rationed as we were in the 1940s to one egg per person per week, and a smidgen of butter, my mother described her memories before the war of feathery sponge cakes and cream-filled meringues, of dinner parties every week in her parents' house (my grandmother was 'At Home' each Wednesday), and unlimited staff—a cook and a kitchen maid, a parlour maid and a chauffeur.

1

My grandparents lived in a tall brick house in Hampstead, filled with staff. My grandfather, Louis, made a very comfortable living from importing the best cigar tobacco. His ability to judge the quality of a leaf in the tobacco auctions in Africa was legendary. My grandmother, Emily, had a beautiful collection of diamonds, emeralds, sapphires and rubies. Her daughters remember how wonderful she looked in evening dress when she came in to them to say goodnight. She was among the first to swap a horse and carriage for a car, although her chauffeur was still inclined to say 'Whoa' when he was teaching my aunts to drive.

I never knew Grandpa Louis Leverson [I have two distinguished Leverson relatives I often boast about: writer Ada Leverson (Oscar Wilde's friend whom he called 'the sphinx') and the composer Gerald Finzi.]—he died when I was four. I have a memory of a white-haired old man with a stick, coughing into paper handkerchiefs and throwing them on the grass. My baby sister Priscilla used to crawl after him and retrieve them, like an eager puppy.

My grandmother, eighteen years younger than her husband, was a tremendous influence in my life. 'Milly', as she was always called, was kind, and loving, and humorous. She had the gift of making every day a treat. She taught me intricate Victorian games of Patience, and music-hall songs, 'Any Old Iron', 'Knocked 'em in the Old Kent Road', 'Pretty Polly Perkins of Paddington Green'. She enchanted generations of children in the family by turning a handkerchief into a mouse, and making it leap up her arm. When, in her old age, she had a cataract operation in Moorfields Hospital, London, all the

2

children in the ward would cluster round her while she recited poems and told them stories. I can still remember great chunks of Lewis Carroll, 'The Walrus and the Carpenter', 'Jabberwocky', 'You Are Old, Father William'.

My grandmother loved children. But I believe that I, as her granddaughter, saw more of her than her own daughters did when they were young. The four girls were brought up by nannies and under-nannies, and my mother, Katherine, and her sisters, Nancy and Jane, were sent away to school, Cheltenham Ladies' College and Roedean. It was not a spoiled childhood. Katherine and Nancy, for example, were invited to a fancy-dress party, and went as the little princes in the tower, in curling blonde wigs and velvet suits. They implored their parents to let them keep their costumes afterwards, but my grandparents, who could well have afforded to buy them, refused.

When they grew up the girls were put on ferociously strict allowances. When my mother was a student at art school she could only afford an apple for lunch, and used to walk home across Regent's Park because she had not enough money for the bus fare. My grandfather left a good deal of money when he died, but tied it up in a trust to protect his daughters. From what? Their own wild extravagance? Spendthrift husbands? Since they inherited his puritan sense of economy, the protection was quite unnecessary. And it led to my father being deeply troubled about money when I was young. Clearly, my grandparents believed money was dangerous. So, perhaps, they thought sex was also dangerous, and protected their daughters by pretending it didn't exist.

3

I have pictures of my mother, Katherine, as a child. All four sisters were extremely pretty— Katherine at eighty-nine still is. She has dimples, a charming up-turned mouth, large green eyes, and crisp curls. To my great disappointment I inherited none of them. All the same, people say we look alike.

Her earliest memories, until her parents hired Nanny Hefford, were happy. Nanny Hefford had previously worked for a family where she had singled out one child as her scapegoat. Then she suffered a nervous breakdown. She seemed to recover, and joined my grandparents. My mother became her scapegoat.

Mother remembers one Christmas Eve, aged about eight, she was lying awake when she heard Nanny's feet outside. 'Is it Christmas yet, Nanny?' she called. 'I'll give you Christmas,' Nanny said, and smacked her viciously with the back of a hairbrush. Mother cried herself to sleep. Her friends told me that when they came to tea Nanny would always find a reason to deprive Mother of jam on her bread, or a piece of cake, to humiliate her. Eventually, her oldest sister, Marion, told my grandmother, who passed on the complaint to Nanny: 'Marion tells me you are unkind to Katherine.' 'Well,' Nanny said, 'she can be very difficult.'

She still can. The middle child, scapegoated for years by a sadistic nanny, it is not surprising that she still gets frustrated if she feels ignored, and she is possessive of those she loves. But I have always adored her. Even when she has been at her most difficult, sulking for days, or saying unspeakable things about her sons-in-law, I love her for her

4

wicked sense of humour. She makes memorable malapropisms, and, although they are probably accidental, she enjoys the effect. My father liked the moment she gazed gloomily at herself in the mirror and complained of the 'crow's nests' under her eyes. She looks up in the sky at a helicopter, and says, 'There's a hovercraft', or at a hang-glider, which she calls 'a glide-hanger'. Now she is in her eighties she says she is suffering from 'Axminsters'.

She is a brave woman. Recently, when I was attacked by reporter John Ware, she wrote an excellent letter to the *Sunday Telegraph* in my defence. Intrigued, they sent a reporter to interview her, and she enjoyed herself greatly, referring to Ware as 'John Thingummybob'. She is physically brave as well. In her late eighties a vast ovarian cyst was discovered in her, with eight pints of fluid inside it. The doctors feared that surgery would cause her to crumble. She survived the operation triumphantly. On one visit to her in hospital I brought her a meringue, and she attacked it with relish, undiminished by the fact she was having a blood transfusion at the same time.

She and my father were utterly different. He was an intellectual, a scientist, with a passion for music, Wagner and Mahler above all. He became head of the pioneering Lines and Designs Department of the BBC, working to Lord Reith. He had worked for Marconi's before the BBC, but it was an Italian firm, and, when Mussolini came to power, the company decided it could not employ a Jew in a senior position.

Anti-Semitism was unselfconscious in the 1930s, even in Britain. At one top-level meeting in the BBC a member of the Post Office staff referred

5

disparagingly to 'those long-nosed buggers'. Nothing was said at the time, but when my father returned to his office he found a messenger already waiting for him, asking him to go to the Director-General's office. He did, and Reith apologized fulsomely to him for the anti-Semitic slur.

Father's department was responsible for developing television, so we had one of the first sets after the Second World War. He played rugby, climbed mountains, was one of the earliest visitors to the Glyndebourne opera house in the 1930s, loved the paintings of Stanley Spencer and used to visit Cookham regularly to admire the murals there. He could solve *The Times* crossword in an hour or two, and taught my son, Joshua, chess.

By contrast, my mother never did well academically, and was deeply unhappy at Cheltenham Ladies' College, where her parents sent her to improve her table manners. But judging by the skill with which she has managed the stocks and shares she inherited I guess she would have been a successful businesswoman. That, of course, was out of the question. I was brought up to believe that any sign of greed was vulgar, so discussing money or food was infra dig.

Television was fairly vulgar, too, so our first set—in order that it should not interfere with conversation—was kept in the hall. Vanity was a vice. My father used to say that my sister, Priscilla, and I had lost all sense from the moment we first saw our own reflections in a mirror. He said it as a joke, but you must remember that he was the lone male in a household of three women, within the greater matriarchy of my grandmother and her four daughters. If he had secretly longed for a son, and

6

was disappointed to have two daughters, he never revealed it, until my own son, Joshua, was born. Then he asked that one of Joshua's middle names should be Rantzen.

My grandmother, Emily, had made no secret of the fact that having girl after girl infuriated her. She gave her youngest daughter, Jane, the plainest name she knew, out of pique. Jane was a gorgeous baby, and turned into a lovely child, with huge eyes and a cloud of soft, dark curls. As the baby of the family she was adored by everyone, especially the nannies, and my grandmother often told me that Jane had become her favourite name. Her daughters also completely converted her to girls. I was her first granddaughter after three grandsons, and I revelled in being spoiled by her.

*   *   *

I was born just after Dunkirk, in June 1940. My father's older brother, Joel, [Author of *Little Ship Navigation.*] (Lieutenant Commander Rantzen, who was a skilled yachtsman), took his little boat across the Channel to pick up some of the British soldiers stranded on the beaches. My mother's family had moved from Hampstead to Berkhamsted, Hertfordshire, to escape the bombs. My father was still working for the BBC in London, and was there when the bomb fell on Broadcasting House. He was famous in our family for the fact that when another bomb fell a few doors away from my grandparents' house where he was sleeping, he rushed to the window just as it blew in. He was lucky to avoid being badly hurt.

But then he was not the most practical scientist.

My mother never asked him to mend any machine, because when he put it together again there were always one or two pieces left over. He invented the spout-less teapot because when he was washing up he could never clean the inside of the spout. I pointed out that a teapot without a spout was really a jug. Then he invented an oscillating wall-fire. My mother had bought a wall-fire for the kitchen, but he was worried that when we pulled a string to switch it on, we would drag it off the wall and set fire to ourselves. So he mounted it on a flexible metal strip. When we pulled the string it swung down, snapped back to the ceiling and flipped backwards and forwards for some time. At least it used to entertain our school-friends during dull teatimes.

Father was absent-minded. He used to leave the house in odd socks, sometimes in odd shoes. He was once asked to be best man at two weddings on the same day, and calculated he could just do it. Sadly, he left the first wedding before the speeches, one of which he, of course, should have made. That was his brother's wedding, and the bride, my Aunt Fred, never forgave him.

He wrote two books about a mathematical theory that came to him in the middle of the night. This was based on statistics, and explained many of life's mysteries—for instance, why human beings evolved to a height of five to six feet. His theory could also be applied to weather forecasts, and to creating more effective deaf aids. He persuaded a laboratory to make a prototype hearing aid for him to try. When we went on holiday together to Greece he swam out to sea wearing it and, in spite of his stately breast-stroke, it disappeared to the bottom of the ocean and was too expensive to replicate. So we will never know if it could have created a revolution for the deaf.

His theory also proved the existence of God, at least to Father, although he disliked organized religion. He used to tell me that the ten commandments were pragmatic and practical, for how else could a wandering tribe in the desert stay together without being reduced to anarchy?

*   *   *

We were—and are—a Jewish family. My grandparents were among the first Liberal Jews in Britain, utterly Anglicized. Our services were almost completely in English, and I never learned to read Hebrew. My grandmother celebrated a traditional Victorian Christmas, with a tall tree, and delicate glass ornaments—birds with spun-glass tails, and brilliant baubles that caught the light. Our Christmases used to mystify some of our more Orthodox Jewish relatives. My Aunt Nancy married into a very observant family. Her son, John, asked by a school-friend why they had such a little tree, replied, 'It's because we're only Liberal Jews.'

In my home we ate bacon and ham, forbidden foods to Orthodox Jews. And since Father was not keen on services we only attended synagogue on high days and holy days. We never lit candles to celebrate the coming of the Sabbath on Friday nights, as Desmond and I did. And yet, being Jewish still made an enormous difference to my life.

Many people say that the existence of the Nazi

9

death camps was a terrible revelation at the end of the Second World War. Jewish families in Britain were surprised at the scale of the Holocaust, but they knew about the persecution. My parents fostered two children, Suzi and Charlie, who were refugees from the horror of Nazi Germany.

Charlie's mother escaped with him to England, but his father, a handsome red-haired PE instructor, died in a concentration camp. Charlie used to have nightmares, the six-year-old would cry in his sleep and call out in German. Mother used to wake Suzi to try and translate, so she could comfort him. One day my Aunt Jane sent him a postcard. Mother called to him, 'Wake up, Charlie, there's a letter for you,' and he tumbled down the stairs shouting, 'It's from Daddy!'. My mother was very upset, and persuaded Charlie's mother to tell him the truth.

My grandparents paid for Charlie's education, and he was always grateful to them, and to my parents. I was invited to his sixtieth birthday party, when he made a speech honouring them. I found to my astonishment that Charlie had never told his own children that he and his mother had so narrowly escaped from being murdered in Germany, as his father was. Some memories are too deep and too painful to share.

My earliest memory is of waking in the middle of the night, and standing up in my cot, listening to the wail of the sirens—first the warning, then the 'all clear'. My mother thinks I was eighteen months old. I remember the blackout, having to cover windows to make sure no lights showed at night, and asking my father what the sirens meant. When he explained that they were warning us that enemy

10

planes were flying towards us, I asked whether they would drop bombs upon us. 'No,' he said, 'the British planes will stop them.' Fortunately, as far as Berkhamsted was concerned, he was right. But it meant that very early on I understood that Britain was at war. I knew we were Jewish. I knew that we owed our lives to the fact that we lived in England. And I also knew that Hitler hated Jews like us, and would kill us if he won the war.

So, from my childhood I have felt not simply a patriotic affection for Britain, but a deep gratitude. Without the wonderful accident of being born here I would surely have died in a concentration camp, along with my family. I learned to prize the freedoms we in Britain so often take for granted, our democracy, our eccentric institutions, like the BBC, and a monarchy with no real power. I love the English language, mongrel as it is, without the purity of Italian, or French. But English is so much richer and more poetic, with all its synonyms from its many different roots.

When the war ended, and we returned to London, the Hampstead streets were still full of memories of the horror we had escaped. There were bombsites, high, crumbling walls, with relics of rooms still clinging to them. They became dangerous playgrounds for city children braver than me, and they turned a glamorous bright pink in summer with rosebay willowherb. There was rationing—I was five before I tasted my first banana. But, above all, there were refugees from Germany and Poland, many of them concentration camp survivors, some of them driven mad by their experiences there.

As a teenager I read as many concentration

11

camp survivors' autobiographies as I could find, discovering the most brutal depths of human savagery. Some of the books reduced me to tears, but I persevered. I knew the Germans were no different from the rest of humanity, to pretend otherwise would be to share their racism. So what could have turned them into monsters, until they came to believe that Jews, gypsies and homosexuals were sub-humans who should be exterminated like rats? Surely it could not all have been the work of one man, Adolf Hitler, evil as he undoubtedly was?

Slowly I came to the conclusion that we all have the capability of committing these crimes, and that the danger was the total unaccountability of a regime where brutes were promoted and given complete power. I was brought up to believe that the German army was trained to obey orders, whereas the British were encouraged to use their initiative. Rightly or wrongly, I learned to distrust rules. I also learned to loathe the lynch mob, the bully, the snob. Being a member of a minority is the best lesson in tolerance I know.

*   *   *

London was a shock I never quite came to terms with, after my five years in the Hertfordshire countryside. In Berkhamsted our rambling house, 'Whitelea', which we shared with my grandparents, had a big paddock behind it, long grass dotted with white marguerites. In London we moved into a semi-detached house, with a small square patch of suburban garden, bordered with high wooden fences. The pavements of Hocroft Avenue, where we lived at number three, were grey, the nearest shops in Cricklewood Lane were grey—instinctively I longed for green fields and woodlands.

Ironically, the house my parents bought in London was built on a farm where they had both played as children. Traces lingered in the street names. Around the corner from Hocroft Avenue was Farm Avenue, and one of the houses there had recurring subsidence because it was built on an old duck pond. As I walked up the hill every day to the bus stop I used to try and visualize tussocky grass beneath the paving stones, to see it as it had been when my parents were young.

And yet suburbia had its consolations. There was almond blossom in springtime, golden forsythia, and hanging chains of laburnum. My sister and I used to walk our dog around the block, marking each neat garden that we passed out of ten. Lilac was a favourite, and scored high points, but I grew to hate the smell of privet, and, to this day, I could never grow a privet hedge. Nor can I plant French marigolds or busy Lizzies in neat rows. But we learned to ride our scooters and our bicycles in those quiet streets.

We used shrimping nets to trap bumblebees in our hollyhocks, then ran shrieking with delighted panic when they escaped. There were far more butterflies in our garden then than there are now—red admirals, peacocks and cabbage whites—and there were elm trees next door, now long gone. The milkman's horse used to stand with melancholy patience outside our gate, the coalman heaved his sack up our path, trolley buses, with their long antennas picking up electricity from overhead tracks, swept us noiselessly to school, and

I used to help my mother push our clothes through the mangle in our scullery. Would any youngster know what a mangle or a scullery was today?

But, unlike the land 'before the war', it was not a completely foreign world. We had a gas cooker, and a refrigerator, several wirelesses, and, as I have said, a very early television. Sliced bread was a miraculous invention which delighted us, so were frozen peas. 'Fresh' peas from the greengrocer were extremely stale. They had travelled for days to reach the London shops, were hard and yellow, and tasted of tin.

Gradually the old tonics that had kept children healthy during the war—rose-hip syrup, cod-liver oil, a daily teaspoon of sticky black malt—were discarded as unnecessary as our diet improved. Or did it? Today's nutritionists would approve of our tightly rationed butter, eggs and red meat. And, in middle age, I have reversed the clock, put myself back on cod-liver oil and malt, and taken myself off sliced bread.

I realize now what a great influence my family matriarchy had upon me. My oldest aunt Marion was the guiding influence on her sisters. For all their sheltered upbringing, they went bravely out into the world. My Aunt Nancy died in November 2000, lucid and courageous to the end. Selfless and generous, she worked for the Citizen's Advice Bureau until she was eighty-five. My mother at eighty-nine is still a Governor of a school in the East End of London. Their youngest sister, my Aunt Jane (who is also my godmother and was in one of the first teams to open up Belsen concentration camp) was recently interviewed by Stephen Spielberg's archive team, anxious to capture her memories on film. All this, in a generation of women which was thought to be unliberated. If I can emulate half their achievements, I shall be extremely lucky.

CHAPTER TWO

SCHOOLGIRL

I was five in 1945, the year we came back to London, and my parents decided to send me to a school in Hampstead called Sarum Hall. It could have been called Scarum Hall, not because it was Dickensian, I don't think we were ever served gruel, but because it had a genuine child-hating sadist as headmistress, called Miss Webb. Miss Webb liked to make us cry. When she summoned us to her study we knew you had to burst into tears quickly because she would surely keep you there until you did. Why, I wonder? What attracts such people into teaching? Perhaps she got a thrill out of breaking six-year-olds down. But then what motivated my mother's cruel nanny? What drives any child abuser?

My parents sent me to Sarum Hall because it had a good academic record, and, although my mother knew I was unhappy there, my father insisted I should stay. I was only summoned to Miss Webb's study once, something about knives and forks being laid on the table the wrong way round (I was, and am, left-handed). I stood stubbornly looking at my feet while she railed at me. I knew it would be sensible to cry quickly and get out fast, but my pride prevented me. I knew she was bullying me, and I knew she was wrong. I knitted my brows and stood there, stolidly. It was twenty minutes before she broke me down, then, finally, when the tears came, she was mollified, and sent

16

me back to my class, where a sweet French teacher consoled me. Now I realize Miss Webb made her staff as unhappy as she made the girls. The French teacher, Mam'selle, drew a mushroom village to cheer me up, with little doors in the mushroom stalks, and elves dancing round them. I practised copying her, not realizing how useful that would be.

Reading had come easily to me, and from the age of five I devoured every book in our home. My parents censored nothing, kept nothing from me. I read children's books, Noel Streatfield, Enid Blyton, Arthur Ransome, but very early on I also read the short stories of Guy de Maupassant, which gave me nightmares, and a dark blue book by a doctor called Van de Velde, which told me everything I wanted to know about the facts of life, and more. I kept those facts to myself, didn't tell my parents—I didn't think they were ready for them. But in our scripture lessons, when the teacher told us about Adam and Eve, I explained to her that we are descended from monkeys, and asked how Genesis was compatible with Darwin. I can't remember my teacher being pleased with me, but my parents laughed when I told them.

They didn't laugh, however, when I described Miss Webb's current affairs lessons. Israel was fighting for its independence, and Miss Webb told us with fury what the wicked Jews were doing to the gallant British Tommies. While not approving of violence, my father was appalled to learn of Miss Webb's political views, and told my mother I must leave the school as soon as practical. Mother and I were delighted.

The school she found to replace Sarum Hall was North London Collegiate School, Edgware.

17

Northwest London parents all wanted their girls to go there. Set in acres of beautiful grounds, in an eighteenth-century building, it was run by the best headteacher in Britain, Dr (later Dame) Kitty Anderson. I was seven when I took the entrance exam. While we were waiting for our interview with Dr Anderson, (she interviewed every would-be pupil in the school, even the youngest) we were told we could draw whatever we liked. The girls next to me drew their mummies and daddies and dogs. I drew a mushroom village, with an elf doctor arriving on a snail. The teachers were greatly impressed with my imagination and originality and showed Dr Anderson. Thank you so much, Mam'selle. Forgive me if I sailed into a place at the school under false pretences.

Summoned to see the headmistress, I walked into her room with trepidation. Memories of Miss Webb were still fresh. But instead of gazing at my feet, I looked into the smiling eyes of a small, cuddly woman, with kind eyes and projecting teeth, like mine (and my father's). Kitty Anderson was a Yorkshirewoman, warm, charismatic without being stately, brilliant but never pompous, with a genuine love of children. She had the enviable talent of never forgetting a name or a face, and could remember each one of her 900 pupils, their parents and their boyfriends, and all the previous generations she had taught.

But all I knew that first day was that, far from reducing me to tears, she and I laughed together. She made me read to her, and asked me to explain some of the words, then we talked together about the trees I had seen in the grounds, magnificent cedars, with spreading layers of branches that

18

fascinated us both. There were other formalities to go through. I had failed the arithmetic test so I had to retake it, but the mushroom village had been my passport, and the arithmetic teacher was kind and encouraging, and pushed me through. With one bound, so to speak, I was free of the misery of Sarum Hall.

I was tremendously happy at North London, happier than my sister, who followed me there, happier than either of my daughters who went there. Perhaps it was because I took advantage of the opportunities the school offered, some excellent teaching, lovely gardens, a lack of rules, and the chance to write and produce plays and pantomimes, without ever being overawed by the academic standards.

The school, however, could be a problem for the over-conscientious: one of my classmates got 'A's' throughout her time there, was awarded a scholarship to Oxford, but then had a mental breakdown and never recovered. I was protected. I had my mother's irreverent example at home; and Miss Webb's example had taught me that teachers could be wrong. Once, for example, I was asked to write the diary of a monk as homework. I amused myself by illuminating the first letter of each entry, like a medieval document. The teacher put a line through my drawing, and at the end wrote, 'Do not waste your time in this way'. My mother was furious on my behalf. I calmed her down. Why should I mind if the teacher disapproved? The teacher was wrong. Pride, again, but, again, self-preservation.

*　　　*　　　*

I had only been at the school a year when I became ill with acute nephritis. Germs from a throat infection had infected my kidneys. I was very lucky to be treated by Bernard Schlesinger, a paediatrician at University College Hospital (UCH), London, and father of John Schlesinger, the great film director. For some years whenever I met John I used to thank him for the fact that his father saved my life. Patiently he would say, 'I know, Esther, you always tell me so'.

In fact, what saved me was a new discovery, penicillin. It had been used on the troops during the war, but in 1948 was still regarded as a wonder drug. They injected it into my bloodstream with needles that were as thick as horse syringes, and turned my thighs black with bruises. I was in ward 42, the children's ward, looked after by a gorgeous red-haired nurse, Sister Mickey. All the doctors were in love with her, and I fell in love with most of the doctors, especially Dr MacGregor. I remember watching him tip her into a cot, as a joke, and feeling pangs of jealousy. I wondered if he would wait for an eight-year-old to grow up. I don't think he did, but I did once get a letter from him when I was making *That's Life!*, and of course I remembered him. I remember all my unrequited loves.

At least once a week the medical students would arrive in the ward, and the interesting cases would be wheeled into the centre of the room. I was interesting, or at least my urine was. They arranged it in rows of test tubes, and I was fascinated to see how red with blood it had been when I was first admitted, and how it had paled, week by week. The consultant described my case, and the students had to answer questions, while I pretended not to listen. Was it an invasion of my privacy, to have my kidneys so publicly discussed? Certainly not. I loved every minute. They were an audience after all. I tried to look as poignant as I could, listening to every word, while I pretended to be deep in my book. It was all I could do not to correct the students, when they got my diagnosis and treatment wrong.

I caused the nurses a problem when they settled us all for the night because I would tell the other children bedtime stories. My father always used to tell stories to Priscilla and me after he'd put out the lights, wonderful, imaginative tales, so I followed his example. Except that in my case I used to tell the children in the ward Bible stories from the Old Testament, which are, of course, highly dramatic, filled with sex and violence, with heroes with fatal flaws, and wicked villains. I told them about David and Bathsheba, and the judgement of Solomon, and Queen Esther, the first recorded winner of a beauty contest who saved her people from genocide. My stories were very popular with the patients, but not with the nurses. They told my mother they would have insisted that I went to sleep, but because the stories came from the Bible, they didn't feel they could interrupt.

The girl in the bed next to me developed big itchy lumps all over her face, and so did I. She had given me measles. I was taken by ambulance to a fever hospital in Neasden. From my bed there, I wrote a letter to my mother, asking her advice. I had not been given a toothbrush so I could not clean my teeth, and the nurses in the fever hospital

21

didn't always give me the injections I needed. Also the strict meat-free diet I'd been put on in UCH was not being adhered to here, did it matter?

My mother thought it did, and took the letter straight to the sister in charge. After my mother had gone, the nurse came and sat on my bed. She was tough and angry—it was Miss Webb over again. She reduced me to tears, and threatened that if ever I wrote home again with any complaints, she would read all my letters first.

When my mother came on her next visit, I told her the nurse had been angry. But what could she do? Patients and their families are in a difficult position, if they complain, revenge can so easily be taken. I have investigated children in care who were mistreated but never dared ask for help, children in a boarding school owned by a paedophile who kept silent about their abuse, families of old people who died in suspicious circumstances in residential homes, who were anxious, but afraid to make things worse if they complained. I now believe that children, old people, disabled or ill people, everyone in residential care should have someone outside the system, an advocate or a befriender, who can take complaints forward and ensure they are not penalized. In my case, my mother made sure I was transferred back to UCH where I was well looked after once more.

UCH was a grimy redbrick hospital in narrow streets in the heart of the city. Sunlight had never penetrated our ward. Even when the nurses pushed our beds out on to a fire-escape to try and take advantage of a lovely day, the air was thick with soot, and the sheets were speckled when we were

22

taken back inside. The infection spread to my ears, and I had to have a mastoid operation (virtually unknown now, thanks to improved antibiotics) and was wheeled under the street to the operating theatre. I can still remember the frightening, harsh rattle of the stretcher wheels over the cobbles. I had been admitted in March, when the trees were bare. I came out in June, and will never forget the breathtaking sight of a sycamore in a London square, a tower of bright green leaves.

But in spite of the grimness of the hospital, I found it difficult to adjust to convalescence at home. There had been so much bustle and fun on the wards. At home, where I was forced to rest every afternoon, it was lonely and frustrating. I remember so well the sunlight gleaming through my curtains, and the feeling of imprisonment. Perhaps that's why, as a mother, I was always very bad at forcing my own children to go to bed when the sun was still shining. As I got stronger, I was glad to get back to school—even though for months I had to do special exercises, 'remedials', in the gym before classes, to get rid of the round shoulders and flat feet caused by so many weeks in bed.

*　　　*　　　*

My years in north London were interrupted again when I was ten, because my father was appointed Head of Telecommunications to the United Nations in New York. He had, among other things, to set up the complex system of simultaneous translation. He didn't much enjoy working there, was shocked by the open bribery and corruption when contracts were being awarded. His boss at the BBC had promised to hold his job open for him when the two-year secondment was over, but of course he did nothing of the kind. When the two years finished, Dad came home to face unemployment—difficult for anyone with my father's pride and sense of obligation. Perhaps, in retrospect, he should have turned down the chance to work in America because it was too great a risk. But I found it exciting, and have the happiest memories of life on Long Island.

My parents found a white clapboard house in Port Washington, a little seaside town a good commuting distance from New York. In our street, between the houses and in odd corners, you could still find remnants of wilderness, which is always tidied away under brick and tarmac on British roads. But in Ivy Way there were patches of woodland, with thick carpets of bluebells and skunk cabbage, and poison ivy which brought us out in a blotchy rash.

The winter was dramatic, heavy snow covered the sloping lawns. We threw ourselves backwards on to it, and swung our arms up and down to make the shapes of angels' wings. The silence of a night filled with huge flakes falling outside the window was quite unlike the busy London suburb I was used to. So were the hot summers—afternoons spent by the beach, then driving to the drugstore for ice-cream sodas, tall glasses overflowing with coffee and cream. The autumn was gaudy. Where in England, autumn drizzle made leaves crumple and fall in soggy brown heaps, the late Long Island sun turned the maples scarlet.

We carved out pumpkins at Hallowe'en, and

played trick-or-treat round the neighbourhood. I learned to square dance—I can still dosi-doh. The school play at Christmas was *Alice in Wonderland*, and they couldn't resist casting an English Alice, although I was only Alice when she had shrunk. I was always small for my age. I had to learn to say 'nut' for 'not', because, to American audiences, the English 'not' sounded affected and odd. If you listen to Audrey Hepburn you will find that she and every other imported British actor, learned to say 'nut'.

History lessons were a revelation. I was used to starting at 1066, but on Long Island nobody knew or cared about the Normans, the Tudors or the Stuarts. It all began with the *Mayflower*, then, after a quick romp past the Pilgrim Fathers and Pocahontas, concentrated on 1776 with the War of Independence. In which, you will remember, the British were the villains, although my new classmates were very forgiving.

I read American literature for the first time— Mark Twain, Emily Dickinson, Dorothy Parker, Walt Whitman, O. Henry, James Thurber, and loved them all. I was very bad at sport. In one game of softball (a safer version of baseball) the fate of my team rested on my hitting the ball. I missed it, three times.

But, to balance my disgrace, I had a moment of glory. A glassblower came to the school and entranced us by creating a glass heron. Our headmaster decided to hold a poetry contest, in which the winner was to be presented with the heron. For some reason I decided to try blank verse: *Gently blowing on a slender tube of glass, Till a silvery bubble forms, and while It swells, lovely*

25

patterns dance Upon its gleaming surface . . .

I didn't know when each line should end, and asked my teacher for advice. (His name was Mr Cane—we would have snapped that up on *That's Life!*).

I submitted the poem, and was in the classroom when the headmaster came to ask Mr Cane if I had written it without help. He said he thought so, and explained I had asked him how to split the lines. So—and it is still one of the proudest moments of my life—I was presented with the heron in front of the whole school. One of the saddest moments came a few weeks later, when the heron fell off our mantelpiece and shattered.

*　　　*　　　*

We returned to London in 1952, when I was twelve. Another hard lesson was in store. On Long Island I was no more extrovert than anyone else, and nobody thought I was showing off when I put up my hand in class. Back in Britain I had to relearn reticence. I was teased for my new American accent. I had to learn to say 'not' again. When I told my British friends about the American supermarkets overflowing with food, the meat in chilled covered counters, instead of attracting flies and ants on the butchers' slabs, they rebuked me for unpatriotic criticisms. England still had rationing, the Hampstead shops were spartan and food and cooking very plain. In Port Washington they had elected me president of my class, in London they told me to sit down, keep quiet, and stop boasting. Television critics have been known to say the same.

When we returned to London, we bought another semi-detached house in the same northwest London suburb, one block away from our old home. Before school term began I worked at a little 'Dame School', Miss Watson's, in Hampstead. Priscilla was in a class there to learn money sums. We had both come from the paradise of decimal currency—American children did their sums in dollars and cents, which required no special skills to add or divide—but in Britain, in those days of twelve pennies to each shilling, twenty shillings to the pound, sums were elaborate torture. Priscilla had to take an entrance exam to get into Henrietta Barnett Junior School, so Miss Watson had the task of drumming the technique into her. As it turned out, Priscilla effortlessly calculated the columns of figures. She inherited my father's mathematical talents, which passed me by.

Miss Watson was tall and thin, and had created her school in a tall, thin family house in Hampstead. I joined Priscilla in the mornings there, to teach some of the youngest children reading—none of the new trendy methods, they had not yet been invented and discarded, but the old 'c-a-t spells cat' that had worked so well with me in my time, and worked equally well for them. I loved teaching. It was, after all, playing to an audience again, one that appreciated any flicker of humour in the grind of learning, and rewarded me with happy giggles. What's more, their reading improved. It was then that my ambition to become a teacher was born, and it still smoulders in me. Perhaps one day, when the television industry finally spits me out, I will be able to persuade another headteacher to allow me to sit alongside

27

their littlest pupils and go through 'c-a-t spells cat' again.

For some reason, my mother—during this sensitive time in my pre-adolescence—referred to my eyebrows as 'bushy eyebrows'. In a destructive mood I sat in front of a mirror, and shaved them off, using my father's razor. The effect was so horrible I refused to go out for days, and Mum had to invent an excuse for Miss Watson. The eyebrows, despite my aunts having warned me that plucked eyebrows sometimes stayed bald forever, grew back slowly. This baldness had happened, they said, to some fashion victims in the 1930s.

I knew about the thirties because two of our aunts (to be more precise, they were distant cousins), the Meyer Girls, were perfectly preserved flappers. They wore the flat, straight dresses of the time, fringes and kiss curls tucked into pastel hats with low brims. Their voices were husky and upper class like Hermione Gingold. They smoked their cigarettes in long holders. Looking like characters in a Noel Coward farce, they came to tea in our garden, and sat beneath the clothes line. A spider slowly unravelled its thread down towards their hats, and they sat chatting elegantly, oblivious to the descending danger, while I choked with laughter. They were delighted by my reaction, even when they discovered what had caused it.

They were favourites of the family. We loved their company, but I had no ambition to look like them and never shaved my eyebrows again. Indeed, I have remained wary of any of the indelible physical adjustments dictated by fashion—never pierced my ears, or my belly button, or my nose or my tongue. I don't understand why so many people want to put metal studs in their tongues, although when I was interviewed by Paul Merton for his series Room 101, the audience told me, 'It's a sex thing, Esther'. Even so, is it worth snagging the spaghetti on?

*   *   *

Adolescence arrived, and I became as obnoxious as every other fourteen-year-old girl. I knew I was being nasty as I provoked rows, slammed my bedroom door, sulked and flounced. But the surge of hormones prevented either sense or civilization breaking through. One morning, after some pointless squabble with my mother in which I was as usual wrong, I went upstairs, packed my suitcase, and stalked across the hall swinging it dramatically. I went to school without a word, rang my grandmother, and said, 'Granny, I've run away from home, can I come to stay with you?' 'Of course you can, darling,' she said, 'I'll ask Grace to make you meringues for tea.'

Grace was Granny's cook, and could have been the original of Mrs Bridges in *Upstairs Downstairs*. She was sharp-tongued, could be ferocious, was shaped like a cottage loaf, and was a great artist. Her meringues were pale yellow, crisp on the outside, chewy at their heart, and she filled them to overflowing with whipped cream. What a delectable punishment for a runaway. The night I spent with Granny was a treat for both of us. We watched television, played canasta, and had my favourite honeydew melon for breakfast.

I rang Mum from school the next day and said, 'I'm coming home today'. She was indignant. 'If your grandmother hadn't rung me, I would never have known where you were. Your Aunt Nancy says it's quite unfair of you to burden your grandmother.'

Mother always expresses family controversy through the reactions of other members: 'Your father was horrified,' 'Your aunt was very upset,' when she means she is horrified or upset herself. In this case, however, the accusation could not possibly stick. I described my evening and reassured her that Granny had enjoyed herself as much as I had. But it was typical of our family that my greatest act of rebellion should be running away less than five miles, and being rewarded with Hampstead's finest meringues.

Around this time, I started a theatre club for girls in my class who enjoyed plays. We bought the cheapest seats in the gallery, known then as 'the gods', because we sat so high we were surrounded by the gilded statues in the ceiling. The gallery wasn't ideal in those days of cocktail party comedies when ladies wore chic hats, and all we could see from our perch up by the chandeliers was a group of talking brims.

We used to go to the Golders Green Hippodrome, an echoing warehouse of a theatre where West End productions used to try out in front of razor-sharp Jewish audiences. Years later, when my father died in 1992, Mother and I discussed what arrangements to make for his funeral. 'He wanted to be cremated,' she said. The Golders Green Crematorium was quite near our home, but I didn't know if that would be appropriate. 'Where?' I asked. 'I suppose it will have to be in the Golders Green Hippodrome,' said my mother. Her capacity to deliver malapropisms did not desert her, even at the most tragic time.

There was, however, an appropriateness in what she said, because many a play died at the Hippodrome in its time. But not all, we saw Marlene Dietrich triumph there in one of her many farewell, farewell, farewell tours. All I can remember now are her exquisitely choreographed curtain calls: once from the right, once from the left, once flailing her white fox fur, once languidly trailing it behind her, once clutching the curtain as if the weight of the audience's adulation was too much for her, and on and on. I admired the skill but I couldn't warm to her.

I never went to the theatre with a boyfriend. The only boys I knew were my cousins. I went out on a real date for the first time when I was sixteen, with an American boy who was appalled by my innocence, gave me a kind if patronizing kiss on the cheek, and told me about a singer called Elvis Presley he was sure would be popular in Britain when we heard his records.

But, although my love-life was non-existent in reality, my fantasies ran riot. I read *Gone With the Wind* in three days during a windy family holiday in Angmering-on-Sea, Sussex. I walked the beach unaware of the sea or the sky, totally absorbed by Scarlett and Rhett Butler. For two of the three days I was in love with Rhett, then, when their lives took a tragic turn and he let me and Scarlett down, I—like generations of readers—was heartbroken.

To console myself I started to invent romances for my table of school-friends at lunch, telling them tales embarrassingly like melodramatic Valentino films, where the heroines were carried off into the night by a tall, dark, determined hero. My friends took over the serving and clearing-away chores, so that I could continue with the stories uninterrupted. I described champagne, and lingering kisses, while we ate blackened sausages and ginger sponge. Beneath our brown serge uniforms beat the passionate hearts of fourteen-year-old virgins, and you won't find more passionate hearts than those.

I once cheated in an exam (to make things even worse it was a Scripture exam). The other Jewish girls at school were far more Orthodox than me, and sneered at my Anglicized Liberal Judaism. 'Liberal Jews make the best Christians', one told me. Loftily, I said I would take that as a compliment. I had my revenge during one Jewish Scripture exam, when we were allowed to take our Bibles in with us. One question asked us what effect the wandering in the wilderness had on the Tribe of Israel. I decided it must have made them more supportive of one another—after all, a touch of wilderness might have done the Jews in our school some good! But I couldn't find a quotation from Exodus to back me up. So I found an unremarkable verse, 'they camped there by night', and added the words, 'and shared their bread, each man with his brother'. It felt blasphemous, but the sky didn't open, no thunderbolt struck, in fact I had a large tick in the margin, and got an A, the only Jewish girl in our year to get an A. The others were less snooty for a month or two. I didn't cheat again.

At sixteen I was confirmed. Jewish boys get barmitzvahed at thirteen, the religious ritual for which they study hard, which rewards them with a moment of glory when they take a service in the synagogue, and which marks the moment when they achieve manhood. Nowadays Liberal Jewish boys and girls have the same service at thirteen. All three of our children have been through the process, filling Desmond and me with pride, and all three now read Hebrew fluently. Desmond, too, learned Hebrew when he converted—his idea, not mine, inspired by a strong affection and respect for Judaism and the Jews he had known. (His partner, Bill Morton, was Jewish; his favourite boss, Cyril Bennett, was Jewish; even his first wife was Jewish.)

In the Anglicized 1950s Liberal Jewish boys and girls were confirmed together in a service conducted in English, after a due period of study, and having written prayers which we then read to the congregation. I even wore a white dress, very symbolic. One aspect of this rite of passage which appeals to all Jewish children, and is a useful bribe when the studying becomes tedious, is that a deluge of presents arrives. I was invited by one distant relative to come and have lunch with him, and choose a book as a present.

This, however, is a memory I blocked for many of my adult years. It was only when, after ChildLine was launched, and a young journalist asked me if I had ever been sexually abused as a child, that I remembered this 'uncle'. The man himself was not an 'uncle'—that was a courtesy title. He was married, with a young family, and was physically very unappealing. Almost bald, with a straggle of black hair around the back of his head, he stooped, peering through thick glasses. His chin was blue with a permanent shadow. He leered, rather than smiled, as he called me 'bright eyes'.

I am struck now by how vividly I can remember

33

him, given that I tried to bury the memory for so long. He arranged that I should meet him at his place of work, and talked to me kindly. Then, on the pretext of showing me an interesting document, he took me behind the shelves of files, and suddenly grasped my breast and pushed his tongue into my ear. It was horrible, furtive, at first and I didn't quite comprehend what he was doing to me. Then a powerful revulsion swept through me. I twisted out of his grasp and escaped, talking wildly, trying to understand what had happened.

All the way home, alone in the train, I shook and cried. Why? After all, I was sixteen, old enough to get married. But it felt disgusting and incestuous, and I was traumatized. As I ran from him at the tube station, he said, 'Don't tell on me'. But I did, I told my mother straight away.

At first, I am not sure she believed me. She said, 'Typical, Esther, over-dramatizing'.

Still trembling, tears pouring down my face, I ran to the end of the back garden to breathe the air. Inside the house, I could hear my father asking my mother why I was so upset. She said something vague and non-committal. She was probably trying to work out how to assess what I had told her. Although she was accustomed to warning us about 'stranger danger', and had always told us never to talk to strange men, or to walk alone in deserted places, to have an incident like this within our respectable family bewildered her.

In the end, she more or less blocked it, and to my horror still insisted that we should visit his family from time to time. He would come out of the kitchen to greet us, always with that revolting leer as he called me 'bright eyes'. How I would dread those visits, my body shaking with the memory of his hands and his tongue. I would try to escape going, but my parents insisted I should. He had a nice wife and jolly children, and they expected me to be there. So, for a year or so, I was forced to see him from time to time.

Then, when I spent a weekend with a friend in Cambridge, somehow 'Uncle' discovered I was there, and rang to suggest taking me out on the river. My friend was surprised by my reaction of fury and disgust. I rang my mother, accused her of telling him where I was, and laid down my terms. I would never see him again. If she wanted to visit him, that would be her decision. But in the future I would not go with her. And I never did.

Slowly over the years the experience buried itself in my memory. It did not consciously inspire me to protect other children from abuse. When forty years later, the full horror of other children's experience was revealed to me, what they described was so much more hideous—sexual attacks usually repeated many hundreds of time throughout their childhoods, often beginning when they were very young, and usually inflicted upon them by their own fathers—that I never compared it with my nasty 'uncle'. After all, as far as I can tell, my one experience didn't affect my life.

But when, soon after ChildLine was created, the young journalist asked me if I had ever been abused, the fragments of my horror at my 'uncle's' touch drifted up from my distant past, and I remembered the revulsion, the feelings of betrayal and powerlessness, and the plunging disappointment I had felt when my mother dismissed the experience. All the same, when I

35

described it to the journalist, I carefully did not call it sexual abuse because I was afraid that children and survivors would think, as my mother had, 'Typical Esther, over-dramatizing'.

But my scruples didn't make the slightest difference to the reporter's scoop. He began his article, 'Esther Rantzen was sexually abused as a child'. And my friend, Eve Pollard, then Editor of the *Sunday Mirror*, made it worse by creating banner headlines on her front page, 'Esther's Secret Anguish'. I was profoundly embarrassed, but as I could do nothing about it, I could only hope that it might be helpful to survivors of real abuse to discover that I had a little personal insight into their pain.

Looking back, more than anything else it was a desperately lonely experience. I was alone behind those shelves with him, and he seemed monstrous and inescapable. I was alone as I ran home, even more alone as I tried to describe it to my uncomprehending mother, lonelier still as I tried to avoid him, without being able to explain to the rest of my family why. And perhaps that does help me to reach out to the echoing loneliness I hear in the children who ring ChildLine.

*   *   *

The years immediately after our return from America were the financially toughest for my family. As I mentioned, the BBC had promised my father they would hold his job open for him, but when Pop came home he found not only that someone else was securely settled in it, running his old department, but the BBC had nothing else to offer him. It took many months for him to find work with Standard Telephones and Cables (STC), for which he had once worked when he was very young. Those months he spent at home, helping Mum with her chores when he could, were humiliating and frustrating for him because he was unable to earn money.

The fact that Mum came from a rich family just made it worse. Father was extremely proud, and knew his own skills. He had been an inspired head of department for the BBC, they called him 'Tiger Rantzen', and he was popular with his staff. He had a brilliant eye for talent, and could spot ability even in the most junior technicians, who had no paper qualifications. None of this, sadly, endeared him to his own bosses, especially when he proposed ways of saving money by cutting back their empires. He discovered, for instance, that the practice of employing people to switch transmitters on and off for maintenance simply shortened the equipment's life, that it was more efficient and economical to let the machines run constantly. That wasn't popular. My father, like my husband, was adored by his troops, but never ingratiated himself with the bureaucrats who employed him.

Later, my mother would sometimes refer to my father's 'nervous breakdown', but I think she meant his deep anxiety about money during this period. He would fly into rages if he discovered, for instance, that she had bought a dozen French marigolds to brighten the front garden.

When he eventually got the job with STC, it meant he had to have a car to drive to work. He found the oldest, most dilapidated Fiat, which was all he could afford. Enchanted by the doll mascot on its bonnet, we loved it and called it Fifi, but the doors would come off in our hands, and it clanked as Pop pushed it up and down the road to get it started.

In the end my mother's oldest sister, Marion, spoke to my grandmother. Marion was a crucial force in our family. She had explained the facts of life to her sisters when she came back from her honeymoon, aged twenty, having learned them from her bridegroom. She had told Granny that the nanny had been cruel to my mother. Now she explained to Granny that we were badly off—not really poor, because, after all, my parents had been given the house we lived in, but the genteel poverty of the middle classes; too badly off to have a holiday, for instance.

I am not sure what happened after this. But perhaps that was the reason why the four sisters managed to break my grandfather's Trust, and make use of some of the money he had left them. Things certainly improved, and my father was able to buy a little car that worked. And he enjoyed his jobs at STC—first in its research laboratory, and then as its very civilized and intellectual salesman. He would make appointments with generals and admirals in the Ministry of Defence, and tell them of the company's latest inventions.

I have a suspicion that some of the night-vision equipment used by British soldiers was sold to the army by my father. He never told us in detail, of course, because this was high-security stuff. He once said that the space race was based not on man's ambition to explore the universe, but the Cold War imperative to put arms where they could be exploded instantly. One evening, when Mum had 'flu and could not accompany him, he took me to an official dinner, and I sat next to his contact in the Ministry, who spent the night explaining to me the virtues of the South African government and apartheid. I hope my father never discussed politics with the generals who bought his wares.

*　　　*　　　*

As inevitably then as now, my O-levels were followed by A-levels. I resented the treadmill, just as my children do, but what real choice is there? At least I only had to take five O-levels, whereas my poor children took nine or ten. Whatever middle-aged journalists (male) like to say about kids getting it easier these days, I think young people work far harder, and their grades have to be much higher.

I didn't get graded at all on my O-levels—was just told if I had passed or failed. Given my nervousness about maths, it was not surprising that I failed first time, and reacted by sobbing noisily in my bedroom, until Mum rang my headmistress, Dame Kitty Anderson, and returned to tell me to please be quiet, I had only failed by a hair's breadth, and would retake it next term. I did, and scraped through.

During the next two years, I amused myself finding distractions from the boring A-level syllabus. I played a witch in a pantomime (no marks for the critic who says it must have been type-casting), and revelled in the applause. I played the Prince of Morocco in *Merchant of Venice*.

Some months later, I found a mark on my neck. I scrubbed it, but it was immovable. I took it to our family GP, who said it might be ichthyosis, a thickening of the skin, and referred me to the nearest specialist in skin diseases. The consultant and several young doctors peered at my neck. They disappeared in a huddle. Then a nurse came towards me with a kidney basin and some surgical spirit and washed off my ichthyosis—the last relic of my dark brown Prince of Morocco make-up.

In those days (as old people say), if you wanted to apply for Oxford and Cambridge you had to stay on at school for an extra term after A-Levels, to take their entrance exams. I had set my heart on Oxford, since a conversation I had with my father when I was about seven. We were walking around the streets of Cricklewood playing 'Sherlock Holmes, Sherlock Holmes, save my life, save my life'.

Pop had invented this game in which he played the devious villain, Moriarty, trying to hoodwink Priscilla and me, who took it in turns to play Sherlock Holmes, the great detective. It took great ingenuity on Pop's part, because he had to construct a murder tale in which his true guilt depended upon me knowing a peculiar fact—for instance, that the length of a year is 365 and a quarter days, or that a whale is a mammal. Priscilla and I never tired of it, and Pop bravely played along with us until he pleaded for mercy and we agreed to stop.

At this point, I remember asking him: What is the best ambition for anyone to aim for? He said, to continue to learn and to be educated for as long as possible. This was in 1947, when many of my girlfriends, especially my Jewish friends, were brought up by their parents to believe that the point of their lives was to marry well and start a family. My parents always brought us up as if we were boys—to believe that a worthwhile career was important, and that nothing was impossible. So I asked Pop where I should get educated after I had left school, and he said the tradition was Cambridge for sciences, Oxford for arts. From that moment on I set my heart on Oxford.

A-levels were a necessary evil—chunks of Virgil to learn by heart and Balzac novels to plough through, though the English was always fun. I, who always worked as little as possible, managed to pass them, then I concentrated on the Oxford syllabus, focusing on Somerville as my first choice. I liked its radical, unconventional, blue-stocking image.

As the crucial entrance exam came near, I cheered myself up, as usual, by doing something quite unnecessary—another pantomime. I suggested to my friends who were also taking Oxbridge entrance exams that we all needed a distraction, or we would go mad. They, bless them, agreed. So after we had sat the exam papers—and before we had heard if we had been summoned for interview—they put me in the library, and, as I wrote each page, they snatched it from me and copied it out. We had songs, and dance routines—it was a big production. All the school's most senior girls were in my cast and I caricatured them.

My close friend, Caroline Barron, one of the school's most distinguished scholars and now a leading academic, played 'Cinderfella', who was too lazy to go to the ball. I played the Ghost of Upper Sixth Remove, clanking with all the prefects' badges from my class, wearing long brown socks and boat-like Clarks sandals. As a distraction the pantomime worked—and made us laugh. We hardly noticed which of us were summoned to the phone for good news, and which were not.

I was driven by someone else's mother to Somerville, Oxford, loved it, and leaped at the offer they made.

The pantomime went well, too, and started a tradition at the school. I am delighted to say that, to this day, just when exams are at their most oppressive, the sixth form at North London create a revue called *Canons Follies.* Don't let the bastards grind you down, I say, and judging by the very high standards of the productions I have seen, they don't.

*   *   *

I am aware that I am describing a standard suburban childhood. It would be more fun to invent something Dickensian, a childhood spent scraping boots or ducking blows. But it wasn't like that. My parents were loving, and humorous, my sister, Priscilla, was my closest friend, and still is. My memories of school are happy, not just because they allowed me the scope to go my own way, but because the school itself was such a warm, balanced community. Dame Kitty was passionately committed to the democratic virtues, tolerance above all. It was her decision that we had our own Jewish prayers four out of five mornings. And I enjoyed the one day a week in which we combined with the Christian girls for an ecumenical service, when I was also able to learn the majestic hymns from the English hymnal, 'For All the Saints', 'To Be a Pilgrim,' and 'Jerusalem'.

Dame Kitty was a feminist, never strident, but determined we should use every opportunity that came our way. She described to us the battles of the suffragettes to achieve the vote for women, and instructed us always to use it. Although she stressed we should use our hard-won votes wisely, she never revealed her own politics. We guessed that, as a Yorkshirewoman who had made her own way up to the peak of the educational establishment, she could hardly be right wing. But she was against the blanket conformity of the comprehensive revolution, firmly believed that schools should be diverse, and that there should be as many different kinds of school as there are children.

She had taken great care when she interviewed me, and did the same for every child, especially the seven-year-olds. Once she kept us waiting outside her office for a lesson, and explained apologetically that a seven-year-old had been so shy it had taken twenty minutes to encourage her to speak at all. 'I wonder whether this huge community of 900 girls is right for her,' she said. I thought back to the joyous relief I had felt when I was treated so kindly by her, and then accepted in the school.

She taught us current affairs herself, and I remember particularly how she warned us to detect and distrust political propaganda. I still have the book she lent me written by Hitler. He advised politicians always to appeal to the basest instincts, never to the intellect, when they are seeking to sway a crowd. As I read some of today's tabloid jingoism and hysterical nationalism, I remember Dame Kitty's lessons.

Languages were taught by another charismatic

43

teacher, Miss Caroline Senator. Her father had been a penniless Jewish immigrant who mended umbrellas. They lived at various addresses in the East End of London, one jump ahead of their creditors. She got everywhere on scholarships, and passed her enthusiasm on to us. I remember her taking us through the Renaissance, and scrawling on the blackboard over her head, 'All knowledge is one'.

A loveable eccentric, Miss Clay, taught us English. She would perch on the corner of a desk, swinging one leg wildly in its crocheted stockings and sandals. She would bicycle up the drive to the school, head down, singing hymns loudly. Our teachers were almost all spinsters. They had made the choice to be scholars, and that meant leaving their home towns, and sacrificing the chance to marry the boy next door. Perhaps they also belonged to the generation of women who lost potential husbands in the First World War. Either way, they had an enormous family of usually devoted girls to cajole and nag into working hard.

Were they frustrated and irritable, like the caricature of the embittered spinster? Most were the opposite, broad-minded and kindly. But a few were. I remember one maths teacher with very short hair, manly brogues and long fingernails. She was wickedly sarcastic to us, but had a mind so crystal clear that even I could understand the calculations, at least for a moment.

Our breaks between lessons were spent in the gardens of the school, which once had been the great Canons estate. There was a pergola festooned with wisteria—and I have created a miniature version of this outside our country

44

cottage. There was a herbaceous border filled with great clumps of peonies, scarlet blooms with powdery black hearts, white satin cups filled with golden stamens. My peonies in the New Forest are nothing like so lush. I hope the school governors knew how valuable an oasis the gardens were to us, and that they didn't think the gardeners were wasting their skills on 900 spotty schoolgirls.

*   *   *

All in all, my school days were very happy. The one dark side to this sunshiny period of my life was my weight. When I was sixteen my appetite suddenly exploded. Eating disorders were as yet undiscovered, nobody talked then about bingeing. They called what I did compulsive eating, and it certainly was. As an everyday snack between meals I would walk into the larder, close the door behind me, and eat my way through a packet of cornflakes, drenched in full-cream milk and brown sugar. No bowl of fruit was safe from me.

My mother and my aunts must have had the same compulsion at the same time in their lives because they, too, put on weight in their late teens and twenties. They all slimmed down later, as I did. But that was no consolation at the time. Just as everyone else at school was growing curves which they could pack into pointed bras, and were showing off tiny waists in full skirts and wide belts, I was turning into an elephant. A jolly elephant, energetic, full of ideas and quite popular at school, but sitting on the stairs at most of the parties I was invited to.

At seventeen I thought teenage boys were fairly

45

awful, and they thought the same of me. But it would have been a boost to be asked to dance. I had spent hours with my cousin learning the waltz, the quickstep and the foxtrot, but not many partners wanted to know.

Not that I was ready for sex—that was out of the question in those pre-pill days. And immature as I was, although I loved the idea of romance, the reality was not much fun—clumsy groping by boys you didn't remotely fancy but couldn't possibly hurt by turning down. I was relieved not to be involved in the snogging sessions that ended some of the dances. While they disappeared into darkened rooms, I rang my parents for a lift home.

All the same, I minded my weight terribly. Like every fat girl, I used to think that if only I were thin all my problems would be solved. Had I but known, with time, they would be resolved beyond my wildest dreams. But, in my teens and early twenties, I never believed I would meet someone to fall in love with, or that he would fall in love with me, or that we would have children together.

My toothy smile and terrible puns concealed a great lack of confidence. So, while I continued to fantasize about the tall, dark Valentino who might sweep me off my feet, my real love-life was non-existent, and I went on cramming myself with comfort foods—biscuits, cakes and cereals. I even wrote a piece for the school magazine, 'Love at First Bite', about a fat girl who drives a boy away by taking the bunch of roses he gives her, and eating them. I never went quite that far, but almost.

*   *   *

46

In the gap between school and Oxford, I went to work for the first time. One of my uncles owned an advertising agency, and offered me a job as assistant to the art buyer. Uncle Robert thrilled me by saying he'd pay me £8 a week, then thrilled me less by adding that I'd have to work hard for it, 'But that will get rid of your puppy fat'. There are no nice words for overweight, but 'puppy fat' must be among the nastiest. As I continued to hit the cornflake packets, he was wrong about me losing weight, but I learned a great deal, about type-faces, and commuting in trains that crushed me so tightly there was no way of avoiding horrible wandering hands.

My boss, Ken, taught me the office rituals. If you want to read the paper, balance it on an open drawer at knee level in your desk, then if your boss walks in you can look up and invisibly slide the drawer shut. If you answer the phone before he arrives, never give him away, always tell the caller 'he's just popped out for a moment'. And on no account attend the office Christmas party.

I did, and have vivid memories of elderly office messengers being sick in the waste-paper baskets. To escape, I was taken by a suavely attractive Indian rep to a club across the road for a drink. It was not much of an escape. As we walked in, a stripper began to take off her clothes and get far too friendly with a chair. The rep was horrified.

He had looked upon me with some reverence ever since an early conversation when he had said idly, 'I suppose you'd sleep with anyone if you fancied him?' And I had replied, 'Yes of course. Provided I was married to him'. He couldn't believe his ears.

It was 1959. Was I so rare at that time, to be a nineteen-year-old virgin? Most of my friends seemed to be just as inexperienced as I was. For all our exams, and hockey lessons, and pantomimes and prefects' badges, we knew nothing about the rough raw world outside. Yes, I knew the facts of life, but in many ways I was as innocent as my mother was at my age. And none the worse for that.

CHAPTER THREE

OXFORD

For those who are lucky enough to experience them, there is something extraordinary about the university years. They seem to be outlined in gold in my memory, like a bubble in sunlight. And yet it was not all pleasure, not fun all the way. As I write, my daughter Rebecca is an undergraduate at Somerville, and I warned her that she would have more intense happiness there, and more agonizing pain than at any other time in her life.

Why is that? Perhaps because there are no checks and balances. You are entirely enclosed in a world with its own rules, a world in which you can be anyone you choose. A scholar? Some of the best libraries in the world are there for you to browse through, and the finest minds devote themselves to cultivating your intellect in lectures, tutorials and classes. Would you like to try your hand as an actor or a director? There are plays and revues every term, and in my day the best were reviewed by critics from the national press, so they became a stepping stone into the professional theatre and broadcasting. A politician? What better training could there be than joining a student political party, and speaking at the Union, although as a woman I wasn't allowed to join as a member of the Union—what prehistoric times those were.

Zuleika Dobson? Each year there was one girl who, like Max Beerbohm's heroine, became the glamour figure—lusted after, written about in student papers and magazines, starring in Oxford productions.

So whatever world you excelled in, sport, music, beer-drinking, bridge, you could indulge in it, and know you were alongside the greatest experts in the country. But the pressure was on to excel, the heights were dizzy, the plunge was steep. And when you shut your bedroom door, Oxford could be a very lonely place. Particularly when exams were looming, or an essay was due.

Of course I knew none of this when I arrived on my first day in October 1959, my parents' car crammed with crockery, books, and two new prints, a lugubrious Modigliani girl and a comforting Cézanne still-life of apples.

Somerville is an unpretentious sprawl of buildings, nineteenth and twentieth century, with none of the imposing spires, domes and crenellations, nor the medieval quadrangles of the men's colleges. There is a cosiness about Somerville, friendly but not luxurious. The baths and lavatories are shared and basic but at least they are not as primitive as the men's colleges.

I found my room, with my own 'scout' to clean for me every day. I bought my uniform, 'sub fusc' it was called. As I was a mere commoner, it was a soft, black, square hat, and a peculiar, short, black gown to wear for formal occasions. This was handy for wiping pens on, but I envied the scholars who had something far grander. My friend Penny used to leap out of bed and wrap her long gown around her with nothing on underneath. My closest school-friend, Caroline Barron, quickly became the social centre of our year, and a group of us gathered around her, drinking coffee in her room until dawn and beyond, sharing all our beliefs, and hopes, and the tragedies of the moment. It's hard to have secrets in Somerville, your friends see you at every hour of the day and night, and in all your moods. When we all meet again, forty years later, we instantly click back as if no time or distance has come between us, and we laugh, and gossip, just as we did at nineteen.

Work was the first concern, and I had already met our two English dons, who had interviewed and accepted us. My personal tutor was Rosemary Syfret, a kind woman and an inspired teacher. She had not published nearly as much as Mary Lascelles, who was a great authority on Jane Austen, and one of the royal Lascelles related somehow to the Earl of Harewood. Mary Lascelles had very poor eyesight, and we were told she was in constant pain. But none of that excused her nastiness to us.

In one of my first tutorials my friend and tutorial partner, Sarah Hedley, read her an essay, not perhaps the greatest piece of original scholarship, but one she had laboured on for most of the week. She finished, and all Miss Lascelles said was, 'No'. And, once, when I handed in an essay she returned it with the words, 'Miss Rantzen, I must congratulate you on your writing . . .' I could hardly believe it. Did she really admire my style? Could I be the new Jane Austen? She saw my hopeful expression and brought me down with a crash, 'Very legible'.

I once described Swift to her as a cynic. Miss Lascelles turned to me sharply, 'How would you define the term cynic?' I fumbled, she stopped me. 'No. I would define a cynic as one who constantly suspects the presence of an ugly backside.' I looked at her, could this be a joke? She had never given a hint of a sense of humour before. She read my face. 'To events.' Hopes dashed again.

There was a tradition that she would ask her English pupils to tea in the summer, at the end of the academic year. The invitation was for 4.15 p.m. We discussed the etiquette, and decided it would be polite to arrive at 4.20 p.m. So we sat on a wall round the corner from her house and I told my friends the dirtiest joke I knew, about a donkey and a tablecloth. I won't trouble you with it.

We walked down her path and rang her bell at precisely 4.20, and she threw it open as if she had been lurking just inside it, like the witch in *Hansel and Gretel*. 'Ah, here you are at last,' she said, 'I'll just go and warm the scones up again.' The scones were produced, and we sat crumbling them as silently as possible while she told us a story: 'A few evenings ago there was full, round, pale moon in the sky. I answered a ring at my doorbell, there was a man with a full round pale face. "Good evening, madam," he said. "Would you care to buy a copy of the *Encyclopaedia Britannica*?" "No," I replied. "Then would your children care for a copy of the *Encyclopaedia Britannica*?". "I have no children. And I am at present writing the *Encyclopaedia Britannica*."'

In retrospect, I feel a little sorry for Miss Lascelles. She held us at arm's length, was spiny and sharp, could reduce sensitive students to tears, but it can't have been much fun for her either—and she was not, I hear, as bad as Miss Grout. Ingrid Grout was a history don who despised all her students. We suspected it was because they had youth, and love, and she had neither. So no matter how hard they worked, nothing was ever good enough. My conscientious, brilliant friend, Caroline, would doubtless have got the First she deserved, had it not been for Miss Grout. However, if the best revenge is to live well, Caroline was the victor in the end, because unlike Miss Grout, Caroline has not only become a distinguished history don herself, with students who love her dearly, but is a wife and mother, and is still the centre of a huge number of friends who adore her. So there, Miss Grout.

*   *   *

The spirit of Somerville, lively, radical, intense, was embodied in our college principal, Dame Janet Vaughan. She was tall and wiry, with dark hair tied in a knot at the back of her neck. She walked everywhere at great speed, bending over an armful of books and papers. She used to amuse us by keeping her car warm in winter with an old fur coat thrown over the bonnet, but, in spite of this pampering, it seemed very reluctant to start on frosty mornings.

Dame Janet used to see us individually at the end of term, and my friends found the conversation difficult. I discovered the key, which was to tell her a string of anecdotes, sliced into extremely short sentences, so that she could say 'Goodbye' at a full stop, rather than a comma. Once I had mastered the technique she was an appreciative audience, rocking with laughter at the mishaps I described to her, and I would leave to find my friends outside her door bewildered to hear what sounded like a cocktail party going on.

Harold Macmillan was Chancellor of Oxford, and Visitor of Somerville, and once came to dinner in our hall. He was Prime Minister at the time. It was a grand occasion, the dons were in their flowing frocks, like the ones worn by smart ladies in 1930s' cartoons, *crêpe de chine* clinging to stout underpinnings. After the meal, Macmillan rose to speak, but as he looked round the hall at us, he began to weep. It was said that he found it unbearable seeing our young faces crowded in front of him, bringing back poignant memories of his own generation at Oxford which had been wiped out by the First World War.

He had no contact with us during his evening at Somerville, which we thought was a pity. We grouchily retired to the library after dinner, but when we heard his party leaving, we leant out of our window and sang 'For He's a Jolly Good Fellow,' and he turned in the light from the door and waved to us. At our end-of-term interview Dame Janet said that Macmillan had been delighted by our song. These days I am sure undergraduates would have the chance to meet all such distinguished visitors, but I am not sure they would be so polite (or subservient, depending on your point of view).

I was touched and intimidated when Dame Janet asked me to stay a weekend with her a couple of years after I had graduated, it was the first (and last) time anyone unpacked my case for me. It was also alarming when Dame Janet said after lunch, 'Well my dear, I'm sure you have masses to do today, I'll see you for dinner at seven'. I had nothing at all to do, my friends had long left

54

Oxford, so I took myself to the cinema.

While I was with Dame Janet the phone never stopped: other principals of women's colleges were ringing in panic because the men's colleges had just started to take women undergraduates, and it was feared that they would cream off all the best female scholars. The obvious answer was for the women's colleges to take men, but for reasons of tradition and pride and feminist stubbornness, Somerville held out against men for far too long. From being at the top of the league tables for good degrees, Somerville fell like a stone, but has now risen again, both in examination results and in morale.

I kept in touch with Dame Janet throughout my television career, and was thrilled when she took part in my *This Is Your Life*, but there is no question that it was ChildLine, not my programmes, that most interested her. She once said, 'ChildLine is the most important invention in child protection this century, and you must write the history of its creation while you still remember. Nowadays I am always being asked about the creation of the National Health Service, and I have forgotten so much.'

She had been a formidable pioneer, and a member of the Bloomsbury set. As a doctor and a research scientist, she had worked with concentration-camp survivors after the war, and was then commissioned to set safety standards for levels of strontium-90 when the nuclear industry began. 'There isn't a safe level,' she told me. She had been a don when Margaret Thatcher (now Baroness Thatcher of Kesteven) was an undergraduate at Somerville, and both were scientists. She said, 'Margaret was regarded as a fascinating curiosity because she was a Conservative, and there simply weren't any at that time.'

In my time Somerville was left-wing, in that those who were interested in politics tended to be ardent members of the Campaign for Nuclear Disarmament (CND) and passionate supporters of the welfare state. I was hardly a scarlet socialist, more a pale lilac Lib-Dem, had such a party existed. My father, like Margaret Thatcher, mistrusted the 'state', and believed in as little government intervention as possible. He once told me of a visit he had made to a nationalized industry where he saw a shed filled from floor to ceiling with bottles of ink. Someone, some years back, had made a mistake in an order, and received ten times the amount they needed, but nobody had ever dared correct the mistake. So, year by year, the bottles kept arriving, and more and more shelves filled up until the whole shed was crammed with them. He used that example to demonstrate that when nobody's money was at stake, nobody cared about waste. His philosophy had influenced me, though not dogmatically, so that I never went on CND marches to Aldermaston, but neither did I turn out for the Tories, principally because I could never get on with the upper classes.

There were plenty of them in Oxford. They were still (just) known as 'chinless wonders', were mainly at Christ Church, and were rich, noble, and very stupid. When asked why they were given places at Oxford a Christ Church don explained that, since they were going to inherit so much money and power, it must be beneficial for them to come into contact with brains, even if they had none

56

themselves. One young man hired an English don to have lunch with him several times a week, in the hope that he could absorb scholarship with the vichyssoise, and not have to do the work. He failed.

I met some of the lords and ladies because I had some incredibly sexy Somerville friends who were taken up by them. One of my friends, Wendy Varnals, I would dearly love to track down again. She was very bright, read Politics, Philosophy and Economics, and looked like a pocket Brigitte Bardot. Wendy outlined her eyes smokily, like Brigitte, pouted her lips like Brigitte, and had Brigitte's long hair, voluptuous bosom and tiny waist.

Wendy appeared in our first term in a production by John Duncan, (who became a television director) of *Jacques*, an Ionesco play which was entirely stylized, and in which she had to jerk around the stage like a marionette. I believe she even had to wear a mask. Somehow her sex-appeal shone through, and from that moment she was a star on the Oxford social scene. She had been a cockney, and these days still would be. But she suddenly arrived back one term speaking totally differently. I think it was at a time when she had been adopted by Grey Gowrie's set (Lord Gowrie, known to his friends as Greysteil because that was part of his title, but to us nobodies as Grey, was a poet, romantically gorgeous, and eventually got engaged to a lady he had known before he came up to Oxford). Whether it was due to Gowrie or one of the other rich young people Wendy met I will never know, but she suddenly began to adopt the clipped vowels and odd downward inflections of the English upper classes.

After Oxford she had a brief television career as a presenter of *Where It's At* with cartoonist Barry Fantoni, a pop art show produced by Liz Cowley. It was one of the swingiest shows in the swinging sixties, but it had a short life, and then Wendy disappeared, where I don't know. Rumour has her marrying a pop star and living in New York. I do hope it's true. I admired her. She was tough and friendly, and we shared many long evenings discussing life over innumerable cups of coffee. I hope her chameleon capacity to transform herself has kept her happy and successful over the last forty years.

The other sex-bomb in our set is still a close friend of mine, Norma Shepherd. Norma had huge brown eyes, glossy, long, brown hair, slender long legs and an amazing bust. When she sped on her bicycle down the High on her way to a lecture, young male undergraduates would swoon on the pavement. She appeared in a student production of *The Country Wife*, and I can visualize the scene in which she tried to write a letter, smearing herself with ink and chewing the quill. She would have been a star if she had dared try the professional stage, but she didn't.

I couldn't count the number of hearts Norma broke at Oxford. All her tragic swains used to end up on my hearth-rug, pouring their hearts out to me, I was the invaluable ugly friend, three doors down the corridor. I could do nothing to help, but I could—and did—listen, for hours on end. It's a wonder I forgave her the terrible tedium, but I did.

After we graduated, Norma joined the BBC as a sub-editor in News, an important journalistic role, and one that could have led to much higher things.

But she met Benny Herrmann (not to be confused with Bernard Herrmann of the Northern Dance Orchestra), a millionaire composer. He was twenty-nine years older than her, and had a ferocious temper. He was also a superb musician. He had been a musical prodigy in Hollywood, wrote the score for Orson Welles's *Citizen Kane* and for all the Hitchcock movies until the producers, more fool them, decided it was more lucrative to put pop music on the track, and make money from the record sales.

Benny created excitement and suspense with his film scores, which are now regarded as classics, including the frightening violin screams in Psycho. When Norma met him in the sixties he was living in London, shunned by the Hollywood he now despised. I remember once ringing her and saying, 'Norma, my mother has just steamed open one of my letters and read it, I'm finally leaving home. Will you share a flat with me?' 'I'd love to,' she said, letting me down gently, 'but I'm about to marry Benny Hermann'.

Benny was introduced to my mother, and liked her at once. She would cook rich, sweet rice pudding for him, with a delicious brown crust. He said it reminded him of the puddings his mother made for him. Towards the end of his life Benny was rediscovered by hot Hollywood directors Martin Scorsese and Brian de Palma, and wrote the score for *Taxi Driver* and *Obsession*.

Norma told me the story of Benny's hiring. One of the producers had been a trombonist, and made his money from producing a television thriller. They had a convivial lunch, the producer being suitably awed by the grand old man. At the end the

59

producer said, 'Do we have a deal?' Benny smiled graciously. 'Certainly,' he said, 'but I have one condition. That is, that we never, ever speak one word to each other again.' The producer agreed.

Norma described the dub. The producer sat at the very back of the theatre, Benny was in front, conducting the orchestra. After each sequence was recorded, the producer would jot down a note to Benny, 'Mr Herrmann, that was fantastic. It conveyed the mood of the scene perfectly. Thank you'. A runner would dash the length of the theatre, and present the note to Benny, who would read it, and scribble a reply. 'I am delighted and grateful that you enjoyed it. I do hope you enjoy the next sequence as much.' They never exchanged a word.

His score for *Taxi Driver* won the British Academy award. Tragically, Benny was dead by then, but Norma came up to collect it, and as I was one of the two presenters of the awards ceremony (with Roger Moore) I had the great pleasure of announcing that Benny had won the British Oscar.

Although I was deprived of the fun of a flat-share with Norma, after her marriage we began working together. I lied to her to lure her onto our team. She was then leading the merry life of a well-off and popular wife in the artistic scene in London. 'All you're doing is buying gloves and having lunch,' I said nastily to her. 'Come and work with us, it'll be amusing, it'll make you a little money, and you can do it part-time.'

It was amusing, made her very little money, and took every waking moment of her time. She would plough through piles of letters from viewers until she found a gem, which would become, 'I've got no gas', (when some poor viewer was threatened with bills from the Gas Board even though he had only electricity), or, even better, 'I've got no water', (when the Water Board persecuted one of our viewers to pay for the privilege of allowing the rain to land on his roof).

Norma still remembers that letter. It was written on sixteen pages in tiny purple handwriting, and, she was so dreading trying to decipher it, she put it off until the end of her train journey home. But it was worth it, and made *Pick of the Week* on Radio 4, a considerable accolade.

That's Life! ended in 1994, but Norma says she still sometimes wakes with a start, panic rising as she tries to remember which story is taking her where that day. She was one of our finest researchers.

*   *   *

Not that I had any idea what future lay ahead, when Norma and I would try and cram gobbets of Old English poetry and *Paradise Lost* into our heads. When things got tough we would mutter to each other, 'Make from the shaeft, lange geshaeft', the only lines of garbled Old English that still cling to our memory. I don't regret having read Anglo Saxon and Middle English in the original, and attending lectures by Tolkien (not the older Tolkien of *The Hobbit* and *The Lord of the Rings*, but his son). We also went to lectures by Professor Wind, completely off our subject. He was an art historian, and spellbound us by analyzing Raphael's pictures, unlocking the intricate symbolism.

One of the most fascinating lectures I attended

was by the French actor and director, Jean-Louis Barrault. At one point he stopped speaking. Then he continued as if nothing had happened. After five minutes he referred back to that long moment of stillness. 'When I made that silence,' he said (forgive my clumsy translation from his elegant French), 'your souls came out of their bodies, and met mine,' and his hands described the arc in the air when our souls met. He also explained what happens when an audience sits in a theatre, 'You are so close your arms touch, and you are transformed into one great animal, you laugh and cry as one.'

By then I was involved with student theatre and revue. I auditioned for a sexy 'Teddy' girl part in a Caryl Churchill play in my second term. It was not exactly typecasting, but I did my best, cinching my plump waist in with an elastic belt, swirling a wide skirt, and doing my best to rock'n'roll. Dancing has never been my greatest skill, but I got away with it, and was given a role as a flower seller in Giraudoux's play, *The Madwoman of Chaillot*.

By this time I was deeply in love, not just with the theatre, but with a director, Bryan Stonehouse. I met Bryan when I auditioned for him. He was kind, northern, and very attractive. In my memory I see him as a slightly creased James Dean, with full lips and blue eyes. We travelled up to the Edinburgh Festival on the same train. I sat opposite him and watched him fall asleep. His chin dropped, his mouth fell open but I still loved him.

'I never told my love,' as Viola says in *Twelfth Night*, there was no point. Bryan already had a girlfriend, Liz. She was at Somerville, wore smart suits, and seemed incredibly sophisticated. What

62

had I to offer him? I was podgy, naïve, and had two left feet. Bryan was the year ahead of me and had done National Service before he came to Oxford, so he was three years older than me in age, and light years ahead in confidence.

From Oxford he joined the BBC on a trainee scheme for the newly opened BBC2 and became a drama director. Soon after, I heard that he went on holiday with friends to a villa in Majorca, learned to swim there, went out to a beach after lunch, and in a split second was dragged under the waves and drowned.

Years later on *That's Life!* we warned of the danger of currents that can sweep you away even if the water is only knee-deep. I suppose that must be how Bryan died, at the age of twenty-seven. All his friends, his colleagues and his family mourned him. Alone, working as a sound effects girl in radio, I mourned him, too. For a year after his death I used to see him everywhere—I'd be travelling on a bus, would see a man turning a corner, know in my brain that it could not be him, but my heart would still miss a beat.

I remained a virgin throughout my three years at Oxford, although there were some close calls. I remember one summer night in a haystack in Henley. We were there performing a revue in Henley week, with a group called the Worcester Buskins. One of the other members of the cast was Roger Mills, now a distinguished documentary maker. Another was the Zuleika Dobson of our day, Caroline Seebohm. Everyone at Oxford had heard of her, she was fêted in the student press as the most glamorous undergraduate of our generation. When we rehearsed our revue I used to watch her to try and fathom her secret. She was blonde, with straight mermaid-like hair. Her eyes were not simply large and blue, they had an ironic twinkle, and she had extraordinary charm, the gift of making the young men who clustered around her feel witty even when they were faltering and shy. When, many years later, it emerged that the playwright Dennis Potter had fallen hopelessly in love with her, I was not surprised.

I was in the haystack with our double bass player, a dark, lanky gipsy of a boy. We were staying in the barn lent to us by a kindly farmer, but his hospitality didn't include a bed or a bath. The hay made a workable bed, although it did move disconcertingly when the fleas in it decided all to jump together, so we used to douse it in disinfectant to try and kill them.

One day I could stand it no more, so I borrowed a costume from our revue wardrobe, a pink gingham dress and boater, like the ones the debs wore who were watching the rowing, and I walked brazenly into the Catherine Wheel Hotel. The receptionist called out to me as I passed, but I put my nose in the air and kept going. Down one corridor I found a bathroom and locked myself in. Such bliss. I sank into the first hot water my body had touched for three weeks, then someone started to hammer on the door and shouted at me to get out. I cowered in the bath until they tired and left me there, with one final shout that I could have had a bath with pleasure if I'd paid half a crown for it—which had never occurred to me. Too humiliated to find my way back, own up, and pay for the hot water, I slunk out of the back door and returned to the barn. I still owe the Catherine

Wheel half a crown for the most delicious bath of my life.

* * *

In my second year I was elected secretary of the Experimental Theatre Club. By then I was concentrating on writing and performing revues and cabarets. My skill, if you could call it one, was to write new words to old tunes, so 'The Belle of the Ball' became 'One Hell of a Ball'.

When we are dancing, you will sing, you can't sing,
It's oh, such a hell of a ball,
Drowning the band as you mangle my hand
Makes it oh, such a hell of a ball.
Then as you lose every beat, bruising my feet,
I'm compelled to
Hold you so terribly near, you make it clear
Your best friend should tell you
B O -ver confident, B F ervescent
But please don't Be all over me
Go for a Burton please go now for certain
As long as you don't go for me
Then when I'm all on my own, rather than stand
by the wall
I'll be gripped by a drip
Even worse than the first
At this Hell of a Ball.

It wasn't art, but it got laughs. So did 'The Birth of the Blues', which became 'A Berth for a Blue'.

I am going to get myself a guy
To try and stop me getting bored, here in Oxford,

65

If only I can
So if you want this little dame
You only have to play a game
I know exactly who I'll choose
One of the Blues
He'll be my man.
Oh, how I long
For a strong
Handsome man
To belong to, I'm looking for one of the Blues.
Brunette or fair
Any year
First or third, I don't care
Cos I'm looking for one of the Blues.
Any kind of sport, wicket or court
netball or rugby
I'll even go for chess
If you possess
All those muscles to hug me.
And I'll excuse low IQs
Overdraft or abuse
just as long as you're one of the Blues
Pass the word round, I've got a Berth for a Blue.

I loved writing lyrics—it had the appeal of a crossword puzzle. It was a technique that turned out to be useful when I had to write songs for *That's Life!* and it means that I can appreciate the wonderful dexterity of Cole Porter and Ira Gershwin, not that I am anywhere in their class, but an earwig can admire the stars.

Gradually as I performed in plays and cabarets I stocked up enough experience with the Experimental Theatre Club, to be given the responsibility of producing the summer revue.

Oxford put on one big revue each summer at the Playhouse Theatre, and the time came to choose a title for it. We met in someone's room to discuss it. The first suggestion was, 'Kick Against the Pricks'. I objected. Everyone else looked at me. 'What's wrong with it, Esther?' 'It's far too long.' They sighed. Then one turned to Giles Havergal and said, 'Giles, you've got to tell her,' and they all left the room.

My family, as perhaps you will recall, was properly, even primly brought up. My mother had a sheltered life. My father had never been in the army. The worst language he had ever come across was in James Joyce's *Ulysses*, and he kept those words to himself. Although my Uncle Max had served in the army during the Second World War, he later explained that he had been overtaken by the purity of our family—the opposite of having been corrupted by us—somehow his wife's family had expunged the army vocabulary from his memory. So when he heard us all call my sister, Priscilla, 'Prick', for short, he rapidly forgot any meaning other than the injury caused by a needle. My friends suffered for years when Priscilla and I went to the theatre, and I called 'Prick' across the foyer. When the moment came to choose the name of the revue, and I revealed that I still didn't know what it meant, they could bear it no longer. Giles, they decided, was the man to educate me.

Giles Havergal is now well known as the Artistic Director of the Glasgow Citizens' Theatre. In Oxford he was celebrated for creating a black-and-white Ball for Christ Church, taking a revue up to the Edinburgh Festival, and improving my vocabulary. He started gently: 'Esther, you

67

remember the quotation from *Romeo and Juliet:* "the bawdy hand of the dial is now upon the prick of noon?"' 'Yes.' 'What does it mean?' 'That it's twelve o'clock.' Enough. 'Esther, prick means penis.'

I was appalled. My poor sister. The rest of the group filed in. They told me the agonies they had suffered, meeting Priscilla and discovering that she was known to the whole family as 'Prick'. I could see what they meant. My parents were visiting me the following weekend. I had to do my duty by my much-loved sister.

I decided to tackle my mother. So I said I would love a drive out into the countryside. She agreed to take me. The sun was shining, the countryside looked glorious. Neither of us paid any attention. Scarcely was I in the car when I turned to her and said, 'Mother, I have bad news.' She prepared herself, but not for this. 'Prick means penis.' There was silence. We drove on together. Then she started a furious speech. 'Esther, you have the most disgusting imagination. How can you possibly say such a thing?' Sadly, at that moment we passed a pub called The Golden Balls. I snorted. She became even more enraged. 'I heard that. I shall tell your father. What a disgusting thing to say.'

We drove back to Oxford, and I did not bring up the subject again. I think my father may have consulted Uncle Max. However it happened, my sister is now known to friends and family as Cilla.

*   *   *

The natural history of an undergraduate is like a frog's life. The first year is spent in a jelly state,

68

nervous of Prelims (the first-year exam which must be passed if you are to continue your university career), and not sure of yourself socially, so you try a little of everything—sport, drama, the Union, politics—to find which one you enjoy and thrive at. By the second year you have made your choices and found your friends, so like the tadpole you emerge from the spawn and start swimming confidently in your new element. The third year is far more adult and earnest, you know you must grow the arms and legs you will need in your next life, and with Finals you make the great leap onto dry land.

In my second year at Oxford I must confess I did very little academic study, instead I concentrated on appearing in and directing revues, writing for magazines, and in the summer I organized the Somerville Ball.

I am not quite sure why I was chosen for this honour. I felt at the time that someone more socially successful—maybe one of the ex-debs who floated around the college—should have taken it on. Heaven knows they went to more dances than me. This was the time of 'The Twist', when Chubby Checker had just invented the new dance craze, and we were all practising swerving our knees from side to side and lashing out with our feet, such a peculiar movement no wonder it has never been revived. I was never a fluent twister. But it was explained to me that whether or not I could dance was not the point; it was whether we could sell all the tickets and cover the cost.

We were sitting one morning at breakfast in the Somerville Hall, wrestling with large hard-boiled eggs and small thin-skinned oranges, and

69

reminiscing about the uncomfortable snogging sessions of the night before. I looked at the dark wood panelling carved like classical pillars, and studded with forbidding portraits of previous college Principals. Inspiration struck, we'd call it the 'Ball of the Vestal Virgins'. We'd cover the pillars with pictures of caryatids, and put a cartoon of a huge sacrificial bull on the stairs up to the Hall (we knew our Freud). I went to Barbara Harvey, the Dean, who had already taught me a valuable lesson, how to lie when you have to.

Miss Harvey was the disciplinary dominatrix of the college, in charge of fining us for misdemeanours, like being late. At that time the gate was only open until 10.30 p.m. and after that the choice was either to climb in, or to ring the bell for the porter, and risk a fine. Some friends from the men's college across the road, St John's, used to take a rickety ambulance to Stratford-upon-Avon to see the summer productions there. That's how I saw Peter Hall's magical *Twelfth Night*, with Dorothy Tutin as Viola. That's also how I saw Zeffirelli's frightful *Othello*, with Gielgud as the least convincing warrior Moor ever. It was difficult not to giggle, especially as the sets were so huge they left no room for a curtain call. We noticed that the curtain rippled as it dropped, obviously hitting something, and when it rose again, Gielgud was tugging at his wig, mouthing at Desdemona, 'Is it the right way round?'

Good production or bad, there was no way we could get back to Oxford afterwards in time for the Somerville curfew. We did the best we could, the porter let me in with a filthy look, and I was summoned before the Dean. 'Why were you late?'

she said, grimly. She was not much older than we were, but managed to convince us she was very middle-aged. I explained that the time of the performance meant we inevitably arrived back too late. 'Since you have no adequate excuse,' she said, 'I have no choice but to fine you half a crown.' Cash was very short, and half a crown then was the equivalent of £5 now. I felt aggrieved, but she had given me a hint for the future.

The second trip to Stratford also ended late. I was summoned to the Dean again. This time I had a story ready. 'We were on our way, would have been back easily in time,' I lied, 'but then we had a puncture. We were in such an old ambulance, the jack was no good, we had to hail another motorist to help us,' and on and on I went. Miss Harvey looked sympathetic. When eventually I finished she said, 'Well, Miss Rantzen, since you obviously did your best, I won't fine you this time. Please don't let it happen again.'

I left, not feeling nearly guilty enough. But then it was such a stupid rule. I never like any rules much, but stupid rules I have always loathed. Perhaps that moment was the birth of *That's Life!*'s famous 'Jobsworth Award', for an idiotic rule stubbornly applied, 'because it's more than my Jobsworth not to'.

Still, I forgave the Dean everything when it came to the Somerville Ball. I had decided to ask her permission for our classical Greek theme. Could we attach caryatids to the pillars? Miss Harvey thought about it, then made my dreams come true. 'Yes, as long as they are not in the nude.' She'd banned naked caryatids, bless her. I skipped down the stairs, straight to the offices of the student newspaper, *Cherwell.* We organized a photograph of my gorgeous friend Norma, she of the beautiful bust, posing for a talented Somerville artist, Sarah Sheppard. To the young photographer's surprise, I pulled him round to the side, so that the full Norma was silhouetted against the window. She was wearing a tight jumper that hid nothing. The picture went round the world, together with the story, 'Somerville Bans Nudes,' and Norma got fan-mail from a sailor in Florida. The tickets sold out the next day.

My own memories of the Ball are mixed. I had found a dress in a sale for £12, very cheap even then. It was lilac, strapless and heavily boned. A young Latin undergraduate grabbed me tight, and tangoed me up and down the length of the hall. When he released me the dress had revolved, and I had a perfect bust in the middle of my back.

*   *   *

Summer in Oxford cried out for romance. The men's colleges gave glamorous Commemoration Balls, with the top bands, the best cabarets, champagne and strawberries at dawn. As the sun rose we would find a punt, and drift along in the early sunlight, which pierced our eyes like darts. If only Bryan Stonehouse had taken me. The boys who did were fun, and clever, but I wasn't in love with them.

I envied my friends, many of whom were in love—Caroline met her husband, John Barron, at Oxford, Margaret met her husband, George Kenyon. I even introduced two of my friends to each other, Kirsty and Nicholas Leonard. However,

I made the appalling error of telling them how much each fancied the other, putting them off each other for years, until at last they met again away from my interfering matchmaking, and happily married.

There were young men already clearly in training as icons of their generation. The Labour aristocrat, Peter Jay (once Ambassador to the United States, now the BBC's Economics Editor), was President of the Union and heading straight for a First, and was going out with a friendly, clever Somervillian a year ahead of me, Margaret Callaghan (now Baroness Jay). I once slept in Melvyn Bragg's bed, but sadly, only because he was away and I needed somewhere to crash out until Somerville's gates opened the next morning. David Dimbleby was editing the student magazine *Isis*, Auberon Waugh contributed an occasional article. But they were all far too exalted for a gauche, over-enthusiastic trainee luvvy to mix with.

I did contribute to *Mesopotamia*, a magazine with aspirations to be *Private Eye*, but without the edge and wit. I went out several times with *Mesopotamia*'s Editor John Albery, (of the theatrical family), who was a Balliol scientist, and went on to become Master of University College. He was funny and lanky, and we remained friends for years after I graduated, but there was no romance between us. When I did fall in love it was inevitably with someone who didn't notice my presence, or, like Dorothy Parker, 'I loved them until they loved me'.

That is not to decry my friendships. The men I met at St John's were talented and wonderful company. Perhaps I was closest of all to Glyn

73

Worsnip, who years later joined the *That's Life!* team. He had a wicked wit, was tall, thin, sang, danced, and was extremely good to me—especially in that second year when, as I have said, I did practically no work. He used to lend me his essays, but I would leave so little time to read them before tutorials that I could not always decipher his handwriting. What did the dons think, as I stumbled my way through Glyn's excellent piece of scholarship? I am sure they guessed it was not my work, but they politely never mentioned it, and nor did I.

After the summer term ended in 1961 I went to the Lake District's Kendal Festival and the Edinburgh Festival with undergraduate revues. A brilliant scholar from Magdalen College, Richard Jameson, was a member of the cast. In the train on the way to Kendal, we saw that a British Rail cup was not just grimy and tea-stained, it was badly chipped. We threw it out of the window. Richard laughed and threw another cup out of the window, then another. It went beyond the joke. We were uneasy.

From Kendal we went straight to Edinburgh, where we stayed in a Freemason's lodge in a big dusty room on camp beds. Giles Havergal was directing our revue, we performed it in the Cranston Street Hall. [Now, perhaps suitably, a hostel for homeless women.] After one show we decided to walk up the nearby mountain, Arthur's Seat. There we watched the sunrise, and climbed down again, arriving at the local grocer's looking so footsore and pathetic that they gave us bacon and eggs to make a delicious breakfast.

Alan Bennett came to visit us. He had friends in

our company, he was by now working as a don at Oxford, and had come to Edinburgh to perform in the Festival. He was rehearsing a revue with Peter Cook, Dudley Moore and Jonathan Miller. I remember sitting on the stairs with him as he shook his head sadly. 'It will never do,' he said. We were all so concerned for them that we went as a group to their first night, determined to clap and cheer. We did, but we were drowned by the rest of the ecstatic audience. The show was *Beyond the Fringe*, and they went on to huge success in London's West End and on Broadway.

Meanwhile, Richard Jameson was becoming more of a concern for us. In the play which was being performed just before our revue, he played a mad scholar. I remember watching him walk down the Royal Mile in Edinburgh, looking thin and feverish, the veins standing out on his temples, almost unaware of the traffic as he crossed the street.

A day before we opened I went for a costume fitting at Cranston Street Hall. A girl stood at my shoulder, pinning the material. Across the room, Richard was in his costume for the dress rehearsal, wearing a long tattered gown and a straggly grey wig. He was looking at his reflection, drawing large black moles on his face. The girl whispered to me, 'None of us knows what he's going to do next'. He caught my eye in the mirror, turned and walked towards me. The girl froze. He took my shoulders, kissed me hard, then let go and said, 'Now are you satisfied?' 'Yes, Richard,' I said, 'More than satisfied'. We were frightened.

I told Giles, and he had a difficult decision to make. Richard's family were abroad, everyone in

75

the group was in their teens and early twenties. However, Giles managed to find help for Richard, such as it was at that time. I think it included ECT, and some very painful treatments. I have stayed in touch with Richard over the years. I now know that during that summer he suffered the onset of schizophrenia. He is brilliantly articulate about his illness and has taken part in a number of programmes on the subject. He frequently joins the audience of the talk show I make for BBC2. His questions are original and to the point.

Once, by sheer coincidence, Richard's consultant also took part in our show. He told me, 'Richard is the bravest man I know, he understands that the medication he takes blunts his intellect and his sensations, but he recognizes that only through that medication can he live an independent life.'

Richard gave me my first insight into mental illness, and having watched the progress of his schizophrenia I now believe that it has a physical origin, and that one day we should be able to treat it effectively with drugs.

The shows we took to Edinburgh were successful, quite well reviewed, and the hall was packed every night. Liz Norfolk was in the company. She was Sir Mortimer Wheeler's very attractive stepdaughter. He was an archaeologist who had intrigued television audiences not just with his erudition, but also his enormous moustache. I became friendly with Liz, and went to lunch in London with her and her mother. It was a delicious meal, but I was curious to see that Liz was given different food from us, steak for instance. When she was out of the room I said to her mother, 'Make sure she takes care of her health, these tours are very tiring.' Lady Wheeler said nothing, but I discovered that, at great cost to herself, she had decided to allow Liz to have as busy and full a summer as possible.

Liz had leukaemia. She died soon afterwards. Young death is agonizing. The ageing process prepares us gently for it. But to be snatched away from us too early, with no fading, no deterioration, seems unbearably cruel. We all mourned Liz, and marvelled at the courage of her mother, who had let us enjoy so much of her company, when she knew how little time was left.

John Wells was also in our cast. What an odd mixture he was. Funny, acid, a writer as well as a performer, when he left Oxford he created 'Mrs Wilson's Diary' with Richard Ingrams for *Private Eye*. At the same time he was an old-fashioned snob. When he tragically died in middle age, far too early, his memorial service read like *Debrett's*. His first job was as a teacher at Eton. He was always in the company of debby girls with double-barrelled names. That seemed odd to us, in the student theatre, an environment where class distinctions meant nothing. It still seems a paradox to me that a man with such keen eyes, such a sense of the ridiculous, could fall for the pretentious nastiness of social snobbery. But then his close friend Richard Ingrams, too, is a paradox.

I knew Richard at Oxford, he was musical, and introvert, and seedily attractive. It was a shock when Ingrams and his *Private Eye* colleagues decided to target me, and caricatured me for years as the wicked witch of west London. I gather Richard once had blown-up pictures of Desmond and me alongside Jimmy Goldsmith in his *Private*

Eye office, just to remind himself how much he loathed us, in case his anger ever went off the boil. Whatever Ingrams and Wells felt about me later, when we were all students at Oxford together we liked each other well enough.

*   *   *

As our third year started, I realized life was about to become real and earnest. I would have to start writing my own essays, and catch up on all the reading I had neglected. I had aimed myself at the BBC. Why? Nowadays, when you ask young people their ambitions, all too often they will say, 'I want to be famous'. But that was no part of my dream. Mine was to some extent based on my father's experience. He had the greatest respect for it as an institution. I also knew how influential broadcasting could be. The idea of discovering important stories and clothing them in an entertaining format deeply appealed to me even then.

The BBC used to send recruiting officers to Oxford and Cambridge to interview potential general trainees and studio managers. No woman had ever been given a general traineeship, which was intended for the real high flyers. But studio management was more accessible, there were more jobs available, and, even though they did not necessarily lead anywhere, at least it was one way in.

I was interviewed for both. For the general traineeship I was asked, 'Do you consider entry to the Common Market to be a political or an economic issue?' I was completely fazed by the question and ducked it. 'Aren't all politics a matter of economics?' No wonder I didn't get the job. But the studio management interview went far better. I was asked about the productions I had directed, and my enthusiasm for the BBC. You can imagine my delight when I received a letter telling me I had been accepted.

To be on the safe side, I had also applied for a scholarship to a secretarial college in Kensington called Mrs Hoster's. The original Mrs Hoster had been Jewish, and the scholarship was specifically for Jewish graduates (probably that would be an offence against race relations legislation now). As far as I know, no other Jewish graduates applied, so I got that, too. So by the spring of my last year I had two life-lines into the real world.

That just left the last barrier—Finals. How could I avoid disgracing myself? Luckily, one of my friends had the answer. He had gone to the library and looked up every English paper for the last ten years. He then listed the authors who turned up in the papers every year because the examiners could not ignore them, the giants of each century. He gave me a copy of his list and I started to read voraciously. No matter if I hated Milton, had never read Jonson, or could not remember a word of Dickens, I read and learned them now.

The pressure was almost too great. One night I decided I could stand it no longer. I got out of bed, took a bottle of aspirin, and swallowed the lot. There was only one tablet in it. Even so, as I lay down in bed again, I regretted my suicidal urge, and fought unconsciousness. 'Typical Esther,' I hear my mother saying, 'dramatizing again.'

In the morning, back I went to the library,

devouring the classics on my list. I didn't bother with critics, or contemporary writers. I had no time. I simply steeped myself in the authors I knew I would have to write essays about, and learned quotations to cover any possible question. At lunchtime, between papers, I took my books to the botanical gardens, and flipped over the pages, just to remind myself of the sense and feel of my chosen authors. And I took one more precaution. I accepted the part of Gwendolen in a Balliol production of Oscar Wilde's *The Importance of Being Earnest*, opposite Peter Snow.

Peter has charmed television viewers of *Newsnight* and *Tomorrow's World*, and he charmed us equally at Oxford. It is not just that he is tall, square-jawed and handsome. He has a benign vagueness, a smiling patrician manner, whether he is shoving toy tanks through a model of the Sinai desert, or battling with a swingometer at election time.

At Oxford I remember him wandering around in appalling jeans and a cowboy hat, hand in hand with his girlfriend, Alison—a baby cowgirl with lush lips, big eyes and a bouncing bosom. They were a good-looking couple, and Peter was excellent in *The Importance of Being Earnest.* It was not his fault that we were all upstaged by the Balliol cat.

The play took place on a lawn, and during each performance the cat used to walk straight across the stage, climb through a college window, then out through another and cross the stage again. The audience applauded each entrance and exit.

During one performance, my dress (made in the 1920s and found forty years later at the bottom of the Balliol dressing-up box), had a long fringe which knotted itself around my stiletto heels. I stood up and found myself bowed backwards, like a sausage. I hobbled downstage for my next line, 'Do you allude to me, Miss Cardew, as an entanglement?' I clearly was, and the audience gave me my best laugh of the run.

Wilde did me a favour that summer. When Finals finished I had a last optional paper on drama, and I managed to weave into it a great many lines from the part of Gwendolen in *The Importance of Being Earnest.* I got what they described at Oxford as 'a good Second'. Thank you, Oscar.

*   *   *

So there was I at the end of my three years at Oxford, poised to join the BBC and start the rest of my life. There was just the three-month secretarial course to endure first. I was a mutinous student. One of our instructors taught us the following 'office routine': *Always keep one spare silk stocking in your handbag, in case of a ladder. Always arrive twenty minutes before your 'chief', in order to open the office windows, freshen the water in his flower vases, and put the water on the boil for his first cup of coffee.* Even while I took notes I determined that I would be a 'chief' myself one day, and when I was, I would freshen my own flowers.

We were taught to touch-type to music, but my typing was hopelessly erratic. When we were given texts to copy my fingers would tangle on the keys and produce a jumble of letters. Then I would try to hide my mistake and waste valuable seconds searching for a word which contained that jumble, knowing that our teacher would never check the original text when she was proof-reading. Sometimes I would find myself so far behind the rest of my class that I would feel tears coursing down my cheeks.

The humiliation was intense, all around me were sixteen-year-olds who were rattling away, their shorthand immaculate, their typing precise, while I, the only BA among them, fumbled along incompetently. But, as I tell my children, no experience is wasted. When it came to writing thousands of words for *That's Life!* years later, I blessed Mrs Hoster's for flogging me on to greater and greater typewriting speeds. I needed them.

So who was I at twenty-two? A graduate with a good degree, more by luck than judgement, with very happy memories of those three golden years to sustain me, and dozens of friends around me. Still a virgin, still too fat, too fond of puns and terrible *double entendres*, I was living at home once more, and eagerly looking forward to earning a living at the BBC. I had not met the man of my dreams, and envied every pretty, confident woman I met.

I had no idea what life had in store. If you had asked me then if I would ever have a successful career, or get married, or have children, I probably would have answered pessimistically. All those ambitions seemed completely out of my reach. But I enjoyed life so much day to day that it seemed stupid to waste time wishing and wondering. And, instinctively, I felt that somehow, somewhere, the best was yet to come.

CHAPTER FOUR

CORPORATION WOMAN

I left Oxford in the summer of 1962, and came back to my family home in northwest London. My bedroom greeted me like an old friend. But the Cricklewood pavements looked grimy and ugly. As I struggled by tube at rush-hour to the secretarial college in Kensington I was surprised how poignantly I missed the beauty of Oxford. My memory was constantly taunting me with nostalgic moments—a still spring morning when I was walking to New College, and between the grey of the ancient building and the blue of the sky came the notes of a trumpet, or sitting in the huge Christ Church quad at sunset, listening to a spectacular version of the *1812 Overture* echoing around the walls.

These memories sustained me during my frustrating first years at work. For, just as I had been warned by the BBC's recruiting officers, even when I had finished my typing and shorthand course and joined my Mecca, the work turned out to be a grinding series of chores.

Broadcasting House sits in London like an art deco liner, as if Reith had sailed it from Regent's Park up Portland Place and anchored it next to All Souls Church. Its foyer is very like a Cunard reception room, with a big glass entrance and copper lift doors. Somewhere high above street level the Director-General, Hugh Carleton Greene, was on the bridge, in a light oak-panelled office out of sight, and as far as I was concerned, out of mind as well. His was a benign reign—under him talent flourished and politicians were kept at bay, but the class barriers in the Corporation were as great as in any ocean liner, and I was a menial, sweating away in the engine room.

I trained as a radio studio manager. Producers and performers were responsible for all the creative ideas in the programmes. Studio managers were the technicians, the sound-balancers. They placed the microphones, mixed the output, invented sound effects, played tapes and records, cued the artists, fetched tea and coffee. In other words, they fulfilled the role of a stage manager in the theatre.

For me the hardest task was the first—switching the studio on. All the studios were similar, airless, windowless, grubby, filled with ancient equipment, some of it lend-lease borrowed from the Americans during the war. But each studio had a different hiding place for the crucial switch that turned everything on. I used to arrive early, praying that the producer would be delayed long enough for me to find the blessed thing. If he was already there I would walk round as if inspecting everything else, until he put me out of my misery and found it for me.

I was given the scripts in advance, so that I could bring the props and records the programmes required. Physics seemed to dictate that anything that made a loud noise had to be incredibly heavy: huge bolsters that when dropped made the sound of a falling body, great chains to rattle, china to clatter for *Mrs Dale's Diary*, even the boxes for the records were massive, so I would stagger under the load towards the swing doors at Broadcasting House. Unmoved, the commissionaires would watch me approach. Far later, when I became a face they recognized from television, they would jump to open the door for me, even though I had nothing to carry but a handbag. The paradox made me smile.

Much of my training took place at Bush House, home of the BBC's World Service. The Treasury pays for it, and has the right to choose which countries are served, but the BBC jealously guards the independence of the programmes themselves and above all the news. It is an extraordinary partnership, theoretically it cannot work, in practice it does, and, as a result, the BBC has an unparalleled reputation for objectivity and truth-telling around the world.

Although I was the lowliest link in the chain, I was aware of this reputation, and proud to be part of it. But Bush House is a strange place. Most of the broadcasters, of course, are foreign nationals, and in my time they were almost all married men, exiled from their families. Twenty-two-year-old females fumbling around their studios looking for the on-switch were manna from heaven. I was taken out by Turks and Frenchmen, and successfully fended them off, although a blonde friend of mine was painfully bitten by a Brazilian in a lift.

We used to work through the night. I will never forget the surreal quality of the Bush House canteen at three in the morning, when the human system is at its lowest ebb, and we used to try to keep going by inventing vile mixtures: ice-cream in Coca-Cola, with sausage and marmalade on the side—anything to stay awake. Then I would sleepwalk on to the bus back to Cricklewood, and often doze right past my stop. The heritage from those years at Bush House is that I can still sleep anywhere, any time, even standing strap-hanging on a train.

I worked with some outstanding broadcasters at Bush House. The Africans were noted for their precision. They could carry on speaking up to the very second a computer somewhere in the depths of Bush House automatically switched wavelengths. Three weeks after I finished my training, I carried a dozen records into a studio, tripped and watched them slide down the back of the grams deck. The African broadcaster in the studio had seen the catastrophe and smiled reassuringly. It was a fifteen-minute programme of record requests. How could he fill the time? He said there was no problem, so the red light went on, he started talking in Hausa, while I wormed around on the floor with a script, a long piece of wire, anything I could find to hook the records back to my side of the cabinet, so that I could play them.

I failed, the hands of the clock ticked by, and he closed the programme, perfectly on time. I rushed into the studio. 'How did you do that?' I said, overawed. 'What did you talk about?' 'Well,' he said, 'I told them I had a studio manager who was only three weeks in the job, and she had dropped the records down the back of the record player, and now she has a script in her hand and is crawling on the floor, and now she has found a piece of wire . . .' It was another valuable lesson in broadcasting—viewers actually prefer mistakes to programmes. Hence the current popularity of out-

86

takes and bloopers.

One mistake was not tolerated, and we were all given a special course in playing records of the Koran. The readings were recorded on enormous discs which played from the inside out. Every other record played from the outside edge to the centre. It was rumoured that a dozy studio manager had once put the needle on the outside edge of the Koran and played it backwards, thus causing terrible international outrage. At least, among my many mistakes, I never made that one.

My moment of greatest personal power was the shipping forecast. Then I was allowed to fade the whole live transmission off the air, play 'Lillibulero', read the forecast with all its tongue-twisting Heligolands and Fastnets, and then fade the channel up again. I was entirely alone, all the knobs and buttons at my command. I fantasized that if ever my job became completely unbearable I would fade the transmission and give the world my full story, get the lot off my chest. I have always felt the deepest sympathy for continuity announcers who do that, and leave not with a whimper, but a vengeful bang. Sadly, after I left Bush House I never sat in that seat of power again.

*　　　*　　　*

My six-month apprenticeship completed, I was posted back to Broadcasting House. I had already spent a little time there during my training, working on the Light Programme music shows, especially the daily *Housewives' Choice*. It may have been 1963, but the BBC was still firmly stuck in the fifties. I knew that women were no longer dancing in frilly pinnies around the bedroom, content to vacuum under the mattress while listening to a kindly announcer singing along to the most nostalgic of all signature tunes, 'ladidadi, ladidadidadi Dee Dah'. But the programme controllers maintained the myth. The programmes were based on domesticity, the boat remained unrocked, housewives knew their place, which was nine o'clock every morning on the Light Programme.

I still have a real affection for the *Housewives' Choice* signature tune. On *That's Life!* we once filmed an Alsatian dog who cleaned the house, and we gave her that music to work to. The record itself was a nuisance. To get the perfect first note you had to listen on headphones, mark the disc with a chinagraph crayon, turn it back half a revolution, and then fade it up exactly on the note, and you would still risk getting a sick-making 'wow' as it began.

I most enjoyed working with a producer called Jack Dabbs, a cheerful man who put together the best collection of music, cleverly using a great many 'open' requests, 'play anything for my granny'. He was the victim of a lurid newspaper exposé some years later. They claimed that Dorothy Squires had bribed him with invitations to stay with her in return for playing her records. He denied it but, in any case, I thought agreeing to take a holiday in Gibraltar with Dorothy demonstrated an even greater devotion to duty on his part.

Godfrey Winn had his own programme of interviews and music. He was a mystery to me, gushing to the stars he interviewed, while they dimpled back at him. I asked his producer why he was so popular, and was told he was so gentle and effusive that the stars queued up to talk to him. One day, when I was about to play a record on Godfrey's programme, the sound of drilling intensified. Drills appear regularly in the background of BBC radio programmes—for some reason they are part of the chemistry, like white vans in traffic accidents, and rain on Bank Holidays. On this occasion, as I stood at the record player, a drill suddenly came through the wall at eye level. That, I felt, was taking things a bit far.

I applied for a transfer to the Drama Department—not to escape drills, they affected plays as much as any other part of the output—but because it gave me the company of actors and directors, and allowed me to work on exciting productions. I would also have liked to work on entertainment shows, but women were not allowed to, lest they be corrupted by the wicked words used not on the programmes, of course, but in the course of conversation. I had already learned the wicked words, thanks to Giles Havergal, but still the BBC placed entertainment out of bounds for us women, for the sake of our feminine purity.

Alas, Drama presented an even greater threat. Not from the actors, they were courtesy itself. I loved working alongside talents like Martin Jarvis and Andrew Sachs, versatile, unassuming, utterly brilliant. Jessie Matthews, however, was a different case. By the time I worked with her when she played Mary, the star of *Mrs Dale's Diary*, Jessie was a middle-aged lady with an irritatingly high voice, who took up so much space in front of the microphone that it was difficult for me to find room to clink a cup on a saucer, or pour the tea. I was too young to remember her as the toast of the West End, with high kicks like launching rockets and a beguiling smile. But the rest of the cast, the producers, and most of all the listeners, forgave her the fluffs and her absent-minded performance in that early radio soap. She carried her mythology with her into the studio, and, after a while, I, too, lost my impatience.

Robert Morley was another star I found difficult to work with. I know he was extremely intelligent, a fine writer as well as an actor, and he had learned to use his eccentric appearance to comic effect. His sprouting eyebrows, pursed lips, heavy body, and constant expression of outrage had stood him in good stead in many an epic film. But none of this was much use if you couldn't see him, so Robert was unnerved by radio, a new medium for him.

The play in which he was starring was a detective drama in which he took the lead, as a Cambridge don. The trouble started as soon as the read-through began. Robert queried every line, no matter how short. He walked along a sofa, then lay on the floor roguishly, throwing cushions around, with his legs in the air. It was coquettish and funny, in retrospect. But the read-through, which should have taken a couple of hours, lasted a complete day. Robert pretended not to understand the director's instructions, I had to lead him, like a baby elephant, from microphone to microphone. I watched the steady, experienced Drama Repertory Company around him fall to pieces, they never knew if or when their cue was coming. At lunchtime he would disappear for a sumptuous meal at Simpson's, while the rest of us went to the canteen.

On the last day, the day of the recording, Robert arrived a different man. His script was marked up with every nuance and stage direction, he knew perfectly well which microphone to use, his performance was immaculate. I pitied the rep actors, who had no chance to pull their own performances together. Their one moment of revenge was during a scene set at a feast at the high table of his Cambridge college. I was doggedly chopping up pieces of banana on a filthy soundeffects plate for the sound of his knife and fork, and swilling soapy water in a teapot for the sound of the wine. Suddenly Robert grabbed my fork and took a mouthful, then he seized the spout of the teapot and swallowed the lot. It must have tasted foul, but trooper that he was, he didn't falter. The other actors smiled grimly. They knew where that horrible soundeffects china had been, and it wasn't Simpson's.

Dame Edith Evans played the nurse in a radio version of *Romeo and Juliet*, in which I played Juliet. Not Juliet alive and speaking, naturally, but when Juliet died, I was the sound of her falling body. Dame Edith was remarkable, when she arrived in the studio the bored repertory actors all stood, as a reflex, from respect. However, Dame Edith insisted on addressing the green cue light when it flashed, so my job became to hold the light as closely as possible to the microphone. When she said her famous, 'Anon!' to Juliet she covered two octaves with those two syllables, much as she did with her 'handbag' in *The Importance of Being Earnest*. I am delighted to have worked with her.

Only one actor threatened my virtue, and that was Andrew Faulds. He arrived in a studio to provide narration for a programme about mountains, and when I saw him I thought he was a backwoods' explorer. It must have been his bristling beard. I never have been partial to beards. For me, one of the best transformation scenes on film is the moment when the seven brothers shave their chins to please the seven brides. I would happily have stayed my side of the glass window, but at one stage I had to present Andrew with a twig to break on cue, and as I approached he locked eyes with me. I walked back to the control room thinking what a funny old mountaineer he was. I glanced at the script, saw who he really was, and it made sense. Andrew's appetite for women was a legend among studio managers. When the programme ended he asked me out to dinner. I accepted. When I told my mother she asked, 'Why?' And I could only answer, 'Because it's there'.

I met Andrew in his flat. As I crossed the threshold he enveloped me in an enormous hug. As he was wearing sandals he looked more rustic than ever. I extricated myself. He had a big yellow copy of *Fanny Hill* on a coffee table. I had never seen an unexpurgated copy before, and flicked over the pages. He seemed disconcerted, and suggested we eat at Brown's Hotel. The head waiter knew his requirements, 'Your usual table, Mr Faulds'. The table was in a dark corner, so our legs automatically interlocked. As each woman arrived at the bar he would make guesses about her anatomy.

By this time I was gaining confidence. It was clear he was such an expert he would never make me suffer any experience I didn't want, although he obviously thought I would want as much as he could offer. He could have been right, if only he had listened to me. But he didn't. We never connected mentally at all. I babbled away, telling him stories from my life as a studio manager, trying to make him laugh. I failed completely. Each joke was an irritating distraction from the point of his evening—the journey back to his flat.

At last the meal was finished and I thanked him for a stimulating evening. He said, 'You sound as if you're saying a long goodbye'. We left the hotel, and as he stood back to make way for me, I ran. We met years later when he took part in a *Man Alive* debate about the danger of fireworks, by now he was an MP and a doughty campaigner. I tried to remind him that we had been out together, but he had totally forgotten me. 'Did I bed you?' he said, beard jutting. 'No,' I said, with relief.

So the actors came and went, and I paid for their coffee and tea, because, although they earned many times more than me, they never seemed to have any cash on them. Ever since, I have tried to make sure that nobody, no runner, no secretary, no work-experience trainee ever pays for my coffee. Sometimes the actors asked me out, and invariably I enjoyed the evening. They were the best company, funny, gossipy, but no threat to my heart or my body.

That came from John, a drama producer from Northern Ireland. He had piercing blue eyes, and a cleft chin. He was considerably older than me, and had a flaring talent. I watched him produce one play, and I fell. He had a way of enabling actors to reach into their own experience, and find a truth, a depth of emotion that they themselves had not believed possible.

I don't remember any of our times together nearly as clearly as that foolish evening I spent with Andrew Faulds. Perhaps it's because I fell in love with John so quickly and completely. Like Othello, John spellbound me with his reminiscences. He told me stories of the great theatrical director, Tyrone Guthrie, his mentor, who had trained him. He told me of Richard Burton, and Samuel Beckett. He also described to me the bitterness and division of Northern Ireland, the arrogance of the Orange marching season. He used to drink every night away in the pubs around Broadcasting House, and he used most of my wages to subsidize his alcohol. He would sing, his eyes shut, his hand holding mine. I still know the haunting Irish folksongs he taught me. There was one that caught my heart, with its tragic lyric and hauntingly lovely melodic line. It was called 'She Moved Through the Fair'.

My young love said to me, my mother won't mind
And my father won't slight you for your lack of
*   kind*
Then she stepped away from me and this she did
*   say*
It will not be long, love, till our wedding day.

Then she stepped away from me,
And she moved through the fair
And so gladly I watched her move here and move
*   there*
Then she made her way homeward with one star
*   awake*
As the swan in the evening moves over the lake.

Last night she came to me, my dead love came in
So softly she moved that her feet made no din
Then she laid her hand on me and this she did say
It will not be long, love, till our wedding day.

I can still hear his voice, bellowing the words in some bar late at night, giving the notes that unique Irish wildness and poignancy. Although part of my mind knew he was a bully, and a drunk, the poetry and drama seduced me. Then, one night when he drove me home, for some reason I now forget, he hit me. It was a hard blow, a fist to my head. Suddenly, bleakly, I saw him as he really was.

He apologized at once, called himself, 'Black Irish', kissed my feet, begging me to forgive him. I did, at one level. But at another, I was disgusted. Why was this man I admired so much, grovelling? Why had he used his strength—he was a powerful, thick-set man—to hurt me and demean himself?

Suddenly he made me confront my own masochism. Why was I spending night after boring night with him? Why did I allow him to bully me, to spend my money on his drink? In that instant I stopped respecting him, slowly I began to extricate myself. He found another girlfriend. As love died, it was replaced with an anger I found healing. We saw each other once or twice after I joined television. He died comparatively young. Sadly, when I heard, I felt nothing.

We made one memorable journey together to Manchester United, when George Best was playing. John was making a documentary film about him, and we met George just before the match to collect the tickets from him. I knew nothing about sport, but the 'footballing Beatle' was already famous. As we stood together, a big crowd collected around George, pressing towards him at the centre. They were worshippers, but all the same, it was threatening to feel the weight of the crowd, the intensity of their fixation with him. George was probably nineteen, a quiet Belfast boy, he almost whispered to us. I wondered how he could stand the pressure. After the match we went to find him and he pulled up his trousers to show the injuries, the bruises and blood where opposing players had tried to cripple him and put him out of the match. So much for the beautiful game.

I remained a studio manager for two and a half years. Against my will I became almost good at the job, learning to create 'spot' effects, the sound effects which were made in the studio, live rather than pre-recorded on tapes or discs. I was taught how to shake a box of dried peas briskly and rhythmically, to make the sound of an army marching on parade. I discovered that expelling a cork from the end of a bicycle pump makes a tolerable champagne bottle opening.

I even invented the noise of a swooping pterodactyl. I reasoned that not many listeners would have been around at the time, so I felt free to run around a studio opening and closing a baggy black umbrella. For the sound of King Lear's storm, I spun a huge wind machine, and shook a thunder sheet. I just missed the era when the sound of horses' hooves was made by coconut shells, although I was taught to clatter them correctly by Harry Morriss.

Harry ran the 'spot' effects store, and had created lunatic sound effects for the Goons. That

96

thrilled me particularly because in my teens I had made weekly pilgrimages to the BBC's Camden Town theatre to watch *The Goon Show* being recorded. Peter Sellers, already a rich and famous actor, used to arrive in his Rolls-Royce, Spike Milligan,* the writer and genius behind the show, would turn up on the tube. They would join Harry Secombe* [*Now, deservedly, Sir Spike and Sir Harry.] and bandleader Ray Ellington, and mayhem would ensue.

There was far more nonsense going on than the listeners ever knew. Throughout one recording a plastic teaspoon was passed round the cast and then the orchestra. We in the audience would wait eagerly for the catchphrases we loved, 'He's fallen in the water', 'You rotten thing, you have deaded me.'

Why were they funny? I suppose because of their surreal anarchy, the secret language they created, which has suffered through the passing of time, like every cult comedy. Anyway, my mentor Harry Morriss invented the wildly rattling doorknob whenever a Goon had to enter or exit, and he taught me how to make old coconut shells sound like a galloping horse, although my horses were always rather three-legged.

Feet became my forte. John produced a play in which two lovers walked through the autumn countryside. I cannot now remember who played their voices, but I was their feet. I was on my knees with a microphone of my own, two large pillows I had made sodden with many jugs of water, and miles of crackly sound tape. I squelched the tape and pillows with my fists every time they walked over the muddy fields, then stopped again when the mood took them to stand still.

Of them all, my favourite production was a musical version of Cinderella, *The Glass Slipper*, by Eleanor Farjeon. Years after I had left the radio I heard a repeat, complete with my door slams. I listened with some nostalgia.

But not very much, because I was more and more unhappy the longer I stayed. Yes, the company of the actors was delightful, and some of the productions were brilliantly done, but my own work was limiting and very dull. Jobs were advertised on the BBC notice-boards, and I would apply for them, but my CV became less and less inviting because, since Oxford, I had nothing creative to report. My greatest excitements during 1963 and 1964 were a holiday in Greece, and one New Year's Eve party, and neither was suitable for job application forms.

*   *   *

The New Year's Eve party was an act of desperation. Only in Scotland does the New Year arrive with a flourish, everywhere else it is an exhausted anticlimax to Christmas, at least in my family. Whatever we tried to do to enliven it, we ended up drinking turgid mulled wine in front of still more turgid television. So, as 1964 approached, I put up a notice in the studio managers' common room offering open house on December 31, for a bring-a-bottle party.

Party animal as I am, I soon realized this was going to be a lugubrious occasion. I had invited some old friends from school and college, hoping they would mix with my new colleagues. I now

98

know that BBC employees never mix at parties. For some reason, even off duty they find the rumour machine of the Beeb utterly fascinating, and will spend the whole night swapping gossip which is incomprehensible to an outsider. So my friends sat with me in our sitting-room at home, occasionally saying, 'I must just look at the BBC', and venturing out into the kitchen to watch studio managers shouting at each other, getting drunk and being sick.

Somehow I had recreated all the nastiest bits of Trafalgar Square in our quiet little semi in the suburbs. The problem was, once they had arrived, even though the midnight chimes of Big Ben had sounded long ago, they simply refused to go. Not for the last time, I blessed my mother. At 4 a.m. she pulled the vacuum cleaner out from under the stairs, plugged it in and pushed it round their feet. As a hint it knows no rival, I thoroughly recommend it as a way of shifting a limpet-like guest, if you have my mother's nerve. I never offered my colleagues open house again, and they never suggested that I should.

The holiday was a tour round the Greek islands. And here I come to a confession. You may think that the virginity, which had almost become a badge of pride, was lost at last when I fell in love with John. And I would like you to think that. But the truth is more sordid. In 1963, a year before I met John, I went on a National Union of Students' holiday to Greece, to the Peloponnese. It was Easter, the wild flowers were a tapestry on the mountainside, the air was soft and warm. Forget the excuses. I was seduced by the tour guide. He said he was a doctor. I think his name was Chris.

He taught me to say 'I love you' in Greek, and invited me into his bed. He enjoyed the experience more than I did. He was indefatigable. No sooner had it ended than he started all over again, and again, and again.

It was a tiring night, but it had two effects. It finally cost me my virginity, and it gave me a lasting love of Greece which stays with me today.

When I became a studio manager, and was friendly with Patricia Leventon, a talented and attractive actress, she suggested we should go on holiday together. I recommended Greece, only this time, a trip round the Greek islands ending at Samos, where my friend Caroline Barron and her husband John were staying.

We flew to Athens, then picked up an inter-island ferry from Piraeus. We were too late to book a cabin, but even though we had no sleeping bags or blankets, we decided to spend the night on deck. We had some romantic idea about dolphins leaping in the wake, and a night under the stars. It turned out to be a night surrounded by people who had the foresight to bring warm blankets to keep out the cold wind, and their many chickens.

As they snuggled down around us, two weather-beaten old men, both in dark blue sweaters came on deck. Do not ask me why, but I decided they were wearing a naval uniform, so one of them must be the ship's captain. When he suggested we should join him in his cabin where he had a spare bunk, I nobly suggested to Pat that she ought to take up the offer. She clearly thought I was delirious, and refused.

I said, 'But it's freezing out here, why don't you sleep in a warm bunk for a couple of hours?'

100

'I certainly won't share his cabin, you must be mad'.

'No, don't you see, he only means it's his, because the whole ship is his. After all, he is the captain.'

'How do you know?'

I realized I didn't, so we refused and the two men went back to their bunks.

Dawn took years to arrive, but the sunrise was glorious, and we still had just enough circulation, thanks to many tiny cups of hot sweet Greek coffee, to appreciate it. With the dawn, up popped the two old men again, still in their dark blue sweaters. This time they had a different idea. We were due to get off at the second port, the capital of Samos, a town called Vathi. Why didn't we get off at the first stop instead, so they could drive us to meet our friends, and we could see some of the island? I, who by now was completely light-headed, said that sounded interesting. Pat said it seemed insane to her. In the meantime, both men had taken our suitcases and were marching down the gangplank, so we had to follow them.

As the boat pulled out of the harbour even I recognized that it was unusual for a ship's captain to be packing my suitcase into the boot of a taxi, and climbing in the driving seat, while his ship sailed away without him. He and his friend turned out to be taxidrivers with a taste for dark blue sweaters.

As I regained some of my sense, Patricia began to lose hers. They drove us to a beach which was completely deserted, with wonderful white sand and calm blue sea rippling at the edge. The ship's captain suggested we should all take our clothes off

101

and swim. Pat, who is Irish, looked at the water dreamily and said, 'That does sound a lovely idea'. I snapped at her, 'No it doesn't'. I turned to the ship's captain, and said as haughtily as I could, 'Take us to the British Consul'. Caroline had told me that the island of Samos had one of the oldest, and the smallest British consulates in the world.

When the two men realized we were serious, and Pat had turned on them the force of her Celtic temper, they quickly put us back in the taxi and drove on.

This time the ship's captain drove with Patricia sitting next to him, and his friend sat next to me in the back, sucking my arm, which mystified me and left large bruise marks on my shoulder. He made up for it when we arrived in Vathi by introducing us to his sister, a middle-aged lady who gave him a hard look, and then found a clean, comfortable room in her own house for us. Finally, he took us to the British Consul, and left us, wishing us a good holiday, and saying, 'No tell'. We didn't, not out of a wish to protect him, but to save ourselves from the obvious conclusion that we were not just naïve, but certifiable.

Mr Marc, the Consul, was a fascinating character. He had inherited the post from his father and grandfather. Tragically, it was one of the economies of Wilson's government, so there is no longer a British Consul on Samos. Mr Marc even then was very elderly, and had the oldest typewriter I have ever seen (apart from Patrick Moore's, which must have a preservation order on it). It was a Gothic design, a double-decker, with huge round keys. He also had a large portrait of the Queen, and a very weary expression. English girls are not renowned for keeping their heads in Greece, let alone their maidenheads.

He courteously directed us to the hotel where Caroline and John were staying, and they arrived as we did. Caroline was discussing whether it was time for a siesta when John said, 'I can see Esther now'.

We sat together in a square in the centre of the little town, eating rich Greek yoghurt with swirls of fragrant local honey in it, while we regaled them with our daft adventure. The rest of our trip was delightful, and convinced me that Greece is one step nearer heaven than anywhere else on earth.

*   *   *

Arriving home again was landing back on earth with a thump. We studio managers all agreed that radio people were quite different from people in television, and the received opinion was that true broadcasters worked in radio, and that television was trashy. I was not at all sure I agreed.

A friend of mine, Colin Charman, had gone to television and he arranged for me to visit the gallery of *Blue Peter*. Valerie Singleton was making an icing-sugar snowman. When the poor little figure began to wilt under the light, she really did say, 'Here's one I prepared earlier'. Biddy Baxter, the Editor, was very much in charge. She was tall and elegant, and she had once been a studio manager, where the legend was that on hot summer days in the grubby studios she used to cheer everyone up by making sound effects wearing a bikini. She created *Blue Peter*, constantly won awards for the best children's programme, and had the reputation for being ferocious. I have only ever found her charming and kindly, but then many women in television have a dragon image.

There are two possible reasons. One is that it is a myth, designed to keep us amused. The most common question asked of anyone who works in television is 'What is X really like?' If you answer blandly, 'X is charming, professional, easy,' the disappointment is manifest. Who wants to know that Joan Collins is easy-going, we want her to hurl plates at your head, like Alexis in *Dynasty*. Please don't tell us that Cilla Black is funny and warm, we want her to throw tantrums and scream for someone's head. Above all, don't bore us with stuff about how nice Esther Rantzen is. Please tell us she is a bad-tempered bitch.

So it could just be that the dragon images make a better story. However, there is another possibility.

I have worked with one or two talented women who are quite impossible, who don't simply survive in crisis and chaos, but positively prefer it. They will create rows, destabilize teams, reduce researchers to tears because that way their own creative juices flow. Do men do the same? In the early days of television, yes, they did. But fashions have changed. Most men now recognize that frightened people don't think well, that talent needs confidence-building. So it is very sad that some women who are at the very top of the industry still retain the bad old ferocity and rudeness.

One of the most notorious bullies when I first joined the BBC was Mrs Grace Wyndham Goldie. She has been credited with creating the BBC's Current Affairs Department, and for discovering some of its brightest young men. She was also responsible for setting back the progress of women for decades. It wasn't just that she memorably invented the myth that women 'lack the authority' to read the news, and that she swept them off the screen. She undermined women behind the cameras just as unforgivably. Only a tiny handful survived her gender cleansing.

Dame Janet Vaughan, my college principal, who knew Grace well, wrote to her to recommend me. I was summoned to an interview Board. I will never forget it. Grace set out to humiliate me. Every idea I put forward was hacked to pieces, or scoffed at. The men sitting beside her became uncomfortable, but she had smelt blood and nothing would dissuade her. She used sarcasm, and brutal contradiction to make me feel foolish. In the end she let me go.

When I met Desmond Wilcox years later (he was then Editor of *Man Alive*, the pioneering documentary series he invented for BBC2), he told me his one memory of Grace. When he was a star reporter on ITV's *This Week*, Paul Fox had recommended Grace to see him. The interview was after lunch. She asked Desmond one question, 'Why should I employ you on *Panorama*?', then, as he began to answer, her eyes closed and her head fell forward. He claimed that she slowly slid down her chair as he reached the end of his answer, and started to breathe heavily. He waited for the next question, but it didn't come, so he tiptoed out. He never did join *Panorama*.

My last sight of Grace was in the hospitality room of a talk show hosted by Malcolm Muggeridge. She was one of the guest speakers.

She walked round, blustering, then focused on the girl who was organizing transport and was extremely rude to her. The room was filled with her protégés, now very senior men in the television industry, looking at her with accustomed fear. For a moment, they had regressed and become her juniors again. But also in the room were the programme researchers, young people who owed nothing to her, but had come out of curiosity, having heard of this towering figure, and were now seeing a bad-tempered, unpleasant, old woman. Their disappointment was palpable. I, who had met her before, was not surprised.

As far as television histories are concerned, Grace's legacy to the BBC was a strong, lively Current Affairs Department. As far as I was concerned, it was to frighten all the men she trained so deeply that they dared not promote another woman, just in case we all turned out like her.

*　　　*　　　*

At the end of my visit to *Blue Peter*, as Colin Charman took me out of the control gallery he could see I had fallen in love with television, with the danger of it, the challenge. I longed to be part of it, but I had to go back to work in radio.

Knowing my frustration, a friend of my mother's, Dr Alice Heim, who was a psychologist working in Cambridge, sent me a cutting from an East Anglian newspaper. The local television station there was looking for a 'Miss Romper Room,' to become the presenter of a new children's programme which was already a success in America. They asked for applications, with a photograph. Chris, a studio manager friend, took a careful picture of me, hiding my double chin. It worked. I was invited to Norwich for an audition.

The studio was filled with four-year-olds, ready to romp. Lined up to audition were a dozen trim, pretty girls, and me, neither trim nor pretty. I gravitated to the children, and we played happily together. Then I was asked to tell a story to camera. I chose 'Little Red Riding Hood'. All went well until I reached the point when the wolf follows Little Red Riding Hood through the woods. Then memories of Andrew Faulds assailed me. 'Be careful with wolves,' I told the camera, especially in the woods, you never know what they'll be up to. If they invite you to dinner, don't go.'

Later in the canteen, I met the American guru and guardian of Romper Room. She explained to me the segments of the programme, all strictly laid down, the 'Do Bees' and the 'Don't Bees'. I felt it sounded narrow and constricting. 'Can't I vary it a bit?' I asked. She shook her head disapprovingly. That—and the wolf in the forest—cost me the job. One of the girls on the team told me the children had voted for me, but the guru, rightly, chose a Norland Nanny, who became a popular local celebrity in East Anglia. I reluctantly returned to the footsteps in gravel and squeaking doors.

*   *   *

My next job in radio drama was to work on a production by Betty Davies of *Waters of the Moon*. Betty was a very experienced drama producer, always impeccably made up, and for some reason always in a large hat. She was a stickler for detail. At one point in the script there was the sound of a distant skating accident. My view was that all the listeners would hear would be a far-off scream. Betty's view was that they should also hear the thud of flesh on ice. The senior studio manager put down a shiny wooden plank. I fell on it until Betty heard the sound she wanted. It took eight falls.

I limped out of the studio and up to the office, where I wrote out my resignation in triplicate. I put all three copies in the post. My personnel officer told me I need only have done it once.

There then followed the most dispiriting six months of my life. I signed on at the labour exchange, and picked up my dole from the office my actor friends recommended. I hated it.

With no reason to get out of bed I stayed in it. My poor parents watched as I slept longer and longer. It gave me a taste of the morale-bashing misery of unemployment which I have not forgotten. My Oxford friend Nicholas Leonard was very helpful. He had just started a magazine in Ireland, and he asked me to write some articles for him. At least that got me out of the house. Finally I swallowed my pride and did something I had always vowed I would never do, I pulled the only string I had.

At university we all knew that one of our friends in the Oxford Theatre Group, John Spicer, had a mother who worked in the BBC. It was said she had rather a boring back-room job, but she had helped other women get jobs in television. I wrote to John. He told me to ring his mother, and, in fact, kindly put a word in for me first. So, to my great relief, when I telephoned her she immediately agreed to see me.

Joanna Spicer was one of the most remarkable women employed by the BBC during the sixties. She ran a one-woman guerrilla campaign designed to infiltrate women into the entirely male-dominated structure. Unlike Grace Wyndham Goldie, a senior woman executive who used her power to keep women out, Joanna Spicer used hers to make sure that women at least got a toe inside the door. She was Assistant Controller of Programme Planning, which does indeed sound boring. In fact, though, her job included assessing all requests from producers for researchers, and research was the best entry point for anyone new to broadcasting.

I went to see her in her pleasant, airy office on the sixth floor of Television Centre in Wood Lane, then, as now, the power level of that strange bagel of a building. The glassy sides encircle a central fountain, on which is precariously balanced a naked bronze statue of the fictional character, Ariel. The fountain has never been allowed to flow, because the constant trickling sound affected executive bladders. All the offices look inwards, so competing bosses can ignore the outside world entirely, and watch each other across the courtyard. David Attenborough, when he was a controller, used to play games with his colleagues. He would put a bottle of Malvern water on his desk, to see how soon competitive bottles would appear on theirs. Joanna Spicer never, as far as I could see, took part in these virility duels.

I was extremely nervous when I met her, but she put me at my ease. She asked me about my time in Oxford, about the performing, directing and

109

writing I had done there, and then asked why I had not applied for the BBC2 intake, as the new channel was recruiting creative staff. I explained that was because I already had the offer of studio management. I also described my frustration in a job where everyone around me was being asked for ideas, and I was opening and shutting doors or falling on wooden planks. At the end of the interview she said she would ring me in three weeks.

I thanked her, left, and went home without much hope. By this time it had dawned upon me that she was the most senior woman in the BBC, and that it was very unlikely she would have the time to ring me. But I was wrong. She rang the very day she said she would, the moment she arrived in her office. It was extraordinarily compassionate of her. She must have known how desperately I was counting the days until she telephoned.

The news she gave me was that no producers had put in requests for researchers, so she could not help me by making any introductions. However, she herself needed a clerk in her Eurovision department, not a creative, production job, but at least a job, and at least in the television service. Would I accept? Of course I would. I thanked her, put the phone down and danced around the room. Without a doubt I owe my career in television to Mrs Joanna Spicer.

When I went to work for her I learned more about her. A couple of years earlier, when Ned Sherrin made a pilot for his first satirical programme, *That Was the Week That Was (TW3)*, he had run into trouble. A group of Conservative women had been invited to debate with the acerbic columnist, Bernard Levin. He had ruffled them so considerably that Conservative Central Office complained to the BBC, and the pilot was referred up to the very peak of the television service, to the most senior programme controllers.

Joanna's office was, as I have said, on the sixth floor, so she was invited to their viewing. She enjoyed it and she laughed. Her laughter made the difference between a pilot cancelled, and a series commissioned. When you think that series became, for many people, the embodiment of the irreverence of the sixties, you can see why I say that Joanna was among the most remarkable and influential women of her time in the BBC.

By chance, just before Joanna Spicer offered me a job, as I lay moodily in bed I had read a newspaper advertisement for a post in radio Current Affairs. It was to work on the lunchtime news programme, and I had applied without any hope, knowing I was the wrong sex, had no experience in news or current affairs, and had a CV filled with reminiscences of my time at Oxford, and a dreary vacuum ever since. But my theory has always been that nobody wants you, when nobody wants you, but when one person wants you, they all want you.

Now was my chance to put the theory to the test. I rang my old personnel officer, the one who had told me I need only have resigned from studio management once. He was unobtainable, so I left a message. 'When I applied for the radio news job,' I said, 'I left out one fact, which is that I have now been offered a job in television.' I left it at that, not mentioning, of course, that the job was as a clerk.

He rang me back straight away. 'Esther, thank

you so much for your call. You will be receiving a response in the post, but ignore it, it's just a standard reply.'

I did receive it the next day, it was a formal turn-down. But the same morning, he rang and summoned me for interview. I went to an office in Broadcasting House where I met the Editor of the programme, one of the grand old men of radio news. His first question was about the television job I'd been offered, and when I admitted it was only as a clerk, his eyes glazed. I was wasting his time.

He asked me a few more questions, but I knew he wasn't listening to my answers, and he knew that I knew. Neither of us cared much. He had already dismissed me. But I had proved my point. He only interviewed me because someone else had decided to employ me. He wasn't interested in my CV, nor in my past experience, nor my future potential. When somebody wants you they all want you, at least for interview.

I didn't care. I had a job in television. I joined Joanna Spicer's department in the spring, and at once my immediate boss, Janet Goldspink, caught pneumonia and had to take three weeks off work. I had already learned her filing system, so for the next week I methodically sorted each request for a broadcast link, and filed it alphabetically by date and country. I hadn't quite grasped that between receiving the telex and filing it meticulously, there should have been another process—Action.

After a week of this, a bewildered Mrs Spicer rushed into the office with a sheaf of complaints in her hand. 'It seems,' she said, 'that broadcasting has ground to a halt all over Europe. Do you know why?' I showed her my filing cabinet, crammed

112

with perfectly indexed telexes, not a single link had been booked. She was very kind about it. But it must have made it easier for her to let me go before my contract ended.

When Janet recovered from her pneumonia, she invited me to drinks in the BBC Club with her friend Jennifer Jeremy. Jennifer had some news. Ned Sherrin had asked if she would join the team for his latest satire show, *BBC3*, but she had turned him down. She had just been promoted to production assistant (one rung higher than researcher), in Obituaries, and she didn't think it would be wise to take demotion and become a researcher again.

I put down my gin and tonic with a jolt, and asked her to repeat what she'd said. She did. Did I argue with her? Did I suggest that Ned's was the most brilliant team in television, and that she was crazy to turn down the chance of joining them—especially for the gloomy routine of making Obituaries? To my shame, I did not. I just apologized to them both, left my gin untouched, ran upstairs to my office, and wrote out a job application to Ned. I had friends on his team already, and mentioned their names as references. I did not mention that he had already broadcast a sketch I had written which had got him into a good deal of hot water.

This had been written when I was still at Oxford at the time of the *Lady Chatterley* obscenity trial. I was producing a cabaret evening for the Experimental Theatre Club. For some reason, very late one night, I had started to read *Peter Pan* by J.M. Barrie, and found it crammed with innuendo. For instance, Peter never wants to grow up, he wants to go to Kensington Gardens and 'play with the fairies'. I decided we ought to put Peter Pan on trial for indecency. Gordon Honeycombe, later a newscaster for ITN, made a wonderfully appalled counsel for the prosecution, reading aloud lewd passages from Barrie.

My friend, John Albery, had passed my sketch to Ned, without actually mentioning that I had written it. It became part of a notorious edition of *TW3* which was broadcast on 13 April 1963. David Frost in his autobiography says it was probably my sketch that inspired Stuart Hood, the Controller of Programmes to say 'The programme was criticized towards the end of the run for smut, and this is something which we will be keeping a very sharp lookout for . . . We have seen what the mistakes on the last series were and it will be my hope that those mistakes will not be repeated'.

That was a gift for the puritans who were gunning for the BBC in general, and *TW3* in particular. It almost cost Ned and the viewers the next series of the show. So although I knew nothing about the row, it was probably a good thing I didn't boast to Ned I had written that sketch, nor does David Frost know. I've never told either of them, to this day. Best not to, I feel. I wouldn't want to be caught with my Peter Pants down.

*   *   *

Ned summoned me for interview a day after he received my note, at eight-thirty in the morning. I remember the suit I wore—dark red tweed—I must have looked at least fifty. I treated myself to a taxi, and on the way rehearsed in my mind all the

114

answers to the questions I had tried and failed at previous BBC Boards. What would I put in tonight's *Panorama*? Is the Common Market a political or an economic question? Ned asked none of them. He had already checked me out with Ian Davidson, his film director, and Ian, who had worked with me on several student revues and cabarets at Oxford, was generous with his compliments.

All Ned asked me was, 'When can you start?' My head whirled. 'Now', I wanted to shout. But I was still under contract to Mrs Spicer. I explained my dilemma. Ned smiled. Ever since the *TW3* viewing they had been fond of each other. He rang her in front of me, and arranged to give her lunch in return for my early deliverance. He offered me a six-month contract, at a pittance of a salary. I told my personnel officer, and he was concerned. 'I might be able to get you a better contract, Esther,' he said, 'with more security in another department.'

'But this is the programme I most want to work on,' I said. 'I really mustn't let this chance go by.'

Say what you like about my taste in red suits or my rude sense of humour, you have to admit that when I get my big break, at least I recognize how lucky I am. The next six months taught me more about television than any other period of my life, were more fun, were more terrifying, and were more memorable.

CHAPTER FIVE

RESEARCHER

Ned Sherrin's offices were converted bedrooms in a row of terraced houses in London's Shepherd's Bush. How sad that a name which conjures up green fields, lush branches and flocks of sheep, should be so misleading. Shepherd's Bush can't have seen a real shepherd for centuries. When I went to work there in 1966 it was grimy and untended, pieces of newspaper flapped across the pavements, traffic ground around the edge of the Green on its way somewhere more pleasant, Kensington or Notting Hill.

Shepherd's Bush Green was only notable for a very large underground public lavatory (now oddly converted to a snooker club). Every now and again the local council made a valiant attempt to smarten it up, with shrubs and new lamps, but it was all inevitably beaten down by the exhaust fumes and city dust. None the less, some of my happiest years have been spent in a poky house in Lime Grove, and the battered old Shepherd's Bush Empire, converted to the BBC Theatre, home of *That's Life!*.

Lime Grove Studios themselves still had a dingy glamour about them in the sixties. Once they had been the home of Gainsborough Pictures, and legend had it that in her lithe and slender prime Jessie Matthews had danced 'Over my shoulder goes one care' on a film set there. Beside the reception there were a couple of oak-panelled rooms where the old film producers no doubt set up their casting couches. I wonder what happened to all that oak when Lime Grove was demolished, in 1993.

It made sense to raze it to the ground. The building was riddled with asbestos, and when *That's Life!* was housed there, officials used to walk through our offices to the flat roof outside, and skim the air-conditioning tanks for legionnaires' disease. There were creaking lifts, with heavy iron doors, and long corridors where cats sat like dozing security men, giving me a long stare as I passed, always at a run, usually laden with papers and photographs. The canteen was notorious, vegetables drowned in greenish water, everything else burned to a crisp.

But for all the discomfort, Lime Grove had atmosphere, years of adrenalin and sleazy show-business had been absorbed into its flaking walls. There were still studios, *Top of the Pops* came live from Lime Grove, and I once saw a very young Tom Jones in the club there. He had more hair in those days, and much more nose. I met him many years later, when he made a record for ChildLine— if anything, age had increased his sex appeal.

I arrived in Ned's offices on my first day in October 1966, promptly at nine, and, as Mrs Hoster's had taught me, my pencil was sharpened, my notebook ready. If Ned had wanted his windows opened, or his flowers freshened, by Heavens I would have done it. As it happened, he didn't. In fact he wasn't there. He had already left for a game of squash, and a 'power' breakfast. There was a briefing note on my desk.

Ned used to arrive in the office well before eight,

sort out all his post, write out his instructions, and be out before any of his staff arrived. He is a strange mixture: a Tory satirist, a Somerset farmer's boy turned sophisticate. His height makes him intimidating, especially when he tucks his chin in and stares down his nose like a superior heron, then lets out a bark of laughter, or a sniff and a smile.

I was nervous of him then, indeed I still am, but he was the best boss I could possibly have had. If I was working within my experience and capabilities, he was instantly bored. It amused him to give me more and more difficult jobs to do. He was always on the phone to political informants who were feeding him gossipy titbits for his last satire show, *BBC3*—my job was to check them out. One morning he called me in. 'Commander Courtney,' he said, 'we're running a competition for the biggest bore in parliament and he's been nominated. Do some research and let me know what you think.' I left, overawed by the challenge, but determined not to let him down.

There are no short cuts in research. If you leave one stone unturned, that will turn out to be where the maggot is hiding. I found the necessary *Hansards* in a library at the BBC, and day after day I worked my way through Courtney's entries in eighty-six volumes. He was certainly loquacious. As I ploughed through the columns of tiny print, I got to know Commander Courtney, then Tory MP for Harrow, very well. He had a fixation about the Soviet Union, and its satellite countries. He had business interests which frequently took him there, and when he returned he used to ask questions in parliament about the dozens of staff in all the

118

Eastern bloc embassies, cooks, cleaners, drivers, all of whom had diplomatic immunity and were probably spies.

It may have been tedious for the razor-sharp journalists in the public gallery, but Commander Courtney was making a point. After a week in the library I returned to Ned, believing I had failed miserably. 'I'm sorry,' I said, 'but I haven't found enough to justify Commander Courtney winning the award as the biggest bore.' Ned said, 'That's fine,' and seeing how crestfallen I was, added, 'Don't worry. It's as much a researcher's job to knock an item down as to stand it up.'

Whenever I undertook a chore of this profound tedium, I used to recite to myself the words Miss Senator, my French teacher, had chanted like a mantra, 'No experience is wasted'. Difficult to believe at the time, it turned out to be true. Two years later I was working with the writer/performer John Bird when a national scandal broke, and Commander Courtney was at its centre. The KGB had produced scandalous photographs of him in bed with a Russian girl. The photographs destroyed his marriage and his career in an instant. My mind went back to a speech I had found in *Hansard*, when the Commander had warned his fellow MPs of the hazards of doing business with the Russians.

At an official dinner he had turned to the Russian secret service man who followed him everywhere. 'Boris,' he had said, 'I know your job is to discover my secret weakness. Why don't I make it easy for you, and save time. My weakness is for beautiful blondes.' I could visualize Boris writing it down obediently, then procuring a blonde for him, and taking up his position with a camera hidden behind the bed. Alas for Commander Courtney, he had diagnosed his own weakness accurately. But it was a thrill for me as a researcher. I produced my notes for John Bird, and that quotation, suddenly made topical by the scandal and Courtney's resignation, became an item in another satire programme.

*   *   *

Back in 1966 there were plenty of chores for me, working for Ned, as the lowest and most menial researcher on the programme, but I loved them all. I was in television—the budgerigar had escaped from the cage. For many years whenever I returned to Broadcasting House to take part in a radio programme I felt as if I had hopped back behind bars. But Television Centre in Wood Lane was an Aladdin's cave, filled with treasure—and the occasional genie of the lamp, such as Ned, or Huw Wheldon, or Duncan Wood, producers who created innovative television masterpieces, *TW3*, *Monitor*, and *Steptoe and Son.* Let no-one say there never was a golden age of television, there certainly was, and I was lucky to be there to witness it.

The treasures I discovered were the extraordinary skills and crafts collected in Television Centre. The wig-makers, who delicately wove real hair into nineteenth-century curls. The make-up artists, not only patching up pop singers' hangovers and politicians' bags, but changing John Bird into Harold Wilson one week, and George Brown the next. There were racks of clothes in the costume stores, dresses Jane Austen would have delighted in hanging next to science fiction space suits. Some stars' clothes were stored on the rail, discarded after a 'Special' or a 'Spectacular'. I once wore a Petula Clarke 'gown' of flowing pink silk for an edition of *That's Life!*. Now the clothes have been auctioned off or consigned to a skip, the wig-makers and make-up artists all gone freelance. And the golden age? Some of us feel it is long gone, too, and today's outpourings seem tawdry and repetitive by comparison.

But the studios themselves are still there. Even empty, they are as fascinating as the boxes you pile on a birthday table. You can sense the magic that is contained in them. Without scenery or lighting the studios are just great warehouses, their ceilings hung with lamps and bars, circled with high gantries, their walls latticed with wires and pipes. Their floors are uniformly grey, awaiting the paint which will turn them into marble or wood, completely flat so that the cameras can glide smoothly over them. The cameras themselves are herded together in a corner, until the crew arrive for rehearsal. Then the switch is thrown and suddenly they turn, rise, fall, swoop to catch a performer's lifted eyebrow, or an acrobat's leap.

Overnight the sets are carried in and built to a designer's plan. But the instant the performance is finished, the crew begin to pull them to pieces, and all that skill and craft is destroyed in a few hours, to make room for the next set waiting to come in. Whole houses are created in a studio, or at least the particular angles of a house the director has asked for, the front of a staircase, the painted glimpse of a conservatory through a window.

Reality is mixed with illusion. Examine the scenery of a classic play, does that look like a precious ormolu candlestick on the mantelpiece? It probably is one—there are firms that hire the most beautiful antiques to television companies. Does that table and desk for a talk show look like nothing you've ever seen in a real home? That's because the designer will have created it, and it's likely to have razor-sharp edges, and legs that protrude and trip up the hasty presenter. If she is female, and partial to short skirts, she had better clamp her knees together when she sits down, because television sofas are notorious for throwing women backwards to reveal a distracting flash of knicker.

Off the main studio are the make-up rooms. I have watched Julian Clary sitting as still as a Buddha while his acolytes teased his hair and painted his eyelashes, and he watched and waited for the perfect image to emerge from their hands. No such perfection has ever been possible when they work on my reflection, sadly. In the quick-change costume room next to make-up, the women designers are straightforward and businesslike, ironing, steaming, adjusting seams and trying vainly to conceal the unwieldy radio mikes all performers must wear these days. By contrast, the male dressers are camp and gossipy, and seem to spend most of the day telling wicked stories about which star demands a special massage before he goes on set to sing, and which other star always pees in a sink in make-up to impress the girls there with his dimensions.

The rehearsal completed, the studio audience arrives, bemused at first by the machinery that surrounds them, which of course never appears on screen. They are invariably astonished at how small the studio is (the impression of a huge hall can be created by perspective and clever lenses), and how surprisingly small some of the performers are, too. (I had always dreamed of achieving five-foot-ten, but nature and my mother's genes stopped me at five-foot-four. Television mysteriously adds those inches. I am told I look six-foot on the screen, and invariably when I first meet people I have to apologize for my lack of height.)

The red transmission light flicks on, the floor manager in his headphones shouts like a sergeant major, 'Quiet in the studio, one minute to titles'. No matter how often I hear that command, my spine still straightens, my lungs inflate, the adrenalin begins. Not because I am nervous (sometimes I am, facing the interrogator Clive Anderson, for instance, or rashly agreeing to sing for Carol Smillie). But because television has for me the thrill of theatre, I know we are broadcasting to one or two viewers, sitting on a sofa, probably eating fish-and-chips together with the sound off. But the potential is there to enchant them, to make them laugh or cry, to share vital information with them, and to reach millions upon millions of sofas, across the nation, from Budleigh Salterton to Buckingham Palace. Nothing has diminished the thrill of the television studios for me, even though I have walked through them for thirty-five years.

In 1966, although I had no idea what the future held, I recognized that television was having a real social effect. It was vibrant and alive, and it fanned the winds of change that Prime Minister Harold Macmillan had identified. Macmillan felt that fresh unsettling blast of cold air in Africa, in countries on the brink of independence (and it is significant that, during apartheid in South Africa, television was banned, because it brought people together, and asked difficult questions).

The same wind blew through Britain in the sixties, and each new gust of thought, from feminism to student liberation, was analyzed and amplified in our television studio. Ned's programme, *BBC3*, was a mixture of sketches and discussion. If a subject was alive with controversy, it was included in our show. I knew how lucky I was to be part of the production team, even a tiny unprepossessing part. I was so grateful to be working for Ned that when Eleanor Bron lost her knitting (a frequent occurrence), I volunteered to find it. When John Bird decided to play Lord (Roy) Thomson, and make-up couldn't find any spectacles with thick enough lenses, I gladly combed London for an optician who was prepared to go into his garden shed on a Saturday afternoon, and grind some glass for us.

I once appeared on the programme myself—or at least my hands did. Ned was creating a parody of a Hollywood musical, and the pages of an elaborate book had to turn to illustrate time passing. Ned looked with disfavour at the hands of the scene men as they turned the pages. 'Could we have someone who looks less like a horny-handed son of toil?', he asked. Colin Leslie, the floor manager looked at me, 'Try Esther's hands', he said.

My hands passed their audition, the crew were amused by my delight. I rang my parents and told them that my hands were about to appear on television. They were kindly, and simulated excitement. At least it was evidence that I was working on the show. For the first five weeks I failed to get a credit at the end of the programme, because Ned had forgotten me entirely. Once again it was Colin who caught sight of me and said, 'Shouldn't Esther be included in the final credits?' So I was.

About the same time I mustered up the courage to ask Ned if I could invite my parents to the studio audience of the show, and then to Hospitality afterwards. Ned was astonished that I should even ask—each week the room heaved with hangers-on and friends of friends. I explained that my parents were great admirers of his work, and he graciously agreed, but, when they came, my father, dear, absentminded Dad, let me down.

I poured them a glass of wine, then led them over to the huddle where Ned was holding court. I asked his permission to introduce them. Mum shook hands and smiled courteously, then Father held out his hand to Ned and said vaguely, 'And who might you be?' I can't remember what Ned said, I was trying to bury myself in a wall. Taking parents to Hospitality can be risky. Some years later when Eartha Kitt took part in a talk show of mine, my mother walked up to her afterwards and said, 'All right then, Eartha, give us a song'. She didn't.

*   *   *

By far the worst moment during my six months was when Ned walked into my tiny office and threw a script down on my desk. It was a song about Rhodesia, which was then struggling for independence. 'I never want to see the singer,' Ned said. 'Illustrate it with captions all the way through,

125

three by fours,' and he walked out. I rang every photo-agency, every relevant embassy, every magazine, anywhere that might have suitable pictures, then worked alongside our director, Darrol Blake while he selected the shots. He chose thirty-eight.

Then I rang Peter Agland, whose job was to turn the photographs into captions mounted on cardboard. (Peter went on to work with me on *That's Life!*, his wife, Sue Barr, works with me on our BBC2 talk show, Peter is Captain of the *That's Life!* cricket team. We met and first worked together in 1966, and still do, almost forty years later. What stamina the Aglands must have.) Peter asked me what size the thirty-eight captions had to be. I remembered what Ned had said, 'Three by four'. Peter was bewildered. He explained to me that 'three by four' was the ratio of the television screen, three high by four wide, but not the actual size of the captions. 'Most captions are ten inches by eight,' he said. 'Fine,' I said.

That Saturday I was out of the control room on an errand when the message reached me, Ned wants you. I ran up the stairs. Ned turned to me, so angry it was like being caught in the blast of a flame-thrower. 'I told you I wanted them three by four. I meant three-foot by four-foot, otherwise the cameras can't move on them.'

The hotter Ned became, the cooler my brain was. What was the solution? Could we have them remade? Not a chance. The sequence was being pre-recorded that afternoon. Darrol stepped in, 'Have a look, Ned, I think these will work anyway, even without a move.' We put them in front of the cameras, they did work, almost.

At the end of the song I longed for the lens to drift into the sunset at the back of the shot. Instead it stuck, static, on the wide shot of the landscape because my caption was too small. Ned turned to me, 'You see?' I did. I was pure blotting paper. Every decision he made taught me something. I didn't for a moment blame him for his anger. I agreed with him. My job was to get it right, and I had made a mistake. The scene-boys tried to comfort me, 'If they had been three-foot by four, we could never have changed them fast enough.'

I was unconsoled. On one of my many errands that day, I walked the length of Lime Grove, blinded with tears I wouldn't let anyone else see. Thirty-eight captions wrong in one song. Eventually I cheered up enough to boast to Peter Agland, 'Surely nobody could have made more mistakes in three minutes'.

But all in all it was a blazingly happy time for me, working for Ned. I never minded that I didn't exist for him. I once walked into his office at six in the evening. He was sitting with his feet on his desk, surrounded by the rest of the team, happily gossiping. 'Is it all right if I go home, now?' I asked. He looked round at the others. 'I don't think anyone would notice,' he said. I wasn't crushed, he was right. His show was the centre of the universe, or so it seemed to me, and I was a tiny fragment of dust on the comet's tail. It was, after all, the programme on which the F-word was first said. And I was there.

Ken Tynan had been invited into the studio to talk about censorship. The show was live. To illustrate the taboos current in the theatre, Tynan said the forbidden word, 'Fuck'. Ned spun in his chair to face the team. We were all sitting on high chairs, like starlings on a wire, along the back wall. 'Is that some kind of a record?' he said. It was. The next morning he told me to collect all the cartoons from the newspapers, and pinned them up on his notice-board. Next week the audience doubled.

I remember the day David Frost gave a famous breakfast party at the Connaught Hotel. Everyone was there: the Prime Minister, Lord Longford, Robert Maxwell. I don't think Ned had been invited. He had replaced Frost with John Bird on this latest satire show, and their friendship had become slightly distant, so Ned read the reports of this extraordinary gathering with rueful fascination.

Once I was alone in Ned's office when the phone rang. I answered it. 'Warren Beatty here,' said a charming American male voice. Fat, eager Esther melted. I put on my huskiest voice in reply, 'Good morning, Mr Beatty'. And he really did say to me, 'What's new, pussy-cat?' Is it any wonder I thought Ned's office was the centre of the universe?

I only had one disappointment—meeting Caryl Brahms. Brahms and Simon had written a cluster of brilliantly funny books together, *Don't Mr Disraeli*, for instance, and *No Bed for Bacon*. Then Simon had died, and Ned had started a writing in collaboration with Brahms. I had always visualized her as a brisk, funny, trim little woman with bright white hair and humorous eyes. She wasn't. She wore dark glasses, was short, dumpy, and craned her head upwards like a tethered hawk surveying the skies. None of which would have mattered, but her soft voice was invariably delivering judgements which were cutting and sarcastic.

Legend has it that during the rehearsal of one of

her musicals, someone became so exasperated that they emptied a glass of beer over her head. The scene-boys and I used to fantasize that we'd put her on roller skates and push her from one side of the set to the other. Not kind, but then Caryl wasn't kind. Lynda Baron (who later became one of the stars of *Open All Hours)* was the singer on the show, and for one programme she recorded two takes of a song Caryl had written. Ned turned in his chair to Caryl. 'Which take do you prefer?' She sighed dramatically. 'The first one was sharp.' 'Yes?' 'And the second one was flat.' It was the only time I saw Ned angry with her. 'Well, you've got to pick one.' She did, with heavy reluctance.

*   *   *

I shared my dilapidated office with Mike Hill, assistant producer on the show. He had been in the navy, and explained to me that he had been an alcoholic. I admired him for his courage, he was a steadfast teetotaller at that time. I also admired him for his gossip, 'It's best to know everything that's going on, otherwise you put your foot in it, are rude about someone's best friend,' and for his vocabulary. As I walked into the office for the first time, he was scattering the C-word all over the phone, swearing at a wrong number. Once he was so incensed by a crossed line that he cut through the phone line, then had to invent the story of an unlikely accident with a pair of scissors for the engineer who came to repair it. He told me years later that he and Ned had discussed me, once, briefly, and decided I was a Jewish virgin. He was not altogether right.

129

My Jewishness was not in question, although it did puzzle the team. I went to Ned for permission to take a morning off to go to synagogue for Passover, one of the High Holy Days. Ned looked mystified. I explained about the Exodus from Egypt, and the fact that we still celebrate our liberation. He said, 'How do Jews celebrate Easter?' I thought for a moment, then stretched my arms out wide, like a crucifix.

At that time I was seeing a good deal of my synagogue. I had begun to run a youth club there called Phase Two, for people of my own age, in their twenties and thirties. For many years there had been a club for teenagers, called the Alumni, which had been very popular. But now it was waning, there was nothing at all for the next age group, and the congregation—nervous of the repercussions of intermarriage—wanted to create a place where young Jews could meet. The Jewish community in Britain has survived the Holocaust, but has been decimated by assimilation. Each marriage to a non-Jew is almost certainly a family lost to the religion.

I didn't feel particularly religious at that time, my childhood faith had dissipated and become agnosticism. I was having a passionate affair with John, a Belfast Protestant, my younger sister was about to marry a Catholic. But I was a frustrated producer, and if I couldn't put on shows for the BBC, I'd make them for the Liberal Jewish Synagogue.

I was invited to Phase Two's first committee meeting, where a tall, young New Zealander, called Brian, was elected Chairman. He had a mannerism I have noticed since in many chairmen. He used to welcome the audience by rebuking the people who were there, for the failings of those who had failed to turn up. (I was once introduced as guest-speaker by a lady who said, 'I am very disappointed to see so few people here, especially since there were many more people for last month's speaker, and he charged us £2,000.' I, waiting to speak, and not having charged them a penny, was less than thrilled.) I noticed our guest-speakers wilted a bit at our Phase Two meetings when Brian pointed out there were only twenty-five people in the audience. Up till then they had thought it quite a respectable number.

After half a dozen meetings Brian himself had had enough, and my cousin Roger and I offered to chair the club jointly. It was fun. I resolutely refused to create purely social meetings, because it seemed to me that when the only point is to find a partner, it kills the evening. You need to be there, ostensibly at least, for a different purpose. So we invited a galaxy of guest speakers, all donating their precious Sunday evenings to us free of charge, and regularly attracting eighty people or more to hear them. Ned came, of course, and actor Kenneth Griffiths whom I had met with John, and Barry Humphries, and comedy writers Barry Took and Marty Feldman, and eventually Desmond Wilcox, but that was not for a couple of years. We had controversy with flat-earthers, and psychic researchers, with Fascists and Communists, and marriage-brokers. Looking back, without realizing it, I was creating the mix for a daily talk show.

Some of us on the committee set up a disabled club called the Out and Abouts, which meets at the synagogue still, under the guidance of an ex-Phase

131

Two member, Jenny Abrahams. I will never forget going to collect some of the members for the meetings, and discovering how much poverty and isolation can be created by disability. Some of them had no other outing during the week apart from our mixture of tea, bingo and a sing-song around the piano.

I ran Phase Two with Roger for two or three years, and wrote a pantomime for them, (*Cinderella* again, with Roger noble and memorable as an ugly sister, and with music by Stanley, a very musical dentist my mother approved of, with a large motorbike she did not.) I gladly sacrificed my spare time, energy and enthusiasm to Phase Two, but what Alfred Marks asked of me was a bridge too far.

I had written to him to ask if he would consider speaking to the club. He rang me at my Lime Grove office. At that time he was not simply a very successful comedian, he was also acting in a Northern comedy in the West End. His voice on the phone was deep and smooth as oil. He said I should come to the theatre, see the play, and talk to him afterwards about the club. I said I'd love to, and I'd bring my co-chairman, my cousin Roger. He said that would be impossible, there was only one ticket. I had to go alone. I've never enjoyed sitting in the theatre by myself, but the play was good, and Alfred was excellent. He played a bluff, honest, sensible Northerner, and, the way you do, I began to believe those were his attributes and warmed to him. I did notice, when I went round to the stage door, that the very old doorkeeper who took my name rolled his eyes skyward. Clearly he thought he was in for a long night.

I was directed to Alfred's dressing-room. He was in an elegant dressing-gown, and, eccentrically, still had on the wig he had worn for the play, grey hair cut short *en brosse*. Alfred was famous for his black eyebrows, his large, eloquent brown eyes, and his almost total baldness. Obviously he preferred the wig, because he sat opposite a mirror, glancing approvingly at himself from time to time. His dresser, a young man, finished hanging up his stage costume, said goodnight, and left. Then Alfred began to make a pass at me. Untender memories of Andrew Faulds assailed me. Enough already.

I was not the slightest bit nervous—there is nothing more vulnerable than an elderly comic in a wig—but I was exasperated. Why did he drivel on? I knew that the only qualities of mine that attracted him were that I was young and female. He knew nothing else at all about me. The desperate thing about 'Don Juans' is that they are so driven. Not for one moment do they relax enough to enjoy a woman's company. She is merely a target. If they don't score, they count it a failure.

Nothing I said to Alfred about the play, or about Phase Two, deflected him. In the end, I was tired. I used my final weapon, I started to cry. At once he pulled his dressing-gown tightly around him (Lord knows how little he was wearing underneath it), got up and offered me a pretzel from a paper bag on his dressing-table. I didn't like them then, and I definitely do not like them now. He demanded a kiss on his cheek in return for a speech for Phase Two. That I could manage. As I left, the stage-doorkeeper looked at me with surprise and great relief. An early night, this time.

I wasn't sure, after that, whether Alfred would

133

agree to speak at the synagogue, but he rang and confirmed the date. He arrived twenty minutes late, and avoided my eyes all night. He spoke well, and left promptly, still without a word to me, but cutting me dead with great dignity. I thought his pomposity made him seem even more foolish.

My romantic life at this time was not at all successful. I nursed a small crush on John Bird, not that he ever realized it, and I would have been humiliated if he had. He was the smartest, brightest star on television at that time. His impressions of the politicians were extraordinary, combined as they were with brilliant scripts, many of them his. But he mixed with the rich and famous, and I was overawed and tongue-tied whenever he came into the office to joke with Mike Hill.

In Hospitality after the very last show I introduced Ned to Chris, the photographic assistant on the programme. Chris was thin, pale, and rarely saw the light of day. He worked for Peter Agland at Atlas Photography, processing the still photographs that were used on the programme. Ned was a stickler for quality. He used to reject still after still, and I would ring Chris toiling away in his dark room and sweet-talk him into trying yet another print. By the time we broadcast, Chris was exhausted, and would sit next to me in the gallery, shaggy-haired and blinking in the light, like some little nocturnal animal. At the end of the series I felt the least he deserved was a word of thanks from Ned. 'Ah,' said Ned to me as Chris held out his hand, 'your boyfriend, is he?'

Chris and I were equally insulted. I explained that each time Ned had said, 'Send that back to Atlas Photography and tell them to try again', Chris had burrowed back into his dark room and tried to reach elusive perfection. Ned looked surprised. He had assumed as we sat side by side behind him, seemingly inseparable, that ours was a personal, not a professional relationship.

However absent-minded Ned was about my private life, he was whole-heartedly generous when it came to my work. Not only had he given me my first most important chance to join a production team, and then constantly stretched my imagination, forcing me to learn as much as I could about television programme-making in six months, he then wrote a glowing report about me. He himself was leaving the BBC to make feature films for Columbia. In his career in television he had always ensured that the talent he discovered, both in front of and behind the camera, would be recognized and prosper. He could do nothing more for me, so he tried to make sure that Current Affairs Group would value me after he had left.

Somewhere in the BBC machine, however, is a steel ruler, designed to rap its staff over the knuckles whenever they risk feeling confident, or, heaven forbid, loved and respected. The ruler swings like a pendulum. You're reaching great heights? 'Fine. This will teach you how far you can fall. Smack. Let's see you scramble out of that one.'

I was dazed when Ned's report was read to me. I think he called me the best researcher he had ever worked with during his time in television, which was more a reflection of his generosity than my talent. And my reward? The next job the BBC gave me was as a clerk, filing a jumbled mountain of 23,000 black-and-white photographs. It took three months of the swelteringly hot summer, and I

135

hated every moment.

* * *

After the Deputy Head of Department had read Ned's paeans of praise to me, Paul Fox (since knighted for his huge contribution to broadcasting, but Head of Current Affairs Group at the time), decided to extend my contract and send me to the nightly evening current affairs programme, *Twenty Four Hours.* The Editor was a charismatic journalist, Derek Amoore. Amoore was little, wiry, wore sunglasses constantly, made brilliant films, and couldn't work with women. He once explained to me, 'I understand fellows, they have bits that stick out. But women have holes. And I don't understand them.' The result was that he would greet us with a cheery, 'Take your knickers off,' but there the conversation would end. This was further confused by his taste for drink. He was an alcoholic, but somehow none of us thought of him as needing help. Evening after evening he would be poured into a taxi, only to slide out of the door on the opposite side, and try to drive his way home.

When Paul gave me to Derek, the only job Derek could think of for me was putting the programme's huge collection of photographs into alphabetical order. So I was left with six enormous filing cabinets, in a narrow office at the front of one of the Lime Grove houses. The sun shone temptingly in through the Venetian blinds, and next door my friends were making programmes. It felt to me like solitary confinement. I made it less solitary by asking for a secretary, and was given one, a charming ex-beauty queen from Zanzibar, called Philomena Peckett. With her beside me, life was almost bearable. I ordered some stationery, and found brown envelopes that fitted the photographs. We stuck them down, slit the sides and made sturdy pouches. Then I ordered some index cards, and started filing and cross-referencing the 23,000 pictures. No experience is ever wasted, Miss Senator? It's hard for me to pick the worthwhile lessons out of this one.

While I was filing away, I saw in *Ariel*, the staff newspaper, an advertisement for a job on *Woman's Hour* as producer of the books they used to serialize. I applied and was given an interview. One of the members of the Board was Joy Whitby, whose husband, Tony Whitby, was Amoore's deputy on *Twenty Four Hours*. A day later, Tony came in to see me, wedged in as I was by filing cabinets in my narrow office. 'Joy says you did a good Board,' he said.

'Not good enough,' I said, having just read my rejection slip.

'She says they didn't give you that job because she thought you would have more opportunity in television.'

I grunted ungratefully. 'You mean she wouldn't give me a job on the finest magazine programme in any medium, because she didn't want me to miss the chance of filing 23,000 stills. Thanks.'

Tony smiled at my heavy sarcasm, and told me that when he first joined the Foreign Office he, too, was given a fearful chore, sorting out all the tiny little flags into their colours, red, blue, yellow, green, so that they could be arranged on the maps again.

'How long did you have to do that?' I asked.

'Three weeks or so,' he said.

My six months felt even more like a life sentence. I met Paul Fox in the club. He asked kindly how I was getting on. I explained what I was doing. Tony Whitby, standing next to me, reminisced about the coloured flags in the Foreign Office, Paul nodded. Perhaps they were right, everyone has to complete an apprenticeship like mine, Jacob toiling in the vineyard for seven years.

One day, the door opened, and Brian Winston rushed in. Now he is an eminent professor, writer of many books, television guru and expert in the politics of the media. Then he was an old friend from Merton College, always breathless with enthusiasm for some new idea, working as a trainee director for *Twenty Four Hours.* He had known me at Oxford, and sympathized with my incarceration with the filing cabinets. He'd visit me from time to time, much as one visits a wolf pacing up and down its cage. He could sympathize but couldn't set me free.

This time, however, he was carrying a copy of the *Daily Mirror.* I asked what he was doing. 'I'm our expert in Crime,' he said. I must have looked surprised. He shrugged. 'Someone has to be it, and Amoore picked me. There's been a series of gangland murders among the car-thieving syndicates south of the river, and Charlie Brown is the key to it.' I had no idea what he was talking about. Furthermore I suspected that he, a nicely brought up Jewish boy, had no idea either. He pointed at the front page of the *Daily Mirror.* There was a picture of the funeral of the latest murdered gangster, and a guarded reference to one of those present, Charles Brown from Leighton Buzzard.

'I've got his address from the phone book, I've ordered a car, I've persuaded Amoore to let you go to Leighton Buzzard and get Brown into the studio.' On a macho programme like *Twenty Four Hours*, the important thing was always to 'Get Your Man'. Reputations rested on it. I looked nervous. 'Go on,' he said, gesturing at the piles of stills and envelopes, 'Anything's better than this.' He was right.

The drive took some time, because the driver was a compulsive gambler, and had to stop at every garage to make a phone call and discover how much he had lost in each successive race. He had lost his watch, and several other prized possessions by the time we reached the address Brian had written for me on a scrap of paper. I asked him to wait for me by the gate while I walked up the path, knocked on the gnarled wooden door of a thatched cottage, and when there was no reply, opened it to reveal two of the oldest men I have ever seen, sitting by a fire in the dark, playing dominoes by the flickering light of the flames. Neither of them looked like a South London gangster to me.

'Charlie Brown?' I asked.

'That's me,' one of them said.

I couldn't bring myself to ask what he knew of the gangland syndicates, so I smiled, backed out, and got into my car again.

We drove past another cottage, this time with Police Station written over the door. We stopped, I knocked, and a young policeman in his carpet slippers with a spaniel in his arms opened it.

'I'm trying to find Charlie Brown,' I said, waving the *Daily Mirror*, without much hope. How could a sleepy village bobby know anything about gangland

139

syndicates?

'Ah, you mean Shooting Brown,' said the policeman. 'He lives round the corner, but you won't find him in. He took the morning bus to London. His wife and children are staying in the vicar's house across the road. He'll be back on the six o'clock bus, or maybe the seven o'clock.'

I thanked him, drove to the house he'd shown me, and rang Brian. He told me I had to stake Brown out. I had never attempted a stake out before. But it seemed to be crucial if I was to get my man.

I asked the driver to move up the road and park just around the corner, so that Brown wouldn't see us when he walked home. But that meant I couldn't see Brown either. The hell with subterfuge. We parked right outside his house, where a mysterious man in a hat with a pulled-down brim was lingering, examining the wood of the lych-gate. I watched the man, trying to look as if I was gazing at nothing in particular. He came towards me and banged on the window. I rolled it down.

'Are you the police?' he asked, flatteringly.

At that moment I must have looked like an embarrassed schoolgirl. 'No, are you?'

'I'm the stringer from the *Daily Mirror*. I've been sent to get a picture of Charles Brown.'

We compared notes. Both of us decided to wait for the six o'clock bus. Nothing happened. We waited on for the seven o'clock. I didn't tell the stringer about the wife and children staying with the vicar across the road.

Promptly at five-past-seven, a man came down the road towards us, carrying a box that could have been a hairdryer, but could have been a gun. I jumped out of the car and called out to him, 'Mr Brown, I'm from the BBC, can I talk to you?'

He lifted the box, then shifted it back under his arm. I could hear a camera clicking behind me, the stringer was getting the pictures he needed. I explained that I'd been sent to invite Charlie Brown to take part in a studio interview with Cliff Michelmore, to disentangle the complexities of the gangland wars south of the river. He looked blank. 'I'm afraid I know nothing about that,' he said, and shut the door firmly in my face.

I rang Brian, who was disappointed, and we drove back to London, to find Derek Amoore, Tony Whitby, Paul Fox and several young executives from the programme waiting for that night's transmission. As I came into the office they chanted at me, 'Failure!'

I took it as a challenge. 'Not yet,' I said.

I went upstairs to an office, and rang the vicarage, asking for the vicar's wife. I had seen through Charlie's front door that the carpet was worn, the walls weren't painted, the house was dark and cold. If he had anything to do with crime in south London, which by now I strongly doubted, it obviously didn't pay. I said to the vicar's wife, 'Can you pass a message to Mrs Brown? Tell her that the BBC will pay for an interview, not a great deal, but expenses, say £25. And then if you come to the studio you can tell Cliff exactly what you said to me, that you don't know what he's talking about.' She thanked me. Charlie rang me back. We agreed that he should come to the studio the next day, and I went down to tell Brian. He was delighted. I had got my man, but I was quietly furious with the lot of them.

The next day Charlie negotiated with Brian for the £25, which at least was something for the children. As Cliff put question after question to him, he shook his head, saying, 'I'm afraid I know nothing about all that'. Cliff declared the interview a waste of time, and it was never transmitted. I saw Charlie Brown to his car, and he winked at me.

'What were you doing in London?' I asked.

'Getting a new hairdryer,' he said.

I went back to my filing cabinets.

*   *   *

One of the senior researchers on the programme was Tony 'Get Your Man' Summers. He was handsome, and full of the required machismo. Since then he has written many successful books, including one on the death of Marilyn Monroe. Then he had an unrivalled reputation for finding the most difficult, elusive interviewees and persuading them to take part in the programme.

It was the time of the seamen's strike in the Port of London, shipping was at a standstill. Harold Wilson caused pandemonium by naming the ringleaders of the strike, ten Communist seamen. As the news came over the speaker in Derek's office, the door burst open under the impact of Paul Fox's stride. 'There's your programme, Derek,' he said. Derek hastily undraped his legs from the radiator and agreed. Tony Summers was dispatched to get them, Paul stood in the centre of the office with his black book of contacts and phone numbers. I was impressed that the Head of Department was prepared to do anything to help put the show on the air.

Tony Summers rang to say, as usual, that he had indeed got his men. Robin Day was booked to do the interviews. The dock employers refused to sit at the same table as the seamen, so Robin tiptoed, like a portly waiter, with his clipboard between them. After the programme the two sets of guests, employers and seamen, went to separate Hospitality rooms. I joined Tony, and looked up at him like a spaniel puppy. 'However did you get them all?' I asked. He gazed down at me loftily. 'I have a contact at Congress House,' he said. 'He gave me an address in a back street in the East End. I persuaded someone there to give me another contact,' the story went on, leaving me awestruck. He had so many contacts, and so much initiative.

The night wore on in Hospitality. One of the seamen flung an arm round my neck. 'See that young man there,' he said, gesturing at Tony across the room. 'We were all in parliament, listening to Wilson naming us, then we went over to St Stephen's Tavern, and he came in. He said to me, "I'm looking for the ten Communist seamen, do you know where they are?" "Yes," I said, "I'm one and the other nine are standing by the bar." '

I take two lessons from that. Firstly, if a gormless young researcher tries to pick your brains, she deserves all she gets. Secondly, Tony always was creative, even when he was working for the BBC.

Eventually the photographs were filed, every one meticulously cross-referenced, and I wrote a memo to Derek Amoore. I explained that the photo library had been in chaos when I found it, one file for Philip, for instance, another for Prince, another for Duke, another for Edinburgh, and it would only take five minutes for it to deteriorate back to that state. Someone would have to take charge of it, to make sure the filing system remained intact.

Derek called me in. 'I've read your memo,' he said, in his sharp staccato bark, 'and I agree. You're elected.'

My face dropped. Could he be serious? This was not an apprenticeship after all—it was a life sentence. Derek justified his decision, 'You said the system would go back to chaos if nobody looked after it, I agree, you're elected.'

I left without a word and ran to Brian Winston's office. There, I stamped around saying every bad word I'd learned at Oxford and from Mike Hill. He asked what was wrong, and, when he heard, sent me to Derek's deputy, Tony Whitby. I told him of the conversation. Tony paled. He had not been made to sort flags at the Foreign Office for life. He told me to go back to my filing cabinets which had been moved to Derek's outer office, and promised he would think of a way to release me.

I trusted Tony. He somehow stayed sane in the lunacy of a daily current affairs show. I can't say the same for Derek. One of his odder habits was to while away the hours in the office with target practice with an air-gun. He once tried it in front of the BBC's investigator, an ex-policeman, who lunged across the desk and grabbed him by the collar, shaking him until he dropped the gun.

Sadly, I was not trained in combat, armed or unarmed, so he knew he had nothing to fear from me. As I sat gloomily by my newly created, deeply loathed photo library, Derek balanced an aerosol can on a cabinet just over my head and started to shoot at it. I was past caring. I couldn't even be bothered to jump when he pulled the trigger.

When Tony came in, I still didn't look up. Tony managed to look surprised to see me there. 'Oh, is that Esther, why is she still there? I thought she'd finished her filing.'

'She has,' said Derek, 'but she thinks someone's got to look after her photo library, so I told her she's elected.'

'Ah,' said Tony, cunningly, 'isn't she rather expensive?'

'Is she?'

'She's paid as a researcher, and that's a clerk's job. Why not ask our programme clerk to look after the photo library as well?'

Derek looked worried. 'But what can we do with Esther?'

Wrong gender, you see. He had no such problems with the men of my age. He easily found jobs for them.

'Don't bother about that. I'll take her. She can help me,' Tony said easily.

There followed another wonderful six months. Tony trained me to copy-taste the news stories coming in over the wires from the agencies. After a while he asked me to script short items, particularly the 'and finally' jokes which ended the programme. Once, oh joy, I wrote a topical song which was performed in the studio by professional musicians, and which made the team laugh. Derek, brilliant man though he was, educated by Jesuits and pursued by his own demons, had no idea how to employ a woman graduate. Tony, himself the husband of one of the most successful women in radio or television, Joy Whitby, had no problem at all.

*   *   *

From *Twenty Four Hours* I was posted to a brand new programme, *Your Witness*, produced by Tony Smith, who is now President of Magdalen College Oxford. Tony was, and is, delightful. Dark, with a permanently worried expression except when he exploded with laughter, I once watched him empty the whole contents of his in-tray into a wastepaper basket. 'If it's important, they'll write again,' he said. He created a great many programmes, indeed he was one of the founders of Channel 4, and is credited with inventing its philosophical basis, of innovation and independence.

Your Witness, presented by Ludovic Kennedy, consisted of a single subject debated for an hour—the existence of God, for instance, or the continuance of the public school system. To add drama, two barristers presented the cases for and against, each one called witnesses, and a jury of solicitors decided who had won.

It was a fascinating format. I remember contributing ideas for witnesses. Our rabbi, John Rayner, gave moving testimony for the existence of God, most of his family having perished in the concentration camps. The crux of the debate, as ever, was how a caring God could possibly allow such evil in the world. At the end of the hour, Ludovic Kennedy put the question, does God exist? We joked that if the jury voted the wrong way, God would punish them, and the overhead camera would fall on their heads. Fortunately, God won.

My job in each programme was to find

appropriate evidence on film. I drew largely upon *Man Alive*, which was the only film archive of first-hand experience. Uniquely at that time, instead of relying upon experts, they went to the people who were involved and knew only too well what it felt like. The much ridiculed question, 'How do you feel' was the catalyst for wonderfully expressive interviews, just as it is now the most used tool in counselling.

In order to gain permission to broadcast clips from the programmes I had to have many conversations with the Editor, Desmond Wilcox. As far as I can now remember, he never turned me down. My job was also to find a studio audience relevant to the subject. Because the camera was in the ceiling, every seat was visible and had to be filled. I used to infuriate the studio audience by dancing for joy when I discovered we had too many, and some had to watch in an airless Hospitality room. At least there would be no empty seats to blame me for.

Two of the barristers we booked remain in my memory, for very different reasons. One was a young unknown, selected by Tony Smith to defend the public school system. He did so with such brilliance that he caught the eye of a Conservative Party looking for a bright new candidate. His name was Geoffrey, now Lord, Howe.

I was talking to Geoffrey in the Lime Grove Club when Desmond Wilcox, who had been dubbing a *Man Alive* film there, came in for a drink with his team. It was the first time we had met. Desmond claimed he was impressed by my legs. I was wearing fishnet stockings, and he said I had a hole in them. Was I ever that slutty? Perhaps so.

Yesterday's sluts become today's respectable matrons—how sad for their husbands.

The other barrister I remember vividly was also a Tory, a Scot, and a dandy. He designed his own square bowler hat. He wore idiosyncratic suits and waistcoats, and I fell in love with him. His name was Nicholas Fairbairn. Maybe he, too, was a Don Juan. Certainly I didn't realize he was married until it was far, far too late. Unlike Alfred Marks and Andrew Faulds, he combined a powerful sexual appetite with charm and humour. Best of all, he laughed at my jokes.

How did he seduce me? He took me to lunch at the Ritz. He gave me a long-stemmed red rose, and, when the menu arrived, barely glanced at it. 'I think Beluga caviare and Krug champagne,' he said. I defy anyone to disagree with that suggestion. I had never eaten Beluga caviare by the potful before. The waiter reverently spooned it out, arranged little heaps of hard-boiled egg yolk and finely-chopped onion, and brought racks of deliciously warm toast. The Beluga consisted of huge succulent globes that exploded on the tongue. If ever there was an aphrodisiac meal, this was it.

Nicholas took me to some lord's house where he was staying, and the rest was inevitable. At the end of the afternoon, I climbed into a taxi and went back to my family, who were all gathered to celebrate the Jewish Festival of New Year. If I was absent-minded, it was because I was dreaming of Nicky, of the castle he was restoring, and the cases he had won by proving that the police had concocted their evidence.

Later he, too, became a member of parliament, making headlines for his extraordinary statements about women—saying, for example, that a skirt was a gateway, an open invitation. He was often retained to defend rapists, and did so most successfully. Although Mrs Thatcher promoted him to Solicitor-General for Scotland, so notorious did he eventually become that he had to resign.

I lost touch with him completely soon after *Your Witness* ended, but just before his death in 1995 I read of his illness and sent him a bunch of roses. He sent me a card in reply, suggesting we meet. We never did. I did, however, once interview his daughter in our talk show. I didn't admit to her how well I knew her father. Nicky was outrageous, his views indefensible, but I can understand why so many women found him irresistible. I did.

Charm, of course, has nothing to do with virtue, nor is it the same as physical good looks. It is the capacity to entertain, and to find you entertaining, and it is dangerous. My sister, the social worker, warned me that charming people often use it as a weapon to manipulate and get what they want; that you should measure them by what they do, not by what they say. And she is right, as usual. All the same, naughty as it was, I have no regrets about my brief affair with Nicky. Yes, he broke my heart a little, but we had fun, and the sixties were a decade for fun.

CHAPTER SIX

BACKING INTO THE LIMELIGHT

After Ned left, the BBC tried to create one more satire programme, *The Late Show*. It had a wonderful team of writer/performers: John Bird, John Fortune, John Wells, Barry Humphries and Eleanor Bron. But Huw Wheldon appointed as producer Hugh Burnett, a man who on paper looked ideal, but turned out to be a disaster. He was a superb documentary film-maker, he drew wryly ironic cartoons, so why didn't it work? Perhaps it was just that he was a stranger to the team. Perhaps he was nervous of them, and with satirists, as with all man-eating animals, it is fatal to show fear.

Whatever the reason, the team of writer/performers would never work in the office if they could help it. They would meet in each other's homes to write, and would occasionally ring me, the only researcher, for a fact, a prop or a picture. Most of the week I would sit alone in my office, and Hugh would sit in his, as if we were drifting on the *Marie Celeste*. Every other office was deserted. Sometimes Hugh would visit me, and ask pathetically if I knew where the others were. I used to say no, because I didn't.

Unsurprisingly, given the circumstances, the show was a disaster. It taught me a terrible television truth, that it takes just as much hard work to make a bad programme as a good one. Everywhere I went people would say to me, 'You know what's wrong with your show,' and I would say, 'Yes', just to keep them quiet. But I didn't—none of us did. Each week we would meet briefly in Hugh's office, at his request, to try and discover why it wasn't working. The discussion would roam over every possibility, would reject all answers, and focus on a detail. We would leave Hugh's office having concluded that the problem with the programme was the boom shadow on the second shot. But the real problem was that the team had no ringmaster to crack the whip and convince them they were funny, or that the scripts were clever enough. John Bird would write a sharp, witty script, then complicate it and elaborate it until the sketches became incomprehensible.

The tragedy was that it was made by a collection of marvellously inventive people. Barry Humphries was only known then as the caption writer for *Private Eye*'s 'Barry McKenzie' comic strip. But he had invented a frumpy Australian housewife called Mrs Edna Everage who appeared for the first time on television, on *The Late Show*. She was so shy that she used to introduce herself on the show with a bat-like shriek, 'Excuse I'. She was very dowdy in those days, dressed in a lumpy coat and dented hat from BBC wardrobe.

Edna and I have had similar careers. In a sense we were both caterpillars in those days, with no real hope of becoming butterflies. I would never have dreamed that I could have a career on the screen. Edna, of course, has been far more successful. Now she is a Dame, she has become a world superstar, and spends the equivalent of my yearly salary on a few of her frocks. In some ways she has been my role model. When I first had to

151

wear glasses at the age of forty, I chose bright red, heart-shaped frames—very Edna. At my worst, my dress sense, including an unfortunate sequinned period, and a strange one-shouldered season, was also influenced by Everage. Maybe I am bolder than I was then. Certainly she is. No more 'Excuse I', now that Edna is the toast of Broadway.

Barry has changed, too. I met him after one of his hit shows in the West End. He was tanned and glowed with success. His manager told me a story about his relationship with Edna. Barry has a fear of heights. They had rigged up a hydraulic lift which could raise him right up to the dizzy level of the gods, to look at the paupers, 'little paupies', shivering there. In rehearsal Barry simply could not climb into it. But when the wig and the dress were on, and Edna had arrived, she clambered on to it without a backward glance, and winged her way up to the ceiling of the theatre, carolling with glee.

Barry when I first knew him was a pale, sensitive aesthete—well, partly. He was a fund of knowledge about art and literature. He collected fine glass, and was the reverse of Les Patterson, the foulmouthed Australian 'cultural attaché' he invented alongside and in counterpoint to Edna. However, like many aesthetes before him, he used to drink crème de menthe by the pint. Drink taken, he would 'moon' mercilessly. He never mooned at me, but legends spread of the threat of the Humphries buttocks. Once Lord Snowdon was having dinner in a local west London restaurant when Barry noticed him there, went to a public phone box, and rang him, pretending to be Princess Margaret, demanding to know when he was coming home. Snowdon was trapped in the restaurant for hours, terrified that Barry was lurking outside about to 'moon' at him.

Even sober, Barry had a passion for practical jokes. Many of them involved Russian salad—the chopped vegetables in salad cream obtainable in tins. He would either empty a tin surreptitiously into a sickbag when he was travelling on an airplane, then retch into the bag, pull out a spoon, and eat it. Or he would conceal a paper-bagful in a litter bin, wait until some likely victim was passing, and retch and eat that. But not, as far as I can remember, on the show.

There were other gems. John Bird and John Fortune improvised together exactly as they did more than twenty years later on Rory Bremner's programme. For their work on Rory's show they won BAFTA awards. On *The Late Show* they sank without trace. Perhaps, as Ned has said, once the Tories had lost the election, without 'thirteen years of Tory misrule' to deride, satire just needed a rest.

Or maybe at that wild time the satirists themselves needed a rest. It is said of the sixties that if you can remember them you can't have been there. I remember them with nostalgia, but I admit that by the standards of any serious swingers I wasn't there at all. I loved the music, the Liverpool sound, and the Kinks, and Alan Price and Georgie Fame. I loved the fact that England was the cool place to be, that the fashion world was guided by Carnaby Street. I looked the part, I wore miniskirts and hot pants, I back-combed my hair and wore heavy eyeliner. But I never smoked marijuana, and took none of the mind-altering drugs, LSD or purple hearts.

Those were not decisions taken on moral

153

grounds, but because I am frightened of chemicals of any kind, and terrified of losing control of my own perceptions. For the same reason I have never drunk a great deal—the sniff of a cork makes my head swim. I was drunk once, at my own birthday party. I walked around in a wide-brimmed pink hat given me by a friend, then took it off and was sick into it. That ruined the party, and the hat, and I never did it again.

Sex, as you will have noticed, was something else again. Not that I have ever been wildly promiscuous. You could count the number of lovers I have had on one hand. Well, perhaps two. My taste in men was sometimes flawed. Far too many scoundrels joked their way into my bed. I find laughter difficult to resist, and being outside British territorial waters also seems to erode my inhibitions, as it does for so many English girls.

*   *   *

An extraordinary event happened to me when I was twenty-five. I began to lose weight. I was working every minute of the day at the BBC and with Phase Two. My work was creative and satisfying. I had neither the time nor the desire to eat compulsively, 'binge' as it's now called. For years I had been on one crazy diet or another, the grapefruit and cottage cheese diet, the cauliflower and cottage cheese diet. All they did was put me off cottage cheese. Nothing made me thinner. But now, without any effort, I felt the pounds fall off me. I would stand on the scales, shutting my eyes out of habit to shield myself from bad news, and open them to see the needle had dropped from ten

154

stone to nine, then to eight and a half, then to seven stone twelve.

At that point I could tell I was in danger of losing too much weight. Although I had never heard of anorexia I could feel the thrill of becoming really thin, and I consciously made myself eat. I settled at about eight stone two. I remember meeting Michael Palin and Terry Jones in the Reception of Television Centre and had the pleasure of watching them jump with surprise. They had known me fat, and assumed that was how I would always look. Suddenly I had a jawline, a waist, my ankles had emerged, so had my eyes, from the flesh that used to bury them. My thighs had thinned down (a crucial improvement in miniskirts) and somehow elongated. Nothing would ever make me beautiful, with my irregular teeth and long chin, but I had become much more presentable. My new look startled my old friends, it startled me just as much. Desmond often said, 'I fell in love with a plump brunette, and ended up with a stringy blonde.' I know what he meant. Inside I will always remain a plump brunette.

Your Witness came back for a second series, and I was at once taken to task by the two assistant producers on the programme. I was still the researcher, the most junior of the production team. The two men lectured me. I must go to Tony Smith, they said, and ask him for promotion. I went, but I found it difficult to make my own case. I knew Tony was fond of me, but that made no difference to his assessment of my skills. Yes, I was a good researcher. But he could only promote me if he genuinely believed that one day I would make a competent producer, and frankly he didn't think I

155

ever would.

It was like hearing the men in the *Twenty Four Hours* office chant 'Failure' at me. I liked Tony a great deal, I couldn't argue with him, but my resolve hardened. I would prove him wrong. The phone rang in my office. It was Desmond Wilcox. He was looking for assistant producers with studio experience, and I had been recommended to him. Would I have lunch with him? Like a shot, I would.

Desmond (like Tony Whitby) was a rare television employer, he was gender-blind, and he believed women should be promoted for their talent. Desmond was prepared to give women opportunities and responsibility at a time when few other male bosses in the industry would. As a result he collected female refugees: Jenny Barraclough from ITV, Pat Houlihan from Light Entertainment, Shirley Fisher from Presentation. They were all talented directors and producers behind the cameras. But he went further and even employed women reporters on screen in *Man Alive* (Angela Huth, Jeanne la Chard and Gillian Strickland) when the popular myth among television executives was that viewers objected to them. Women's voices were light and irritating, and women's faces were distracting and lacked authority, so the legend went. Desmond didn't agree. Nor, it turned out, did the viewers.

I was in Desmond's office when Jenny Barraclough arrived, furious, because her editor in ITV had removed her voice from the commentary of the film because it was 'too light'. Desmond said, 'I know how talented you are, Jenny. Of course you can join us. Would you like to direct or report?'

Jenny chose to become a director, and made the

heartbreaking, award-winning 'Gail Is Dead' for *Man Alive*. It was the profile of a child who had grown up in care to become a pretty, clever, hopeless junkie who died in her early twenties. Jenny also filmed a pioneering portrait of Holloway Prison for which she won a BAFTA. She was extremely pregnant when she went up to collect her award, the first woman film director to win it. I thought she looked glorious. What an achievement, not only for her, but for Desmond's employment policy.

Scarcely had I joined Desmond's team than Tony Smith asked me to return to Current Affairs for another programme he was creating, called *At the Eleventh Hour*. He gathered about him yet another extraordinary mix of talents. The poet Roger McGough was in a band called The Scaffold, with artist John Gorman and Paul McCartney's brother Mike. Tony recruited Richard Neville, a glamorous rebel from Australia who was the Editor of Oz magazine. He hired an actress I had seen and admired in the Cambridge Footlights, Miriam Margolyes. Some of the music for the show was written by Ray Davis of the Kinks. Heavens we were 'hip'. Tony Smith is now a pillar of the establishment, President of Magdalen, the very Oxford college singled out (quite unfairly) by Gordon Brown for an attack on élitism. But then Tony was the pied piper, leading a raggedly band of anarchic rebels, in a programme which should have worked, but didn't.

There were very interesting pieces in it, Ray Davis's songs, Roger's poems. The show was rude, and lively, but it was out of joint. So, although it may have been fun for us to put together, it was not much fun for the viewers.

Having once blocked my promotion, now Tony gave me my first opportunity to write for a programme on a regular basis. Most of the team created their own material, but we lacked a showpiece for Miriam Margolyes, so I put together a 'Jewish mother' monologue for her. It was inspired by my own mother, so it should have been funnier. The first monologue was about medical programmes. I had come downstairs one evening to find my mother and my sister watching *Your Life in Their Hands*, both wearing duffel jackets back to front, so they could put the hoods over their faces if it got too bloody. Who would ever believe a scene like that could be real? My monologue was attacked by a couple of Jewish writers as anti-Semitic. There was a sensitivity about creating a Jewish comedy character—after all, the Holocaust was still only twenty years away.

Miriam loved to shock. Short, round, with large dark eyes and a rollicking laugh, she is now rich and famous, working as often in Hollywood as she does in film and television in Britain. She is noticeably proud of her big round breasts, indeed she has been known to pull one out to enliven a dull moment.

Tony took Miriam and me to Bloom's, the kosher restaurant in Golders Green. There was a long queue. Behind us were a small couple with two large sons, Craig and Douglas. The parents used their bony elbows to nudge their way past us and grab the first free table. Victoriously they strode towards it as Miriam bellowed after them, 'The trouble with that man is that he has a very small penis'. By then, we were at the front of the

158

queue facing the Head Waiter. I sighed. We'd waited all that time, and now Miriam had got us thrown out. The waiter looked at her more in sorrow than in anger and told her, 'Madam, when you said that, every man in the restaurant, even the chef in the kitchen, looked down at himself in dismay'. We had our meal, thanks to the new tolerance of the sixties, or perhaps to the Jewish sense of humour.

We soon discovered there were limits to the BBC's sense of humour. From time to time an American, Harvey Matusow, came to the office to contribute ideas. He once explained to me that there were moments in life when things got so bad, you could only laugh. 'One morning,' he said, 'I had the day off, so I was sleeping late. I was wakened by my wife ringing from Mexico. She said Harvey, divorce is so easy here. Why don't I just drop in to the office on the corner and get one? At eleven, my lawyer rang and told me that my appeal against sentence in the McCarthy trial had failed, so I would have to go to jail. At two, I had a call from the advertising agency where I worked saying "Harvey, as you've got the day off, we suggest you don't bother coming in again. Ever." What could I do? I'd lost my wife, my job, I was going to jail, I could only laugh.'

Harvey's tale was more dramatic than most people's, but all the same he gave me the germ of an idea. When the washing machine breaks down, and the loo blocks, and the car runs out of petrol, what do you do, but sit in the middle of your flooded kitchen floor, laugh, shrug and say 'That's life!'.

Harvey also brought with him from the States a

joke about President Lyndon Johnson (I have heard it said of every President since). 'How do you know the President is lying? If he scratches his ear, he's telling the truth. If he rubs his nose, he's telling the truth. If he moves his lips, he's lying.' Why not retranslate this to Harold Wilson? We did. He complained furiously. Hugh Carleton Green instantly took *At the Eleventh Hour* off the air. We had only been due to run one week longer, but with our rudeness and untidiness we had been trouble all through the series. Had we been as skilled and successful as *TW3* he might have defended us, as it was, he didn't.

*　　*　　*

Back I went to *Man Alive*, to find myself in a hornet's nest. Desmond had transferred the programme from being a film-based documentary to a film and studio mix. None of the rest of his team had made studio-based programmes before. I had, so they thought I must have come to teach them how it should be done. It rapidly became clear to them that I was only a jumped-up researcher, given my first promotion. Alas, filled with unjustified confidence, I strode around the office, giving them the benefit of my wisdom. No wonder they hated me. I would have, too. They did, however, take their hostility a bit too far—they sent me to Coventry. Nobody spoke to me in the corridor, no-one sat next to me in the canteen.

Then, one day, a researcher, John Pitman, strolled into my office, sat down, and we began to gossip together. I told him tales of the daftness of Current Affairs, he told me stories of his time on

160

the *Daily Mail.* Once he had been writing about lipstick, and wanted to find out how many are manufactured each day in Britain. Nobody had the figures he needed. So he made up a number. To his interest, his statistic appeared over and over again in other papers over the next few years. He had created what Norman Mailer called a 'factoid', an invented fact that takes on a life of its own.

We had a pleasant ten minutes, then John strolled out of my office as casually as he had arrived. As he left he said, 'You're not bad, Ranters'. Such was the odd chemistry of *Man Alive* that, from that moment, everyone smiled at me in the corridor, sat with me in the canteen. I had become so accustomed to being ignored, it was days before I noticed.

Desmond sent me on a production course, not before time, as a trainee director. I learned to write commentary, fitting words to picture without duplicating what the viewers could see for themselves, or indulging in the 'Look at Life' style of simulated surprise, 'Oh, gosh, what have we here?' Huw Wheldon was one of our lecturers. Huw was a tall, benign Welshman, with a long nose, a chin like Mr Punch, and humorous eyes. He had been a television presenter himself, creating a programme for children called *All Your Own.* It was famous for a moment when one child's pet owl ate another child's pet mouse. He also created the most famous of all arts programmes, *Monitor*, on which film-makers like Ken Russell and John Schlesinger worked.

When I heard him lecture he was the BBC's Director of Programmes, and his influence pervaded the whole television organization. He was

161

humane, in an organization which all too often can be as bleak as a granite wall. He was an intellectual, without any snobbery. He said, 'Always assume in your viewers maximum intelligence, minimum information. Don't take any fact for granted, but never patronize. Remember you're tense, and anxious to get the programme right. Your viewers are relaxed, and comfortable, and thinking far more quickly than you.'

I have learned that viewers are also very much more observant than producers realize. Years later I was cutting a film for *That's Life!* about songs to celebrate the spring. I had waited outside Harrods with my stick mike (as I explained to my studio audiences before the show, do you know why they call it a stick mike? Because I took it out on the streets and policemen would tell me where to stick it), when I met a man with a lovely tenor voice, who sang to me. I must have watched that piece of film half a dozen times, the rushes, the rough cut, the fine cut, the rehearsals and finally on transmission. But only the day after the programme broadcast, and the phone calls started, did I take the film out again and see what millions of viewers noticed at first sight, that behind the singer was a desperate toddler, whose mum rolled down his trousers, and let him pee in the gutter, discreetly, just behind the singer's shoulder. How could we have missed it?

Wheldon also said, 'All programme making is story-telling.' It may sound obvious, but it's strange how easy it is to forget the crucial construction of every story: beginning, middle and end. And he said, 'You'll never be a producer until you have made a programme so wonderful that everyone, even the lift-man in Lime Grove' (long gone, even in my time), 'comes out to shake you by the hand, and a programme so bad that nobody will sit with you in the canteen in case the subject comes up.'

Wheldon was one of the innovators, the man who inspired much that was great in that time of classic programme-making. He told us that excellence was our aim, whatever kind of programme we made. Although he made arts programmes himself, he equally adored comedy, be it *Dad's Army* or *Fawlty Towers*. He was always amused by the casting of *Dad's Army*, Arthur Lowe as Captain Mainwaring, far more common than John Le Mesurier, his second in command. He also valued the fact that there were only twelve editions of *Fawlty Towers*, all written by John Cleese and Connie Booth, as one of the cast told me, 'writing off their marriage on the backs of envelopes'. Wheldon said if they had been working in the US, a stable of writers would have taken the idea from them, and exploited it to death. As it is, it is repeated over and over again to huge audiences, and as I write is still playing to audiences of over eight million.

Wheldon believed that broadcasting should be accessible, but that did not mean tacky or playing to the lowest common denominator. He would judge a programme firstly by its aim. Was it a worthwhile attempt? And if so, then he would allow for gallant failure. He knew—as we all discover, sadly—that the best way to learn is from mistakes. Lord Hill (Charles Hill, once the radio doctor, eventually promoted to become Chairman of the Board of Governors), once told me that if only Huw had listened a little more, and talked a little less, he would have been 'alpha', and been appointed Director General. Was that the resentment of a curmudgeonly Englishman, faced with the easy fluency of Welsh 'hwyl'? If so, it was the BBC's loss. Huw was one of the best DGs the BBC never had.

For our final exercise on the training course we had to create a programme, and direct it in the training studio. I invented a *Woman's Hour* with a live studio audience. I made the audience practise putting on false eyelashes, and vote between two identical twins, one dressed as she would wish, the other dressed as her mother wanted. I had invited some high-powered political women to join the audience, thinking they would have strong, articulate views. They had, but no sense of humour. Although I had included a serious debate for them to take part in, they were appalled by some of the frivolous items, and wrote in dudgeon to the highest level of the BBC and complained. I met Paul Fox later at an official function. He told me that their complaint had ricocheted around the rocky crags of the hierarchy, nobody recognizing the programme they were describing, until at last he realized it was only a training exercise, and I was to blame for it. Had he not seen me toiling over the dusty filing cabinets for so many months, he might have been furious. As it was, he was only mildly irritated.

*   *   *

When I returned to my home in *Man Alive* there were changes on the way. Bernard Braden had made a deal with the BBC. He and Barbara Kelly were making a situation comedy for the Light

164

Entertainment Department. He also agreed to make a consumer programme, and Paul Fox, now promoted to Controller of Channel One, decided to give it to Desmond Wilcox's department.

How short television memories are. Some people, I know, have forgotten Bernard Braden, still others have never seen his work. But I believe that in that era of innovation, Bernie was a great original. He was a Canadian actor who had great success as a broadcaster, first of all in radio in the popular comedy programmes, *Breakfast With Braden*, and *Bedtime With Braden.*

Then, almost accidentally, he had invented consumer television programmes. He told me that he had come across a true story from a friend, about milk bottles delivered, or I suppose misdelivered, week after week. He told it on the air, and was astonished by the response, so the next week he had included stories from the viewers, with a reply from the milk company. So the genre was born. He had invented a platform for the viewers' voices, for the stuff of real life to be shown on the screen.

Bernie was the perfect teller of these tales. Because he was Canadian, he couldn't be pigeon-holed into a class or a region. Because he was used to comedy, he took the stories he told lightly, but mixed them with serious journalism. He had created the programme for ATV, one of the independent television companies, it was called *On the Braden Beat.* The only glitch arose when he made a commercial for Campbell's Soup. As a performer he didn't see why he shouldn't be paid to say the words. He didn't claim to be a professional consumerist. His team thought

165

otherwise, and told me later that the advertisement had seriously damaged the credibility of his programme.

All that was in the past. When Desmond was given the task of creating a new consumer programme for Bernie at the BBC, he talked to me about the people I knew. In Current Affairs Group I had met John Lloyd, a writer and producer who worked on the old *Tonight* programme and with Bernie in ATV. Bernie got on very well with John, who was now a freelance. Desmond met John, liked him, and hired him.

John Lloyd died at thirty-six, of pancreatic cancer. From 1968 until his death in 1976 my working life was bound so closely to him that I called him my guardian angel. Imagine a Welsh Woody Allen, a little wisp of a man, with a constant half-smile, and when he knew there was a joke on the way, a light in his eyes of sheer joy. I loved providing research for him. He would lean back in his chair, his legs draped over the corner of the deck, and then transmute my dull pages ('not another eighteen-page epic, Esther, it's only a fight over a pair of boots'), into wit and wisdom on the screen. He would fuel himself with innumerable pints of beer and packets of cigarettes, but then we all smoked.

In the late sixties there were scare stories about cigarettes causing lung cancer, but the tobacco companies always denied them and blamed air pollution. Addicts that we were, we wanted to believe them. In 1970, when I first heard the statistics from the Channel Island of Jersey, where the air is pure and clean, cigarettes are incredibly cheap, and lung cancer tragically common, I could

166

kid myself no longer, and gave up. But in 1968 I, like everyone else I knew, was smoking twenty a day.

John Lloyd met John Pitman, and, sharing a sense of humour, they got on together at once. We had the nucleus of the team. All that had to be decided was how to make the show.

John Lloyd said to me, 'Bernie reads autocue so well, all we really need to do is put one camera in front of him, give him the stories to read, and there's the programme. But, unfortunately, if we did this, the production team would fall asleep. So, we need to find something more inventive.' He then told me that on one of the ATV shows, a researcher, Gordon Watts (who was to become one of my more eccentric Editors on *That's Life!*), had come back into the studio and reported what he had discovered to Bernie, recreating in the show what had happened in the office. 'The researcher told Bernie the story, he was unimpressed and asked the difficult questions', John explained. 'Now, you used to perform at Oxford, how would you like to present your own research on the show to Bernie?'

It sounded fun, if unlikely. After all, John Pitman was a better bet than me. He was already training to become a reporter, and could certainly make the films for the show. However, we started to put the pilot together.

Not for one moment did John and I think we would survive the pilot in an on-screen role. I knew enough to realize that the point of a pilot is to try out ideas and people, and that the bosses almost invariably change the presenters, whatever else they decide to keep. Neither of us took the pilot seriously. I was hoping to train as a director, and one day become a producer. John was on his way to making serious documentaries. Even so, it was disconcerting to go to make-up, see my friends the make-up artists there, and sit down myself in front of the mirror with its traditional show-business border of lights.

As the audience came into the studio, it was strange not to be in my normal place in the control room. Bernie did his warm-up ('If your hands perspire when you applaud, we can't afford towels, but a woolly dog will pass among you from time to time and you can wipe your hands on its back') and the show started. I was used to that ritual. But instead of being perched behind the director in the gallery, watching the screens flick and change, this time I was combed, lipsticked and polished, and sitting behind a desk beside John Pitman. At least he was there, secretly clutching my knees as I grabbed his, for comfort, under the desk. And at least I was familiar with all the studio equipment, cameras, floor manager, props. All the same, when my cue came, and I opened my mouth and spoke a couple of words, my own voice echoed in my head and nothing made sense to me.

Then an astonishing thing happened. I looked at Bernie and I saw in his eyes that he was really listening to me. I cannot tell you the difference that made. He broke through the shell of fear that paralyzed me. I knew that if I stopped, or garbled my words, or forgot my facts, he would help me out because he was genuinely listening.

I hope I learned that crucial lesson. When I interview people, I always look straight into their eyes, so that they can read in them the knowledge that I am really interested in the story they are telling me. You may think that goes without saying. Perhaps it should. But (naming no names—Clive Anderson) there are interviewers who are only waiting to strike like a snake, and deliver their own witty next line. Other interviewers (too many to name), have a list of questions on a card and simply work their way down through them. But Bernie was sharp, funny, and listened. So on that pilot, and for many weeks later, he saved my professional life.

*   *   *

Neither John nor I professed much interest in the fate of the pilot. The series, which was part of the BBC's deal with Bernie, had already been commissioned. We knew we'd be working on it as researchers. We were certain that the bosses would be dismissive about our own performances on it, and that we would be replaced by experienced professional reporters. We weren't. Not that the bosses were enthusiastic about us, it was as if they hardly noticed. Because we were in the pilot, they seemed to assume that we would be included in the show. John and I were incredulous, but carried on. If they hadn't noticed how inexperienced and slightly pathetic we were, we weren't going to point it out to them. We were too busy working on stories.

Desmond had come up with an idea for my first investigation. He put his head round the door, said 'white slavery' and disappeared again. All I knew about white slavery was a cruise my mother had been on in her youth, when a young man had embraced her on the deck by moonlight, and she had felt the point of a needle in her side, and immediately assumed she had been drugged and would be bundled up and sent into the harems of North Africa. So she struggled free, and dashed to her own cabin, where she lay down prepared to fight unconsciousness. Twenty minutes later she was still wide awake, so she examined the lining of her fur jacket, and discovered the cleaners had left a long pin in it.

That was the closest she or I had ever been to the white-slave traffic. Now I had to try and find it in London. Far from being hidden under a stone, it was there in the open, waving at me. I rang the Foreign Office, and a press officer told me to look in Stage, the theatre paper, for advertisements for dancing girls in the Middle East. There they were, 'No previous experience necessary'. A woman from Equity told me that they would take anyone female under the age of forty. Even if you sang like the Hound of the Baskervilles, they'd still give you a job. I did, so I was the ideal candidate to test the audition process.

The man from the Foreign Office told me that British consuls were constantly having to rescue the girls who answered those ads and took jobs abroad, otherwise they ended their lives as toothless, penniless old crones stranded thousands of miles away from their friends and family. What a fate. I applied at once.

I have noticed that you seldom hear of Ralph Nader's mother. Nader puts his life at risk many times in his investigations on behalf of the American consumer, but does his mother leap into the ring and interpose her body? Where is Roger Cook's mother? Does she rush forward when some

170

brutal gangster is about to break his ribs, and hit him over the head with a saucepan? My family is different. When my mother heard I was about to launch myself as a potential white slave, she was horrified. What was the BBC putting me through?

I tried to calm her. I showed her the advertisement for dancers at the Kit-Kat Club in Beirut, top money, no experience necessary. The auditions were being held in a respectable rehearsal room in Great Newport Street. They even had a phone number. Mother wasn't mollified. She rang Desmond. He agreed to send John Pitman to wait outside, in case I was drugged and rolled up in a carpet. So John had to spend a couple of hours sitting on a doorstep in the West End of London, ready to pounce on any carpets being carried past him.

Inside the audition room I met the man in charge of the troupe, Pan Theodossiou. That was his real name, his stage name was Taki Bengali, and he was President of the United Arab Republic Magic Circle. He asked me my age. I said twenty-five. It was a lie. I was twenty-eight. Taki looked at me—at least I was clearly under forty. He told me to sing. I gave him a 'Hound of the Baskerville's' version of 'I can't give you anything but love, Baby'. He asked me to stop, and explained that my job would also include *consummation*. This was a technical term that meant consuming drinks with the customers after the show. If it led to any other kind of consummation, Taki didn't go into details.

He offered me the job, twenty-eight pounds a week. Spangles beckoned. It was quite good money. I liked Taki. There was a fatherly quality about him, and, as I have said, I always preferred

171

older men. I accepted. The phone rang. Taki answered, looked confused, then handed me the phone. It was my mother.

I said everything was fine, and I was just leaving. On my way out I passed a resigned John Pitman, smoking his thirtieth cigarette, cursing Desmond Wilcox for sending him out as chaperone when he had serious research work to do.

Back at the office I hit the phones. I discovered that the trick hidden in the 'non-Equity' contract Taki had given me was that whatever the girls ate or drank, plus the cost of the accommodation, would be deducted from their fees. So they invariably ended up in debt to their management, who took their passports so they couldn't fly home. Quite soon the girls would be encouraged to try to pay off their debts by agreeing to more strenuous kinds of *consummation*, which led in the end to their becoming toothless old crones knocking on the doors of the British Embassy. I even found a girl, with all her teeth, but with quite a frightening story to tell, to whom this had happened, and whom we flew home to describe her experience.

In the first programme I described the audition, Bernie encouraged me to sing two lines of 'I can't give you anything but love, Baby', and declined to let me sing any more. The girl we flew back was evidence of the dangers I had managed to avoid, thanks to the powerful combination of my mother and John Pitman. *Braden's Week* ran for four years, then *That's Life!* ran for another twenty-one. But a part of me still hankers for my lost life in spangles.

*　　　*　　　*

Why did *Braden's Week* work so well, when the satire shows I had worked on after Ned's departure were failures? Not because the performers or the writers were cleverer or more talented. But television relies on chemistry. John Lloyd and Bernie between them created an alchemy which took the ordinary stuff of life and made it sparkle. John Lloyd once told me that anyone could find a good story:

'Stories aren't difficult. But a television programme has to be greater than the sum of its parts. You must make a place the viewers want to come to, so that even if a particular item bores them, they have faith that in a moment or two something will happen which they will enjoy. It's the frame that counts, the setting. If you can create that, you'll have a programme people will want to watch.'

That's still true. Whether it's Richard and Judy's morning show, or *Have I Got News for You*, the successful recipe is based on relationships between the presenters, atmosphere—a set of intangibles that together build success on screen. Sadly, unlike a recipe, it's impossible to copy them by the book. Instinct makes a great cook, and instinct makes a great producer.

In our studio Bernie and John created the atmosphere of a happy production office. It was reality, but it was also carefully constructed illusion. Bernie had been an actor. He could convey a natural relaxation on the screen. In life he often seemed melancholy, but when the red transmission light went on he was genial and warm, and built a strong relationship with all the rest of the team. I am not for a moment implying it was a

173

false impression. In some ways, the red light liberated Bernie, made him the person he could be when the tension of real life was lifted.

John Pitman and I were simpler souls, basically what we seemed—researchers who enjoyed our jobs, were excited by the journalism, and (at least as far as I was concerned), loved the glitz of a studio audience and a wider audience of eight million viewers. John always claimed to hate all that, and as soon as the series finished he went back to his first love, documentary-making. I used to accuse John of backing into the limelight. He accused me of begging people to ask me for my autograph. I can remember being at Heathrow with my mother, she turning to a porter and saying, 'Would you like my daughter's autograph? She's so natural'.

At first I was supposed to handle the studio items, while John presented the films, but in the end we just took the first stories that came our way. Which is why I tackled the Gnome-nobbler of Folkestone. It was a no-news week that week, especially when it came to the film stories we needed to end the show. John had made a memorable film the week before, of a road-planner who had decided to take down a hedge round a field, so that drivers could see the on-coming traffic. Sadly, that created many more accidents, since drivers were now distracted by what the hedge had previously concealed; in the field a randy bull was servicing many cows. Somehow Pitman had enticed a woman in a tweed suit to say to him, 'I think it's a load of bull'. Simple stuff, but it pleased us and our viewers.

This week, however, we did not even have a

randy bull, nothing at all, until John Lloyd read a story in the *Evening News* about a phantom gnome-nobbler. I rang the Folkestone journalist who had sold them the story. He didn't sound too keen on us setting out to meet him straight away, but we were desperate, otherwise there would be a five-minute hole at the end of the programme.

There were two journalists behind the phantom gnome-nobbling story. We met them in a pub, and now I realize they, too, must have had a tough no-news week, as they drove together round Folkestone, with nothing to look at but garden after garden filled with plastic gnomes. Gnomes were everywhere—especially in one big front garden, which was crammed with rockeries, a different little statue peeping out from behind every stone. So they had written their story in the Folkestone paper about a phantom nobbler, and the lady who owned the big garden, read it, believed it, and put barbed wire all round her rockeries.

When we arrived with our crew, the journalists led us proudly to the lady's garden. James Clarke, our director, zoomed in and out of the vicious-looking barbed wire protecting the gnomes for a sequence to be covered with sinister chords of music, a sort of Noddy version of Jaws. Then the gnome-owner went inside her house, and was filmed at her Hammond organ playing 'Home Sweet Home', or as I said later to Bernie, 'Gnome Sweet Gnome'. I interviewed her, and she insisted on talking to me with her back to camera, so that nobody could recognize her in the supermarket, follow her home, and start nobbling.

Then I interviewed a man who, according to the

journalists, was a gnome manufacturer, although from his uniform he appeared to be an ambulance driver. He had rosy cheeks, ears that stuck out, and looked a little like a gnome himself. When I asked whether he thought the nobbling was politically inspired, perhaps an 'Anti-Vietgnome' demonstration, he didn't blink, just politely said he didn't think so. After the interview I asked why he didn't cavil at the question, and he said he just thought I couldn't pronounce Vietnam, so it would have been impolite to comment.

We finished our interviews, and I realized that not only had we failed to find the nobbler, we had not discovered a single nobbled gnome. No gnome had actually disappeared—in fact, no gnome had been desecrated in any way. James took a spare gnome to the beach, where he filmed it bobbing up and down with ripples breaking over it, a sad little sequence over which, of course, he put tragic music. Thus two bored Folkestone journalists and a BBC team contrived to make a five-minute item out of not much news.

Back in the studio after our film, Bernie encouraged me, rashly, to make as many gnome puns as I could in two minutes, I got through 'A rose by any other gnome,' but when I reached 'Are you a gnomo-sexual?', he cut me short. That went a little too far, and he said to me afterwards, 'I didn't think you'd say that.' No doubt I had been corrupted by my days in satire.

*   *   *

At the heart of *Braden's Week* were the classic consumer stories we told. A girl wrote a letter to the programme about her boots, saying the first time she had worn them they had fallen to bits. She took them back to the shop, which offered to send them to SATRA, the shoe trade's research laboratory. Back they came with the standard reply: it was the owner's fault, the boots had been worn from the inside. She protested to the shop. They said, 'But madam, you have been walking in these. In the rain.'

It seemed to me that there must be a law saying these boots were made for walking, even in the rain. I rang the Law Society. A man in the press office was astonished by my question. 'Before I answer, Miss Rantzen, what do you intend to do with my reply?'

'Put it on the air. Tell our viewers.'

'Let me get this straight. You are asking me to give you the advice free of charge, so that you can hand it out to your viewers and thus deprive my members of work—my members, who, being solicitors, charge their clients for such advice, and incidentally pay my salary.'

I could tell he wasn't enthusiastic.

When I rang the Consumers Association I had the first of many enjoyable conversations with David Tench, the legal advisor to *Which?* magazine. He took a very different view:

'Of course there's a law, it's just not used very much. The Sale of Goods Act 1893 states clearly that if you buy a pair of boots, or indeed any other goods, they must be fit for their purpose and of serviceable quality. And that you are entitled to rely upon the skill and judgement of the person selling you those goods. So even if your viewer has the most extraordinary feet, with extra long toes, the shop assistant should have spotted that when the boots were fitted.'

I quoted him on the programme, with suitable illustrations of our viewer's bare toes. The floodgates opened. Boots, shoes, pots, pans, tables, chairs—our viewers had been lumbered with an incredible variety of goods that fell to bits as soon as they arrived home, and the shops had refused to refund their money on the equivalent grounds to 'You've been walking in these.' So David and I concocted a letter for our viewers to use, to put the shops on notice:

> *Dear Sir,*
> *Further to my complaint about the faulty . . . I purchased on (date), please let me have the address of your registered office, in order that I may take a writ out against you under the terms of the Sale of Goods Act 1893.*

We knew it was a good letter when an official from the Lord Chancellor's office rang and asked for a copy, for his own use.

We dictated the letter on the air. We had an 'after-care' department to answer viewers' letters, and they sent out hundreds of copies. The government was nudged into setting up small claims courts, so then we adjusted our letters to include a reference to them. I learned that fair dealing depends on two things, a good law so that unfair dealing can be punished, and good information so that the public know the law is available to them. Had David Tench not disinterred the Sale of Goods Act 1893, and had a television programme not existed to tell consumers how to use it, boots might have continued to fall to pieces without remedy.

I also learned that professional organizations owe their loyalty to their members, and most are little help when a member of the public goes to them for advice or protection. The Federation of Master Builders was the worst. In spite of its name it was no proof of quality, no protection whatever from the cowboys. As far as I could see all it did was provide an imposing logo for its members to display, and cheap holidays for its members to enjoy.

The General Medical Council was as bad. When we exposed doctors who created terrible injuries using lasers which they claimed would remove tattoos, but which in fact caused full-thickness burns, the GMC did next to nothing to follow up and act upon the complaints it received.

The Law Society let our viewers down again when on *That's Life!* we were inundated with complaints against lawyers who were incompetent, negligent, even fraudulent. I might have turned against the whole profession, had I not seen the greatest lawyer of my generation, Lord Denning, in action.

I was pursuing a double glazing con-man at the time. There are fashions in con-men. In the sixties and seventies they were busily selling exorbitant contracts for home improvements, wildly overpriced and installed by cowboy builders. People were earning just enough to want to make their homes more comfortable, and install central heating, or loft conversions, or double glazing. So they became vulnerable targets for high-pressure door-to-door salesmen.

In the eighties, the con-men became ecological and were selling water softeners and solar panels. In the nineties, they moved in on the charities, pretended to sell advertising space on wall maps in aid of a local charity, or organizing fund-raising events, from which a tiny percentage went to a good cause.

This new century began with the greatest con of all, the 'millennium bug'. It never existed, of course. But the world fell for it, and employed high-priced consultants to frisk all their computers for bugs, in case civilization blanked out at midnight 2000. Probably the idea chimed in with our fears that the world was about to end. After all, we are more fascinated than ever with the oldest con of all, astrology.

The most effective way to irritate Sir Patrick Moore is to call him an astrologer instead of astronomer. Patrick says horoscopes are complete rubbish, and he should know.

Why—when night after night they tell us with complete conviction what the day will be like tomorrow, and day after day they are proved completely wrong—do we believe our weather forecasters? Even after Michael Fish solemnly addressed camera, reassuring a viewer that hurricanes do not exist in Britain, only to be blown off his weather map the next day by a gigantic hurricane, we still believe them.

Why do we rush to believe feng shui? Or buy a face-cream that pretends to erase wrinkles? Or try a diet that claims to make us lose weight without eating any less? Or send chain letters that claim to bring bad luck if the chain is broken? Our native gullibility provides a good living for con-men, and

180

for the consumer journalists who expose them.

Back in 1969, I had been contacted by a whistle-blower who was working in a disreputable double glazing company. He told us stories of door-to-door selling by salesmen on high commission: terrible lies were being told to the punters to persuade them to sign expensive contracts, followed by even more terrible workmanship when the windows were put in, if they ever were. Some customers were just left with vandalized houses, windows removed, brickwork damaged, and no double glazing installed at all.

The salesman who came to us said the office phones were constantly shrilling with customers trying to obtain their windows, trying to have their homes repaired, desperately trying to get their money back, but nobody ever answered them. He brought with him a list of the most aggrieved customers. We often found, when a company was treating people particularly badly, that someone in the office would be quietly taking notes, waiting for the chance to blow a whistle on the operation.

I printed some questionnaires, and sent them to the customers the man had named. We had a hundred replies, most of them telling appalling stories, so we rang the company for its response. At once the BBC lawyers contacted us. It was Friday. The show was due to transmit on Saturday night. But the company had taken out an *ex parte* injunction. That meant, unless we went to court to lift the injunction, not one word of my research would be broadcast.

A couple of hours later we arrived in our barrister's chambers in the Temple, I with my arms full of supermarket bags brimming with

181

questionnaires. To demonstrate the evidence for our criticism of the company, I spread them all out over the lawyer's floor. They were amused, and quite impressed. The barrister was Brian Neill (later Lord Neill, who was to cost me dear nearly thirty years later, when I took out a libel action of my own).

Once I had satisfied the barrister that our script was defensible, we went to see a judge in chambers to have the injunction lifted. I sat next to our lawyers, but understood not one word of their discussions. Much of it was in Latin, and they seemed to be talking about the case of a nineteenth-century butcher. What that had to do with our television programme I could not imagine, but clearly it was a precedent, and we won, that round at least. The other side immediately decided to appeal.

All this, as I said, was on a Friday, and we only had twenty-four hours before the programme was due to go on the air. So we trooped round to the Appeal Court straight away, and I sat down and prepared to be mystified again with stories of Dickensian actions involving butchers. We were in a panelled room with a high bench, on which were sitting three immensely old men in wigs. The judge in the centre was talking to a man standing in the body of the courtroom. The judge was saying, 'Now, do you understand what this means, Mr Smith. You can go on with your action, you have every right to go on, but if you do go on, and you lose, it will cost you a great deal of money.'

The judge was speaking slowly, clearly, and in English, rather than Latin. He had a slight rustic accent. I whispered to the BBC solicitor next to me, 'Who's that super little old man in the middle?' 'That,' he hissed back, 'is Lord Denning.'

I had never heard of him, but I should have. The legal profession at that time was a monument to the English class system, but even so, Denning, the son of a Hampshire draper, had through sheer force of intellect won his way to the very top. Not only that, but he had retained his humanity, his sense of humour, and his common sense. They say that no other appeal judge has created so much precedent, nor had so many of his own judgements reversed.

Our papers were handed up to the little old judges, sitting like three wise monkeys on their high bench. They glanced at them for a moment. Then the barrister for the other side started his argument, which was that his client should be allowed to see the script before we transmitted. If that principle had been established as a precedent by the Appeal Court it would have been a disaster. Denning interrupted him, apologizing, but pointing out that time was short:

'Your client knows very well the nature of the programme,' he said. 'In his own statement he refers to the complaints they have received from his customers. In this country we have an important freedom, the freedom of the press. With it comes responsibility, they must be accurate. If they are not, your client can sue them, with all the vigour he can muster. But that does not give him the right to prevent them from broadcasting, it must not encumber the freedom of the press.'

He finished. The two others judges sitting beside him hadn't spoken. He looked at them, and they both murmured their agreement.

'What would have happened if they had disagreed?' I asked our solicitor.

'They sometimes do. But that never makes any difference to Denning's style. He always gives judgement like that.'

With that, we trooped out again, and were free to broadcast. Our case went down in the law books, establishing the valuable precedent that scripts do not have to be handed over prior to broadcast, and I became an ardent fan of the extraordinary Lord Denning.

*   *   *

On *Braden's Week* I discovered also how complex and difficult unravelling a consumer story can be. A couple came to see us who had been employed as office cleaners. Strictly speaking, they were self-employed. A company called Canadian Office Cleaners had sold them contracts to clean offices in London. The couple had used their life savings to buy the contracts. The problem was that no matter how hard they worked, they simply couldn't make a living. They were now badly in debt. We went through the terms of the contracts. They looked clear and above board. The couple told me the hours they worked, all through the night, every night. They seemed honest, hardworking, and completely exhausted. I began to realize why.

Canadian Office Cleaners employed salesmen who went from office to office, offering to undercut any cleaners they already employed. Once they had obtained the contracts, Canadian Office Cleaners took its cut, and passed the contract on to the cleaners who were then obliged to fulfil terms which forced them to work at a loss. By the time they had paid for their transport and their cleaning equipment, they were out of pocket.

Once again, I constructed questionnaires, and asked the couple to find as many other clients as they could, to fill them in. With my trusty supermarket carrier bags overflowing with dozens of replies, I went to meet Mr Canadian Office Cleaner, who turned out to be a sentimental con-man.

There are three kinds of con-men, in my experience: the witty, the ruthless, and the sentimental. This gentlemen moved himself to tears with descriptions of the valuable work he had done with the alcoholics and down-and-outs back home in Canada. I am more gullible than most, and my eyes filled sympathetically. I went back to the office concerned that we might be exposing a philanthropist. John Lloyd laughed at me, and assembled a tough script from my research. From that story I extracted another valuable piece of consumer advice. If someone is offering you a business franchise, no matter how copper-bottomed it may seem, ask to meet a few of their satisfied customers before you sign on the dotted line.

The wittiest con-man I met on *Braden's Week* was a television repair man round the corner from our office. A woman rang us from her home in North London. She had had a television set that had broken down, and when she was travelling to visit a relation in west London had found a repair shop *en route* in Shepherd's Bush. She took it there, leaving her phone number so they could let her know when it was ready for collection. Instead, they rang to say that it was irreparable, that it would only cost her money if they drove across London to return it to her, so would she like to leave it with them? It seemed sensible, so she agreed. A few days later she was visiting her relative again. As she passed the shop she saw her own television with a 'For Sale' sign on the pavement.

I asked how she had recognized it. She said her son had amused himself by decorating it with flower transfers, and there it was, the prettiest telly in Britain, and the most recognizable. She parked her car, disguised herself ('How?' I asked. 'I put my hair up and my glasses on,' she said) and went in to ask the price. It was £30, quite expensive, even for a telly as pretty as that. She walked out and rang us.

I rang the shop, asked for the owner, and told him the story. He paused for a moment, then said, 'It's a fair cop. You've got me'.

I needed more, so I chanced my arm.

'Look,' I said, 'this isn't a major exposé, why don't I send my photographer round? You can apologize to our viewer, and she can have her pretty telly back with your best wishes, and I'm sure our viewers will love you for it.'

To my delight, he agreed. Our photographer took many pictures of him leaning over the pretty telly, his hands outstretched, begging for forgiveness. The audience laughed. Even our complainant enjoyed it. That kind of con-man I have a soft spot for, no matter how I try to harden my heart.

*   *   *

186

Sometimes on *Braden's Week* the 'baddy' would agree to come to the studio. Robert Maxwell came to defend his door-to-door salesmen from Pergamon Press who were persuading people to buy encyclopaedias they couldn't afford. He was bluff, and bullying. We didn't take to him.

But Victor Ross was a different matter. It was a period when big companies, like *Reader's Digest*, were just computerizing, and the results were chaotic. We had dozens of complaints about *Reader's Digest*. One woman had been waiting six months for the magazine, without receiving a single copy; another had a hall lined with them. Men kept staggering up her garden path with heaps of them, and she couldn't stop them being delivered, however hard she tried. We took pictures of their plight.

John Lloyd told me to persuade someone from the company to come in and answer the complaints. I rang *Reader's Digest* and explained. Their Press Officer said, 'You'll want our Mr Ross'. I asked if I could speak to him, to try and assess how he would answer Bernie's questions. The Press Officer put Victor Ross on the line. He was soft-voiced and diffident, very different from Robert Maxwell. I went back to the Press Officer. 'Are you sure he'll be up to this?' The Press Officer was sure.

What I didn't know was that Victor Ross was a born performer and knew exactly how to use the cameras. He came into the studio, and sat quietly while we told the stories of fearful persecutions by *Reader's Digest*, complete with pictures of viewers cowering beneath piles of magazines. Each time Bernie turned to Victor Ross, Victor found his camera, and addressed it: 'Mrs Jones, what can I say? This is terrible. How could we do this to you? I apologize, most sincerely.'

I think he even managed to squeeze out a tear. As *Reader's Digest* story followed story, the attitude of our studio audience changed. Why were we tormenting this poor man? Couldn't we tell how much he was suffering? Bernie cut the item short, and John and I were vaguely aware that things had not gone quite as planned. Afterwards Victor Ross joined us for a drink in Hospitality and smiled at me, 'Was I up to it?' he asked. 'More than up to it,' I said.

Holidays have been a constant theme on all the consumer shows I have ever worked on. Back in the sixties, package holidays were becoming very big business. Clarkson's were piling them high, and selling them cheap. There were rumours that they were only making half a crown profit per tourist (the equivalent of twelve pence today). The tiny profit margin had two results. One was that two weeks in Spain became affordable to almost everyone, and tower blocks sprouted along the coast, with pubs and fish and chip bars on every corner. The other was that the waiters treated these low-price customers with contempt. It was service with a snarl, the food and accommodation were basic, and complaints were rebuffed.

When, after an avalanche of complaints, we started to criticize Clarkson's, their management was aggrieved. Why weren't our viewers more grateful for the chance to go abroad at these bargain prices? How, otherwise, could they have a holiday in the sun at all?

But I could understand why. They'd been sold a

tricycle as if it were a Rolls-Royce. And a holiday is even more precious to us than a Rolls-Royce. It's the fortnight we save up for and dream about all year. If the dream becomes a nightmare, if the hotel is revealed to be a building site, the food makes us sick, the bathroom is full of cockroaches, it's more than just money down the drain. Our most cherished hopes are crushed and trodden into dust, and we are furious.

It's no good a tour operator turning round and saying, what did you expect for the price? We expected what you told us when we booked with you—the sea on our doorstep, Spanish sunshine on our balcony, reward for all those months of grinding work and drizzle through a British winter. The pictures in the brochures set up their own expectations. Nobody tells you in advance that this is a cut-price holiday, so it's going to be nasty.

Although, having said that, I did once on *Braden's Week* come across an unusually frank holiday camp owner.

We had received a number of complaints about a peculiar camp on the Isle of Wight. Some of our viewers had stayed there and brought back stories of living in army barracks, surrounded by concrete gun emplacements and barbed wire. We sent a photographer, and he brought back pictures of an unconverted army camp, a relic of the Second World War. We could hardly believe it. We tried to get a response from the owner, a boiler-maker who lived in the East End of London, but he lay low and said nothing. So we asked a local journalist to comb through the local council minutes, and he struck gold.

A few months earlier the owner had appealed

189

against his rates, and was quoted in the minutes as explaining why he should pay less: 'Mine,' he said, 'is a horrible holiday camp'. And he went on to describe the concrete, the barbed wire, the barracks, the gun emplacements, the lot. I carolled with joy when I read it. Researchers dream of moments like that, when we have our baddy convicted out of his own mouth.

* * *

Braden's Week was a very satisfying programme to work on, the journalism was exacting, and worthwhile. We were receiving sackloads of post from viewers asking for our help. Our subject matter felt very much more relevant to the stuff of their lives than most programmes I had seen or worked on. Not only that, although I didn't realize it, I was serving an apprenticeship as a junior television personality.

A *Daily Express* photographer perched me on the edge of a desk, then laid himself down in the corner of the office, so the photograph made me look as if my legs were ten miles long. I was asked to be a judge in *Nationwide*'s 'Cook of the Realm' contest, the winner was a farmer's wife, Gwen Troake. I remembered her some years later when I needed an outstanding cook for my documentary series, *The Big Time*. I also remembered one of my fellow judges, Fanny Cradock. She, as befitted an expert chef, stalked the *Nationwide* studio, giving very little away. As she passed me she hissed,

'Darling, I have just discovered there is something in these dishes which is the most deadly poison.'

190

I was alarmed. 'What, Fanny?'

'I couldn't possibly tell you. That's my professional secret.'

'But you must, as a judge I've got to taste everything.'

She glanced at an elaborate cake.

'The underside of that ivy garnish is covered with the most poisonous dust.' I didn't lick it.

It may have been risky, but being a television personality also had its privileges. In 1970 I was guest of honour at Dalbeattie Civic Week, and had to crown the Civic Queen (John Lloyd sent a crew to film me—and ambushed me on the programme with embarrassing shots of me having to crown her twice. I'd put it on the wrong way round the first time).

I was driven in cavalcade through the little Scottish town in Kirkcudbrightshire, in a procession whose pace was set by the slowest walkers, the fancy-dress contestants, most of them muscular Scottish men in dangly earrings and high heels, pushing prams. They kept falling off their heels, which halted our procession, I waved regally at a passer-by who waved back, and we were then left for five minutes staring at each other until the cavalcade crept on its way. As the local paper put it, 'The crowds were several thick in some places'.

I had a glittery dress made for the occasion, and was enjoying the glitz of it all.

Then, suddenly Bernie threw a large Stork-shaped spanner into the works. He made a commercial.

CHAPTER SEVEN

LOVE AND MARRIAGE

Although I have described the fun, and the satisfaction of my new job on *Braden's Week*, I have not so far mentioned the most fundamental change that had occurred in my life. I had met my future husband. Not that I realized it straight away. Working for Desmond Wilcox, who was Head of General Features Department, I knew he was charismatic, that he liked women, and was married to a colleague and friend of mine, Patsy Wilcox. Until I worked for him, I had no idea that their marriage was, from his point of view, extremely unhappy.

Can any outsider judge the health of a marriage? Time and again I have been astonished when a seemingly strong, happy marriage has shattered. People have great skill in preserving a public face, when in private they are destroying each other. During our friendship, nothing Patsy ever said to me gave the slightest hint that her home life was difficult, in fact, quite the reverse. She fell in love with Desmond when they first met, in 1949, and stayed in love with him for the next fifty years.

They met because Patsy had been working on the local paper in Edgware which Desmond joined as junior reporter, his first job in journalism. He was fresh from National Service, and eager to explore the new world he found himself in. He was also eager to explore a woman, but in the unswinging fifties opportunities were very limited.

192

Dennis Norden has memorably described the *mores* of those conventional times, when, as he says, men had to keep their feet on the accelerator and the brake at the same time. Good girls did not have sex before marriage, and Patsy was a good girl.

She and Desmond married in 1954, when Desmond was twenty-two, and, although they had been engaged for four years, he had never got as far, he says, 'as twanging her suspenders'. But, as they drifted inexorably towards a wedding, the delightful prospect of sex was not enough to convince him that marriage was in fact what he wanted. He told me that the night before their wedding day, he walked up and down the bank of the Thames, desperately worried that he was doing the wrong thing.

Patsy, a little older than he, was far more mature than he was. She had been brought up in the old-fashioned Jewish tradition that educated boys, but still maintained that for a girl marriage and having children should be the first ambition. True, Desmond was not Jewish, and also true, she had a career of her own. But she still believed that her identity as a woman depended on being married, and Desmond was the man she set her heart on.

Desmond, on the other hand, was at the threshold of his career, and his horizons were about to change dramatically. Almost at once he was appointed as the *Daily Mirror*'s foreign correspondent, and started to roam the world. He met Hollywood stars, multi-millionaires, presidents and rebel leaders. He parachuted into Suez, was bombed in Hungary, and rode on a mule through the mountains of Central America. He met women—ambitious, talented, unencumbered women. By now, the fifties had given way to the sixties, the old moralities had been blasted aside with the invention of the Pill, and Desmond was in his element. With his blonde hair, the clean, smart look he had learned in the army, and a remarkable way with words, no wonder so many women took pity on the handsome, lonely, foreign correspondent, miles away from his home and family.

All the same, over the years, ostensibly, the Wilcox marriage flourished. They had three terrific children together, and created a comfortable life in their homes in Orpington and then in Kew. But the marriage was never, for Desmond, a satisfying partnership.

Why not? Patsy was intelligent and a good journalist. Desmond was generous, supportive, and believed in marriage. But throughout his time with Patsy—and he was married to her for more than twenty years—he felt he was with someone who depended upon him, and whom he loved in return, but was not, alas, in love with. He was a passionate, caring man who needed to feel committed, heart, mind and body. For him, his marriage to Patsy was a relationship to which he was tied by family responsibility, rather than by desire.

*   *   *

Years before he met me, Desmond had left Patsy to live with a woman who is now very widely respected as an expert on broadcasting. She was funny and clever, and very attractive. But she, too, was married, to a man who drank heavily. They had

194

children, and she could not bear the knowledge that they would suffer without her, so she went back to her husband. After that relationship, Desmond had a number of close friendships, but always on the basis that 'What goes on on location, stays on location'. Until he met me.

It is extremely painful even now, more than thirty years later, for me to face the fact that I broke Desmond and Patsy's marriage. I deeply regret it. Without me, their marriage might have ground along from day to day, like many others. Desmond would have found it endurable, and probably would have continued to play away from home. But the fact was that Desmond and I recognized in each other the exact qualities we both wanted, and needed. We should have resisted each other. But our love for each other was overpowering. We had found what we had both subconsciously been looking for—physically we were perfectly suited, and, even more important, mentally.

My experiences with men had up to then been bruising and unfulfilled. Desmond was my lover, my father-figure, my teacher, and, to my astonishment, he said he loved me, too. I had no idea that would lead to our own marriage. I assumed that was impossible. But I certainly knew I had fallen head over heels in love, and I stayed in love with him for thirty-two years.

I remember the moment he caught my mind and therefore my heart. It was in the unromantic setting of a viewing room, with half a dozen people, in a tiny hot cubicle, with a deadline to meet. I was sitting right at the back, Desmond was watching the rough cut of a *Man Alive* film. He stopped and

195

started the heavy Steinbeck machine, showing the editor where to cut a scene, where to let a sequence breathe, where commentary would be necessary, and I was spellbound. I had never worked with film before, and I could see that he was turning an ill-shaped collection of rushes into a sharply-focused beautifully presented film. *Man Alive* was winning all the television awards at that time, and Desmond was the inspiration and the leading craftsman behind its success. I came out of the room dizzy with the amount I had learned in that hour, and deeply impressed with the man who had taught me.

A few days later, Tony Smith asked me to go back to the Current Affairs Department to join his team making his late-night show, *At the Eleventh Hour*. I went to Desmond's office to ask permission. He was reluctant to let me go, even though I committed myself to returning to *Man Alive*. In the end he said, 'All right, you can go on one condition. That you go out to dinner with me'.

I should have said no, but I said yes. Now I can look back on more than thirty years of conversation, laughter, some moments of agony but many more of ecstasy. We had three children, two weddings and twenty-three years of marriage. For all the pain we shared—and caused—I'm still deeply glad I said yes.

We talked urgently, as if we had a lifetime to catch up, all through that first evening together. I learned what an extraordinary man he was. He had survived so many adventures. It was like listening to the hero of a Victorian children's book. Desmond tended, like many good storytellers, to improve his punchlines. Some people, therefore, doubted the truth of his tales. My experience is that the more unlikely it sounded, the truer it was.

He was brought up during the Second World War in a cottage in the Cotswolds. With his father away in the army only earning £4 a week, his mother, Alice May, had very little money to feed and clothe three sons. Desmond, the oldest son, kept rabbits, and sold them to eke out the family income. Under his care they bred well, like rabbits, and the local hospital began to depend on the meat for their patients. For Desmond's tenth birthday, his mother gave him a scythe, so that he could cut the grass he needed to feed his flock—seventy rabbits by now. For Christmas lunch the family would eat vegetables from the cottage garden and two succulent roast rabbits.

When his father, John Wilcox, returned from the war as a Lieutenant Colonel there was instant conflict between them. In many ways, Desmond had become the man of the family, and the provider. John was a tough little man, bossy and controlling. When he tried to discipline Desmond by beating him, it was the last straw, and Desmond ran away to sea.

At first he went to the Outward Bound sea-school, training on a four-masted schooner, the *Pamir*, as a sail-training apprentice. He learned to scramble up the towering masts to adjust the sails and the rigging, while they swung out over the sea. At the age of sixteen, his training completed, he signed on as a deckhand in the merchant navy, on a tramp steamer bound for Africa. It was a grim life, hours of chipping away at rust and repainting metal, then having to guard himself from the sailors who waited in the showers for the golden-haired, pink-and-white deckhand.

Desmond was so utterly miserable that he used to stand at the back of the boat gazing at the wake, nerving himself to jump off, but he never did. Instead, when they docked at West Africa he joined a white hunter, and worked with him on safari, looking after the guns and polishing the bullets. But when they returned to the port, the hunter persuaded him to sign on again, and he took the same tramp steamer back to Britain.

He had cut his leg on some wire. The wound festered and became gangrenous. They had no doctor on the boat, nor anaesthetic, so the second mate operated, cutting away the gangrene following instructions over the radio from a surgeon in England. Instead of anaesthetic, they gave him a bottle of rum to drink, and pushed his fingers in his mouth to bite on when the pain became unbearable. He had the scars all his life.

He was taken to a London hospital when he landed back in England. His father found him there and arrived at his bedside with a list of possible careers. As an architect himself he was fed up with explaining to friends that his oldest son was a deck boy. He gave Desmond a choice of acceptable professions: architect, doctor, lawyer, journalist. All of them meant going back to school, and then university, except one—journalist. After doing his National Service in the Parachute Regiment, Desmond joined the local paper in Edgware, went from there to the *Daily Mirror* under Hugh Cudlipp, and from there to ITV as a reporter/producer on *This Week*, where David Attenborough spotted him, and persuaded him to create *Man Alive* for the newly invented BBC2.

As Desmond described to me his career I

realized that he had battled through to success without any of my advantages. I had been a middle-class child, with a secure family life, which led me comfortably to Oxford and then into the BBC. He had left school at fifteen, run away from home, and without a degree or any strings to pull had carved out a career in broadcasting. He dazzled me with his achievements. I also realized that he was accident-prone.

When he was working for the *Daily Mirror*, to pick up a little extra money he also worked on Saturdays for the *Sunday Pictorial*, a tabloid that specialized in exposing villains. They had uncovered a fiendish trade in pet cats, which were being kidnapped and sold to laboratories for vivisection.

Desmond went with a photographer to snatch a picture of the gangster who ran the trade. He and the photographer had perfected a trick on previous investigations. Desmond was the driver, and would honk the car's horn very loudly, the gangster would look towards the car with a suitably startled expression, and the photographer would get his picture. It had worked perfectly up to now. But the cat-napping gangster spotted what they had done, leaped into his car and followed them. As Desmond climbed out of his car, the gangster drove at him, trapping him with the bumper and breaking his thigh-bones, then cracked him over the head with a car-jack.

Desmond lost consciousness, and woke to discover that his legs were in traction, and that he was blind. The gangster had damaged his optic nerve. The *Mirror* paid for him to be operated on by the world's finest surgeons—in a series of

199

delicate operations, a Swiss doctor restored his sight. Then McIndoe, the world-famous plastic surgeon, repaired the damage to his face. The gangster spent a long time in jail, but for many years sent Christmas cards to Desmond, promising to finish the job when he was released.

Desmond's life made mine seem incredibly dull. Even more seductive was his gift for inventing imaginative insults. He once told me that I had 'all the sexual allure of a rotting log'. When I was late for a date, he said I was like 'a half-dressed elephant waiting for its cue'. I don't myself understand what levels of masochism these insults touched in me, but they certainly made me laugh, and that, as I have said, is very difficult for me to resist.

I also loved the way he was the first to defend any vulnerable individual or minority. Not only did he fight valiantly for women to have equal opportunities in the BBC, he was equally determined that racial minorities should not suffer prejudice—Jews, for instance. His first wife, Patsy, was Jewish, so was his business partner, Bill Morton. He once punched a man, knocking him downstairs for an anti-Semitic remark.

I especially admired the way he tolerated my mother, even enjoyed her company. The first time he brought me home after dinner, it was late, and she greeted him sitting on the stairs in a bath towel and bath-hat. They compared notes about bath oils, and on the next visit he brought her a large bottle of Badedas, a luxury she had never dreamed of.

Our courtship took place in the theatres and restaurants of London. Desmond was far more sophisticated than me, and used to enjoy late-night dinners. I got hungry far earlier, and my stomach would rumble so loudly that other members of the audience would glare at me with irritation. One evening, during the interval of a play, Desmond suddenly disappeared, only to reappear minutes later, breathless, carrying an enormous salt-beef sandwich on rye. He had run to Soho and bought it for me. Around me in the theatre bar, diamond-studded American women drew their minks around them and salivated. One of them sighed, 'What a man'.

It was almost impossible for us to find time alone together, although we stole one weekend in Paris. I was so nervous that we would be recognized at the airport, that, although it was a fiercely hot day, I insisted on wearing a long black mackintosh, a black scarf over my head, and black sunglasses. Desmond pointed out I looked much more conspicuous like that.

Paris is said to be the most romantic city in the world, certainly for us it was. We walked beside the Seine, bought prints from the *bouquinistes*, with their stalls of old books and engravings, and listened to the music in the Madeleine. Yes, there was guilt, for both of us, but there was the joy we felt just being together.

We found another week in Ireland, and drove together round the wild coasts of the Dingle peninsula. We saw the windswept beach where St Patrick landed, ate fresh oysters from Heron Cove, staying mostly at bed and breakfast hotels, where we drank tea and ate soda bread.

Occasionally we would go on location together. Once for a *Man Alive* programme I had invented a sequence called 'Beyond Your Means'. It was a discussion between three couples, all in debt. One lived in a council house, one in a leafy suburb, and one in a stately home. They compared notes on the best ways to save money.

'It's all very well if you don't mind having bits of old furniture,' said the man from the council house to the stately home owner, looking contemptuously at the antique chairs around them, 'but we like new things ourselves.'

After the recording, Doris, the production assistant, tiptoed up to Desmond's bedroom and made him an apple-pie bed. Hidden in the sheets was a hairbrush as big as a porcupine. I admit he didn't know anything about it until he came down to breakfast the next morning and she told him what she had done.

By this time the whole of his team knew of our relationship. They were tolerant—many of them knew of his unhappiness at home. Angela Huth, who had been a close friend of his before I joined the team, was kind to us both. She was a friend of Princess Margaret, had an English rose beauty, with honey-blonde hair and shrewd blue eyes. She was an observant and witty reporter; now she writes novels and plays. She also had a feline sharpness. She once examined a dress I was wearing, 'I do like that Mary Quant frock,' she said. 'What a pity she isn't making anything as pretty this year.' But although our friends accepted us as lovers, that did not mean we accepted the situation ourselves.

It was a relationship filled with deceit, Desmond had to lie to Patsy to be with me. She was my friend, so I lied to her, too. I don't defend our behaviour. Over and over again Desmond and I would try to give each other up, to stop seeing each other. Perhaps other, stronger characters could have succeeded. We failed. I had been to the Wilcox family home, and met their children. Neither Desmond nor I could bear the thought that they would get badly hurt if he left home. The children themselves have told us since that they might have preferred him to leave, rather than subject them to the anger and rows they lived with for years at home.

There seemed no way out of this classic triangle, without hurting everyone. One day, after one of our separations had broken down, and we met again in tears, we made a deal. We would wait until our relationship had lasted ten years, Desmond would stay with his family until then, which would mean his twins would be sixteen, his older daughter eighteen. Then, if we were still in love and wanted to get married, he would leave home. We didn't quite make the ten years, but we tried.

*　　　*　　　*

It was actually about eight years later that Desmond and his family suffered a terrible Christmas. For some reason Christmas puts a particular strain on fragile marriages, perhaps it is the pressure-cooker effect of everyone being in the house together, with no work to call them away or distract them. Desmond rang me from a public call box and said he had left home. My heart stopped. What should I do? It was the moment I had dreamed about.

In some ways I—a spinster in my thirties living away from home—was a walking blasphemy to

203

traditional Jewish values. When I had been on *Braden's Week* a year, the *Jewish Chronicle*'s television writer, Hyam Corney, came to interview me. I was twenty-nine and had just left home to live in a flat on my own. 'Why is it,' he said, 'that you never married?'

About the same time, I decided to go on holiday to Israel, visiting it for the first time. I was moved, impressed, and bullied wherever I went. When I sat by myself in a hotel restaurant and ordered a meal, the waitress asked me, 'Why is it you never married?' When I asked directions to the beach, the swimming pool attendant asked me, 'Why aren't you married?' When I took a taxi to the station in Jerusalem, the driver said, 'How come you're not married?'

I could have told them I was married to my career, but they would not have understood. I could have said I was going out with my married boss, in which case they would have understood, but would not have approved.

*   *   *

What did my own extended, respectable family think of my long affair with my married boss? They were torn. He wasn't Jewish, but they could cope with that. Of course, they disapproved. But they also admired and liked Desmond. There was a time when my mother nagged me constantly about my relationship with him. Then Desmond sat down with her, and said to her, 'You know I want to marry your daughter'. He never actually proposed to me, but he did at least propose to my mother.

I didn't believe we would ever get married. I

always thought he would stay with his family, for the sake of the children. Even when he rang me on that December night to say he had left home I was unsure that was what he really wanted. Of course, he came to me that night. We clung to each other. He was certain we should stay together, that our lives belonged together. I believed him, my heart told me he was right. But my head, my conscience would not be persuaded. So I forced myself to tell him that I thought he should find a flat of his own, neutral territory, so that if he wanted to return to Patsy, he still could.

He borrowed a house from a friend for a little while. Soon after his death, I found a letter he wrote thanking her:

I have been most grateful, most, most, most grateful, for the shelter that you offered me at a time when I most needed it. The path of whatever it is called not only doesn't run smooth, but appears to run up hill and dangerously all the way. I am sorry only that I am not able to report that the emotional thunder storm is over. If it doesn't end soon I shall take steps to walk out from under it. It really can't go on like this. At the moment four people are unhappy to no good purpose, and something must be done to ensure that at least one or two achieve some kind of happiness, whatever the cost to the others.

It is clear from this how lonely he was, and how desperate that we should be together. But still I insisted he must live on his own. I was, I suppose, trying to justify myself, to prove that the marriage had died, that I hadn't torn them apart. So, with typical efficiency Desmond found a flat in Chelsea with two bachelors, where he cooked and sorted the laundry for himself, far better than I could.

One of his extraordinary skills was that he could walk into a nasty hotel room, adjust the lights, put his favourite photographs around the frame of the mirror, and suddenly make it look pretty and welcoming. He did the same to the flat he found. Sometimes when I came to him late from the office I would find him waving a kitchen spoon, apron round his waist, grumbling that 'the Yorkshire pudding was going up and down like a yoyo' because he had been adjusting the oven to make sure it was perfect.

I was spoiled, of that there can be no doubt, and my women friends envied me. Desmond was handsome, impeccably dressed, brilliantly talented, no wonder he won my family round.

And yet I forced him to spend eighteen long months living on his own, while I wondered why I was punishing him, and me. In the end I could stand the separation no longer. He had by now been to his lawyer, and there was nothing that could mend his marriage. He moved into my flat. By then we had been in love with each other for eight years.

As he unpacked his cases, put his razor in my bathroom, and meticulously hung his clothes in my wardrobe, we were both coming home. Patsy was furious and bitter, all the more so because now she knew of the eight years of concealment and duplicity. But at last there was no more subterfuge.

The BBC knew officially as well, because as soon as we made the decision to move in together, Desmond went to Huw Wheldon and told him. The BBC Board of Management discussed us. We were a serious problem. Desmond was my boss, and by now I was presenting and producing *That's Life!*, one of the BBC's most popular and successful programmes. The Board decided that if we combined our personal lives, we should separate our working lives. It moved the whole *That's Life!* team to Current Affairs Group.

Although I missed the exhilaration of working with Desmond, in many ways I was happy about our professional parting, and was frankly far happier there. It made me independent, and I was seen to be standing on my own feet. Nobody could accuse me of owing my success to my love affair with the boss. (How the fact that we were constantly in the nation's top ten programmes could have been due to Desmond's influence, I don't know, but some people managed to draw that conclusion. Jealousy is beyond reason).

The BBC's decision may have been right for the programme and for Desmond's department, but it was torture for Patsy. She herself was also working in Current Affairs Group. We were now in the same building in Lime Grove. She could not drink in the club, eat in the canteen, walk down a corridor without risking meeting me. She had lost the man she loved, now she was even denied the safe haven that work might have provided for her.

That decision turned the knife in her wounds.

*　　　*　　　*

Desmond was keen, even before we married, that we should have children. I had more or less put the idea out of my mind, thought I was destined to spend the rest of my life as the other woman, and single. But Desmond persuaded me, and in 1976 I became pregnant. I kept it secret. *That's Life!* was in full swing. I knew there would be huge press interest, and condemnation. Single mothers were very uncommon then, let alone single-mother television presenters.

The programme broke for one week, at Easter, when I was three months pregnant. I arranged a holiday in Crete, with my sister and her family, my parents and Desmond. During that week, on the one Sunday I was not in the studio recording *That's Life!*, I had a miscarriage, and lost the baby. One week earlier, I would have been in the studio. One day later, I would have been at Athens airport. The body has mysterious ways of taking decisions, that never touch our minds.

We had just seen a midnight procession of candles, one lit from another, a wave of light rippling down the main street of our Cretan village, as the tragedy of Good Friday's crucifixion was symbolically replaced with the light of the Resurrection. Greek Orthodox Easter is a mystic celebration, religious and pagan at the same time, with the rebirth of the Saviour, and of spring. I went back to our hotel, and the pains began. At first I had no idea what was happening, but my sister knew, and stayed with me.

Desmond and I had nicknamed the baby growing inside me 'Mike', joking that if the viewers noticed my developing bulge, we would explain that it was a radio mike, concealed under my dress. Now he sat outside my bedroom in tears as I lost Mike.

Watching Desmond's grief and bereavement, suddenly I too wanted a child as desperately as he did. I went home and told my GP what had happened. 'Some people,' he said, 'say you should wait before you try again, but I don't see why you should.' (I was, after all, thirty-six—quite old for a first pregnancy.) We tried and, to our joy, succeeded.

When I knew I was pregnant again, I went to my gynaecologist, George Pinker. He consulted his notes. 'I see you had a previous appointment, but cancelled it. Why?'

'Because I lost the baby.'

He was horrified. 'But all the more reason why you should have come to see me. I would have examined you, probably operated on you to make sure everything was clear.'

He need not have worried—the evidence was in my womb. Emily was thriving.

George Pinker told me to take care this time. Absolutely no travel, not even by train. And at three months he ordered me to take complete bed-rest, to get over the most dangerous time, when we had lost Mike.

*   *   *

On a bleak, rainy February day, when I was forced to stay cosily in bed, we were staked out by Fleet Street. Patsy had sold her story to the *Daily Mirror*. That morning, I opened my copy of the newspaper to find us spread across the centre pages, and, as I did so, the doorbell rang. We had moved to a little town house in Chiswick. At our porch were a cluster of six or seven journalists and photographers.

Desmond had to go to work, so he pushed past

them, without a word. A friend, the musician Tony Kinsey rang. We wrote songs together, and he needed to see me. He knew I was in bed. I explained there was a crowd of reporters at the door.

'How do I get past without them questioning me?' he asked.

'Put a pencil behind your ear, carry a clipboard under your arm, and say you've come about the central heating,' I suggested.

It worked. They let him through without a murmur. The weather grew worse. Snugly tucked up in bed, I asked Tony what the reporters were doing. The *Evening Standard* reporter had a motorbike, so he volunteered to get Chinese food for the rest. They were huddled miserably in the cold, I was safe and warm, and not allowed to go downstairs, let alone out of doors. I felt slightly sorry for them, especially as I had an even better story for them, secretly growing inside me. But only slightly sorry.

But that kind of secret must out, eventually. Emily survived the first three months of my pregnancy, and carried on thriving. We had an amniocentesis test, and discovered she was a girl. Mr Pinker told me her gender in a roundabout way:

'Do you want to know?' he asked.

'Yes, please,' I said. It seemed absurd that he should know, the lab assistant should know, without us knowing, too.

'It's on the feminine side,' he said.

'What do you mean?' I asked, suddenly anxious. 'You mean it's neither one nor the other?'

'No, Esther,' he said. 'She's a girl.'

'Then why didn't you say so?'

'Because for many of my patients that would be bad news.'

Of course, Mr Pinker was the royal gynaecologist, and for many of his coroneted patients, the baby had to be a son to inherit the title. How foolish. Jews do these things differently: you are only a Jew if your mother is Jewish. If you must make these gender distinctions, I think the Jews err on the right side, but then I would, wouldn't I.

I managed to hide Emily's growing presence by wearing smocks, and bigger smocks, until I was seven months pregnant. I even presented *Start the Week* on Radio 4, one of the guests being Richard Ingrams, Editor of *Private Eye*, without him noticing the 'story' under my voluminous dress. But eventually a gossip columnist rang me from the *Daily Express*, he'd heard I was expecting a baby.

I rang his Editor, Derek Jameson. I explained that I needed twenty-four hours—we hadn't yet told Desmond's children, we didn't want them to learn it from the papers. And we were negotiating Desmond's divorce, to try and get married before the birth. Derek was kind, 'I know what you mean, Esther, I'm a bastard myself.' He gave us twenty-four hours, and we told the children, who took the news calmly.

The next day, instead of leaving Derek with his scoop, we put out a statement to Press Association. I was due to go to a meeting at Television Centre, and as I arrived, a group of television writers were leaving a press launch they had attended. A number of them were friends. I waved to them, they waved back, all eyes on my stomach. The news

211

appeared in all the papers. Derek Jameson forgave me, but said he would never be so kind-hearted again, the gossip columnist has loathed me ever since. Hell hath no fury like a journalist deprived of a scoop.

When Patsy heard that the baby was due, she generously agreed to a quick divorce. Whatever her feelings about me, she had no wish to make the baby suffer. In those days there still was a stigma on illegitimacy. We put the wedding together in three weeks, so that Emily would be born in wedlock, just. Sarah Carr, a classy friend of ours, had read Patsy's angry article in the *Daily Mirror*, and regarded it as an official announcement of our engagement. She came out to dinner with us, and said to Desmond, 'Time to buy Esther a little sparkler'. He looked perplexed, so I explained, 'Sarah means an engagement ring'.

Desmond said, 'But I've bought Esther a turquoise ring already, made by the Hopi Indians'.

Sarah looked appalled. 'Semi-precious!'

'But it goes with a turquoise necklace.'

I tried to be helpful. 'White goes with everything.'

So we went to buy an antique diamond ring. My mother went with us, and startled us all, when the ring was produced, by taking a jeweller's loop out of her handbag, screwing it into her eye, and examining the stone under the lens. I told you Desmond was tolerant.

The wedding itself was at the Richmond Register Office. Desmond was quite calm. I was terrified, and shaking. Only the touch of his hand steadied me enough to get me through my responses. Outside, a reporter from the *Evening*

News was circling like a hornet, asking my family whether they minded the fact that I was obviously eight months pregnant. I was wearing a very large blue chiffon dress, I have it still, with a royal blue cloak. I had the look of a very happy whale.

Years later, when Emily was four, she saw a picture and asked why I wasn't wearing white. I explained the significance of white, and that she was inside my tummy, so obviously white would have been inappropriate. When she realized I had told her something naughty she rolled around on the floor, chuckling. Then we heard Desmond's key in the front door.

'Ask Daddy the same question,' I said mischievously. She came back even more amused.

'What did he say?'

'He said there were two reasons you didn't wear white. One was that you got married in a Register Office. And the other he'd tell me when I was eighteen.'

The wedding reception was at Searcy's at the back of Harrods. Our family and friends and many BBC colleagues drank champagne with us. My father made a speech graciously explaining to the BBC executives how they could run the organization more effectively. A friend sent a telegram saying, 'We knew you had it in you, Esther'. I wrapped up slices of wedding cake to take to my antenatal class. Sadly, I have no pictures of the party at all. Desmond, who spent his working life surrounded by cameras, seemed to dislike them in his private life, and I must have forgotten to book a photographer. Fleet Street had one of its many strikes that day, but it ended at lunchtime, so when we returned home we found a clutch of photographers at our door. We rolled down the window as we approached, and one of them offered us the choice. 'It's up to you, Esther and Desmond—either you can put blankets over your heads and run to the front door, and we'll take pictures of you looking like bank robbers, or you can invite us in, and we'll take nice ones you'll like the look of.' Put that way, we invited them in, and gave them a glass of champagne.

Our honeymoon was brief, a weekend in The Old Bell Inn, Hurley, on the Thames. It was early December, we drove through silver frosted countryside, listening to Mike Oldfield's *Tubular Bells*. Perhaps it wasn't the romantic wedding little girls dream about, but then I wasn't a little girl. I was enormous, and enormously happy. We both were. The happiness still felt fragile to me, like the frost in the hedgerows, and the music as delicate as winter birdsong. I still couldn't believe, that after all the pain, we were together.

When we arrived at the hotel, nobody knew we had just got married. The next morning, the waiter who brought us breakfast asked us for our autographs. I signed proudly, but he wasn't satisfied. I'd written, 'Esther Wilcox'. Our pictures appeared in that day's papers, so the news spread, and the Austrian chef said he would make a special wedding feast for us that night.

When we arrived at the restaurant, on the menu was Desmond's favourite meal, roast lamb and raspberries. But we had pledged to eat the chef's feast. The first course arrived on a silver plate, carried high over the diners' heads. It was a pyramid of smoked salmon, with cream-cheese dollops along it. I said to Desmond, 'That's

Freudian'. I had seen nothing yet. The second course was an enormous Austrian sausage, with two wrinkled cabbage-leaf pouches either side, stuffed with rice. I couldn't stick my fork into it. Pudding was a strawberry pyramid of ice-cream, once again decorated with dollops of cream. We laughed, and remembered that Freud himself was Austrian.

There was so much ice-cream left over that when we went to our room I rang my sister and asked her and her family to tea the next day, to finish it. Did I mention how tolerant Desmond was? I can't think many men would welcome in-laws joining them on their honeymoon.

*   *   *

We had to get home quickly after the weekend because Desmond's twins were living with us. (His older daughter, Cassie, was with her boyfriend.) Desmond and I had decided to move into his family home in Kew. That had been a very difficult decision. We had supposed that Patsy would want to live with the children in the house, and that Desmond and I would help to support them there. But Patsy decided she wanted to live on her own. Teenagers are never easy, and Patsy had a demanding job. She employed a housekeeper, who told us that their life in Kew had been bleak.

Unexpectedly, Desmond received a letter from Patsy's lawyer saying that her health had deteriorated badly. She was suffering from stress, and could not, therefore, look after any of her children. She suggested we should buy the children a flat, a 'separate living unit'. But the twins were

215

still only fifteen, and I thought they were far too young to be cut adrift. So we decided to buy Patsy a flat to live in on her own—a very pleasant flat in a block overlooking Richmond Park—with a spare room in case she wanted the children to stay with her from time to time. She didn't.

Desmond and I moved into the family home in Kew, and lived there with the twins. That meant the least possible disruption for them. They stayed in the bedrooms they knew and loved, with all their friends still able to phone and visit them easily. It was difficult for me to create a relationship with them at first, given the poisonous background to the marriage, and the high level of hormones swirling around—they in the midst of puberty, me in the last stages of pregnancy. I instituted family suppers, so that we could get to know each other. The children tolerated me with remarkable patience, and I grew to like and respect them. They were kind to me throughout my three pregnancies—I have very fond memories of Claire, my younger step-daughter, firmly closing the curtains and making me take my afternoon rests—and sweet to the babies when they arrived.

But all the same, for me that house in Kew was filled with malevolent ghosts. When I had postnatal depression after Emily's birth, I thought I saw Patsy like a black bat, flying in and out of the wardrobes. We redecorated the house, and tried to make it feel different, but in my mind it was always the home Desmond had shared with Patsy, and I was relieved when we moved to Hampstead.

After we married (and I will later describe the ferocity with which our colleagues in our department responded to our marriage) the twins

216

continued to live with us for several years, until we were able to buy a little flat for them, around the corner, near enough still to be able to use the washing-machine and the fridge. I enjoyed their company, and tried to be friendly and supportive, as my aunts had been to me. We still get on well, but I know it must have been difficult for them to be part of a split family at open war, especially since Patsy refused to allow me to be mentioned by any of them, or even be invited to their weddings.

Patsy was inconsolable and remained angry and bitter until the day she died. Although I steadfastly refused to discuss her publicly, she once told a paper that I was worse than the cancer that eventually attacked her. I had instigated the break-up of her marriage, she said, I was the guilty party, I had betrayed my friendship with her, and she would never forgive me.

I only had one more conversation with her—when I had been married to Desmond for twenty years, at the time of his sixty-fifth birthday party. Patsy had just been diagnosed with melanoma. I knew she was undergoing a painful, unpleasant course of chemotherapy. Her daughter Claire had just had a baby girl, and I was going to fly them over from Singapore, where they were living, to be guests of honour at Desmond's surprise party. I thought Patsy would be pleased to see her latest granddaughter, too, so I rang to ask what date would suit her? Her voice was acid:

'Please never speak to me again, Esther. If you wish to make arrangements, do so through your assistant.'

I tried to explain. 'I'm organizing a surprise party for Desmond, but I can arrange the date so that

217

Claire and her baby can stay with you, either before or after it.'

We agreed a date, but, in the event, Claire and her baby were unable to fly to Britain. Patsy nevertheless rang Desmond on the morning of the party, to wish him many happy returns. I stood like a statue in the bedroom. The surprise had been perfectly set up. Desmond had no suspicion there was going to be any kind of celebration, indeed he had forbidden me to arrange a party because he was so morose about his great age. I had taken a delight in disobeying him. Why shouldn't he be proud of being sixty-five and surrounded by his friends and family? I whispered to the children that Patsy was on the phone, they realized what was happening, they too stood rigid with horror. Was she going to wreck the surprise? She waited until her last sentence to him, 'Enjoy your party'.

Desmond came off the phone, 'What party?' he asked. The children and I gazed at each other with horror. Emily was already ill, with the chronic fatigue which was to rob her of eight years. Somehow she mustered the strength to sob wildly (she would have made a great actress), 'I can't have a party. Don't have a party. It's not fair.' We rushed to console her.

'Don't be upset. We don't know what Patsy meant. We know you're too ill for a family party.'

Whether Desmond guessed the truth I don't know, to this day. If so, he decided to play along, and was properly astonished when dozens of his friends greeted him at Chewton Glen, the luxurious hotel we save for our most special occasions. Whatever I have done to Patsy, and I know how reprehensible many of my actions have been, I still

218

think giving away a surprise birthday party is as mean as shooting a decoy duck.

Patsy died, unforgiving, in November 1999. From her I learned that bitterness rebounds. She gloried in it. She spent the latter part of her life, as Robert Burns said, 'nursing her wrath to keep it warm'. From time to time I read of others who, like Patsy, turn the undoubted wrongs they suffer into an integral part of their identity, almost as if they fear healing and moving on. She was a clever, attractive woman, with a successful career, a comfortable home, many friends and three children who loved her. And yet she convinced herself that none of this counted. For her, the failure of her marriage was the most significant fact in her life. It need not have been. She was fifty when she divorced Desmond, with more than twenty productive, active years to come. She took great satisfaction in loathing me to the end, and yet I believe she would have enjoyed far more happiness if she had taken to heart the proverb, 'the best revenge is to live well'.

*   *   *

For a while the press reminded their readers whenever they wrote about me that I had been a marriage-breaker and I used to tease Desmond by saying he had made me a 'nay-word'. But as the years rolled by, I almost forgot how scandalous our relationship had been at the start. I became shrouded with respectability. People began to refer to me as an 'institution', which made me feel like a remote and ramshackle psychiatric hospital.

I even began to collect a few honours, which I prized, didn't deserve, but am certainly not going to

219

hand back. I received awards from the Variety Club, from the Royal Television Society, from BAFTA, an OBE from the Queen, and a Gotcha from Noel Edmunds. I was asked to become patron of several charities, which I regard as a great privilege. One of my most memorable invitations came from a small charity for disabled people in the Midlands.

The Chief Executive wrote and said they particularly needed help in improving their profile with the media. I asked my p.a. to try and obtain some more information about their work, so she contacted the Board of Trustees, all admirals, generals and lords lieutenants. By return the Chairman of the Board wrote a letter to me which frothed on the page. They certainly did not want me as a Patron, he said, they had no idea why I had been approached, how could they possibly have on their notepaper the name of a woman who had fornicated with a married man?

By now twenty years had gone by, and my scarlet notoriety had faded to pale pink in my mind, but obviously not in theirs. I was taken aback, and frankly rather offended. Then I thought of the perfect revenge. I wrote to the Chief Executive, copied to the Chairman, thanking him for his kind invitation and saying I would be delighted to become a Patron. Clearly he was right, I said, they desperately needed help to improve their skills in dealing with the media, especially television presenters.

There was a pause. Then I had a crestfallen reply from the Chief Executive explaining that their plans were now on hold, because they were restructuring. I never heard from them again. I do hope they found the Patron they were looking for. And I certainly hope he or she was whiter than white.

*   *   *

While I was writing this chapter, I remember Desmond turning over the pages and encouraging me. 'Go on,' he said, nervous that I would lose confidence. Autobiography is more exposing than running naked through the garden on your fifty-eighth birthday. I know. I've done both. So I went on writing, and finished this chapter with a paragraph I thought summed up our life together. I said:

'Now that Desmond and I have become Darby and Joan, who used to be Jack and Jill, we have, thank heavens, passed the stage in our lives when we tumbled down and broke our pates on every obstacle life threw at us. Life is slightly more peaceful. In our family home in Hampstead we are literally "the folks who live on the hill", enjoying our trips to the local bookshops, the Chinese restaurant, the theatre, the movies, the walks on the Heath. Most precious to us, we have discovered painfully, are the health of those we love, and the friendship of those we care about. We are like any other old couple, arguing amicably our way round the garden centre, choosing tulip bulbs and garden seats. What a dull pair! But just to reassure you (and me) that we have not entirely lost the insanity of our youth, we still create surprise parties for each other, still dress up in fancy dress when the occasion demands it, still tell awful jokes at each other's expense. And I'm afraid I still make puns. You can't have everything.'

A few days after Desmond read that paragraph, he died. Now when I read it myself, still raw with losing him, I can hardly believe how crassly I understated what we had together. Perhaps I was trying to underplay the drama, to point out that, in spite of the bitterness and turmoil created by our early years together, we had found tranquillity at last.

And indeed the turmoil continued. In later chapters I will describe the birth of our children, my postnatal depression, the way in which Desmond was forced to resign from the BBC, and how he built a new career as an independent producer, reinventing himself and pioneering a caring, selfless journalism that will be remembered as long as television itself is remembered. But now that I have to draw a line at the end of our partnership, facing the cold truth that we will never laugh together again, or make love together, or share the joy of the children's company, or our friends' companionship, perhaps I can sum up a little more adequately where our love story took us.

Desmond and I were partners, and our partnership was complete and all-consuming. Physically, intellectually, emotionally, we adored each other. If I had done the conventional 'right thing', run from him and refused to become the last straw that broke his precarious marriage, I would have missed the most valuable relationship of my life. I have lost him now, the gap he leaves seems unbridgeable, for me, and for our children. That is the price of the kind of love we shared—when it ends, the pain is agonizing.

But, as I will describe, the last months we spent together were especially beautiful, and I have those indelible memories. Around my neck is a silver locket with a tiny lock of his hair inside it. (Our daughters also have one each.) Next to his hair is a picture of the two of us standing together in our sunny spring garden, under an arch of roses, waist-high in buttercups. He brought the gold of love, and laughter and sunshine into my life. That is what we shared. That is what I will always remember.

CHAPTER EIGHT

BRUNETTE TO BLONDE

When *Braden's Week* started it dawned on me, slowly, that I should take my new career as a television reporter seriously. I still thought I would go back to producing, but it was fun for a year or two to try and learn new skills in front of the camera, instead of behind them. I was twenty-eight, and, although I never had the gloss and glamour of today's young women presenters, I suppose I blossomed as I fell in love with Desmond. Most people take on a special shine when they are in love—and Desmond's love gave me much more confidence. I needed it.

From 1968 onwards, appearing regularly on television made me all too aware of my many physical drawbacks. My father had trained me to believe vanity was a vice. But now the camera was on me I knew that in order to communicate effectively I should try and be as attractive as God would allow. The first decision was easy: I had been a brunette—in my mind I still am—but my fine brown hair looked heavy on screen, so I asked the hairdresser for golden streaks, and I went from brunette to blonde.

The rest of my defects were far more intractable. My smile, which I had never seen before, having always been behind it, I now recognized as a problem. Not just my prominent teeth, but acres of gums flashed whenever I laughed. I decided that all I could do was make jokes about them before other

224

people did, and the penalty was that for thirty years journalists labelled me 'toothy Esther Rantzen'. I had inherited my dental drawbacks from my father, but I forgave him because he had also handed on to me his legs, which I had often admired as he paddled on our holidays together. His legs were marble white, but long from the knees down, with elegant ankles. I wore fashionable short skirts to make the most of mine. I made up my eyes with masses of mascara to try and distract from the teeth, but there wasn't much I could do to focus on my one other good feature, my back. (Michael Aspel first pointed out that I had a good back, which depressed me because it meant that I had been facing the wrong way on television for years.)

With all my efforts, and advice from professional make-up artists, it was clear that I could never be regarded as beautiful, as Joan Bakewell was on BBC2. So it is odd that I became one of the first woman reporters on BBC1, and later the first (and I believe, the only) woman producer/presenter in the BBC.

I cringed when I saw myself on screen, but told myself I shouldn't be ashamed of my looks—after all, most women are not beautiful. Why shouldn't an ordinary woman's face be represented on the television screen? There are few enough in the media, in newspapers, magazines or commercials. The tyranny of physical beauty, born of the age of the camera, makes young people feel inadequate, and the old feel deformed by their age. It's such an artificially manufactured image. I have watched a top photographer retouching the picture of a lovely nineteen-year-old model to make her neck so thread-thin it could never have supported her

225

head. No wonder our teenagers are beset with eating disorders, trying desperately to look like the impossible supermodel images they see around them.

It was particularly brave of John Lloyd and Bernie Braden to put me on the screen in the sixties, because women on BBC1 at the time were used as decorative ornaments. There were no women at all on the serious programmes. In Light Entertainment they smiled, wore very little, and said less. Colin Charman, my friend from studio management days who went on to become a producer in Light Entertainment said to me, 'For some reason, Esther, you are the only woman on television who doesn't annoy my wife'. We were in the BBC Club at the time. I said, 'If a man walked in now, wearing nothing but a leopard-skin thong, flexed his muscles, said nothing, but walked out again, that might irritate you'.

That was exactly how they used women in Light Entertainment, to take the magician's cloak, point to the scoreboard, or kick up their legs in a long line of Television Toppers.

When I started to appear on *Braden's Week* I made a rule with the BBC Press Office that I would never be interviewed for a fashion item. I hope that doesn't seem self-important. I didn't want anyone to notice my clothes because I was fighting to be considered a reporter, on equal terms with the men. It was also true that I didn't enjoy buying clothes at all, in those days. (Unfortunately— thanks to the advice I have received over the years from BBC costumer designers—I now do, and the effect on my bank balance is catastrophic.)

For my first appearance on *Braden's Week* in

226

1968 I put together the nearest thing I could find to a man's suit—a blue tunic and skirt—with the idea that I would put a different blouse underneath it every week. After the third week, a man rang the BBC's Duty Office with a plaintive request, 'Please will Esther Rantzen wear something different?'. The next week I did, so he rang to thank me.

Being one of the first women on television, I felt a special responsibility. My parents had brought me up on a story of one of their close friends, a brilliant woman who—having competed with all the best men in Britain—was awarded a scholarship. Three weeks later she got engaged, and told the authorities she would not take up the scholarship after all. The authorities met, and wrote into their terms of reference that they would never award it to a woman again.

I recognized that I mustn't fail, must make the most of the chances that were given me. Not only must I live up to the aspirations of the women in our audience, I must not let down the men who had given me pioneering opportunities, because if I failed and was sacked, it would be even harder for the women following behind me.

*   *   *

Other doors were beginning to open, even in the male-dominated Current Affairs Group. Michael Bunce, the Editor of the new early-evening programme, *Nationwide*, invited me to join his team, between the series of *Braden's Week*. I was one of three women whom Buncie booked in rotation, like a harem, Sue Lawley came from Plymouth, Suzanne Hall came from Norwich, I

227

came from *Braden's Week*. The programme had been created by Derek Amoore (he of the air-gun). It was an ambitious and original idea, a nightly magazine programme, to which all the regions contributed, and which was broadcast nationally.

Derek was the first Editor of *Nationwide*, and it had some very peculiar moments. One of the early reporters was a programme-scheduler, Alan Shalcross, who became a gifted producer, but was never destined to become a presenter. I will never forget his look of complete panic as a camera advanced upon him, red light blazing, but no script on his desk or words on the teleprompt. He gasped, and fell silent. Alan could ad lib marvellously in the office or the bar, but when live television fell upon him it choked the words in his mouth. Only a few can rise to that occasion—Cliff Michelmore is one, David Dimbleby is another. Their trick is to recognize that viewers infinitely prefer television cock-ups to programmes, so to enjoy the moment with them.

Michael Bunce, who invited me on to the team, had taken over as Editor from Derek Amoore and when he did, comparative calm descended on the programme. It was still quite nervy—two interviewees would arrive in the studio simultaneously, and it was the luck of the draw whether they would be put in the right seat. If not—and this happened more than once—Bob Wellings would interview A about railways, and I would interview B about the biggest marrow in the world, when it should have been the other way around. People rarely contradicted us, even when we called them the wrong name, and gave them the wrong job description. They just put it down to the

228

madness of live television.

It wasn't mad, exactly, but it was accident-prone. Once I had to demonstrate a newly compulsory addition to the standard motorcar, the windscreen washer. I tried it on rehearsal, it worked perfectly, spraying the screen with water. I tried it live on the air—nothing. All the water had been used up. Buncie ticked me off, I thought unfairly, for not making sure my props were in order.

On another occasion, Professor Meredith Thring came into the studio to demonstrate his latest invention, a wheelchair that went up and down stairs. This time the item was to be pre-recorded in the afternoon. I rang Angela Huth's husband, Quentin Crewe, a writer and broadcaster who was a wheelchair user, and he told me that if the invention really worked it would revolutionize his life. He explained that stairs are the problem, they prevent people in wheelchairs from crossing roads, getting into trains and buses, living in unadapted houses, going to the theatre. If only they could climb stairs in a wheelchair, life for many disabled people would be vastly improved. Quentin agreed to come to the studio to test it.

Professor Thring was a superb example of the great English eccentric. He arrived in the studio, his white hair vertical, as if blown in on a gust of air. His trousers were in bicycle clips. There was a tremendous clanking sound behind him, and one of his students brought in the wheelchair. Each wheel had large flapping flanges attached to them. Our designer had built a staircase for us in the studio. Quentin was sitting in his wheelchair, looking with horror at the Heath Robinson contraption. I quickly came to his rescue. 'Would you like me to

229

test it, rather than you?' Relieved, he nodded.

So we recorded a brief interview, then I got into the chair and tried to continue to talk to Professor Thring. He couldn't hear a word I said over the thud and roar of the machine, flopping and crashing its way up and down the staircase. The team was, nonetheless, very pleased with the item. I was in the gallery when it transmitted, and for the first time I saw the angle of the cameras up my very short skirt. 'This item,' said the director; 'is about Esther's thighs.' Had my gender impeded an important item about wheelchair access? Or (as I hope and believe) had my short skirt saved a catastrophic item?

Clothes were a nuisance. They assumed an importance in those early days which I still think was misplaced. Once they cost me a job. I had enjoyed my time on *Nationwide*, so I was very pleased when Michael Bunce rang and asked me to make some more films for them. Was there anything I would particularly like to cover? Yes, there was. I said, 'I'd love to go to Belfast, and make some films about the Troubles.' Michael was quite taken aback. 'I'm not sure it would be appropriate,' he said. At the time there were no women war reporters. 'The problem is, what would you wear?' I spluttered that I didn't think that was a problem at all, what did the men wear? But I wasn't sent to Belfast, then or ever.

Jacky Gillot was a friend, she became the first woman reporter on *News at Ten*, and she found the same uneasiness. She once told me that to be treated on equal terms she had to dress in heavy tweed, wear thick brogue shoes, and certainly had to learn to shove the men out of the way. They were not going to make way for her.

I remember meeting a producer on *Tomorrow's World* in the BBC Club. He said, 'Do you know anyone who could be our first woman reporter?' I had comparatively recently graduated, and a number of my women friends were attractive, articulate, and knew their science. I wasn't sure if they wanted a scientist, so I said, 'What kind of woman are you looking for?'

'Certainly not an Esther Rantzen,' he said.

I said, 'I can understand that, but which aspect of Esther Rantzen are you trying to avoid?'

'The trouble is, Esther, when you're on the screen I'm always aware that you're a woman.'

'This may come as a surprise to you, Andy, but whenever Richard Baker's on the screen I'm always aware that he's a man.'

I told him that what he was looking for was a man who could pass as a woman, at least in long shot. Funny now, in these days of 'in your face laddettes', to look back. Young women now shout like lads, swear like lads, but wear tiny tight dresses with their erogenous zones well on display. That would have frightened the producers of *Tomorrow's World* out of their jockstraps.

I am not a good feminist, I admit. I have never been politically extreme. I have always believed in evolution rather than revolution. All the same, looking back I recognize I was one of the pioneer career women who pushed back the frontiers, not as a conscious decision, but because of the patterns in which my life fell. Many of my contemporaries at Somerville had married early, I married late. Then that was rare—now it is commonplace. Most of my friends had their babies in their twenties. I had

231

mine in my late thirties and early forties. That, too, is now more common. I had already reached a position of some seniority in my job when I started my family, so I became a working mother. I saw no reason why the new experiences that were opening up to me in my private life, should not be reflected in the programmes I made.

Until the mid-seventies, not just the media, but the whole of public life was driven by men, and male values. The prejudice affected every class, all cultures. I remember trying to sell the concept of consumer protection to a group of male trade unionists. They were dismissive, 'You'll just be discussing the price of lipsticks'. Yes, we were, among other subjects, and why not? Given the wide range of stories we investigated, why not look at the price of cosmetics? Women spend money on them, and deserve fair dealing.

So, along with our stories about con-men selling home improvements, we debunked slimming pills, and anti-wrinkle cream. We discovered that the pots in which face-creams were sold had false bottoms, so they looked twice the size they really were. Rimmel, owned by relatives of mine, was one of the offenders, and Bernie greatly enjoyed the moment when I had to reveal that I had rung up my own Aunt Rose Caplin to complain.

We tackled the craze for make-overs. A viewer from Northern Ireland sent us two articles in which several women had completely changed their hair and make-up with professional help. The photographs were identical, but mysteriously one was from an American magazine, the other was British, and they listed quite different cosmetics. I rang the women themselves. They said the

232

American version was accurate, and that the make-overs had changed their lives, made them far more confident and sociable. When I rang the British magazine's beauty editor she confessed that she had bought the article and listed whatever cosmetics roughly matched, and were being promoted at the time.

Such cons still exist, particularly in the multi-million pound beauty industry. I discovered from my friends in hairdressing that they buy and sell 'credits'. When you see the name of a hairdresser under a picture, you cannot be at all sure he or she has really done the hair. When I started on *Braden's Week*, none of the male programme-makers would have noticed, or cared, about such swindles.

Throughout my career I was to find many serious stories affecting millions of women, which male-dominated television had ignored. I had postnatal depression after my first baby, Emily, was born. I was unprepared for it, had never been warned, had not read about it, nor seen any programmes about it. As a sufferer I helped to make a programme about it with producer Ruth Jackson, and set up a network of support groups, the 'Meet-a-Mum Association' which still exists today, and of which I am still president.

When I wanted to breastfeed my babies, at once I encountered the prejudice against breastfeeding mothers. I was lampooned in the press for it. It was said by an inventive gossip columnist that I had breastfed in front of Prince Charles, (absolutely untrue, unless he was hiding in a cubicle in the ladies' loo). But I could see no reason why women should have to breastfeed in a lavatory, uncomfortable and unhygienic as that was for both mother and baby. We told stories on *That's Life!* of breastfeeding mothers who were thrown out of restaurants all over the country, from Harrods to a local health food shop, all this while the *Sun* newspaper gloried in pictures of women's breasts on page three.

During the eighties, not only were women struggling free of their stereotypes, the 'new man' was admitting that he too wanted to be involved in his children's upbringing, and why not? Better for him, better for the whole family. Jean Rook, 'the biggest bitch on Fleet Street', completely disagreed with me. She had based her career on being tougher and stronger than the men around her, and adamantly opposed the thought that men should be present to watch the birth of their babies. But she was an anachronism.

On *That's Life!* we ran stories highlighting the problems all new parents face, the impossibility of taking a toddler in a buggy on a train or a bus, the shops that put children's departments up long flights of stairs. Our young men reporters took part in a nappy-changing contest. We campaigned for safer children's playgrounds, and for proper seat belts in school buses.

I don't wish to imply that male television journalists were entirely insensitive to women's issues. That would be sexist, and unfair. Desmond, when he worked on *This Week*, tackled cruelty to children. On *The Braden Beat*, Bernie had composed a moving description of the vicious bullying that deaf children can suffer at school. But there is no question that my new role as wife and mother in my private life sensitized me to these issues in my work. For example, in 1982, just after my son Joshua was born, we made a special ninety-minute programme *Having a Baby* which highlighted some of the dangerous practices which caused death and disability in babies, and the fact that women would like some choice in the way their babies are born.

In 1983, we created another special programme about stillbirth, *The Lost Babies.* Hospital staff at that time did not recognize the cruelty of taking dead babies away like garbage, and burying them in unmarked graves, without even a photograph for the parents to remember them by. That has changed, now photographs are taken, parents are allowed to grieve for their babies, still-born babies are allowed their own graves and their own memorials. If I had not experienced motherhood, I believe I might not have understood the importance of these stories.

And, of course, in 1986 *That's Life!* tackled the painful subject of child abuse, ChildLine was launched, and my life changed totally.

*   *   *

In 1972, I had no idea of the peaks and troughs ahead of me. I have never planned my career strategically. How could I? It would have been absurd to contemplate a career as a television presenter, when there were so few women on the screen, and even more ridiculous to think of being a producer/presenter. There simply weren't any. Not only that, but a crisis had hit *Braden's Week.*

Bernie was, you remember, among many other things in his career, an actor. Although he had invented consumer programmes on television, a part of him still thought of the script as a series of speeches, like a play. When the manufacturers of Stork Margarine came to him and asked him to deliver some speeches for them in a commercial, he did so, without telling anyone at the BBC in advance. It happened between series. He was not under contract to the Beeb, and saw no reason to turn the offer down. When the BBC discovered what he had done, all hell broke loose.

I admired and respected Bernie, and I was devastated. I felt he had betrayed the show. He once told me, 'Esther, you have eyes like the "Midwich Cuckoos" as if the BBC has brainwashed you'. In a way it was true. The public service ethic had indeed been part of my blood stream, and I had been trained to believe that consumer journalists, even puny little researchers like myself, are perceived by the viewers to be trustworthy, and independent. We are human, alas, and not infallible, and with the best intentions we sometimes make mistakes, but we must not become salesmen for any product, nor sell our integrity to the highest bidder.

There are people who will think this is pompous nonsense. When the row broke over Bernie's head, many of the public were mystified. The words he had been asked to speak by Stork Margarine were true. What was the problem? Many years later, Carol Vorderman thought the BBC was crazy when they objected to her making a commercial in the style of *Tomorrow's World*, the programme she was presenting. Still later, ITV appointed Caron Keating to present their consumer programme, *We Can Work it Out* even though she made commercials for a milk product. So it shows that not everyone would agree with the BBC bosses, that Bernie had undermined the credibility of our programme. But I understand the BBC's view, that presenters of consumer programmes should be seen to be independent of all commercial pressure, we must not be involved with product placement, or advertisements of any kind.

Occasionally these days I am in an awkward position, when a company gets into a partnership with ChildLine—for instance, when a new toothbrush was launched, and £1 went to ChildLine for every brush they sold. I did my best to publicize the promotion (as the Tooth Fairy, of course— pictures which occasionally come back to haunt me), but each time I wore a ChildLine sash, and made it clear I was supporting the cause, rather than praising the bristles. It's a tightrope, and Bernie fell off it, or rather he jumped, with great force.

I walked into his office when I found out about the Stork commercial, and asked, 'Why, Bernie?' He looked at me as if I was a foolish child. 'Because there is no other way to make that kind of money in one afternoon.'

I still didn't understand. He was one of the highest paid performers on British television. Did he really need the money? What I didn't realize, until one summer when I met him in the south of France, was that among his closest friends were Sean Connery and David Niven. Bernie had a nice villa, with a swimming pool, a little way back from the coast. Niven, whose villa we visited with Bernie, had a palace overlooking the bright blue sea, and servants wearing white gloves. Film stars' salaries made even highly paid television stars look like paupers.

Riches are all comparative. Years later I discussed this with Richard Stilgoe, who wrote lyrics for Andrew Lloyd Webber. At that time he had written part of the opening chorus of *Cats*, and told me how much he made from it. I gasped as I calculated what Andrew must make from the whole score. Richard said, 'But Andrew still doesn't think he's rich. He can only afford his collection of pre-Raphaelite paintings. The friends he visits in Hollywood have walls lined with original Monets and Van Goghs. By comparison with them, he's almost poor.'

I am happy to say that Lord Lloyd-Webber is catching up fast. Musicals such as *The Phantom of the Opera*, and *Cats*, and the others bring in far more money worldwide, than puny offerings like *Titanic* in the cinema. But Stilgoe's point was valid, I think I am poor next to Cilla Black, Bernie thought he was poor next to Sean Connery. The commercial was a way of making money quickly.

Desmond was extremely fond of Bernie, and, as Head of Department, now had the tricky job of trying to keep *Braden's Week* on the air, when bosses like Paul Fox were determined to sack Bernie. It took delicate negotiation. At one moment Desmond was warned that by defending Bernie, he was putting his own job on the line. Desmond argued that, since there was no reference to commercials in Bernie's contract, it would be unfair to fire him. He persuaded Bernie to write a letter saying he had no idea the BBC would object. The show stayed on the air, but damage had been done. It turned out to be the last of the series.

238

I was relieved when the row was resolved, I loved working on the show. We had built up to an audience of eight million, not bad for a programme transmitting at eleven-thirty on Saturday night.

For one programme Frankie Howerd was the guest. I met him in the make-up room. He stared at his own face in the mirror, his mouth drooping in a grimace as he tugged at the bags under his eyes. 'Do something to disguise these, darling,' he said to the make-up girl. She did her best. On the show Frankie wrecked her subtle artistry. 'Look at these,' he said to the camera, 'come on, zoom in, just look at these bags.' Obediently the camera zoomed in to photograph the bags in minute detail. The make-up girl sighed—she'd done her best. Then Frankie pulled out a briefing note Bernie had put together for him, and read it aloud. Interrupted with incredulous oohs and aahs, and 'titter ye not', he turned it into a comic masterpiece. Bernie wept with laughter. We finished the recording and, for once, watched it broadcast. Frankie was just as funny the second time. John Lloyd glanced at the clock as it transmitted—we were appalled to see it was almost midnight. 'Ridiculous waste,' he said to me.

I got to know Frankie quite well, he came to my birthday parties, and we asked him to appear on *That's Life!* as often as possible. I can see him standing on the lawn of our country cottage on a hot June day, wearing an appalling gingery wig, rivulets of sweat coursing from under it and down his face. He used to chase any young men on the team around the garden, and they would arrive at my side panting and disbelieving. Could such a comic genius, in the middle of a party, really have tried to seduce them? They forgave him. I was concerned about the deep drifts of depression that seemed to engulf him from time to time. Why is it that those who amuse us so much have to pay such a price themselves?

During the last series of *Braden's Week* I attempted to get us into the *Guinness Book of Records*. We were tipped off that in a pub in the West Country they were going for the 'ferret down the trousers' record. It was agonizing to watch. A man pushed a ferret down inside his belt, and we saw the sharp claws glinting through the tweed. It was down there several minutes. It felt like hours to us watching, and I cannot imagine what it felt like to the man in the trousers—let alone the ferret.

James Clarke (of gnome-nobbling fame) was the director. He took the close-up shots of claws through tweed, then turned and orchestrated the crowd, waving at them to gasp histrionically. Gasps turned out to be his speciality—he went on to direct soft porn films. We never got our record entry in the *Guinness Book*, not because the ferret didn't stay down there long enough, it did, but because the McWhirter brothers believed it would encourage others to follow suit, and there was a risk of tetanus.

If my private life was eventful, so was John Pitman's. He was vox-popping outside Harrods, as I did for twenty-one years on *That's Life!*, when a lady in an estate agent's office came out and invited him to an orgy. No such thing ever happened to me. He went, and described it to me later in the canteen. I think quite early on he had made his excuses and left, or at least that's what he told me. I was clearly impressed with his sophistication, so he became even more sophisticated, and told me of an orgy he'd heard about where Mandy Rice-Davies was present.

'There was a fly in the room, so they put honey on her boobs,' he said, 'and bet which one the fly would land on.'

'How disgusting,' I said primly.

'Rubbish, Ranters, you don't think it's disgusting at all.'

'I do.'

'Why?'

'It must have made her jumper all sticky.'

He laughed. I have always enjoyed making Pitman laugh. He knew he was leaving the show at the end of the run, because he was going to make documentaries for *Man Alive*. I knew the show would have to change, the bosses had decreed that they were bored with the format.

*   *   *

Bernie had a mulish stubbornness, not always, but every now and again he would take a position and be unshiftable. For instance, he was convinced you could only do comedy in the light, and refused to work in dark sets. In a sense he was like the Walter Matthau character in *The Sunshine Boys*, who insisted that the letter 'k' was funny, as in 'cupcake'.

Bernie was equally adamant that on our programme only one person should address the viewers. It was his show, only he talked to camera. All the rest of the cast should talk either to him, or to each other. It seems a tiny point, but it infuriated the bosses, David Attenborough and

Paul Fox. It meant that neither John Pitman nor I could ever present our research directly to the audience, we always had to answer questions from Bernie. This had the effect of sometimes making Bernie appear extremely dim, with questions like 'What happened next, John?' when he knew perfectly well what happened. Worse, the viewers knew he knew. Bernie, as I have said, had been an actor, and for him this was dramatic licence. For our bosses it was nonsense, and they decreed it must change.

John Lloyd took Bernie out to lunch and tried to persuade him to make this simple alteration to our format. He failed. The answer seemed to be that we should devise a new programme, starring Bernie as the only presenter. John Pitman was leaving the show anyway, I suggested that I should leave it, too, on camera that is, but join the production team of the new consumer programme. I admired Bernie so much, and by now was so addicted to consumer television, that would have suited me perfectly.

We worked out a format that put Bernie alone in front of the studio audience, linking pieces of film and tackling the kind of consumer investigation and interviews we had shown on *Braden's Week*. Desmond tried to sell the idea to Bernie, he failed. Bernie said he thought it sounded like a reduced version of the show we had already been making. He revealed that he'd been asked to launch a new television channel in Canada with a *Braden's Week* show transmitting twice a week, and that he'd decided to accept the offer. He also made another series of commercials for Stork Margarine. Although I was downcast and disappointed at the time, Bernie's decisions turned out to be bad for him in the long run, and good for me.

Barbara Kelly was convinced at the time that Bernie was the victim of a plot by Desmond and me to knife him in the back. Perhaps she still believes it. Even though she knows in her heart that Desmond put his own career at stake to defend Bernie when he made his first Stork commercials, the conspiracy theory was too tempting. But she was completely wrong. The facts are these. Bernie made the decision that rather than change the format of *Braden's Week*, he would go to Canada, and make another commercial. If that decision turned out to be disastrous, that, as they say, is show business. It is very hard to know which way to jump, many great performers have made the wrong move at turning points in their careers.

I had already made a disastrous mistake of my own, a terrible chat show. Paul Fox had been to America, and had seen an interview programme in which two women jointly interviewed a single guest. I later read the account of the storms behind the scenes of that show. I wish I had read it before I agreed to this strange idea. As it was, Paul suggested that Harriet Crawley should share the show as the other woman interviewer—she was the beautiful young daughter of former MP Aidan Crawley. The show was to be called, *She and She;* John Lloyd produced it, and for once was unable to save it. Fortunately, only six episodes were commissioned. I can't say the atmosphere between Harriet and me was ideal. The press implied that we disliked each other—that was untrue, but we had nothing in common.

Our first interviewee was Enid Bagnold, the

243

author of *National Velvet*, one of my favourite children's books, who had never given a major interview before. When she came to the studio we discovered why. Enid was very elderly, and crotchety. She had refused to meet any of the team before the programme. The theory was that I should read her autobiography, so that I could lead her through her life, while Harriet dropped in a few inspired questions. Unfortunately, that meant I knew Enid's life better than Enid did. Every time I reminded her of an incident, or asked her a question about someone she had met, she denied all knowledge of it. Harriet did no better, Enid failed to hear most of her questions. It was a surreal first programme.

We staggered on to the end of the series, our last show featured Barbara Castle, then a senior minister in the Labour government. Before we booked her, I was invited to dinner with Harriet's parents. I felt overawed by the grandeur of it all. After dinner, Aiden Crawley took me to one side and said, 'Why are you interviewing Barbara Castle? There's a much more interesting woman in Parliament you should invite.' I asked whom he meant. He replied, 'Margaret Thatcher.'

I was astonished, Mrs Thatcher at that time was comparatively unknown to the public, and seemed to me to be dull by comparison. I had met her once, she made a speech in which the words rattled along with a light, high, mechanical fluency, like a sewing machine. I told John Lloyd of Aiden Crawley's suggestion. He was bemused by it. As it was, Barbara was a wonderful guest, sharp, funny, and kind to me.

A poisonous attack on me had just appeared in

one of the periodicals. It was my first experience of being criticized not for what I did, but for what I was, my looks, my voice. The Masai in Kenya used to believe that the camera steals your soul, and would not allow tourists to photograph them. The venom in that review stole my confidence from me, even though my sister, Priscilla, explained, 'Because you appear on television, people think you are two-dimensional, that you have no blood'.

Barbara Castle had clearly read the review. She came into makeup, glanced at me, and said, 'Don't worry. That's the sort of attack politicians have to put up with all their professional lives. It'll be someone else in the firing line tomorrow'. I was touched.

The series ended. I went back, with relief, to *Braden's Week.* We decided to hold a press launch, always a dangerous decision. The press usually enjoy the food and drink, but ignore the press handout, which they rightly assume is just a blurb, and spend their time trying to find the story they suspect the BBC is trying to conceal.

In this case, a tall elderly *Telegraph* reporter was clearly startled to see me. He said, 'I thought you were working on *She and She*?' I explained that had just ended, and I was on the new series of *Braden's Week.* He took another drink and said, 'I saw the interview with Barbara Castle. I didn't like the question you asked about why she had no children.' I said that Barbara herself had not minded at all.

That weekend I opened the *Sunday Telegraph* to find a large story claiming that *She and She* had been axed. The BBC, it claimed, had taken the programme off the air after complaints from viewers about the insensitive questions to Barbara

Castle about her childlessness. As I was reading it the doorbell rang. My flatmate, Deirdre Macdonald, herself a journalist for the *Scottish Daily Express*, opened it to find a man who put his foot in the door and said, 'Good morning, I'm from the *Sun*. Can I speak to Esther Rantzen?'

I pulled a dressing-gown around me, asked him in, and made him a cup of coffee. I was wearing no make-up, and hoped my pallor would appeal to his compassionate side. Things started badly. 'I'm a heavy from the *Sun*,' he said grimly. He was extremely thin and delicate-looking, but I didn't dare contradict him. He asked me about the axing. I explained the series was due to run for six weeks, had run for six, the original press release had described it as six, I couldn't have made any more, because I was now making *Braden's Week*.

He said ferociously, 'What about all those complaints, then?' I said as far as I knew there had been no complaints, there was just one *Telegraph* writer who had said he had disliked the interview. The Heavy nodded, his tone changed. 'I thought it was odd, no mention of phone calls or letters of complaint. The reporter must just have been making lineage, a bit of extra cash selling a story to the weekend paper.' Then he said, 'Look, I believe you, but would you mind if I stay a bit longer? There's a car downstairs with its engine running, and if I go back to the office now, the Editor won't believe I've grilled you enough.'

I gave him another cup of coffee, then he left. Up to that point I had always believed that the broadsheet newspapers were to be trusted, but that the tabloids made things up. I found, not for the last time, that it ain't necessarily so.

Crucially, I had met a producer, Peter Chafer, who believed that a new consumer programme could be created in the wake of *Braden's Week*. Peter had worked in Current Affairs Group, then moved to the Religious Programmes Department. He and I made two documentaries together, one on Jehovah's Witnesses, one on the Mormons. Both had their dangerous moments.

Early on in our research about Witnesses, they had withdrawn all cooperation from us. Jehovah's Witnesses are incredibly tightly disciplined. The moment that decision was made, we knew we could no longer film any practising Witnesses, so we based our documentary on interviews with ex-members of the cult. From their testimony I came to the conclusion that they provided a community for the lonely, and an incredibly full and busy life spent studying, at meetings, and evangelizing on the doorstep.

They also demanded a real talent for belief from their followers. At the time we made our film, they thought the world was about to come to an end in 1984, a brief ten years ahead. When the heavens streamed with blood, as a Jew I would be doomed, so I had many phone calls from Witnesses who desperately tried to save and convert me. They didn't succeed, but they did teach me a valuable piece of information. If you want to get rid of a voluble Witness standing at your front door, tell him you have been 'disfellowshipped'. That's the equivalent of excommunication, and Witnesses are forbidden to speak to anyone who has been cast out of the cult, so they will turn and run.

For our film we realized that we had to show a religious service, but of course we couldn't film a real one. So we reconstructed a service (no hoaxes, we told our viewers exactly what we were doing, and why.) We used a congregation of ex-Witnesses to perform it. We even had an ex-minister to lead them. Everyone was on edge, the prayers and readings had worrying memories for many of our congregation.

The minister stood at a lectern in a BBC conference room. It was a sultry, breathless summer day, the sun was hot on the windows. Ken, a little, elderly cameraman, moved the minister a step backwards from the lectern, so that he could be seen. Then Ken walked back to his camera. As he did so, Eric, our equally elderly sound recordist, asked the minister to say a few words, shook his head, and went up to move him a step closer to the lectern, so that he could be heard.

Eric returned to his headphones. Meanwhile, Ken had just reached his camera, and was squinting down the lens. To his surprise, the minister was obscured by the lectern again. Ken muttered, got up, and moved the minister one step back so that he could be seen. By this time, Eric had adjusted his headphones, and asked the minister for a few more words. He couldn't hear him. Eric, tut-tutting with irritation, got up and moved the minister a step forward again.

All this was in front of a room full of entranced ex-Witnesses, their anxiety forgotten, watching Ken and Eric push the minister forwards and backwards. We hoped it would go on for some time longer, but, sadly, as Eric moved the minister forwards, Ken reached his camera and turned round just in time to see him.

It was very hot. Tempers were on a short leash.

Ken shouted something rude at Eric. Eric flung down his headphones and rolled up his sleeves. Ken advanced towards him. It was almost fisticuffs, until Peter slowly rose from his chair and said 'Gentlemen, please. Not in front of the customers'. To everyone's disappointment, Eric and Ken found a compromise position for the minister, and the service began.

The film was a success, so Peter and I were asked to make another about the Mormons. I was fascinated by this New World version of Christianity. Joseph Smith, the founder, was lynched by a furious mob who disapproved of his doctrine of polygamy. To his disciples, Smith's death guaranteed him immortality. His successor, Brigham Young, led the Mormons to their eventual home in Salt Lake City, Utah, and we followed in their footsteps.

Although officially polygamy was no longer part of the doctrine, we were told that there were still Mormons who practised it. Peter and I were given an address of one polygamous Mormon in the hills outside the city, but when we drove there, as we got out of the car we heard a bullet whistle over our heads. Not being war correspondents, we got straight back into the car and drove to our hotel. There I had a message, to meet Brother John in the local library.

I sat at a table, and round the bookshelves came a very large man. John was six-foot-six tall, dressed in cowboy gear, with a stetson and a bootlace tie fastened with an ornate silver brooch. He had a big handsome rosy face, and he called me 'Little lady'. I blushed and fluttered, and we were invited back to his home, where he said one or two of his own little ladies would be waiting to be filmed.

We arrived, and walked into a sitting-room, filled with wives. One of them, a slender woman with dark hair and eyes, introduced herself to me, 'I'm Sister Susan, John's first wife'. I smiled, and shook hands. She led me round to shake hands with the others. 'This is Sister Anne, wife number two. Sister Joanie, wife number three. Sister Glenda, wife number four. Sister Margie, wife number five'.

We reached a middle-aged lady. I held out my hand. The woman didn't take it. 'I'm Margie's mother, and I don't like any of it.' She was mother-in-law number five, had just arrived unexpectedly, for tea, and discovered four other wives she had known nothing about. She left, outraged.

I interviewed the five wives, and they explained to me the advantages of their way of life, how they took the chores in turn, the housework, the cooking, the gardening. Sister Susan invited me on a tour of the house. Each bedroom had a double bed, and a different wedding photograph on the bedside table; different brides, that is, same old bridegroom, smiling broadly.

Brother John had a gym in the basement full of keep-fit equipment. I could see why. We ended up in the kitchen, where Susan made me a cup of tea. Peter was in the sitting-room, talking to Brother John, man to man. Susan and I were alone together. She fixed me with her intense dark eyes. 'Sister Esther. Have you ever wondered why God has sent you here to us? Why God has kept you in your unmarried state to this day?' She gazed at me deeply, hypnotically. I suddenly realized that she was John's recruiting officer. I got up quickly.

'Thank you so much for the tea,' I said.

Scrambling my handbag and my notes together, I blundered like a panicking carthorse into the sitting-room and said to Peter, 'I had no idea of the time, Peter, I've made another appointment for us in town, I think we'd better leave'.

Peter was surprised by my urgency, but I was on my way to the car. Brother John shook me warmly, too warmly, by the hand, I waved to the little ladies, and we drove away.

'What's the hurry?' said Peter.

'One minute longer and I would have been wife number six,' I said. 'And my mother wouldn't like any of it either.'

That film turned out well, too, and Peter began to talk to me about another project. Perhaps together we could create a successor to *Braden's Week*? Like me, he had worked for Ned Sherrin on satire shows, and loved the razor edge of creating a programme whose humour was based on real life. By this time Paul Fox had been replaced by Alasdair Milne as Controller of BBC1, and Alasdair agreed to commission a very short series from Desmond's department, six weekly programmes, to be transmitted in the height of the summer, when nobody watches.

It was a kindly decision. At least then we could fail quietly, when not too many viewers would witness our humiliation. I often wonder how I would have felt if I had known that those six weeks would turn into twenty-one years, and become not so much a programme, more a lifetime's vocation?

CHAPTER NINE

THAT'S LIFE!

I have dared to call *That's Life!* a vocation. How offensive that must seem to those who have sacrificed their lives to a great calling, the teachers who work in sink schools, doctors who save lives, social workers who protect the vulnerable, nuns who tend the dying. Meanwhile I, a television 'fat cat', have been primped and cosseted, dressed and made-up by experts, have been paid hundreds of thousands of pounds, have been sent round the world to meet the most fascinating people—how dare I dignify my self-indulgence with a word like 'vocation'?

The truth is (and my agent fought and screamed at me for twenty-one years to prevent me sharing this secret with the BBC), I would have paid them to allow me to work on *That's Life!*.

At one time I was offered one million pounds by ITV to leave *That's Life!* and work for them. Turning down a million pounds is a unique experience. In case you are ever tempted to make the same decision, I should warn you that the immediate sensation after you've done it is to kick yourself. I remember putting the phone down and saying to myself, 'What an idiot you are, Rantzen'.

The offer had been to present the nightly news magazine programme in London. Jeremy Isaacs was running Thames Television. I liked and respected him, knew the programme would be excellent, but it was not *That's Life!*. I can't pretend to you that the money wasn't tempting.

In retrospect I should have asked ITV to send the money round with a couple of security guards. I would have put all those bank notes on the shelf in my larder, made myself a cheese sandwich, sat on the wooden kitchen chair and counted it, like Scrooge. I've never seen one million pounds in one place. Then the next morning I would have asked the security guards to take it back to Jeremy, and would have signed on for another series of *That's Life!*. Do you see what I mean about a vocation?

Some years after that offer, my agent rang me at our country cottage and said, 'How would you like to be the Controller of BBC1?' I assumed he was joking. He wasn't. Bill Cotton, then Managing Director of BBC Television, had put my name forward as his preferred candidate. I talked it over with Desmond. He pointed out that ChildLine, the children's charity I helped to found, needed my constant input, and that as Controller I would have very little time to devote to it. He also pointed out that *That's Life!* was riding high in the charts, and I still loved working on it.

I went to see Bill. John Birt had just hit the BBC with the force of a combine harvester, and Bill loathed what he was doing to creative people. Michael Grade, who I believe has a unique gift for spotting talent and commissioning good programmes, was Director of Programmes, and he disliked Birt viscerally.

With all the possibilities whirling in my head, I waited in the Reception of Television Centre. I had not made up my mind. I had two letters in my handbag. One thanked Bill and accepted. The other also thanked him, but refused. His office

253

rang down for me. I rode up in the lift to the sixth floor, still undecided. As I sat down in the chair, I reached into my bag and pulled out the refusal.

Was it ChildLine that pulled my heart away from this unique challenge, of becoming the first woman Controller, of running the most important television channel in the world? Or was it *That's Life!*? Was it fear that I would be such a high-profile appointment that the vultures would circle me ready to pick out my eyes at the first misjudgement? Or was it the knowledge that life at the top of the BBC's pyramid in its state of civil war would be unpleasant and destructive? I suppose all these played their part, but I also know that if I had not been working on *That's Life!*, I would have accepted the job with alacrity. I was wedded, body and soul, to my extraordinary mongrel of a show.

Some critics will find that a peculiar admission. They have labelled it 'the programme with talking dogs and rude vegetables'. But then they called me 'toothy Esther Rantzen' long after my teeth retreated and became civilized. As I sift through the files of stories we covered on *That's Life!*, I find a unique catalogue of life in Britain during two decades—the funny, the tragic, the wicked, the ridiculous. It was a celebration, week by week, of so many different aspects of our viewers' lives. Health issues, safety issues, what went on in prisons, in psychiatric hospitals, in local councils, in schools. The con-men, the altruists, the eccentrics, the 'jobsworth' officials, the sinners and saints.

We took on the medical profession, the legal profession, the trades unions, even the BBC itself, on behalf of our viewers. We worked incredibly long hours, six or seven days a week, and the reward was that forty-minute romp on Sunday nights was watched by up to twenty-two million viewers. At one stage we were the most popular show on British television, we were the most watched consumer programme in the world. Yet we did it without putting live sex on the stage, or giving a million pounds away in vision. And, although we were sharp, we were never cruel.

If you hated the programme, you will think my assessment deranged. But I loved it, and I believe nothing has replaced the work it did, or has come near the achievements of the programme over the years.

Not that many people would have spotted our potential from our first show in 1973. Peter Chafer, the Editor, and I had worked out a number of different consumer items. I came up with the title. For me, it expressed that moment when everything goes wrong, and all you can do is giggle, shrug, and say 'That's life!'. (It also became a rod for my back. When I ran out of petrol, and tried to pour a few drops from a can into my tank, as each car pulled out and passed me, the driver rolled down his window and shouted, 'Ah well, Esther, that's life!'. So they did when I tripped on a paving stone, or my umbrella turned inside out. Each person thought he was the first and only one to shout it at me, so I had to smile, and nod, and keep my two-fingered wave firmly in my pocket.)

Peter incorporated into our mix of consumer stories many of the elements in Ned Sherrin's satire shows, notably the musical stings, produced live by Dave Lee's band. Dave himself wrote our signature tune, which has proved a nice little earner for him

255

over the years. In our first series it was sung, by Hyacinth Bucket, actress Patricia Routledge. It makes odd hearing now, with lyrics by Herbert Kretzmer, who wrote the words for *Les Misérables.* That was a masterpiece. I'm not sure our signature tune was. For the second series we dumped the words, and Tony Kinsey, our musical director, arranged it for a brass band. The presentation team was not a great success, either, for that first series.

I was alongside actor George Layton, from *Doctor in the House*, and Bob Wellings from *Nationwide.* Bob was charming, affable, and hated the studio audience. Viewers who knew and loved him from his work on *Nationwide* were uneasy to see him in this new format. George was a very gifted actor, viewers had also enjoyed his work in situation comedy, what was he doing in consumer journalism?

All the same, the show had energy, and some original ideas. The 'Heap of the Week', for instance, was a film in which each week we found a machine that drove its owner mad and we invented an elaborate and spectacular end for it. On our first programme a champion explosive expert, 'Blaster' Bates, blew up a broken freezer belonging to comedian Colin Crompton.

Our audiences grew, little by little, and the letters arrived by the sackful asking for help and offering ideas. Alasdair Milne extended our run, from six to ten programmes, and told Desmond he would recommission the series. Bless him for seeing some promise in our unprepossessing baby.

However, Alasdair made the condition that we must change our presentation team. The three of

256

us looked so uneasy together. Everyone agreed with him. I went to Peter Chafer with two proposals. First, that I should be made Producer, working to him as Editor. Second, that we should return to the John Lloyd format that we had tried and tested on *Braden's Week*, using two unknown reporters alongside me, who would be dedicated to us.

Was this naked ambition, so that I could dominate the screen? I would prefer to think it was clothed ambition. The truth was that I was the only member of the production team who had any experience of consumer journalism, and I knew from my four years on *Braden's Week* that it is very difficult.

John Lloyd could have produced the series, but he said he didn't want to spend his week with us in the office. He only wanted to write the show. By this time he was spreading his wings as a freelance, trying his hand as a drama and comedy writer as well. Peter Chafer himself had never worked on a consumer show before, and was sometimes at a loss to know how to brief a researcher on a particular story. I was being called upon to make a producer's decisions, without having the authority to do so. When Alasdair heard of my request, he called me into his office, and asked me to justify it. It was tough, like being hauled in to explain myself to the headmaster.

'Why should I allow you to produce this show?' he snapped at me, sharply.

Even though I would not be the senior member of the team, Peter Chafer was my boss as Editor, it was a blasphemy at the BBC to allow the presenter a role as producer. I cleared my throat nervously,

257

and tried to explain what I had learned from Bernie's experience.

'Presenting a consumer programme is a unique role. You are asking viewers to trust you. You become the face of the production team on the show, and off it. You are asked to speak to professional bodies, and justify any criticism you make on the programme. When Bernie made his commercials for Stork Margarine, the BBC was furious because they felt he carried the authority of the show. Why not make me the producer in vision? Then when I introduce an item, or give the viewers advice at the end, I can do so with the genuine voice of the programme. And let's do the same for the reporters. Give them jobs as researchers. Ask them to come into the office every day as members of the team. Let's do away with the 'us' and 'them' of presenters and production team. Let's all work alongside each other. That's how I learned my craft on *Braden's Week*, and that was why I could deliver the research on the screen with conviction.'

I knew I was on trial. My instinct was that this was a very important moment. If Alasdair had turned me down, I would have had to choose between being a presenter and a producer. He looked at me. Alasdair is a Wykehamist, and a Scottish puritan, a combination of steel and granite. But his sharp manner disguises a kind heart. He knew I had served my apprenticeship behind the cameras as well as in front, he agreed to let me try and combine the roles.

I had a second challenge—to convince Peter that we should repeat the experiment that had worked so well on *Braden's Week*, and find completely unknown reporters who would be ours and ours alone. No memories of other programmes and different contexts. It was a risk, but if it had worked once it could work again. We decided to hold auditions.

I rang my Oxford friend, Glyn Worsnip. He had been brilliant in undergraduate revues, he could sing, could imitate any kind of voice or accent, had lean, dark, good looks, and a sharp wit. But he was dedicated to becoming an actor, and when I rang he was working with a stage production of *The Canterbury Tales*. Diffidently I asked if he would be prepared to do an audition for us, to see if he liked the material. He agreed, without much enthusiasm, really as a favour to me. From the moment he sat at a desk in the studio it was clear the cameras liked him. So did the production team. We invited him to join us, he agreed. I was thrilled.

The second reporter was a surprise. Kieran Prendiville had joined the team as a researcher from the Oldham News Agency. He was an excellent journalist, with a dry sense of humour. But I had never thought of him as a performer. John Lloyd told me Kieran wanted to audition. I was incredulous. But audition he did, and he, too, was instantly successful in front of the cameras. He had instinctive timing, and was the perfect foil for Glyn. We had our two reporters.

*   *   *

We had decided to adapt John Lloyd's format for *Braden's Week*, except that we made the crucial change Bernie had refused, turning the reporters to camera. We also decided to use newspaper

259

misprints as punctuation. Nowadays those wonderful mistakes are all too rare—modern technology seems to have eradicated most of them. Then there seemed to be an endless supply, sent to us by our dedicated viewers. 'Thought for the Day: I will lift up mine eyes, for in thee we thrust'—you know the kind of thing.

On *Braden's Week* the misprints had been read by a radio announcer, Ronald Fletcher. His urbane manner, white hair, impeccable dinner jacket, gave the daftness an extra flavour. On *That's Life!* we hired Cyril Fletcher. Not, as Paul Fox mischievously claimed, because the BBC booker had called the wrong Fletcher. But because I had met him on the Radio 4 programme, *Start the Week With Richard Baker.*

My father had always adored Cyril's humour. His deep musical voice was perfect for the Odd Odes he recited. 'Pin back your lugholes. Odd Ode number one coming up', he would announce, and my father would settle back with delight. So I was intrigued when Cyril arrived very early one Monday morning in the radio studio to talk about his pantomimes. We chatted together after the programme, then I raced back to the office and ran into Peter's office. He, too, was a fan of Cyril's. I made some phone calls, Peter met Cyril and he was booked.

How simple that sounds. In fact, it was a fluke, a lucky break for us and for Cyril, because we worked for Desmond, in a factual department. If our programme had come out of Tom Sloane's entertainment empire, I would have known that the official view was that Cyril was washed-up, burnt out, past his sell-by date. The entertainment bosses neither knew nor cared that Cyril was still successfully touring the country performing his one-man show. Occasionally, fans like my father would say wistfully, 'I wonder what happened to Cyril Fletcher?'

What happened to Cyril was that he went out of style with the handful of bosses who guard the threshold to television studios. It's not a conspiracy, although it can seem like one to the performer on the receiving end. It's simply that at meetings and away-days the bosses chat together, and reputations are made, or broken. It's irrational, and subjective, but give them the name of any performer and they will tell you at once if he's in or out. There are usually a dozen names at any one time who are in. The rest are out.

But at least in those dear dead days in 1973, producers who had a broader agenda, and a more flexible approach, could choose who took part in their programmes. Now the controllers demand to know who they are, and veto everyone who appears.

Fortunately, none of the bosses questioned our choice of presenters, and not knowing that Cyril was officially out, we brought him in. He was a great asset to the show, not least because he brought with him the affection of the older generation of viewers. He stayed with the series for eight years, and over those years Cyril and Betty also became much prized personal friends.

Betty Astell is a remarkable woman. She is a celebrated beauty, was a film star before the war, and when she met Cyril it was love almost at first sight, and they have remained friends, lovers, partners. Cyril invited Desmond and me to their house in East Sussex. It was a perfect neo-Georgian manor, set in a wonderful garden. From the rose garden you looked out over a field of buttercups, which Cyril allowed a local farmer to cut as hay on condition he never used a chemical, herbicide, pesticide or fertilizer on it.

I must have a mind like a magpie, because now from our rose garden at our cottage, we too look over a field of buttercups grazed by the local cows, on condition no chemical is ever used on it. Cyril taught me to judge a rose by its fragrance, which he said was 'the soul of a rose'. He told me of Sissinghurst, with its white garden, a heavy white Louis Philippe rambler rose hanging in clusters in the apple trees. In our garden, Louis Philippe has turned our apple tree into a thick crown of white petals.

Betty is not only an actress, a writer and a director, she is an inspired cook and a considerable interior decorator. She and Cyril gave Desmond and me an invaluable piece of advice. They said if ever you have a lovely day together, buy something, a trinket, a tiny ornament, it needn't be expensive. Then each time you look at it, the memory of that day will fill your mind. I have a mirror that Desmond and I bought on our honeymoon in Henley, little glass grapes we bought in Venice, an ornamental box from the Taj Mahal, a china cherub from Windsor, and each one evokes memories of wonderful days spent together.

Cyril had a secret, and I hope it is not disloyal of me to reveal it now. He called it 'Flatley', and it arrived with him every Sunday, carried reverently in its own cardboard box. It was a little black toupee, and it was glued on for every performance.

Why, I was never sure. Without it, Cyril looked exactly the same, to my eyes. Perhaps it was a talisman.

It came into its own on the night of the ten dogs in the studio. A viewer had rung to complain about pellets called 'Scentoff', which were supposed to prevent dogs from dropping 'messages' on the lawn. Our viewer found that for her dog they acted in reverse, as a magnet.

Clearly, we needed a scientific test. I suggested we should invite ten dogs into the studio to see if the pellets attracted or repelled them. My boss Peter Chafer was scathing, 'You're just finding an excuse to get ten dogs into the studio, Esther'. I pleaded guilty. God smiled—occasionally He does demonstrate an engaging sense of humour. In this case, He prompted Desmond to say after rehearsal, when our Floor Manager had insisted all the dogs were to be kept on leads for safety reasons, 'That's not a fair test. The dogs have to be taken off their leads so that we can tell which way they want to go'.

I looked nervously at the Floor Manager. However, faced with an adamant Head of Department, he didn't argue. God seized the opportunity, and as the red light went on, one little bitch came into season. On the command, 'Unleash', the most glorious chaos ensued. Five dogs pursued the bitch, she fled into the audience, they roared with delight, the soundtrack of the programme is like a storm at sea. The other five leaped around the stage.

An enormous Airedale bounded up to Cyril. He cowered back in his chair, one hand protectively over his head. The Airedale galloped back towards me.

As I gazed about at the mayhem, a scene-boy hissed from behind one of the pieces of scenery, 'Look there, Esther'. The Airedale had one leg cocked over our potted palm, and a huge lake was spreading around it. The cameras focused on it, and yet another gale of laughter went up from the audience. I managed to shout at Cyril, 'And finally, Cyril?'. He took the cue. 'And finally, Esther, we've been sent a letter from the Post Office apologizing for a missing parcel. The letter actually read, "pissing parcel".' The perfect last joke. I took my chance. 'Well, I'm afraid there have been quite a few dogs missing all over this studio. Sorry about that—goodnight.'

I wasn't sorry at all. Word of mouth spread through the nation, and the next week we had our highest audience ever, twenty-two-and-a-half-million viewers, all of them turning on to see what the dogs would do next. Alas, all we had to show the viewers was a dead potted palm, unable to withstand being watered by an Airedale.

After the show, Desmond had to defend the dog riot from our irate bosses who said he should have done something to restrain them. 'Like what?' he asked plaintively. 'Are you saying I should have run after the Airedale with a cork?'

One of them also wondered why Cyril had cowered back in his chair, with one hand over his head. The answer, of course, which Desmond did not reveal, was that Cyril was protecting Flatley.

Cyril was a great support to me. His judgement on the scripts was good, I found his company delightful, and so did our viewers. So, in 1982, I was upset to be summoned to see Alan Hart, then the Controller of BBC1, to be told that Cyril would

264

have to go. I argued. It was no good. Alan gently pointed out to me that he was in charge of the channel, and his mind was made up. The story leaked to the press, and something in one of the stories convinced Cyril that I had been responsible for the decision, or had failed to fight it adequately. I tried to tell him the truth, that I had fought until Alan Hart made it clear to me that my arguments were pointless—he had made the decision and I would have to live with it. Cyril moved to Guernsey, and I saw less and less of him.

Some years after Cyril left, the time came for his eightieth birthday. Obviously we wanted to celebrate it. I plotted with our film director, trying to find a way of presenting Cyril with a surprise birthday cake. I needed a disguise, but my teeth are always the give-away. What about a bee-keeper costume, a big straw hat with veils all over my face? At the time there was a very nasty plague infesting bee-hives, it had originated in Austria. The director suggested I should become an Austrian bee-keeper, and by the strange rules of *That's Life!* that seemed logical enough.

Our film director was Mike Porecki. Mike used to be an assistant film editor, brilliant pictorially, but almost too enthusiastic. He used to shoot many rolls of film before he was satisfied. I am sure he has learned caution and economy since, but I used to plead with him in the cutting room, 'Please Mike, ask yourself, why am I shooting this?' Mike rang Cyril and explained that he was making a pilot gardening programme and wanted to star Cyril in his Guernsey garden, with an Austrian bee-keeper talking about the new bee plague. Cyril agreed.

I scripted the rest of *That's Life!*, then flew to

Guernsey by a late afternoon plane, ready to film the next day. I was greeted with a message to ring the office. The lawyers had pulled one of our main stories, would I please write another to replace it. We had known that would be a possibility. I had all the research in my suitcase. I sat up with a typewriter, clacking away until four in the morning, then fell exhausted into bed.

The arrangement was that Mike would ring me to talk about the shoot at about midday, a hairdresser would come to put rollers in my hair, and I would join them on location in Cyril's garden at two. Knowing how late I had been working, Mike decided not to ring me. He was happy enough, filming flower after flower in Cyril's beds. Cyril thought he was mad—Mike couldn't tell a rose from a nasturtium, but insisted on filming every blooming thing. Petals against the sunshine, raindrops on the sepals, butterflies on the bough, Mike shot them all.

Back at the hotel, the hairdresser arrived outside my bedroom door, knocked timidly, I snored on, and he left. At last, at two, the phone rang by my bed. It was the production assistant. I sat bolt upright, 'What time is it?' He told me. I leaped from the bed and into my clothes, with a raging headache. He arrived at my door with a plate of smoked salmon sandwiches in one hand, and a box of heated rollers in the other. I stuffed the sandwiches in my mouth, complete with parsley and black olives, stuck a roller in my fringe, and climbed into the bee-keeper dungarees.

If we didn't start filming immediately, we'd never make the plane home, and Cyril's birthday wouldn't make the show. As we ran to the car, I was still knotting the veils round my head. We reached the corner of Cyril's road, then rang Mike, as we had arranged, to say we were in position. Mike's voice was dreamy. He was in a flower-induced trance. 'We've only got three or four more set-ups to do,' he said, 'we'll be ready in twenty minutes.'

'Ready or not, Mike,' I said, my rage only slightly muffled by yards of netting, 'I'm coming in. If we don't shoot this film now, we'll miss the plane.'

'But I'm getting some beautiful shots.'

'Can I remind you, Mike, that the roses are only being filmed to convince Cyril it's a gardening programme. We are not really going to show them. Please, *please* ask yourself, *why* am I filming this?'

I put down the phone, climbed out of the car, and, in my white welly boots, stamped into the garden. Cyril was there in his gardening hat. Betty was fluttering round the edge of the lawn. I shook hands with Cyril and said, 'Gut Afternoon' in what I hoped was an Austrian accent. I then retired behind a shrub. Cyril began making a camera statement.

As Mike and I had planned, each time Cyril started, I came out from behind my shrub with a question. The first time he was interrupted, Cyril was amused. The second time, he was less amused. The third time, he expostulated. The fourth time, I found my wrist gripped in iron fingers. Betty had arrived my side of the shrub and was holding me down.

'Betty,' I whispered urgently through yards of veiling, 'it's me, Esther. We're doing this to surprise Cyril.'

She recognized me, and dropped my hand. As I

267

emerged from the shrub, so did she, with a dancing movement that sent her gliding towards Cyril. When she got near enough she hissed at him, 'Cyril, stay calm, it's Esther Rantzen'. Cyril didn't hear a word. I thought the time had come for the denouement. As he was beginning yet another camera statement, I unwound the netting, took my hat off, and wished him a very happy birthday. The crew brought on a sumptuous birthday cake, champagne popped, Cyril made a sweet speech, I paid tribute to him, and the filming ended.

We caught the plane back to London—just—Mike cut the film, and we sat together to watch it. To my surprise the whole denouement was in a very wide shot, no close-up of me emerging from the veils, no close-up of my tribute to Cyril. I asked Mike why. He pulled out the close-ups and we watched them together. As I smiled affectionately at Cyril, an enormous black olive skin from my sandwich lunch worked its way over my right front tooth and stayed there. I looked like the Witch of Endor. It clung there throughout my charming speech to Cyril.

I looked at Mike. I didn't need to ask why he had failed to warn me, why he didn't tell me to remove the black olive. It was his revenge for my foul temper. That was a lesson learned. Never have fisticuffs with a film director. For once Mike had known exactly why he was filming me, with one black tooth. I was lucky he didn't send it as an out-take to one of Denis Norden's blooper shows.

*   *   *

We quickly established the elements of *That's Life!*.

First of all, the *vox pop*. [From the Latin *vox populi*—the voice of the people.] Every week I would go out on to the streets with a film crew, asking questions, offering passers-by the opportunity to sing, dance, wiggle an unusual muscle, or taste some disgusting piece of food. That provided us with a light start to the show, and established very firmly that ours was a programme in which ordinary people were the stars. At the heart of the programme were our investigations into faulty products, or dishonest contracts, exposing con-men and poor service. We would lift the mood with a song by Victoria Wood, or Jake Thackray, or Richard Stilgoe, and would end, as we had begun, with a light film, the portrait of a memorable character, or a talented pet, to send our viewers happily to bed.

For the first few years we transmitted very late indeed on Saturday nights. Then in 1976, not for the first time, I was summoned to see the Controller of BBC1. By now, Bryan Cowgill had the job. Bryan had been a notoriously tough Head of Sport, and was a very successful Controller, competitive, and determined to win against ITV. I went to see him with my Editor, John Morrell.

Bryan frightened us both by saying, 'How would you like to move to Sunday night?'

As a Jew, I was nervous. 'We are quite a rude programme. Isn't Sunday a religious night?'

Bryan was clearly startled by my transformation into an Archbishop and replied,

'Mornings are for religion. I intend to run you after the nine o'clock watershed.'

That sounded fine to me. And it appeared to be fine for our viewers, too. Over the weeks our audiences built, until a journalist rang and said, 'How does it feel to be in the top ten, Esther?'

I was astonished. 'Are we?'

We were. Bryan was jubilant, and protected us from the worst ITV could throw against us. When they scheduled James Bond on Sunday nights, he started us one minute after it ended. Our audiences continued to climb.

Then tragedy struck us. By this time I had been moved from Desmond's department to Current Affairs Group which had provided us with a number of different Editors, Michael Bunce, for example, and George Carey. Good as they all were, the programme was built week by week by two of us, John Lloyd, who wrote it, with me as producer. I told John I regarded him as my guardian angel. Suddenly he became ill. He was always a tiny, fragile man. One day he arrived in our office, sat at the typewriter to read the research, then doubled over with pain.

I rang the BBC nurse, and took him to the 'San', a small, dark room. He sat on the bed. The door burst open, an Australian nurse fell through it, clutching an oxygen tank. She stared at John, obviously expecting him to have passed out on the floor. She was so ferocious he jumped to his feet, stammering that he was sorry she'd been troubled, and that he was quite all right. She told him to go home straight away, and said she would order him a taxi. John lived alone. He let himself into his flat, then collapsed on the bed.

Our film director, Pat Houlihan, a close friend, offered to go to his home with a bowl of soup. I said that would be an excellent idea. She couldn't rouse him to let her in. In the end she managed to break in and found him, clearly gravely ill.

Meanwhile, I was struggling with the script. John was a magician. Over the years I had watched him spinning lumps of research into a beautiful strand of script—now, somehow, I had to do the same. Reception rang, a journalist from Nigel Dempster's gossip column had arrived to ask me questions about my relationship with Desmond. I was unruffled. I knew I had such a difficult job ahead of me, writing a complete forty-minute script, that I would outlast the most determined Fleet Street newshound. I did. I was there until two in the morning, our devoted team alongside me. I wrote the programme not because I wanted to, but because I had to, otherwise there would have been a forty-minute hole in the schedule of BBC1.

The next week I visited John every day. His flat was bare, cold and inhospitable. Desmond lent him a comfortable chair, and a thick, soft rug to wrap around him. He seemed to rally. The X-rays revealed an ulcer. We thought that must have been the problem. For the next couple of weeks I continued to write the scripts, John watched them broadcast and advised me on each one. That item was too long. That dialogue should have been kept to two voices, not three. I was grateful, but I longed for him to get well and come back.

One blessed Thursday he did. I saw his legs draped over the typewriter as I walked up the stairs to his office, and sighed with relief. Next day I watched him from my window as he walked across the yard at the back of our office. Every step he took was an effort of will, his body was being propelled by courage and spirit alone. My optimism faltered.

Before long, he was in hospital. I went to see Brian Wenham, the Head of Current Affairs Group, and told him how desperately worried I was. I asked him to send a message to Alasdair Milne, an old friend of John's. 'Please tell Alasdair to visit John soon—he may not have much time.'

Alasdair came to dinner with Desmond and me a few days later. 'I hear you're being dramatic about John's illness,' he said.

I was hurt and embarrassed. 'Am I?' I said, hoping he was right.

I rang the BBC doctor, who had seen John. 'Is everything being done for John?' I asked.

The doctor was reassuring. 'Yes, it's just that John himself is convinced he has cancer.'

I was appalled, John had never said so to me. But he was right, as people so often are. It was cancer of the pancreas. Ten days after he was admitted to hospital, John died, aged thirty-six.

I went to see him before he died, his humour was constant, his spirit indomitable. He explained to me that the X-ray had only revealed the ulcer.

I said, 'So it hid the . . .' My voice trailed away.

'Yes,' said John. 'There was no sign of it.'

We were both talking about a tumour, but he refused to put it into words, and so did I.

John Pitman and I produced a tribute to Lloyd, performed in the theatre of the British Academy of Film and Television Arts. We showed clips from the programme he had created. I felt robbed by his death. I wish I could believe in heaven, and that John Lloyd is there, turning out scripts to amuse the angels, I suppose now his legs would be draped over a state-of-the-art word-processor. But I can't make that leap of faith.

All the same, for weeks after John died, he, my guardian angel, continued to look after me. I would sit at his typewriter with sheaves of research next to me, and implore him, 'Come on John, I need your help'. And as I rolled the first piece of paper in, I would hear his voice in my head, dictating the opening lines. Dear John, I miss his wit, his humanity, that naughty gleam in his eyes still.

*   *   *

It was through John's perception and instinct for character, that Annie Mizen became a national icon. One cold winter morning I had been sent to film our *vox pop*, in the market in the North End Road, Fulham. It was a dreary day, drizzling, and we had a grumpy crew. The cameraman wanted to be back in his office, warming his feet by the fire. In those bad old pre-Birt days he was paid just as much as a stand-by cameraman as he was for lugging his heavy camera round the streets in the rain. 'Anyway, you're just making fools of people,' he said, sullenly.

Shivering, I got out of the van and filled half-a-dozen glasses—three with cider, three with champagne. Our task that morning was to discover if people could tell the difference. After about five minutes, a little old lady bustled up. She was wearing a brown felt hat, and her glasses gleamed with anticipation. She didn't notice the camera. She told me later that when she saw the crowd she thought there was a fight, and she wanted to get to the front to see who was doing what to whom. As it was, she found me, with a tray of full glasses.

I handed her one: 'Would you like to try this,

273

madam?'

She took it: 'I don't drink, mind', she said. 'Only Freeman's.' She took a deep gulp, then drained the glass.

I asked, 'Do you know what that was, madam?'

She looked at me enquiringly.

'That was champagne,' I said.

A huge smile spread over her face, and in the middle of that grey, drizzly street it was as if the sun had come out, she was so thrilled.

'Champagne!' she exclaimed. I can hear the joy in her voice now. 'Champagne! I haven't had that for years!'

'Have another,' I said.

She took it and drained it.

'That was good.'

'Have another,' I said.

She shook her head. Her cheeks were rosy, her eyes bright. 'No thank you. I don't drink, only Freeman's.'

We finished filming and drove back to the office. We cut the film, and our audience laughed at Annie's infectious delight in the champagne.

When I went out again the following week, the same day, at the same time, I decided to go back to the North End Road. Sure enough, the same little old lady in the brown hat arrived. She suffered from painful arthritis in her hands, and had a weekly appointment at the local hospital. The street market was on her route. This time I was handing out caviare.

'What's that?' she asked as I handed it to her. 'Mouse's droppings?' She took a large bite. 'It doesn't taste like it, not that I've eaten mouse's droppings.'

I came back to the office, and before I viewed the film with the editor, I asked John Lloyd's advice. 'I've met the same little old lady,' I told him.

A standard Current Affairs producer would have cut her out, rather than show her again. John said, 'If she's as good as you say, run her for what she's worth.'

So I did. Once again, she gave the best interview of all.

In our next film, we tried to discover whether the public could tell the difference between whisky and brandy. I thought we might as well take our film crew back to the North End Road, same day of the week, same time. Along came Annie, still protesting that she didn't drink, only Freeman's, still downing it by the glass.

'Whisky makes you frisky,' she sang to me, and got thoroughly mixed up as I tried to explain to her which was which.

Each time I explained it, of course, I had to give her another swig to make sure she got them the right way round. Heaven knows what the hospital thought when she arrived there eventually for her treatment, flushed and singing. This time when our studio audience saw her on the screen there was a rustle of recognition, Annie was becoming a star.

She was eighty-four when I first met her, she died at ninety-two. By the time she had appeared a dozen times on our show she had become a national institution, signing autographs and opening fêtes. On the day of our last recording, Norma Shepherd went to pick her up in a taxi, telling her Esther wanted her to come for a drink. Annie was dressed in her Sunday best, but Norma persuaded her to put on the brown hat and coat she had worn in every programme.

At the end of the programme, Norma brought her down from the Hospitality Room to the wings of the stage. We were recording in the Television Theatre, once the famous music hall, the Shepherd's Bush Empire. As I finished the previous item, Norma pointed me out to Annie, 'Esther's over there, Annie, go and meet her'. Annie walked on to the stage, and saw the audience for the first time. They recognized her at once and roared a welcome. She sat down in a chair beside me, and we watched a selection of interviews she'd given us over the past twenty-six weeks. The team drank her health, the show ended. But Annie stayed on the stage, and kept our audience entranced for another forty minutes with her jokes and her stories.

It is a truth widely disregarded by those who make programmes that the very young and the very old have a dangerous charm about them which enables them to steal any show. The very young are dangerous because they are so unpredictable. I remember once interviewing a child on *Children of Courage* who instead of answering my question said to me, 'You've got a big lump of spinach stuck in your teeth'. What could I do, except ask her to remove it, which she did, with her fingernail.

The old are dangerous because they don't care any more what anyone thinks of them. Once I took some stewed octopus tentacles out on the street. An old lady took one look at them and said, 'That looks just like my old man's doo-dahs'.

As I said at the time, he should be easy to recognize.

But Annie became a star not simply because of her great age. Whatever 'character' means, Annie had it by the lorry-load. She told me her teachers thought she was clever at school, and wanted her to stay on. But she had to leave at fourteen and earn a living, which she did, as a cleaning lady, all her life. I thought it was a wicked waste of her sharp intelligence. But she was completely uncomplaining. Having enjoyed her career as a cleaner, she enjoyed her new career as a television personality even more. Her greatest pride was that she had cleaned the studios of Madame Vacani, who taught the royal children how to dance.

I met Annie's daughter, who became the schoolteacher Annie herself might have been. Years later her grandson Toby came to work on our production team. Annie carried his picture with her everywhere, and used to show it to me when we met in the street.

I am only sorry we met so late in her life. Age certainly didn't wither her, nor stale the infinite variety of her wit, but it eroded her hip joints, and one day she was found in her flat, having fallen and lain with a broken hip for sixteen hours in the hallway before anyone found her.

The hospital patched her up and sent her home, but she fell again.

One of our viewers owned an old people's home by the sea, he offered her a place there. Desmond and I went to visit her. She was pleased to see us, but she had lost the sparkle in her eyes, her sharpness. As we left, we turned to wave. She was at a window high above us, waving back from behind bars. She looked like a prisoner. I sensed I would never see her again. I never did. But wherever I go people still ask me about 'that wonderful old lady on your programme, Annie'.

*   *   *

I spent twenty-five years on the streets, filming interviews for *Braden's Week* and *That's Life!*. In spite of the fact that I always asked strangers cheeky questions, standing much too close to them, in all that time I was only physically attacked twice. Once in the seventies, by a junkie on the King's Road; the second time by a parking warden.

A judge had said, as judges do, that in his experience parking wardens are incredibly old and ugly. John Lloyd sent me out to find out if that was true. Sadly, it was. I rang in a panic after an hour, 'Help, John,' I said. 'Every time I find a parking warden, she is always middle-aged, grumpy, and in a horrible uniform with an extremely nasty hat. It's not funny to tell an ugly old lady she's ugly and old. It's cruel.'

We discussed the dilemma, and John suggested that I should reverse the question and try to make a commercial advertising the beauty and sweetness of parking wardens. So off I went again, this time asking them about their favourite poems, and flowers and songs. I found a nest of parking wardens behind Oxford Circus, where they were swarming like yellow and black striped wasps. I walked up to a warden and asked him for his favourite poem. He took my microphone from me and hit me with it.

When we put together our parking warden ballet for the programme, the plump little ladies in uniform putting tulips under car windscreen wipers

278

were professional actresses. I'd had enough of the real thing.

As you will have noticed from Annie Mizen's forays into champagne drinking, and whisky and brandy comparisons, quite a number of our *vox pops* involved food and drink. You might like to try one of the most revealing of these round your own dinner table. If you blindfold your guests, and serve the wine at the same temperature, you'll find it oddly difficult to tell the difference between red wine and white. It's also hard, we discovered, to tell Stork from butter, or Pepsi from Coca-Cola.

My favourite game was to take out dishes of snails, removed from their shells and delicately simmered in butter and garlic by the great French chef, Michel Roux. Passers-by would be asked to shut their eyes. I would spear the little black rubbery morsels, place them in their mouths, and wait until they'd had a good chew before I told them what they were. The snails came out again far faster than they went in. My least favourite game was handing out dishes of bat stew.

Our film director for that particular item was Adam Curtis, who went on to be garlanded with BAFTA awards for his documentaries. When he worked with me, he was a wicked cherub, with dark, curly eyelashes and a devilish smile. It was with great pride that he managed to track down tins of bat stew—heaven only knows where. As I'm sure bats are an endangered species I suppose it's only fair that they won this particular round in their history.

Off we went to the North End Road again. Perhaps I should say at this point that we conducted our *vox pops* all over the British Isles,

279

from Manchester to Brighton, from Belfast to Cardiff, from Norwich to Glasgow. Our only failure was in the West Country. West of Bristol the blink rate went down, the reply time went up, the answers were so slow I found myself snoozing on my feet. I'm not commenting on their IQs, they were doubtless thinking faster than the speed of sound, it's just that the sounds they emitted were incredibly slow, and laced with many an 'ooo-arr', much like the Worzels. So, when our deadlines were tight it was tempting to play to the cockney strengths, and go round the corner to Fulham.

Not that we were popular there with the barrow-boys. They hated us. They claimed that the crowds we attracted prevented them from making any money. I had my doubts. I suspected that many of them were far wealthier than any of us. However, I didn't argue with them. They got on with their job, and I got on with mine, until one fatal day in 1981, when the ribbon-seller complained to the local bobby. (The ribbon-seller wasn't my favourite person since the day he'd called me a 'fat Jewish c***'. Perhaps it was a kind of achievement to invent a sentence of three words which managed to be simultaneously fattist, anti-Semitic, sexist and obscene.) The policeman strolled up to me and said, 'Move along there'.

I was surprised, and explained that we'd filmed on the same corner for eight years. The bobby was unimpressed. 'Move along,' he said, walking away. We moved to the opposite corner. It started to rain, the light persistent drizzle that always seemed to accompany our street interviews. There were fewer passers-by on the second corner prepared to sample my bat stew. So we returned to our original spot. The bobby reappeared. 'Move along, I said, or I shall arrest you for obstruction.'

For a moment I slipped under John McEnroe's skin. I almost said 'You cannot be serious', because I didn't believe for one moment he was. But he was, deadly serious.

'Excuse me, officer,' I said, more polite than McEnroe, but less good at tennis, 'I can't be causing an obstruction because look how much space there is all round me. I'm just handing out bat stew.'

'That's it. You're nicked,' he said, reaching in his pocket for his walkie-talkie.

A Black Maria appeared round the corner from nowhere. Inexperienced at being arrested, I climbed into the passenger seat. The policeman climbed into the back of the van, where, I'm told, prisoners usually travel. As we pulled away from the kerb I rolled down the window and whispered to Adam Curtis, 'Tell Press Association'. Once a journalist, always a journalist. A crowd had collected. I shouted at them, 'If you don't think I was obstructing, would you mind saying so'. From the crowd came the unanimous bellow, 'Guilty, Guilty'.

At the police station a ferocious-looking man was being cautioned. He was encircled with chains, from which knives and knuckle-dusters were hanging. It may have been fancy dress, but I suspected not. As soon as I arrived, the station sergeant stopped what he was doing with the gentleman with the steel jewellery, and started to sort me out.

'I think I should tell you,' I said timidly, 'that nobody has cautioned me.'

He looked embarrassed. 'You do not have to say anything, but anything you do say will be taken down and may be used in evidence.' They took me to a cell. I waited to be strip-searched. I wasn't.

Adam Curtis, gallant to the last, arrived with the van and the police let me go. Adam told me he'd made a rendezvous with the press to meet me outside Harrods. As I climbed out of the van, and adopted a pathetic innocent victim expression, my hair was plastered to my forehead, the rain glistened on my cheeks like tears. That picture appeared in the papers, and cynics in the BBC accused me of setting the whole thing up as a publicity stunt. To which I replied that, had I done so, I would certainly have gone to the hairdresser first.

Researching the law of obstruction I discovered that it's the policeman's catch-all. With our film as evidence, I pointed out to the BBC lawyers how much space there was on the pavement for the crowd to move around me and the crew. They pointed out to me that that didn't make the slightest difference. Even had I been standing on one leg, the policeman could still call it obstruction if he chose. And he did choose.

My case was heard at Horseferry Road Magistrates Court, where we discovered from the court listing that the policeman who arrested me was Constable A Herbert. Just what we thought he was. (In fact PC Herbert was delighted with his new-found fame, dined out on the incident until he retired, and even appeared on my *This Is Your Life*, when we shook hands and forgave each other.)

We showed the magistrates the film as evidence of my innocence (carefully losing the moment when I told Adam to phone Press Association). They watched it courteously, then pronounced me guilty and fined me £15, exactly what they had fined all the other streetwalkers who had been arrested for the same offence. Only the others had not been offering their customers bat stew.

BBC News sent a reporter to interview me after the verdict. I insisted that we talked to each other on the run, in case I was arrested again. I was sad to read a column by Richard Ingrams, Editor of *Private Eye*, who was ruthlessly pursuing me at the time, that when he saw *Esther Rantzen Arrested* on the newspaper billboards, his heart leaped with joy. At last, he thought, justice had been done. I must have been bundled, pale and shaking, down the front path of the home I shared with Desmond, and off to prison, to face a lengthy sentence for being successful on television, in spite of my total lack of talent.

Imagine Richard's disappointment to find I was only facing a £15 fine for obstruction. Imagine how much worse it would have been for him to know that the BBC lawyer insisted on paying the fine for me, as an expense incurred on duty. I couldn't find it in my heart to break the news to Richard. But I shared his delight in the billboards and have them framed in my home to this day.

*   *   *

Looking back, arduous as they were at the time, and I usually interviewed seventy people in a day (I claim now to have interviewed more people than any other television reporter in the world, well over 25,000), the street interviews were great fun. We

283

sang, we danced, a workman played a tune on a long steel pipe, hiding his face in a doorway in case the tax man recognized him, we played charades. I was kissed by drunks from Cornwall to Aberdeen. Occasionally we were revealing, as when I asked people what class they were. Nobody would admit to being upper class, very few were working class, we're all middle class now.

Once I was asking passers-by to sample fruit-flavoured stamps and envelopes. A small man in a tweed hat looked hard at me, recognized me, and said, 'Now that I've got you standing here in front of me, I just want to tell you I think your show stinks'. He got a round of applause, and we kept him in our titles for weeks.

Chris Serle went out to discover if anyone could remember our signature tune (as I have said, although it was wondrously recognizable, I'm not sure of its melodic strength). He found a boy who could sing it all the way through. While he was singing, an old lady in a shower hat came up and asked him what he was doing. He explained he was singing the *That's Life!* signature tune. The old lady looked blank.

'You know,' he explained, 'the show with Esther Rantzen.'

She looked appalled. 'I can't stand the woman. She's *so* ugly.'

She became the punchline of our film, and I decided to put a big brown paper bag over my head and apologize to her on air. On the night the audience laughed so loudly when she said she couldn't stand me that they drowned her comment about my ugliness, so there I was, sitting in a brown paper bag, for reasons they could not understand.

Meanwhile, Desmond was up in the control gallery, seeing the film for the first time. As the old lady appeared in the shower hat, he jumped out of his skin: 'Heavens, she's Patsy's aunt.'

His first wife's aunt got the biggest laugh of the night.

Our most moving moment during a *vox pop* was never transmitted. In 1980 we were making a programme for the Christmas special. Out we went as usual into the London streets for our *vox pop*, but this time I asked an extra question. When the cameras stopped rolling, I said to every old person I met, 'What are you doing at Christmas?'

If they told me they were spending it alone, I asked our production assistant to write down their names and addresses. Then I had my own Christmas treat, on our programme budget, buying a bottle of sherry for each one, and a box of nice chocolates, some fruit, a cake, and other titbits I hoped they would enjoy, with a card thanking them and wishing them a 'Merry Christmas from all of us on *That's Life!*' I packed everything into scarlet Christmas stockings.

Time was very short, so I ordered a taxi to take them to all the addresses on our list, about twenty people. The taxi-driver himself rang me, almost in tears. He said he had no idea such poverty existed. He had gone up rickety stairs, in crumbling houses, and into cold, damp rooms. As he gave them the stockings, the old people were overwhelmed. They clung to him to thank him. There are charities all over Britain packing shoe-boxes for refugee children abroad. I wonder whether at Christmas time we should all be packing stockings for some of our own old people?

CHAPTER TEN

CONS, CAUSES AND CRAZY PETS

When *That's Life!* began, its chief aim was to protect our viewers' purses. We wanted to warn them against buying shoddy goods or services, or being swindled by unscrupulous con-men. The utilities, gas, water, electricity, telephone service, and British Rail, all provided us with hours of innocent fun. Our style was to use humour as the spike to nail the message home, that customers deserved better than they were getting.

One poor man had radiators fitted in his house that began to spout black oil. He told us that in desperation he stuck his finger into the pipe to block it, and rang the builder. 'Come at once and mend these, or I'll sue.' The builder said, 'I hear ducks fart in church', and put the phone down. (Weeks later I met the Duke of Edinburgh, and he offered to discover from Sir Peter Scott, who was also at the reception, whether that was anatomically possible. 'I don't know about the church,' said Sir Peter, Britain's most scholarly expert on ducks, 'but they certainly fart under water. I've seen the trail of bubbles.')

I remember a caravan manufacturer who defended himself against the criticisms of his customers by saying furiously, 'What do you expect? Of course there are dozens of faults, this is a British caravan.' Meeting John Cleese in a restaurant he asked me for the script of that item. Was that, perhaps, one of the tiny sparks that led to the brilliant creation of Basil Fawlty?

At midnight one Friday, when I should have finished the script, Norma Shepherd brought me an irresistible, 'You've got no gas' item. That was how we described stories when a viewer who had no gas was pelted with gas bills, printed first in black, then in red, then with heavy legal threats attached. In this case our poor viewer had done everything she could to explain to them, on the phone and in writing, that she only had electricity, she had no gas.

Norma came to tell me that our viewer had just rung to say the gas men had called, walked into the house, and attempted to cut her off. I wrote an extra item, ending it with 'They looked at her kitchen, they looked at her, and they said, "you've got no gas"'. Emotionally and physically exhausted, I slid from my chair at the typewriter down on to the floor, and lay there. At the time I was extremely pregnant. I opened my eyes to see two security men peering round the edge of the door. They were looking at me with alarm, fearing that I was in labour and debating whether they should send for an ambulance. I scrambled to my feet and reassured them. I should not have written the extra item that week, but I could never resist a 'You've got no gas'.

I could rarely resist a con-man either. They are a fascinating breed. They often have the gift of a vivid imagination, they have charm, are articulate, and sometimes are even hard-working, at least until they have squeezed their poor victims completely dry. Given all that talent, they could make themselves a comfortable living, if they were prepared to be boringly honest. But they aren't.

They far prefer selling a scam to a decent product.

Soon after *That's Life!* began, we uncovered a massive swindle worth many hundreds of thousands of pounds in a credit company called 'Coach House Finance'. I met the man who founded the company in Colchester. He was honest, but out of his depth, and had left most of the running of the business to a smart young salesman called Raymond. At this point he was retired, and Raymond was given free rein. The business doubled and redoubled, until it was taken over by a very large American company.

What nobody realized, except the whistle-blower who contacted us, was that the business was all fictitious. Raymond and his friends were inventing loans on non-existent cars. We were shown some of the application forms, and tracked down the real people whose names appeared on them. They were astonished to see loans for thousands of pounds against their names. We showed the loan forms on the screen, and our viewers tracked down the licence plates—one was on the back of a Colchester bus.

Lord George Brown was on the board of the American parent company, and he warned Coach House Finance that it was on the edge of a 'Watergate' style exposé unless it cleaned up its business. A private detective came to our office and told me that unless I was careful I would end up in 'a concrete overcoat in the Essex marshes'. In fact, I ended up in a courtroom in Essex, giving evidence in Raymond's trial when he was sent to prison.

Mr Guisbers, a Dutch man who used to advertise in local papers all over Britain, offering work at home to people with very little money, also ended up in jail. Often his victims were disabled, or working as carers for disabled relatives, or single parents, and could not afford to lose the money Mr Guisbers took from them. The work he advertised never materialized. The only person to make a profit was Mr Guisbers himself, who would change his name, adjust the scam, and put in another set of advertisements.

By then, the format of *That's Life!* had been bought from the BBC by Dutch television. They were making their own version, and had borrowed Simon, one of our directors. Norma gave him Mr Guisbers's office address. Simon called there, but could only find one courteous man who told him Mr Guisbers had moved on. From the description Simon gave us over the phone, it was clear that the kindly man was Mr Guisbers himself. Finally Mr Guisbers picked an alias which must mean something else in Dutch—he called himself 'Mr Tampon'.

Norma, who had been tracking him through scam after scam, recognized his style at once, rang the office number in Holland, and was told Mr Guisbers had just died. She came and told me. I said she must fly out on a day trip to Holland and present our sympathies. She said tomorrow was awkward. I said fine, how about today? In an hour she was on the plane to Holland, took a car to the address, and presented our sympathy for Mr Guisbers's sudden demise to the man himself, now transformed into Mr Tampon. He laughed, and confessed we had indeed tracked down the right man, Norma flew home and we enjoyed composing a script in which we concluded that Mr Tampon should go to jail, 'be sent up for a long stretch'. He was.

There was silence for some months. Then viewers began to write to us again, complaining about a swindle involving gold bonds. Once again Norma recognized the style, the spelling mistakes, and rang Holland. Surely Mr Guisbers was in prison now? The Trading Standards officers reassured her, certainly he was. Just to check (I did mention that it's the last stone you pick up that has a maggot hiding beneath it), Norma got the name of the prison, and rang them. The Governor spoke to her, yes, Mr Guisbers was inside, in fact he was a model prisoner, all he did all day was sit at a typewriter and write letters to Britain. They took his typewriter away, and added a few months to his sentence. I wonder where he is now.

*   *   *

In case you think con-men have to be masters of disguise, let me tell you about our eighteen-stone, wig-wearing con-man. If ever there was a recognizable man, he was. Far more ambitious than Mr Guisbers, he targeted big companies. He would tell them he was from Saudi Arabia, or India or Pakistan, on a buying mission worth millions of pounds. What he was buying depended on the company he targeted. Sometimes he was buying nurses' uniforms for the health service back home, or school uniforms for local schools, or steel for factories. Somehow he never had his wallet with him, so when he was put up in fancy hotels, and wined and dined, he didn't pick up the bill. But others, his would-be customers, were glad to. Often

290

he would persuade them to advance him a generous sum, then he would move on.

We had many descriptions, including his weight (eighteen stone), and colouring (a dark wig), and very bloodshot eyes. We created our own photofit, and again our viewers helped us track him down. Once he left a hotel at such speed he left his suitcase behind. A viewer sent it to us, and I unpacked it on the air, pulling out an enormous baggy pair of boxer shorts. I warned outsize-clothes shops to be on the lookout for a man trying to replace a pair of knickers.

That Sunday, I asked all our viewers to look at the other end of their own sofas. Was there an eighteen-stone, wig-wearing con-man watching the programme with them? On Monday morning a hotel porter rang us. As I spoke on Sunday, he had looked along the hotel sofa, and there he was. But by the time he rang, the con-man had fled, and as far as I know, was never seen again. (Unless, of course, as Glyn used to say, you know different.)

Slimming was always a productive area for con-men to enjoy at our expense. Most of us think we are overweight, and yearn to find a product which enables us to eat what we want and still lose those extra pounds. One enterprising con-man used to send out a piece of string, and suggest that you tied it tightly around your waist to discourage you from eating. It worked as well as any of the other ideas we investigated.

Kit Miller was a 'wide boy' journalist who at one stage auditioned for *That's Life!*. That would have been fun, to hire a reporter who was an undercover agent cheering for the villains. (I learned from one salesman we exposed that we were required viewing for his company. They'd meet and watch us over a curry on Sunday nights, applauding the cheek of the con-men we quoted. Mr Guisbers was a particular hero.)

When we didn't hire Kit, he went into the slimming pills market. At the time, Sam Fox was a page-three model and the nation's favourite pin-up. She had paired up with an Australian called Peter Foster and was, according to Kit, pregnant. Kit offered a Sunday tabloid exclusive pictures of the cot she had bought, and the cuddly toys in it, for a front-page story about the baby they were expecting together. Except that they weren't. It was rumoured that he had bought the cot and the teddy bears himself. The deal was that, in return for the Sam Fox exclusive, he would be allowed by the editor, Wendy Henry, an article inside the paper praising his latest miracle pill, and giving details of how to obtain it. We exposed the scam, but not before Kit had raked in an estimated two million pounds.

Peter Foster was the least likeable of all the con-men I met. He had cold black eyes, like a lizard. 'Esther Rantzen,' he said, 'I am your worst nightmare.' In a way he was, to him people were walking wallets waiting to be squeezed. He sold 'Bai Lin Tea', a Chinese tea whose magic property was that you could drink it and then eat as much as you liked, and the weight would drop off you. Sam Fox was pictured on all his posters, smiling and praising its effects: 'I lost seven pounds without having to diet!'.

When we mentioned on air the hundreds of complaints we had received that the magic tea simply didn't work, he moved on to a miracle anti-wrinkle cream made of mother-of-pearl, and modelled by Sam Fox's mother. That didn't work either, so he returned to his native Australia. The last I heard he was in prison there, serving a sentence for similar offences.

*   *   *

We often trapped our con-men by using hidden cameras, but the BBC always insisted that we justified their use, and we had to put in a written request, and support it with evidence from Trading Standards Officers or other consumer protectors before it was allowed. In our early days cameras were so large it was difficult to hide them. These days you can secrete a camera in a spectacle case, or on the end of a pen.

Nowadays there is the Broadcasting Standards Commission (BSC) to enforce rules protecting privacy. And certainly, since technology has developed so far, and recording equipment has been miniaturized, privacy is a serious concern. But, in my view, the BSC has shown itself to be irrelevant to broadcasting, and out of touch with reality. I believe in protecting people's privacy as far as their private life is concerned. But if a crime is being committed, or if someone vulnerable is being made to suffer, the BSC should surely not abet a cover-up.

I made a programme in which we used a hidden camera to film a brain-damaged patient in a hospital. We did this at the mother's request, on a day when a fête was being held in the grounds, and the public were invited. Idiotically, the BSC declared the film to be an invasion of the hospital's privacy. Why should an institution or an organization be protected against the accountability of a camera?

There have been ground-breaking programmes revealing the cruelty that occurs in some institutions. For instance, John Willis produced *The Secret Hospital* in 1979 using exactly the methods we used—secret cameras hidden on visitors on a day when Rampton Hospital was open to the public. In the nineties, *That's Life!* filmed in mixed wards to show primitive conditions there. The BSC's ruling would prohibit that filming, if they had the power. Fortunately they cannot censor in advance, and equally fortunately, sensible programme-makers disregard their more absurd and counter-productive rulings.

In the seventies, when some of the most expensive swindles were home improvements, central heating and double glazing were almost invariably sold by door-to-door salesmen, in unwitnessed transactions. Since nobody could check what the salesman promised, how he described the product and its price, and what sleight of hand he used to obtain a signature on the contract, it seemed sensible to film him in action. That was always a complicated feat of organization. Where could we hide? The salesman would invariably walk all over a house, looking at windows and walls in every room. Not only did we have to build wardrobes and garden huts big enough to hold me, a crew and a load of equipment, we had to construct them in a few hours, and somehow fit them into normal homes.

To film one salesman, our director built a garden shed the size of a small aircraft hangar in a tiny garden. It was pushed right up against the kitchen window, and the tenant upstairs objected. When Henry Murray, the director, explained to her that he would take it down the next morning, she was quite satisfied, and strangely incurious. She didn't ask why in that case he was building it at all.

We filmed salesmen offering their customers all kinds of fake bargains—typically, 'Sign now and you will have the chance of becoming a show house, which means you get a fifty per cent discount', and 'This will only cost you the price of a packet of fags a week,' (not such a bargain these days). The hidden cameras helped to show our viewers how timid and ingratiating the salesmen were, how they wheedled their way into people's homes, and how butter wouldn't melt in their mouths. Far from being brash bullies, they appealed to the customers' sympathy, who might not have been so sympathetic if they'd heard the salesmen referring to them as 'gophers', and witnessed the glee with which they pocketed their huge commissions.

The first time I jumped out of a cupboard to reveal to a salesman that he had been filmed, and asked for a response, he smiled at the camera, smoothed his hair, and told me how much he enjoyed the programme. Some of the con-men positively enjoyed their five minutes of fame—and, sometimes for the next few weeks, would advertise their product, 'As seen on television'. But little by little we had an effect, the Consumer Credit Act was brought in with clauses to protect a consumer's right to change his mind the next day. And our viewers heeded David Tench from the Consumers' Association when he said, 'If something sounds as if it's too good to be true, it probably isn't true'.

I profited personally from our campaign to clean up the door-to-door selling industry. One of the salesmen rang the BBC and left a message with the Duty Office, 'I know where Esther Rantzen works, and I'll be waiting for her there, to punch her teeth down her throat'. I went to our Organizer's office, with the log of calls in my hand. 'Glyn,' I said, 'may I have a carpark pass, so that he can't catch me walking in the door?' He sighed. I had been parking in the carpark for months, but only on the strength of a pass I had drawn myself, carefully colouring it with red ink. The security guards knew I had forged it, but let me in with a grin. I wasn't nearly senior enough to be issued an official pass. But now I was endangered, I could have one.

*   *   *

Like our viewers, we loved animals. Indeed, *That's Life!* was influential in protecting some animals from cruelty. Not enough, when you look at modern farming methods, but at least we brought about some change. For instance, when I was on location for an interview with a farmer, I happened to see a tiny calf lying in a darkened barn, in a pen so small he couldn't move.

I mentioned this to a researcher, and he discovered the reason. Consumers prefer veal to be white meat, so veal calves were fed a diet deficient in iron, housed in the dark, and in pens so small they couldn't move, to prevent them developing muscle. Our audiences responded with such anger to the pictures we showed that the so-called 'veal crates' were outlawed in this country. Sadly, that simply means that nowadays veal calves are reared abroad, under just such cruel conditions. Only the British consumer can change the situation worldwide, by insisting on pink veal.

We criticized the Kennel Club, for preserving the painful inbred deformities regarded as 'beautiful' by pedigree dog breeders. Snobbery is a strange vice. Unpleasant when it divides society, it is downright ridiculous when it decrees that a dog must have its tail docked, its ears clipped, otherwise it is not 'good' enough. Dog breeders have been genetically modifying breeds for years, sometimes with terrible effect. Did you know that the bulldog's head is now so large that few puppies can ever be born naturally, and have to be born by caesarean section? The bloodhound has been bred with deformed eyes, to give it that lugubrious expression. The dachshund is profoundly disabled, bred for centuries to have artificially shortened limbs. Nature keeps trying to correct these deformities, so the only way the breeders can keep the breeds 'pure' is to inbreed them, but that also means other disabilities are introduced, like weakened hip joints.

The snobbery attached to pedigree puppies has also pushed their price up, and created a squalid black market in puppy production. We exposed puppy farms: collie bitches kept in squalid conditions in barns on remote Welsh farms, their puppies taken from them far too young, then sold in puppy supermarkets. Many of them die very young, catching diseases from each other, and never developing the immunity they would develop if they were allowed to stay longer with their mothers, in healthy conditions. Meanwhile the

297

poor little mother bitch is made to produce litter after litter of so-called 'pedigree' puppies. All this in a nation which prides itself on caring for animals.

I tried to persuade my production team that we should also expose the ghastly cruelty of 'foie gras', the delicacy produced by force-feeding geese until their livers explode. Since I first discovered how it is produced, I have never been able to bear the taste of it. But the team felt our viewers would be too upset by this grisly trade. For the same reason we never exposed the horror of battery chicken farming. I try only to eat free-range eggs, and organically produced meat, but it can be difficult to obtain and labels can be misleading. Once again, it will take pressure from consumers to take the factories out of factory farming.

At least, thanks to Parliament, which outlawed the hideous tradition of chaining sows down so that they couldn't stand, British pigs are well treated now. But humane methods are expensive, British pigfarmers need our support if they are to stay in business. It is up to us to buy British bacon, for our pigs' sake. It may cost us a penny or two more, but we humans have so much power now over the rest of creation, I believe we also have the responsibility to protect all creatures from avoidable pain. Not only that, but now we have the pleasant sight of fields dotted with tiny huts, with pigs contentedly rooting around them, rather than these interesting intelligent animals being herded together by the thousand in great tin warehouses.

I am not a vegetarian, nor do I oppose animal testing for medical purposes. How else would Ben Hardwick (the toddler dying of liver disease for whom we campaigned in 1984) have had his transplant, if the surgeons had not been able to practise their techniques on animals? But BSE has taught us that nature will take a terrible revenge if we break her laws by feeding grass-eating cattle the minced brains and offal of other animals. Compassionate farming brings its own rewards— the food it produces tastes better, and is better for us.

It was no coincidence that Desmond and I bought a cottage in the New Forest, where ponies, pigs and cattle can wander where they choose, have right of way on the roads, and graze on the grass verges. We always loved watching them roam free, and enjoyed coming across groups of cattle placidly standing in the shade, holding up traffic which never gets impatient, as drivers do in city gridlocks. We also delighted in piglets—their impudent little tails curling over their backs—exploring heaps of mud by the roadside; and ponies, with their enchanting foals trotting in the spring sunshine beside their mothers, like long-legged baby ballet dancers.

In spite of our team's affection and care for animals, in 1988 *That's Life!* was accused of cruelty to a white Persian cat called Mimi. By the time we met Mimi she was long dead. In fact, our first meeting with her was when one of our researchers pulled her out of a black rubbish bag. Mimi belonged to Elsie Athaide, and Elsie had loved her dearly. So dearly that when Mimi passed on to the great mouse paddock in the sky, Elsie had her stuffed.

It was some time before the taxidermist returned Mimi to Elsie, and when she arrived, she was in a black rubbish bag. Elsie unwrapped her. Whereas in life Mimi had been graceful and elegant, with long soft fur and big blue eyes, Mimi stuffed looked bedraggled and ruffianly, one ear up, one down, her head askew, her eyes asquint, her legs crooked, as if she'd had a night on the tiles with an overenthusiastic tom. The team laughed, our Editor, John Morrell, did not share our amusement. 'You can't show that,' he said, 'it's in the worst possible taste.'

Spare a thought for our Editors—all of them. What an impossible job they had, trying to impose taste on a team which delighted in being rude. Not by today's standards, of course—these days we would be regarded as prim. We had no four-letter words in the show, for instance, although we were often sent them by our viewers. For years, pinned up on our notice-board was an article about a prize-winning Chinese chef, as the headline said, '*The Best Fu-Kien Chef in Manchester*'. That was never transmitted.

Nor were some of our rudest vegetables. In the seventies John Morrell had to stare glumly at the week's harvest, all sent to us by our viewers, all shaped more or less like masculine personal parts, and decide which parsnip could be transmitted, and which went too far. I remember a lively debate with his successor, Ron Neil, in which he said a tomato with a phallic projection was obscene, and I maintained it was just a tomato with cucumber ambitions. An unnoticed effect of the European Union has been that these vivacious vegetables which used to be sent to us by the hundredweight, no longer seem to be on sale anywhere. Doubtless their dimensions break Common Market rules.

John stifled his scruples about Mimi and allowed me to write her story into the show. I enjoyed writing that script. I built it as poetically as I could. Elsie's feelings about Mimi required it. After all, I pointed out, she had stuffed her cat for the same reason that Shah Jahan built the Taj Mahal, as a permanent memorial. I reminded our audience how beautiful a white Persian cat can be, and we found a meltingly lovely picture from a calendar of favourite cat pictures. Then I slowly pulled down the edge of the black rubbish bag to reveal Mimi, transmogrified. As I did so, I said, 'That's let the cat out of the bag'.

When the audience saw her, a roar of laughter rolled round the studio, and echoed across the nation. Les Dawson, a few years later, told me it was the funniest thing he had ever seen on television, a rare tribute, coming from him. But at the same time, the BBC switchboards jammed.

That was on Sunday night. Monday was officially our day off, but I came into the office early, just in case there had been trouble. As I did, the phone on my desk rang, it was the BBC's accountability programme, *Open Air*. They liked to pick controversial topics from the night before. We had forty complaints about Mimi, and *Open Air* needed someone from the programme to defend it. I was there almost before they put the phone down.

As I went into make-up I decided for the only time in my life to lie on television, brazenly. And so I did. They showed the whole offensive section of the programme on *Open Air*, including the Taj Mahal and the calendar picture, then Mimi herself was revealed. An irate viewer came on the line: 'Miss Rantzen, that was disgusting. To laugh at that

301

poor cat. To turn it into a figure of fun.'

I looked with as much sincerity as I could into camera. 'I can only apologize. We had no idea the audience would respond like that. I would never have done it, if I'd realized they would laugh at Mimi.'

It was an outrageous lie. The lady was not dim, she spotted it. 'Don't give me that, Miss Rantzen. You knew. I heard what you said, "that's let the cat out of the bag".'

'Nerves, I'm afraid, pure nervous reaction,' I said. And then trying to get back on to firmer ground, 'And in any case, it was a consumer item. We made the point that under the Sale of Goods and Services Act, Elsie was entitled to get her money back from the taxidermist.'

'That's no good. Fining's not good enough. He should be stuffed himself.'

'Now let me get this right,' I said. 'You are saying we were cruel to put a dead stuffed cat on the programme, but nothing is bad enough for the taxidermist. He should be killed and stuffed himself.'

'That's right,' she said defiantly.

As I walked from the studio I met Peter Weil, the Editor of *Open Air*.

'Thank you,' I said. 'That was a unique glimpse of our audience's reaction.'

John Morrell had been right, but I am still bewildered by the outrage he and some of our viewers felt. Mimi was after all very dead. And she was not my grandmother. Had I put my grandmother stuffed on the show, and badly stuffed at that, I agree that it would have been bad taste. But I have the feeling I am only making you

302

think the worse of me, especially since now you know that, like President Clinton, I have lied on television. But unlike President Nixon, only the once.

*   *   *

In 1979 one of our film directors, Nick Handel, rang me at home. Imagine a very tall animated sapling, arms flailing like branches in a high wind, black hair tossing, black eyes gleaming—Nick was launched through life by his own enthusiasm. I am extremely proud of having recruited him into television, where he has produced *Children in Need*, and countless successful documentaries.

When I first met Nick he was producing a programme for GLR, the BBC's local radio station in London. I sat in the waiting room, watching him answering listeners who had rung in response to a quiz, and I was impressed by his charm. He got rid of each caller neatly and quickly without hurting anyone's feelings. When it was time for me to be interviewed by the presenter, and I mentioned my previous career making sound effects, Nick dashed into the studio with the props I had mentioned— armfuls of sound tape for crackling leaves, a jug of water and a cushion for footsteps in mud, and, before I could protest, I was on my knees in the studio, making the sound of lovers walking through autumn fields. Or at least their feet.

The most important quality for any film director is the capacity to charm birds off trees, and persuade people to do things they might have refused had they been warned in advance. Nick passed that test with flying colours. We were

303

putting together a new production team at the time, so I rang him and invited him to join us. He turned me down, explaining that his one ambition was to become a Light Entertainment Producer for Radio 2. But Nick had left school at sixteen to become a tea-boy in the BBC, had no degree, and in those days the producers were chosen from Oxbridge graduates. Nick was turned down for the job he had set his heart on, and came to us instead. We were delighted to have him. One night, when everyone was exhausted and tempers were fraying, he climbed into an empty sack and jumped all over the office in it.

On the occasion he rang me at home, however, he was less exuberant—sounded worried. We had been contacted by a man who said his dog could talk. Nick was there on location. He told me, 'Now that we've seen the dog talking, we're worried that it might look a bit cruel. He's got the dog's lower jaw in his hands, and he waggles it up and down.'

I said, 'What's the dog's tail doing?'

'Wagging.'

'Then make sure we have plenty of shots of the tail, in case viewers are worried.'

Paul Heiney, the reporter, was also anxious.

'Tell you what,' I suggested, 'film it, and if it looks too cruel we can always junk it.'

So they filmed the most famous dog ever transmitted on *That's Life!*, Prince, the dog that said 'Sausages.'

The idea of featuring talented pets had come to me two years earlier, in 1977. I don't think I ever suspected what richness we would discover: the pussy who played ping-pong, the horse that could count, the crow that drank beer and had to walk home, and the dogs who did everything, the housework, bricklaying, playing football, singing, and, as Prince proved to us, talking.

One of our viewers sent me an entry from an American encyclopaedia showing that Thomas Edison's dog had also talked, but that had been long forgotten. And no other dog had Prince's vocabulary. He could growl the words 'jersey', 'Elvis', and even 'Esther'. But it was his 'Sausages' that caught the public's imagination. For years after he appeared on the programme people would growl 'Sausages' at me in the street.

We found two more talking dogs. One said 'Hello Mum'; the other said 'I want one'. We managed to create a surreal conversation between all three, but Prince was the clear winner. He even made a record. Sadly Prince is no more, but nearly twenty years after his death a new commercial has just been screened, and in it a dog asks for 'sausages'. So he has achieved a certain kind of immortality.

What all our pets demonstrate is not so much the talent of British pets, as the craziness of British pet-owners. They spent hours teaching their animals to answer the telephone or read labels on cans of dog meat.

During our twenty-one years on the air, we tapped into a national vein of eccentricity in a hundred other ways. We found, for example, cohorts of body musicians, who played tunes on themselves. They hit their skulls with spanners, identical twins hit each other's faces to create a melody, a nurse played on her patients' bodies with syringes (less erotic than it sounds), a drummer played William Tell's overture on a pencil clamped between his teeth, and a rugby club mimed Glenn Miller perfectly. In their muddy sweaters, and with ears bandaged, they played invisible saxophones, standing and sitting with the precision of Tiller girls. There was a jolly farmer who played music on the cow clusters normally used for milking cows, a man who played 'Amazing Grace' on the gears of his fork-lift truck, and a woman who played watering-cans and petrol pumps.

We nearly got thrown out of Kew Gardens one lovely spring day, when a group of schoolgirls offered to play recorders on the programme. We filmed them in the deep blue haze of a bluebell glade, but when the Kew authorities discovered they were playing with recorders stuck up their noses, they withdrew permission and asked us to leave. We managed to pacify them, and finish the film.

We held competitions to find the wildest laugh in Britain, and invited the winners to our last show. I remember walking away across Shepherd's Bush Green on that hot summer night, with a sound like a cocktail party with jackals and donkeys wafting out of the open window of our Hospitality room.

We had another competition to find the most accurate Trimphone soundalike. The Trimphone produced an irritating bubble of sound, and we discovered that otherwise sane men all over the country could whistle through their lips and produce the same noise. Adam Curtis (of the many BAFTA awards), and I worked out an elaborate way of choosing the winner. We put a crate in a shopping mall, put a real Trimphone on top of it, asked our contestants to hide inside it, and the one who deceived the most passers-by into answering the phone was the winner.

Where have the eccentrics gone, now that television has lost programmes like *That's Life!* and *Nationwide*? Is life now so fast and furious we have no time for them? If so, that is a matter for deep regret. What is this life if, full of care, we have no time to do something completely daft? Our eccentrics were an integral part of the programme.

We made a memorable film about a plumber who collected loo handles, the light shining through the chains and sparkling on blue, emerald and ruby-coloured glass handles. We made another about Christine, who loved the taste of wood and paper, and who blindfolded could tell the difference between the tabloids and the broadsheets, just by chewing on them.

Glyn Worsnip demonstrated two useful recipes we were sent by our viewers, for 'Steak Manifold' and 'Washing-up Machine Trout':

Take one steak, wrap it in foil, stick it on the manifold of your car and go for a drive. Take a trout, stuff it with butter, mushrooms, tomatoes and herbs, wrap it in foil, and put it in the washing-up machine. Drive for ten minutes, complete the washing cycle, and there's a perfectly cooked meal for two.

Our audiences instantly joined any game we offered them, for example, the bread basket survey. Someone sent us a picture of a bread basket (presumably stolen from a baker's van), being used as a window box. Suddenly our post was full of pictures of bread baskets being used as playthings in a gorilla's cage, swings in a playground, or sledges in the snow.

Another viewer, having forgotten a friend's address, drew a picture of his friend's house, and his letter arrived safely. At once our viewers sent us letters with pictures of my teeth as their only address. They, too, arrived. We reached a stage when we had to broadcast a plea from the British Dental Association, as every letter addressed to them was delivered to us instead, by weary postmen who thought if it mentioned teeth, it must be for me.

One of our most useful surveys was inspired not by us, but by the talented South African songwriter, Jeremy Taylor. He wrote a song called 'Jobsworth'. It was dedicated to all the unhelpful officials who insist on sticking to the letter of a stupid rule, 'Because it's more than my job's worth not to'. Our designer created a Gestapo-style hat as our Jobsworth Award, and our viewers nominated dozens of worthy winners. My favourite was the parking attendant who watched a husband carefully helping his wife from the car to the hospital door, she being in the last stages of labour, and because he had parked in the wrong bay, clamped him. Alas, without *That's Life!* to draw attention to such crassness, this kind of behaviour reigns supreme and unchecked nowadays.

*   *   *

I have a soft spot for the *That's Life!*'s campaign to Get Britain Singing. I'm not sure why the idea came to me. Perhaps I was standing in a queue surrounded by particularly gloomy people, and it seemed possible to cheer them up, if we hid our cameras, played music, and encouraged passers-by to join in. On one occasion we actually achieved a miracle. We were filming in a garden centre, Adrian Mills was dressed as a scarecrow, when a lady in a wheelchair was pushed past him. The music sounded, Adrian jerked into life, and danced towards her, singing cheerily. She leaped out of the wheelchair and ran.

I was watching the uncut rushes of another of these musical extravaganzas, filmed at the Liverpool Flower Festival on a grey, cloudy day. Our reporter Bill Buckley was dressed as an elf. Bill is gay, but had not as yet decided to 'come out'. As an elf, Bill was on the very outer limits of 'camp'. He was wearing long, grey pointed ears (definitely unappealing. I made a note to tell make-up to choose a more cheerful colour next time— pink, perhaps, or green), wrinkled tights, and he skipped down the hillside, kissing passing men on the forehead. I remember suggesting to Christine Pancott, our film editor, that it might be wise for Bill to take a closet on location in future. Just then Bill himself rang. 'Hello, Bill,' Chris said, 'Esther wants a word with you', and passed the phone to me.

'Hello,' said Bill in a fragile voice, 'You wanted to speak to me.'

'Bill,' I said, 'I know you're not 'out', so do you think it's advisable, when dressed as an elf, to kiss strange men?'

'I was very careful only to pick very unattractive old men,' he said defensively. I didn't pursue it.

'What did you ring to say?' I asked.

'On much the same subject,' he said. 'A man from the *Sun* newspaper just arrived on my doorstep and told me that James's wife has accused

309

me of stealing her husband.' James was his partner.

'Ah,' I said. 'And you said, "My private life is my own concern".'

'Yes, I could have said that,' said Bill, in a sad voice. 'As it is, it's going to appear in the paper tomorrow. I suppose that's the end of my career.'

'Why on earth should it be? Not at all,' I said, and instantly rang Gordon Watts, our programme editor.

He got in touch with Bill straight away to reassure him, then came and had a look at the film. In the circumstances he decided we should wait a week before we broadcast the grey-eared elf.

Bill came round to supper with Desmond and me that evening, and we talked it through. His greatest fear was his parents' reaction. Indeed they were so hurt they refused to talk to him at all for several years. I wrote to them on Bill's behalf, but that had no effect. From Bill's point of view this is not entirely a sad story. He had a tiny flicker of pride, he says, that his story was all over the front page of the *Sun*, while the footballer they'd exposed the week before had only been on page five.

He was certainly 'out', and far more comfortable now that he could be honest about his sexuality. And although his parents never completely came to terms with it, in time they healed the breach and began to communicate again. But seeing his pain, I wonder whether people have to sacrifice all their rights to privacy, just because they happen to be reporters on a television consumer programme.

I never actually appeared myself in our Get Britain Singing routines, although my directors did persuade me to try one. We were in a hospital. I was dressed as Florence Nightingale, and they put me in the men's surgical ward. The musical introduction started, I appeared, opened my mouth to sing the first note, and heard a death rattle from the bed by the door. I had never heard a death rattle before, nor have I since, but it was unmistakable. The doctors pulled the screens around him, I took off my costume and refused to sing any more. If I could kill an old man with a single note, how much more damage could I have done in that hospital—and throughout the land?

CHAPTER ELEVEN

CONSUMING PASSIONS

Glyn, Kieran and Cyril were the first of many co-presenters I worked with on-screen on *That's Life!*. They were followed by reporters Chris Serle, Paul Heiney, Gavin Campbell, Adrian Mills, Bill Buckley, Michael Groth, Doc Cox, Grant Baynham, Kevin Devine and Howard Leader. We drew upon a galaxy of comic talent, including Molly Sugden, June Whitfield, Wendy Richard, Cleo Rocas, Jo Monro, Scott Sherrin, John Gould, Kate Robbins, Simon Fanshawe, Barry Cryer and Maeve Alexander. And we recruited musicians who contributed regular songs each week, Victoria Wood for instance, and Richard Stilgoe. For particular items we invited special guests like Spike Milligan, Boy George, Bonnie Langford, Wet Wet Wet, Frankie Howerd and Les Dawson. No wonder our audiences grew until we were the BBC's most popular programme, with such a profusion of stars to draw upon.

Unlike most production teams, when we were choosing reporters we never picked fully grown talent from other programmes, we grew our own. That was the way I had been recruited onto *Braden's Week,* and although it was risky, it paid off. I brag rather too frequently about the number of stars we discovered or rescued from dungeons where their talents were imprisoned out of sight.

Many of them joined us as junior members of our production team. Peter Bazalgette, the most successful impresario in television today, (the man behind *Changing Rooms*, *Ground Force*, and *Big Brother*), came to *That's Life!* as a researcher. Adam Curtis, whom I later watched collect two BAFTAs in one night for his programme *Pandora's Box*, joined us as a researcher at the same time as Peter. Colin Cameron is now Controller of BBC Scotland, but early in his career he came to London to direct our footballing dogs. Pat Houlihan eventually became Editor of the *Holiday* programme, she wrestled with dogs, cats and wood-eating ladies in her time as one of our film directors. Bill Nicholson was our first 'Heap of the Week' director, now he makes feature films, and wrote the deeply moving *Shadowlands* about C.S. Lewis. Ian Sharp also started his film career with us, then went on to work as a director in feature films, including the James Bond movies.

Then there are the on-screen talents. One of our first reporters, Kieran Prendiville is now better known as an outstanding television playwright, having created dramas for BBC1 such as *Ballykissangel* and *Care*. Chris Serle became the presenter of *Pick of the Week*. Bill Buckley is the voice of Channel 5. Victoria Wood is a comic genius who fills theatres all over the country and invents brilliantly original television plays and series. Like an over-proud Jewish mother I could go on and on listing the brilliant talents who worked with me during the twenty-one years of *That's Life!*, and that's exactly how I behaved. Like a dominant, demanding, protective, infuriating, loving, claustrophobic Jewish mother.

But may I defend myself, for a moment? Television is difficult, part of the skill is to make it

313

look easy, which it ain't. Get one detail wrong, and like a house of cards, your programme will fall flat. And yet timidity doesn't work either, if you want to engage the viewers you have to push your luck. If the chicken won't sit in the bicycle basket first time, you must try, try, try again. If it starts to rain when at last the hen's in it, and the shot makes her look bedraggled, and the countryside miserable, then you must go back again and shoot it in the sunshine. (Jane Elsdon-Dew was the director who battled with the chicken and the weather, the film in the end was a little poem, but she went through hell to achieve it. The chicken, before you ask, enjoyed the whole thing.)

It's the same merciless struggle with research. When you work on a consumer programme, the pursuit of the story becomes an all-consuming passion. When Shaun Woodward was researching the story of Ben Hardwick he had no other life at all, he spent every minute of the day with Ben's family. When Richard Woolfe was investigating Crookham Court (a school owned by a paedophile) I rang him when he was in hospital with his wife, who was in the second stage of her labour with her first child. (I will come to both those stories later.)

On Fridays, when I used to write the script, I know researchers dreaded the experience. Not because I was horrible to them, I hope, but because in order to sew together a script, I had first to pull their research apart. Sometimes I would ask them a question to which they had no answer, in which case either they found the answer, or we cut the item. We had to discover the truth. Otherwise, as we found to our cost, the BBC had to pay thousands of pounds in libel damages.

314

What did the team get in return for their hard work? A training second to none in television. The thrill of broadcasting to an enormous audience, and getting the feedback the next day. Most of all, the knowledge that this was worthwhile television. That the fun was skilfully crafted, and based on reality. That the serious content was influential and could change people's lives for the better. What did I get out of it? Forget fame and fortune, I loved the programme, and I loved my team.

The affection that bound us together was sometimes misinterpreted. Henry Murray was one of our first series producers, he was talented, hard-working and exceptionally good-looking. He was also blond and muscular, but I hardly noticed that. I was too busy employing his brain. Others did, though, and years later I discovered it was rumoured that Henry and I were more than colleagues.

The same prurient suspicion fell on Shaun Woodward. Now Shaun is renowned as the Tory MP who masterminded the 1992 election campaign that landed a 'double whammy' on the Labour Party, then crossed the floor to join them. But when I met Shaun I had been appointed a member of the National Consumer Council (NCC) and he was very young, fresh from Cambridge, and working as their parliamentary lobbyist. At the end of one Council meeting he told me that he felt the NCC and *That's Life!* could work together in the interests of consumers, and that perhaps we should join forces on some of our campaigns.

That sounded sensible, so I invited him back to our home in Kew. Over a cup of tea he told me a little about his own background, including his degree, a double First in English from Cambridge. He said, 'I'd really love to work for the BBC'. At that time we were putting a new production team together, so I suggested he should meet Gordon Watts, the Editor. Gordon, understandably impressed by Shaun's consumer credentials and his intellect, hired him as a researcher.

Shaun and I worked closely together on the Ben Hardwick story, then the time came for his first annual report. He came back to the office, his face grey. The executive who interviewed him had said with some kindness, 'The only problem is, Shaun, that your affair with Esther isn't doing your career any good.' This variant of the 'have you stopped beating your wife' question left Shaun speechless. The executive was a friend of mine, and a few minutes later he strolled into the office. I called to him.

'Andrew,' I said to him. 'Can I point out to you that I am a Jewish mother, not a Swedish au pair girl? When I was at Oxford, young men used to reminisce with great affection about beautiful, twenty-two-year-old Swedish women who came to live with them, did a little dusting and ironing, and introduced them to the delights of sex. Terrific. I got bored with the description of the delights, but I believed the stories. However, I am not Nordic, not twenty-two, I'm terrible at ironing, and seducing the young men on the team would be incest. I will nag them, make them eat their greens, praise them when they're good, but I won't have an affair with them.'

Andrew blushed, glanced at Shaun, and said he'd pass on what I'd said to the gossips in the department. But there is a cliché, accurate as many clichés are, that a lie will encircle the earth before the truth has put its boots on. When Shaun moved to *Newsnight*, and got engaged to Camilla Sainsbury, as the news was passed around the office they asked nervously, 'Does Esther know?' Yes, of course I knew, and I was thrilled for them both.

One Friday night, when I was working late on a story with Adrian Mills, the phone rang in the script room, I answered it and a man said, 'It's the *Sunday Mirror* here, Esther, we've been told that you're having an affair with a twenty-eight-year-old man on your team. Is it true?'

Was it, I wondered, an echo of the old gossip about Shaun, who by that time was in his thirties? The script was late, the director was waiting to put cameras on it, I had no time to waste contradicting the rumour, so I said to Adrian, 'How old are you?' 'Twenty-eight,' he said. 'Good,' I said, 'Here's a call for you', and handed him the phone.

As I typed on, I enjoyed watching Adrian blench, then contradict the rumours with his usual charm, while trying not to show how offended he was at the suggestion, for fear of insulting me.

We were like a family, and like all families, we had our disagreements. Gavin Campbell, for example, talented, intelligent, committed to all our causes and campaigns, used to drive the team mad with his unpunctuality. They tried every strategy they knew to get him to a location on time. They sent cars for him, they provided escorts for him, but the unexpected always happened. An old lady would collapse in the street, or a young man lose his wallet, or a dog would be sick, or a squirrel would drop out of a tree, and each unforeseen calamity would create a new delay.

One producer, certain that it would be a fail-safe solution, booked an overnight room in a hotel next door to a location, only to find Gavin was still late because he'd become involved in an intricate dispute with the hotel manager about a chocolate in the minibar. Once Gavin was so late in the office that we moved his desk out onto an iron staircase. He was not amused. But he knew how highly we rated him, and what a tremendous asset he was to the show.

Adrian managed to make an asset of his weakness. Not that he believes he is bad at accents. He has told me, often, of the high grades he obtained at drama school for them. So it's odd that when we investigated a Spanish company, 'Editorial Office', we didn't at first ask Adrian to be the reporter. It was an elegant scam. 'Editorial Office' wrote letters to companies all over Britain, indeed all over the world, bringing them the joyous tidings that they had all won awards. They were vague about the reasons for the honour, it was just for being the best. All each company had to do in return for the award was send an executive or two to collect it.

The executives were then put up in smart hotels, given grand dinners complete with cabarets, not Shirley Bassey, but a military piped band or two, and then presented with a metal blob, a piece of twisted tin to display in a show-case at reception. The catch, if catch it be, is that 'Editorial Office' were not all that discriminating. If your name appeared in the Yellow Pages, you qualified for one of their awards. They made their money from skimming a handsome profit from the hotel bills,

318

and most of the award-winning company executives were happy to put the costs onto their expense accounts.

The first time we exposed the scam on the programme, in rehearsal our reporter Grant Baynham read the Spanish company's poetic description of their awards dinner in a Spanish accent. Our house rule was no funny voices when we were quoting real people. But publicity leaflets were fair game. Grant did well, but he was uncomfortable, so I suggested Adrian should try his version of a Spanish accent. Adrian was quite confident. The more the crew laughed, the more confident he became. There was an oriental quality in his Spanish that added flavour to the script, particularly as he delivered it most seriously.

The item was the hit of the show, and letters poured in from companies who had also received invitations to stay all over the world and pick up their awards. Then we were told 'Editorial Office' were staging an awards night in a grand Kensington hotel just round the corner from Lime Grove. Adrian put on his dinner jacket and went with a crew, nipping through the hotel kitchen to avoid the bouncers. When they got into the dining room, there were so many other video crews recording the event to justify their company's expenses that our crew fitted in perfectly. Adrian found an empty seat and sat down, the other men at the table looked at him enquiringly. Adrian introduced himself in what he still believes to be a Spanish accent. The other men looked astonished. 'My mother,' Adrian explained, 'is Japanese.'

Grant Baynham was not at all pleased when the team played a practical joke on him. He had tried to give up smoking, without success. In the end he suggested that if anyone caught him smoking they should throw a jug of water over him. Without his knowledge, a cameraman filmed him smoking, so we rigged a bucket of water high over his chair, and at the end of the show, we tipped it over him. He disappeared behind the desk, and came up spluttering and shaking his fist. We hoped it was mock anger, but he was genuinely furious. He decided to leave at the end of that series, and I couldn't blame him. But I plotted with our Editor that in his last programme Grant should take revenge upon me.

Without telling Grant that I knew, the Editor crept down in the last few minutes of the show, and handed him a bucket of water. Grant chucked the lot over me. I, who love slapstick, was delighted. But Grant had further revenge in store. He sold his story to a tabloid newspaper, and in it made many scorching criticisms of the programme, and more especially of me. He had every right to express his views. But had he asked me I would have advised against it. Other employers in the industry don't like what they see as betrayal. Understandably, they think that if you bad-mouth one, you may bad-mouth everyone you work with.

Having a big cheque waved in front of you, when income from other sources appears to be drying up, is tempting. I remember when Patsy, Desmond's first wife, was having her angry say in the newspapers, a reporter from the *News of the World* rang me and said, 'I've been authorized to offer you a blank cheque, Esther, for your side of the story.' Fortunately, I had a steady income, and recognized that everything has its price. But I realized then that if money is tight, that kind of temptation must be very difficult to resist. No wonder there is a spate of kiss and tell stories in today's newspapers, and no wonder Grant succumbed to the temptation to quit and tell.

He was the only member of the *That's Life!* team to cricitize us publicly, although those with long memories may remember an even more hostile article about me in a Sunday paper, which looked as if it had been written by Doc Cox. Doc is a fascinating character. By profession he is a sound recordist and dubbing mixer, responsible for the soundtrack on many of the television programmes you watch. By predilection he is a musician with his own band and an alias, 'Ivor Biggun'. In this disguise Doc composes disgusting songs which have a considerable cult following, especially one called 'I'm a Wanker.'

From time to time various journalists would ring me up to draw my attention to this disgraceful split in Doc's personality, just as they would tell me about Gavin Campbell's part as a policeman in a pornographic film, made when he was a hungry young actor. I'm not sure what the other actors had to simulate in Gavin's film because I've only seen his scenes, which are extremely dull. I got quite skilled myself at simulating shocked surprise each time a journalist rang me to expose Gavin or Doc, *'No*, I *can't* believe it, is that really so? I'll have to ask him about that.'

With 'Ivor Biggun' in his life to express all the naughty excrescences in his subconscious, Doc himself is shy, sensitive and invariably polite. I caused him considerable pain when we featured him in our 'Get Britain Singing' spectaculars by

321

suggesting he should dress up as a banana, a tulip or a crocodile, but his woebegone expression added so much to the general joy of the film. Although I know I was a sadist to make him do this, it was in the cause of art, and I was sure our friendship would survive. Until one Sunday morning I opened the *News of the World* and read his article, under the banner headline, '*I'd Like to Strangle That Cow Esther*'.

We were recording the programme that day. When I arrived at the television theatre in Shepherd's Bush, Doc was already there. Looking even more woebegone than usual, he came and sat with me in my dressing room.

'I don't know where they got it, Esther. I haven't spoken to the paper. I never said any of those things.'

I looked at the byline, 'Dan Slater?'

Doc shook his head. 'I think I met him months ago. We had dinner. I may have got a bit drunk. But I still didn't say those things. And he certainly didn't tell me he was working for that paper.'

Normally we would let such things pass without a comment, but Doc was personally distressed that millions of our viewers would be misled into believing that he hated me and the show. So when the programme began we gave him an opportunity to put it right. He declared in no uncertain terms that none of the article was true. As a Sunday night programme we had a unique opportunity to reply, on the same day, and to the same audience. Among them Wendy Henry, the Editor of the *News of the World*.

I recently met Wendy, for the first time, at a wedding in the South of France. We were both in

322

swimsuits, it was a charming social occasion, so I didn't bop her on the nose. Desmond told me that my smile as I limply shook hands with her would have curdled milk. I believe him. Why was Wendy, the first woman Editor of a national newspaper such a caricature of a truth-deaf hack? She was notorious on Fleet Street. She was the Editor that did the deal with one of our con-men that raked in £2 million for him, when he was selling phoney slimming pills and he invented the story for Wendy about Sam Fox's pregnancy that never was.

And now she was responsible for Doc's diatribe. She rang me on Tuesday morning, in a fury:

'I heard Doc Cox say our story was untrue. I have the transcripts of his interview with Dan Slater. He said every word.'

'Send me the transcript,' I replied. 'If we were wrong, we will apologize to you.'

She sent the transcript to me. I could not believe my eyes. She had lifted a word here, a word there. She had omitted the end of the sentence, if it suited her. The headline came from a sentence which read, 'sometimes I will direct a film, Esther will cut it, and I'll think silly cow, she's wrecked it, and I could strangle her. Then I'll see it on the air, and damn it, she was right.'

We decided to put the transcript she had sent us onto the screen, so that our viewers could see for themselves what unscrupulous editing can do. She was quite frank about the fact that she had cut it to ribbons herself and was entirely unashamed. But our studio audience laughed with disbelief, as they saw Doc's words twisted and taken out of context.

All his many tributes to the programme, and his pleasure in working with me had been cut, the fact that we had never had a row in six years, and that he believed my fearsome reputation was based on a sexist myth, all that had gone. When I asked Wendy why, she said she had to cut something, they were short of space. So I quoted her on the air.

But it wasn't just editing for space. In the interview Doc had explained that his first marriage, which lasted ten years, had been broken up when he invented Ivor Biggun, his rude *alter ego*, whom his wife hated. Wendy had decided that was boring, so she rewrote it to make him say that his marriage had been broken up by Esther Rantzen. We showed that piece of rewriting too.

Wendy was crosser than ever. She sent Dan Slater's tape recording of Doc's interview to be edited in a sound studio to make the words fit her version. I met the editor who cut it years later, he told me he had never had such a difficult job in his life. Wendy invited her readers to ring a special number and listen to Doc's interview. One of our team rang it, transcript in hand, and counted the edits. There were forty edits in five minutes. We said so in that night's programme.

These were momentary blips in friendships, some of which have lasted twenty-one years. We still play cricket every year, we attend reunions, we follow each other's careers with interest, we are delighted when chance or arrangement brings us together. Some of us are still close friends in spite of our careers, which make friendships so difficult to sustain. But there was one professional row in my life which wrecked many of my friendships, which split my professional partnerships, and which taught me a valuable lesson.

It happened in 1980, when I was forty.

Ostensibly I had everything. *That's Life!* was more successful than ever. I had two gorgeous baby girls, Emily and Rebecca. What's more, the BBC had decided to move our production team back where we started, and we were once more working for Desmond. Some of our stories were so strong they gave rise to spin-off programmes called *That's Life Reports.* And I was the executive-producer of another series, *The Big Time.* I was busy, successful, had a happy home life, what could go wrong?

Jealousy. It writhes in the gut. It twists values. It turns love to hate, affection to loathing. It afflicted my old friends and colleagues in Desmond's department like a plague. There is a BBC rule which says that husbands and wives cannot work together. Outdated as it sounds, there is method in its absurdity. As Desmond's wife, some of his team believed that I had undue influence, that I had become the power behind the throne. It was untrue, but that's how I was perceived. Nobody could go to him and complain about me, or they thought they couldn't. The normal balance of power was destroyed.

Fearing that, when Desmond and I first told Huw Wheldon of our love affair, Huw had made the decision to transfer me away from his department into Current Affairs Group. After our marriage the BBC management moved us back into Desmond's department, General Features, for the best of motives. Not because I wanted the move, I didn't. I valued the independence of my working life in a different department. But the rest of the *That's Life!* team desperately wanted to return.

Desmond had remained closely in touch with

them, even while we were in Current Affairs group. None of the team was interested in making political programmes because, unlike me, they had not served an apprenticeship there. They had joined Desmond because they wanted to make feature programmes, and to work for him. He was a unique leader. A brilliant practitioner himself, he enabled other talent to shine. It seemed only fair to move them back to his department, and allow them to work where they were happiest, and where the show itself had been invented. It was a disaster.

My husband was a generous, loving man. He cared about the people he worked with. He was vulnerable to them. When they let him down he was badly hurt. They loved him for his openness, but they destroyed his career as a BBC executive. They conspired behind his back, the very people he had helped most were the ones to betray him. They wanted to get rid of me. But they botched the job. Instead of forcing me out, they lost Desmond.

It happened very traditionally, they waited until we were away in Greece, on a short Easter break, then two key members of the department went to the senior management and complained. We returned to find the whole unit in uproar. There was an emotional meeting of the department. Desmond was summoned to see Alasdair Milne, and offered his resignation. It was accepted, and Desmond became an independent producer.

Why did it happen? Why were the department up in arms? In retrospect it all seems petty and pointless. I never damaged anyone's career—the reverse, in fact. I never interfered with any other programme or team member, and, though they all suspected pillow talk, there was none. I was too

326

tired to notice or care what happened outside *That's Life!* and my own busy family.

Michael Parkinson once told me he thought the problem was that documentary-makers in the department had too much time, and too little work. That meant they had hours to fill with gossip and plots. He could well be right. The fact was that the BBC had piles of untransmitted documentaries on the shelf, that is the real reason why they were commissioning fewer from Desmond's documentary-producers. But the frustrated film-makers assumed it was my fault, that Desmond was so busy fighting for my programmes that he had no time to battle for their ideas. They would not, could not, listen to reason.

At the time I said that if a filing cabinet drawer stuck, they blamed me for it. Bill Cotton, who had the nasty job of trying to manage the row, told me his priority was to move me and *That's Life!* into a department where we would be a small fish in a very large pond. He must have felt that our success in a small department had so dominated all the rest of the output that the other teams felt neglected, and therefore consumed by jealousy. I could only watch as the clever, humorous people I had once worked with turned into a mindless lynch mob.

Desmond toyed with the concept of moving with me to commercial television, and we had exploratory talks with Michael Grade, who was then with London Weekend Television. But in the end we decided I should stay with the BBC. It turned out to be an ill wind for Desmond because he became an independent producer, creating for BBC Scotland and later for ITV his enduring, ground-breaking series, *The Visit.* The films he made were moving and inspiring, and culminated in the programme, *The Boy David*, the story of David Jackson, the boy from Peru whose face had to be rebuilt by surgeon Ian Jackson when it was destroyed by a disease caused by malnutrition.

In Desmond the BBC may have lost a maverick, brilliant executive, but the viewers gained an insightful, influential documentary-maker. Not only did his films win prizes around the world, but through them, hundreds of thousands of pounds were raised for charities—some of which were created as a result of his programmes. We should, I suppose, be grateful to the conspirators who caused him to relinquish his climb up the executive ladder in favour of an even more distinguished career making programmes.

I, too, should be grateful for the lesson they taught me. I learned, painfully, that the smiling faces in the office, the men and women who wished me a cheerful 'Hello, how are you?' were not friends. Indeed, some of them were enemies, whose ambition was to poison my career. I had invited them to parties, had believed we were as close as my friends at university had been. I was wrong.

As the row simmered down, after Desmond's resignation, I still had to go into my office. Letters were still arriving by the thousand from our viewers, and there was another series to prepare. I was once again sent to Coventry, as I had been when I first joined the *Man Alive* team in Kensington House. I sat alone in the canteen. Not that I wanted the company of the colleagues who had hurt Desmond so badly. I worked with the ghost of their treachery all around me, hating the building, suffocated by the atmosphere, staring at the car park, longing to escape. I rang my agent, Richard Armitage, and told him, 'I feel like a Jew trying to work in a concentration camp. The war may be over, but the old guard are still here. They are furious that I've survived, and Desmond has gone. They want to be rid of me. I can hardly bear to come in here.' Richard was sharp with me. 'Then let them have their way, let them win. Their one wish is that you should no longer make *That's Life!*. Then they can claim victory, they can say they were right all along, that you can only make the programme successfully when Desmond is protecting and supporting you.'

So I doggedly went into the office, answered letters, planned stories. BBC management decided to move me back into Current Affairs Group, but this time the team were consulted as to whether they wanted to stay in Features, or move with me. Some came with me, others stayed behind. I didn't blame any of them, whatever their decision, nor was I surprised. I knew now that colleagues are not the same as friends or family. I did object quite strongly, though, when some of those who jumped ship attempted to continue to make the programme I invented, *The Big Time*, without me. So instead they changed the format, and it became *In At the Deep End*. But otherwise I wished them well, and left without a backward look.

*   *   *

I was lucky, *That's Life!* was a valuable property, and BBC senior management trusted me. What's more, they found for me in Current Affairs Group

329

a superb Editor, Ron Neil, who was one of the most gifted team leaders I have ever worked for. He went on to create *Breakfast Time*, the first breakfast programme in Britain, starring Selina Scott and Frank Bough. Then he rose to the very peak of the BBC management pyramid, only recently retiring.

We had very happy times together, and I am extremely grateful to him for ensuring the happiness of the team in his care. He was, however, anxious about my role at first. There was no other presenter/ producer in the BBC. He asked Roger Guertin, our film editor, what would happen if he forbade me to oversee the cutting of the films. Roger said, 'That would be disaster.' So Ron let that alone.

But he still questioned every decision I made as producer. So I asked if he would go with me to see our Head of Group, John Gau. When we sat down in front of John, I explained. 'It's as if each time I pick up a paintbrush, Ron asks me what colour I'm using, and where I'm going to put it. I'm beginning to lose confidence.'

By some alchemy, John soothed me down, and at the same time supported Ron's authority. We left having made our points, having been listened to, and having found a formula to work together well. And it did work. Our audiences continued to soar. Ron went from us to *Newsnight*, and then onwards and upwards. He remembers his time with us with great affection. So do I.

*   *   *

Instinct is so crucial, in journalism. Several times in

my life I have stumbled on a very big story. At the time it's impossible for me to explain why I know in my heart, or in my gut, that this moment is going to be one I'll remember all my life. For example, I know exactly where I was when I first heard the story of Ben Hardwick.

It was in January 1984. By this time I had started a family of my own. Previous generations of working women had to pretend that having babies made not the slightest difference to their capacity to be as hard and as hard-working as the men. If women journalists wanted to be taken seriously they avoided 'women's subjects' as demeaning, and by this they meant not only fashion and beauty, but babies and children. The result was that the vast population of mothers were unrepresented in the media. So were fathers who wanted to take part in the parenting of their own children.

Perhaps out of arrogance, perhaps because becoming a mother completely overwhelmed me emotionally, I couldn't ignore the experience, put a damp-proof course between my life and my work. I've never been any good at that.

Emily's birth was difficult. Desmond was at my shoulder; I remember him leaning over watching George Pinker put together an intimidating pair of forceps and saying, 'What are you doing, George, building a garage?' I was given pethidine, a nasty drug, that fragmented my memories and gave them a nightmare quality. As soon as Emily was born they took her away from me and wrapped her in linen, which felt coarse and rough to me as I tried to cuddle her.

When my second daughter, Rebecca, was due, George Pinker said to me, 'Is there anything you'd like done differently this time, Esther?' I said yes, I'd like my baby to be handed to me straight away, without being bundled up, and I'd like some time to pass before they cut the cord and cleaned her up.

Mr Pinker was intrigued, because I clearly found it very difficult to ask these favours. 'Why, Esther? Why can't you ask for what you want? You're a strong-minded woman, what about the hundreds of inarticulate, shy women I see? If you can't ask me, how can they? What's wrong? Should I not be sitting behind a desk?'

I tried to reassure him, and explain that it was not because he intimidated me, it was simply that to me he was the expert—after all he'd been at so many hundreds of births. I'd only been to one.

But I remembered the conversation, and that inspired me to suggest *That's Life!* should mount a special survey into childbirth. That in turn led to a book, *The British Way of Birth* which made the strong plea that doctors and midwives should be more sensitive to parents, and allow mothers more choice in the way their babies are born.

*   *   *

Emily was born a dimpled, blue-eyed baby, with a soft tuft of dark brown hair rising vertically from her head, and a wide grin. Three days after her birth I developed raging post-natal depression. It was easy to diagnose. Whenever anyone asked me how I was, I would dissolve into tears. It lasted six months. My only consolation was to take Emily onto my lap, and listen to the whiffles of her sleeping breath. Her heartbeat on mine was the most soothing sound in the world.

I rang a producer friend, Ruth Jackson, and together we planned a *Man Alive* programme about post-natal depression. As part of the programme, in partnership with *Woman* magazine, we created a network of support groups called the 'Meet-a-Mum Association', 'MAMA' for short. I am proud to say I am still their president, and they still do invaluable work, supporting isolated, depressed mums, and providing them with company and reassurance.

Two years after Emily, Rebecca was born—a very different experience. 'If only,' said George Pinker, 'I could go into business delivering second babies, my life would be so much easier'

Certainly Becca had no trouble finding her way out into the world, no forceps or garage-building, although George did look at her with some surprise and said, 'That's a big one. At least eight pounds.' She was, in fact, nine pounds two ounces. May I recommend big babies? She was plump and delicious, and I knew she could withstand any cold winds, or clumsiness on my part. She, too, spent the first three months of her life in my arms, or on my lap.

When I was in hospital she was always in the bed next to me. Midwives used to burst into my room, gaze accusingly at the empty cot and say, 'Mrs Wilcox, where is that baby?' I would look dreamily at the ceiling, as if I expected her to be floating up there like a plump, pink helium balloon.

One beautiful nurse, tall, black, swan-like, I think Ethiopian, said to me, 'When did you last feed that baby?' Becca was fast asleep at that moment, and then as now, when she's asleep she is undisturbable.

I tried to remember. 'I'm sorry, I don't know. I'm demand-feeding.'

The nurse looked suspicious. 'We approve of demand-feeding. But not more often than every two hours, and no longer than three hours between feeds.'

Perhaps God should have implanted an alarm clock under Becca's skin.

Eighteen months after Becca, Joshua was born. A newspaper heralded his birth with a disgraceful headline, 'At last a boy for Esther'. That was absolutely not what I felt. I was extremely happy with my two girls. But I had been delighted at forty-one to be pregnant a third time. Desmond couldn't believe it.

Together we bought a pregnancy test kit, and I insisted on taking it into the bathroom and conducting the chemical experiment myself. The result was unmistakable. I shouted through the door,

'Congratulations, Desmond, there's a clear ring.'

'Maybe that's because you've done it too fast, leave it for another ten minutes and it may have disappeared,' he shouted back, with typical lack of faith in my technical ability.

I encouraged this view, since it logically followed that plugging in a hoover or finding a duster would also be beyond my fragile intellect. He always claimed that I never knew where the hoover was kept. And that was the way I liked it. However, in this case, I was right, he was wrong, and after ten minutes the ring was even clearer. Eight months later the ring was revealed to be Joshua, and our family was complete.

Without Joshua, there would have been no Ben Hardwick story. Because just before I discovered I was pregnant, David Frost came to visit us in our home in Kew, with an idea. Impresario as David is, he was putting together a franchise for a new breakfast television company. His concept was a television version of the Hollywood United Artists, to combine six of the best-known on-screen talents, Michael Parkinson, Angela Rippon, Robert Key, Anna Ford, Frostie himself and me.

Peter Jay was to Chair the new franchise, which, for the first time, would give us all the chance to amass some capital. The problem with being a television fat-cat, as we all were, was that although by ordinary standards we were high income earners, we had short working lives, and our lifestyles ate up most of the cash. In fact, Desmond and I have always been used to reading our bank balances in red. So to have some shares in the company promised financial security for the first time.

I rang Alasdair Milne and asked his advice. He was honest with me. The BBC also intended to start a breakfast programme, but I was not part of their plan. He advised me to join Frost's consortium.

*   *   *

David's love-life was always a source of great curiosity to the press. At this time he was dating Lynne Frederick, Peter Sellers' widow. The journalists had pursued them to the ski-slopes to try and capture pictures of them both together. On the day the franchise announcements were to be announced, the 'Famous Six' all met in David's house for the news. David took the call from Peter Jay. 'I see. Yes. Any conditions? No.' He put the phone down. He turned to us, dead-pan. 'We've won. Unconditionally.' Parky hugged me. 'Now we've got our eff-off money,' he said, happily.

A worm of doubt squirmed inside me. Was I going to be any good at breakfast television? There was a hammering at the door, a mob of journalists and photographers pushed past the pretty dark woman who opened it. We watched with amusement as they ignored her, and started to photograph us. She was, of course, Lynne Frederick, who they'd chased down the ski-slopes. But today—different story, different quarry.

A few days later, Peter Jay asked to see me. At his franchise interview, the interrogators made it clear that they assumed he had his 'Famous Six' exclusively for the breakfast show. I, however, had told Peter that I must continue to make *That's Life!* as a prime-time programme, probably for ITV, in the evening. *Impasse.* I apologized, but explained to Peter that this was not negotiable. So I would have to leave his team. How would we explain this without destroying the credibility of TV-am's bid?

'Easy,' I said, having just discovered the ring in the bathroom. 'I'll explain I've just found out I am pregnant, and I can't combine breakfast television with a new baby.'

That was how I jumped ship, luckily well before it began to sink, only to be saved by Roland Rat. Someone said at the time that it was the first recorded instance of a sinking ship being saved by a rat. Because, notwithstanding the brilliance of the five famous stars, it was a hairy puppet-rat that attracted the ratings (or the ravings).

During the rough few months that followed I stayed in touch with my friends who were still aboard, and sympathized with the horrors they suffered, before a little-known producer climbed in and saved them. He was, of course, Greg Dyke. But by the time he was recruited Angela Rippon and Anna Ford had both been forced to walk the plank, quite unnecessarily. When programmes fail, it's invariably the producer's fault, but it's always the presenter who gets sacked, usually the female presenter. It's totally unfair. But then I would say that, wouldn't I?

The only person not to buy my Joshua excuse was Mark Boxer, Anna Ford's late husband. When fists started to fly in the TV-am offices we all went out to dinner together. I mentioned how lucky I felt I had been, that Joshua had prevented me from staying with the breakfast programme. Mark looked at me sharply. 'What a shame nobody ever told you about birth control,' he said.

Quite. I had really been saved by an instinct that the mixture of talents David had collected, though perfect for winning the franchise, had not been quite right for the programme. What they needed more was what the BBC had in Ron Neil, a very experienced, populist, magazine programme editor. They hadn't got one. Without that, I thought the talents they had brought together were like brilliant racehorses, harnessed together without a driver. The chariot would be torn to pieces with nobody to use their strengths and steer them in the right direction. And so it proved.

I went straight back to the BBC and Bognor. Bognor, because actor John Judd was putting together the cast for a pantomime, *Dick Whittington*. We met round the table of Richard Baker's programme, *Start the Week*. John looked at me, I couldn't sing, I couldn't dance, I couldn't act, but I had passable legs, and I yearned nostalgically for the days when as an undergraduate I had pranced my stuff before a live audience in the theatre. He came home with me to press his case.

Desmond listened incredulously.

'No,' said Desmond, 'Absolutely not. She has a brand-new baby. She's an investigative journalist. Esther, you can't, you mustn't do it.'

I did it. And how typical of my husband that he not only saw the show two dozen times, not only booked two pink charabancs to shuttle my friends and family to see it at one hilarious matinee, but on the last night he came onto the stage to sing the songsheet in front of the audience.

To understand the nobility of that gesture, you have to know that Desmond was musical, but could not sing in key. When he sang 'Happy Birthday' people thought he had invented a *musique concrete* descant. So it was with dread he heard Kenneth Alan Taylor, our brilliant Dame, announce to the audience of our last performance, 'Ladies and Gentlemen, there is one little boy who has been to more than twenty performances of our pantomime, and he has been dying to come up onto the stage and sing. Come along, little Desmond.'

The cruel spotlight picked him up as he cowered in the stalls. But he came up to the stage like the trooper he was, and spoke the song with impeccable rhythm, like Rex Harrison in *My Fair Lady*. I was so thrilled with him I gave him an enormous kiss.

'Dick', Kenneth the Dame rebuked me, 'Boys don't kiss men. They kiss women.' And he/she kissed me instead.

I loved that pantomime. The glorious sound of children laughing, the wickedness of the cast's (successful) attempts to make me laugh, the ancient jokes, ('Infamy, infamy, they've all got it infamy'), I loved it all. Even when the principal girl went down with flu on the third night, and I had to sing duets with myself, I loved it. It wore me out physically though, I got thinner and thinner. When at last the run ended, (a triumph, according to *Stage*, we had played to ninety-two per cent capacity. Nobody mentioned how tiny our Bognor theatre was, so that wasn't too difficult), I went back to the BBC to make a documentary about stillbirth.

Among the letters that had been part of our *That's Life!* survey into childbirth were a clutch of tragic stories that made me sit under my desk and weep as I read them. These were from women whose babies had died, and who felt they had been punished as a result. The babies had been taken from them, and they had never had the chance to hold them, to mourn them. Nobody would talk to these parents about their loss, the hospital would offer to bury them, but the babies' bodies would be consigned to an anonymous mass grave. All this, I remind you, happened a short twenty years ago. How could caring hospital staff have been so callous to these bereaved families?

We began our research and discovered that there had been good psychological research into stillbirth. We met the psychiatrists responsible, they could not believe our letters. 'But we have published our work,' they said. 'We have proved that mothers must be allowed to see their babies, and have photographs of them, and be allowed to grieve. Surely this cannot still be going on?' But it was.

I interviewed some of the mothers who had written to us. I spoke to the social worker who ran the Stillbirth and Neonatal Death Society, 'SANDS'.

'What if a baby is badly disabled,' I asked her. 'Should the parent still see him?'

'A dead baby is still a baby,' she told me, 'The nurses will wrap a baby if needed, with a hat, or a shawl. There will always be something to see, to hold, a tiny hand, or a foot.'

I spoke to a woman whose husband had been told to redecorate the nursery, give away the cot, pretend the baby had never existed. No wonder she had broken down completely. I went with a couple to try and find their baby's grave in a cemetery in Paddington. We walked in the winter mud between eighteenth-century gravestones. The mist was freezing, and clung to the branches of the bare trees. Between the graves I caught sight of a scarlet, woollen hat—a gravedigger was cheerfully humming to himself as he forked out lumps of dank clay. It was a scene from *Hamlet*. I interviewed the shocked parents as they realized they would never now be able to identify their baby in his pauper's grave.

Then I got back into a car, was driven home, and put to bed for the next three weeks. I had double pneumonia. When I told the doctor what I had been filming, he said, 'If you'd stayed there much longer, a hand would have come out of that grave and beckoned you in.' But the film did its job. We put it on cassette, and it was loaned out to teaching hospitals. It became a training film, and was shown around the world. Now it is standard practice to photograph a stillborn baby, to name her, to bury her in her own grave, and create a memory book for her. A dead baby is still a baby.

*   *   *

Soon my own babies were turning into toddlers. Somehow I juggled motherhood with *That's Life!*. Mondays became the best day of the week. That was when I would take the girls to the nursery school in Richmond, and while they were painting big, bright, splodgy pictures, (they are framed on my bedroom wall to this day), I would sneak away to the local department store and order myself a hot chocolate and a croissant and be a housewife for an hour.

Yes, I know, being a housewife all your life is for some women boring and frustrating. All those creative intellectual powers wasted, they dream of working in a busy office, meeting challenges and earning a fortune. But I dreamed of pushing a supermarket trolley round a food store, and whipping up a Pavlova for supper. Monday mornings were my wish-fulfilment, and girls, I make no apologies for that.

One Tuesday in January 1984, back in the office at Lime Grove, I was standing in the canteen queue waiting to choose between burnt potatoes, and swimming boiled cabbage. The new series of *That's Life!* had been on the air one week. Shaun Woodward, then a researcher, ran up to me. He told me that a production assistant, Gill Bradley, had taken a phone call from a desperate young mother, Debbie Hardwick, whose toddler, Ben, was about to die. He had biliary atresia, a liver disease. His only hope was a liver transplant, but that would require a donor, and there were no donors. In fact, transplant surgery had almost halted in Britain.

Fifteen years ago, in America, a baby with the same illness had been given a liver transplant, and he was still alive, and thriving. But there was no hope for Ben. Why? *Panorama* had apparently terrified the nation with a recent programme that claimed the medical tests for brain death were inadequate. As a result, many people believed organs could be removed from someone who was still alive. The medical profession had protested, they said the *Panorama* claims were based on discredited American tests, but to no avail. The damage was done.

Ben's surgeon, Roy Calne, told Debbie that her only hope of saving her son's life would be if she could change public opinion. She asked how she could possibly do that. He said television would be the most potent means. So she had rung two programmes, the first, an afternoon show on ITV, told her to write to them. The second was *That's Life!*.

I asked Shaun how long Ben had to live, he told me, 'It could be a few weeks, it could be days.' I looked at Shaun's tray of food, and said I didn't think he had time for it. I asked him to go now, find a crew and a director, and film Debbie and Ben straight away. A thought struck me. Joshua was almost exactly Ben's age, and loved the little tubes of bubble liquid we used to blow towards him

342

through a wire loop, so that he could catch the big, fragile bubbles that floated around him. I suggested Shaun should stop on the way and buy some bubble liquid.

He did, and the film he brought back was heartbreaking. Ben, his blue eyes shining with fun, sat in his bath, his hands high over his head, trying to catch the bubbles. His mother, Debbie, was a lovely young woman, and eloquent as people often are when they have rehearsed the words in their heads through countless sleepless nights. She explained to Shaun that for a parent to donate a dead child's organ might become the only gleam of comfort in their darkness.

'Surely,' she said, 'If one child has died, it must be some consolation for parents to know that they have saved another child.'

I wrote the script around the film, then I went home to Desmond and my young family. I hugged them, feeling the children's warmth and strength, thanking God for their health. I talked to Desmond about Ben's death sentence, and neither of us could believe there was any realistic hope that his life could be saved. But all the same, neither of us could quite quench the tiny leap of hope in our hearts.

The film was transmitted on *That's Life!* on Sunday 15 January. The next morning I went to Broadcasting House to take part in *Start The Week With Richard Baker*. To my astonishment, Richard and all his guests were talking about Ben. When I went back to the office, all our phones were ringing. People were offering money to send Ben to America for the operation, other families were ringing to tell us of their experiences. Many of them were saying they, too, had lost children, and that Debbie was right, it would have been a great comfort to them if they had been able to save another child's life.

Suddenly at the end of the week we had fresh news, a phone call from Addenbrooke's Hospital. A donor had been found. An doctor's wife in Nottingham had watched our programme while her husband was in bed with flu. When it ended, she took him a cup of tea and told him about Ben. Until then her husband had no idea that liver transplants were possible on such little children. A couple of days later, he was asked to work on an operation on a desperately ill little boy, Matthew Fewkes, who tragically died. The doctor asked the Fewkes family if they would allow their son's liver to be donated to Ben. They agreed. For years I carried Matthew's picture in my wallet. The Fewkes' example of generosity saved hundreds, maybe thousands of lives.

Exactly one week after our first programme, I rang Debbie from our studio. She was with Ben in Addenbrooke's, waiting for the final tests before the transplant operation could take place. I told her about the avalanche of letters we had received, of the offers of support.

She told me, 'Thank you isn't enough to say to all those people, especially to anybody who could save our son's life by donating the liver of their child. They can give him the gift of life, which is more than I ever dreamed of.'

The operation was successful. A few weeks later I held Ben in my arms for the first time, unable to believe that the miracle we had all prayed for had actually taken place. We filmed him playing happily in the children's ward, then for some reason I asked Debbie to take Ben to the door of the hospital. He wasn't due to leave Addenbrooke's for some days yet. But I had a feeling we needed to show him at the door, that things were going too well, and something was due to go wrong.

Have I mentioned the steel ruler the BBC keep in reserve, for programme-makers they fear are growing complacent? Now they rapped us hard over the knuckles, twice. Firstly, the management decided that Ben's story might end in tragedy, and that therefore we must be prevented from filming him any more. Secondly, they took us off the air.

We felt the first steel thwack on the day Ben left hospital. We were in the *That's Life!* studio, preparing that night's programme. All the press, including a BBC news film crew, had been told that Ben was going home, and they were on their way to take pictures of his departure. Ben was the story of the moment, every news bulletin, every newspaper, was covering each new chapter in his battle for life. Unable to go ourselves, we arranged that BBC news would allow us to share their film coverage.

The news team were well on their way to Cambridge when the cameraman rang our control room. They had been instructed to turn back. A senior executive had decided there should be no more coverage by the BBC of Ben's story. I understand that at an important meeting someone had said, 'Don't they realize the child may die?' Of course we realized that, so did Debbie, so did our audience. That's why the transplant was crucial, that's what gave Debbie her urgency, that's why our viewers were so moved. But that was surely no reason why our audience could not share the moment Debbie had longed for, Roy Calne had worked for, when Ben could at last go home.

But we never had a chance to debate the point, the news crew were on their way back to Shepherd's Bush, and we had lost the sequence. Our language was unprintable, when we heard. But at least we had some pictures we had already shot of Ben in Debbie's arms by the hospital door, and over them we told our viewers the news. The next morning, the newspapers had the picture on their front pages of Ben smiling through the car window. We hadn't. Neither had BBC news.

The second smack from the BBC's ruler was just as hurtful, and even less easy for us to understand. By now we had reached an audience of fourteen million viewers, thanks to Ben's story, and we were still climbing. What broadcasting organization in the world would take us off the air at this point? The BBC would, and they did. They replaced us with a dog show, Crufts.

Perhaps there were contractual reasons. Maybe there was no other available slot to show the magic moment when some high-priced pooch became the dog of the year. As I hope I have already demonstrated, I like dogs as much as most people. But as I watched the tweed skirts and stout brogues of the judges striding round the ring, and the fluffed and shampooed pedigrees pattering smugly to their places, I gritted my teeth as ferociously as a Rottweiler.

We only lost one programme, though to us that week felt like a lifetime. Ben himself came into the studio just before Easter, we gave him a silver balloon to hold, he smiled up at it, and the audience were enchanted. One of our viewers arranged for the family to take him to Malta for a summer holiday, Ben had never been allowed to play on a beach before. I went to London Zoo with Debbie and Ben. We filmed them together in a meadow by the river, and she told us, 'If things went wrong tomorrow, it would still have been worth it.'

When, one year after his transplant, things did go wrong, I was telephoned one night at home in bed by a Cambridge newspaper. The reporter broke the news to me that Ben had died. I had to pull myself together, find an instant reaction, and discover from Shaun what had happened. He told me that Ben's new liver had begun to fail again, they had decided on a second transplant, but his heart had been unable to withstand a second major operation.

I went to his funeral, piercingly painful, as children's funerals always are. We had to rush a programme together to commemorate him, we used 'Ben', the Michael Jackson song he had loved. To it we put the lovely pictures we had collected over the year, of Ben catching bubbles in the bath, riding the rocking horse, playing by the river.

Among our viewers that Sunday was Andrew Lloyd Webber, who rang me to say how moved he was. He talked to Don Black about it. Don, one of the finest lyric-writers in the country, had written the words of 'Ben'. He mentioned it to the singer Marti Webb, who was at that moment recording an album. From these threads a golden chord was woven. Marti added 'Ben' as an extra track to her record, and released it as a single. Her version went immediately into the charts.

Shaun and I wrote a book telling Ben's story, it

347

was published by the BBC and went straight to the top of the bestseller lists. The money raised by the book and the record became the foundation of a fund set up in Ben's memory, the Ben Hardwick Memorial Fund.

*   *   *

Ben's story doesn't end there. Although he only lived three short years, his story changed the face of transplantation in Britain. In Addenbrooke's hospital at the same time were two other children, Matthew Whittaker and Andrew Hardwick (no relation to Ben), who were dying for lack of liver transplants. Thanks to Ben, they had their operations and they are still, as I write, alive and well.

In the last *That's Life!* in 1994, Andrew Hardwick came into the studio. I shook Andrew's hand and remembered what his father, Ron, had told me as his son recovered, 'Andrew takes the medicine, we get better.' Those words often echoed in my head, when my own daughter became gravely ill.

Then, as a surprise in that last programme, the team played me a filmed interview with Matthew Whittaker, from the university where he was studying. As I stood in the studio listening to him, my eyes filled with tears I could not control. It was unbearably moving to see him as a young man, and remember the tiny, skinny child I had met in a hospital ward, keeping himself alive by sheer bravery.

Ben's story had other extraordinary effects. So many millions of viewers were spellbound by his story that we rose in the ratings until *That's Life!* topped the charts at number one. I feel immensely proud that through television a true story of the battle to save one child's life could reach out to so many people in this compassionate country. And having reached so many people, we were able to achieve the miracle that Ben's surgeon had asked for.

We did, for a short time, change public opinion. The rate of transplant surgery doubled. Hundreds of lives were saved. And even when, tragically, Ben died, we were able to create a charity in his name, the Ben Hardwick Memorial Fund, which paid for a paediatric unit in his hospital, and has helped countless other desperately ill children.

Sadly, as I write, the waiting lists for transplants are growing again. So perhaps we should end Ben's story with a quotation that Debbie Hardwick was sent. It was printed on a crumpled and faded newspaper cutting. None of us knew who had sent it, or composed it. It's the last will and testament of a donor. It contains the ideas that inspired the Fewkes family, and so many other people whose names we will never know, but who gave that most generous of gifts, the gift of life.

Remember Me
The day may come when my body will lie upon the white sheet in a hospital, busily occupied with the living and the dying. At a certain moment a doctor will determine that my brain has ceased to function, and that for all intents and purposes, my life has stopped.

When that happens, do not attempt to instil artificial life into my body by the use of a machine.

And don't call this my deathbed. Let it be called the Bed of Life, and let my body be taken from it to help others lead fuller lives.

Give my sight to the man who has never seen the sun rise, a baby's face, or love in the eyes of a woman. Give my heart to a person whose own heart has caused nothing but endless days of pain. Give my blood to the teenager who was pulled from the wreckage of his car, so that he might live to see his grandchildren play. Give my kidneys to the one who depends on a machine to exist. Take my bones, every muscle, every fibre and nerve in my body and find a way to make a crippled child walk.

Explore every corner of my brain. Take my cells, if necessary, and let them grow so that, some day, a speechless boy will shout, and a deaf girl will hear the sound of rain against her window. Burn what is left of me and scatter the ashes to the winds to help the flowers grow. If you must bury something, let it be my faults, my weaknesses and all my prejudice against my fellow man. If, by chance, you wish to remember me, do it with a kind deed or word to someone who needs you. If you do all I have asked, I will live forever.

All my working life I have learned from the programmes I have made. One of the criticisms levelled against me by more 'objective' journalists is that I do not draw a hard and fast line between my life and my work. In this chapter I have confessed that this accusation is true. The story of Ben Hardwick affected me deeply. In some ways it became a model for the creation of ChildLine, because it taught me how effectively television can change people's lives for the better, how it can alter prejudice, and support important causes.

During the telling of Ben's story I interviewed many bereaved families. Recently I, too, have had the experience of sitting at a deathbed and watching someone I loved die. Then I took the decision that I know my generous husband Desmond would have wanted, and I rang the transplant coordinator. She asked me a list of questions. (These days there is, understandably, a nervousness that a donated organ might be infected with Aids. But I didn't find the questions intrusive.) And even though my tough, battered husband, with his scarred corneas and his cut-about heart was sixty-nine when he died, they could still use his eyes, his skin and his bone.

Desmond will be remembered in so many ways by the people who took part in his programmes, by viewers, by friends and family, for all his achievements, both as a man and as a programme-maker. But having lived through Ben's story with him, I know Desmond would be glad that his deathbed became, as the quotation says, a 'Bed of Life'.

CHAPTER TWELVE

CHILDLINE

I am, as I have said, an agnostic. Nevertheless, there have been times in my life when I have felt guided. Forgive me, please, if that sounds conceited. I don't mean that I felt chosen for some special mission. It's simply that I felt as if I was being steered along a particular path without understanding where it was leading. Often the rocky path took me into an unknown country, organ transplantation, for instance, or child abuse. The years between 1984 and 1990 felt like that to me. I hurtled round each bend and bruising corner as it came, and stopped occasionally to take in every extraordinary new view.

While the Ben Hardwick story had the programme in its grip, I caused our Editor, Gordon Watts, to sniff derisively when I said to him, 'Sometimes I feel as if God is writing the script'. He thought I was confusing myself with God. I hope I wasn't, and that I had that distinction clearly in my mind. What I really meant was that God was using us to tell a story, and only He understood where it would end.

In 1984, when Michael Grade came to the BBC as Controller of BBC1, I had just finished a series of programmes called *That's Family Life*. These were transmitted on weekday evenings, between series of *That's Life!*. I found making them intensely moving. We tackled some of the toughest subjects life can throw at a family: the death of a child, disability, the dilemma of a young person who realizes he or she is gay.

Michael was impressed by the programmes, said that we had put on to the agenda subjects that many people find difficult to discuss together as a family, and decided I should be one of the presenters, with Nick Ross, of a new programme he had invented called *Drugwatch*. Drugs were already a frightening problem in California, where Michael had just been working, and he believed that Britain would soon be engulfed in the same desperate battle against them.

Drugwatch was a fascinating programme to make. We suggested to the viewers of *That's Life!* that they take part in an anonymous questionnaire about their own experiences of illegal drugs. They did, by the thousand. In this way we managed to tap into the reality of drug-taking in Britain. We based our programme on their replies, and were able to set up a network of support groups for addicts and their families. Diana, the Princess of Wales, came into the studio to sign a pledge, 'Just Say No'. So successful was the programme that the Editor, Ritchie Cogan, came to me to ask if there was another subject I thought could be tackled in the same way. I said, yes, I thought there was. Child abuse.

For some time I had realized that this was the subject I found most painful to read about. When I saw headlines about the murder or torture of a child, I could hardly bear to read the story. As a journalist I knew I should not have been so timid, and was irritated by my own reaction. One story I did read was the death of a Heidi Koseda, a three-year-old toddler whose body had been found locked behind her bedroom door. She had been dead for two months. She died agonizingly from starvation. Her mother and her mother's partner had thought they were punishing her. They both had mental health problems, and had met when they attended the same special school. Could this death have been prevented? Should that family have been better supported?

I went with Ritchie Cogan to see Michael Grade and put to him the idea of a programme about child abuse. Ritchie suggested that we could create another survey with the help of *That's Life!* viewers, and could ask them whether they had ever experienced cruelty as children. Their answers might enable us to find better ways of protecting children from avoidable pain. Grade listened to Ritchie and me. He could have told us we were crazy even to suggest such a subject for a prime-time programme on BBC1. After all, he has the reputation of an entertainer. But instead he said, 'How long do you want for this programme?' We said ninety minutes. He gave us a slot, and a time. *Childwatch* was born.

The producer on the programme was Sarah Caplin, who is my first cousin. I am extremely proud of her, and shine in her reflected glory. As I write, she is Granada's Head of Features. She combines intellectual brilliance with a show-business talent for attracting audiences. Together we compiled an intricate detailed questionnaire for the viewers, asking about their suffering as children. We received 3000 replies. They made heartbreaking reading. They were written by adults, with the language, perspective and understanding of adults, who were vividly reliving

354

their childhood experiences. Time had done nothing to heal their hurt. It was as if the cruelty had been inflicted on them the day before. Their psychic wounds still bled, and, reading about them, we bled too.

'I was never frightened of walking home alone in the dark, of being raped or mugged. I knew what was waiting for me at home was infinitely worse than that.'

'I was abused and dare I say tortured for the best part of five years. I have not forgotten, I never will forget the pain, anguish and confusion linked to it. Most vivid is the fact that as a 12-year-old no one would listen to what I was saying. They didn't want to hear. What you are telling them they find as unbearable as the abuse itself.'

'The worst moments for me were the nights, four sisters sleeping in one room and all of us wondering who would have to suffer. I used to feel filled with guilt wishing that he wouldn't pick me.'

'It happened to me almost daily. I tried to take an overdose of tablets but it only made me sick. He used to frighten me by saying that my mother would be put in a workhouse, and that I would be put in a home if anybody found out.'

'He used to pull me round the room by my hair and hit me. Then I wet the bed and he came in and took the bed away and gave me an old coat to sleep on. I was locked in my bedroom every day—I could never understand why I couldn't play outside like other

children. At Christmas when all the shops had Christmas trees in them, I used to look in the windows and my only wish was that I could have a tree and a little doll, but my wish never came true. My best time was when I was taken into care, and the first things I saw were that Christmas tree and the doll I had seen the year before. At last somebody loved me.'

'The worst memory I have is when I realized that what my stepfather was doing to me was wrong. My nightmares were always the same. I was being attacked by a man whose face was always blacked out. I would be screaming, but I could hear no sound coming out.'

I still have nightmares, I have no friends, never had a boyfriend, and wish I had died at 15. Please help all the children who are suffering sexual abuse and cruelty, because they will always be left with the mental pain.'

The vast majority of the surveys were from women, most of them describing sexual abuse, many saying they had tried to tell someone (often a school-friend) but had not been believed. One told us she had been so sickened by what her mother and her mother's partner had done to her that she had described it in an essay, and given it to a teacher who she believed liked and cared about her. The essay was returned with red pencil scrawled across every page, and the teacher's comment on her 'repulsive imagination. What on earth made you think this kind of rubbish is suitable material for an essay?' Her cry for help was thrown back in her face.

As we read the surveys, we longed to be able to seize the hands of the clock and drag them backwards, so that we could find these children and protect them from the appalling cruelty they described. But time had taken the children away. The adults they had become still carried the scars. They told us how much they had suffered since; they had agoraphobia, or self-mutilated, many were depressed, some suicidal. Some had turned to crime, or become alcoholics or junkies. Many found marriage impossible; some had become prostitutes. Over and over again they told us they had been robbed of their childhood. What about today's children? We had no doubt the crime—this secret crime of child abuse, which is so difficult to detect and quantify—had continued to this day. How could we reach today's child victims? An idea came to me, so difficult, so challenging, that it almost took over my life.

We had launched our survey on *That's Life!*. I knew we had millions of child viewers, they wrote to us, sent us ideas, and enjoyed our odd combination of seriousness and talking dogs. So after the programme on which we launched our survey, and explained the point of it, we decided to open phone-lines, just in case there were children suffering cruelty who were watching the programme and needed help.

We could only keep the phone-lines open for a few hours—after all, the BBC is a broadcasting organization, not a child-protection agency. I remember clearly the two counsellors who came to our office to tell us of the calls they'd received. The lines had been jammed with children describing current abuse, most of it sexual. It seems that by launching our survey we had given permission for the first time for victims of this most taboo crime to ask for help. The counsellors explained that most of the children had called anonymously. I was appalled. 'We must try and discover who they are,' I said. 'We must stop this crime.'

One of the counsellors looked at me gravely. 'Esther,' she said, 'this is your crisis. You have only just learned about it. But the child has been living with this for months, perhaps years. Distressed as you are, you must tread carefully. If you go in with hobnail boots you may do more harm than good.'

I was unconvinced. 'What harm could we do?'

They described one call. A child had rung to tell them about the sexual abuse she was suffering. Having persuaded her to tell them her name and address, they sent the police round. The front door was opened by the alleged abuser himself, with his arm round the child. The policeman explained why he had called. The man laughed. 'She's always up to something, this one. Tell the policeman it was just a joke, and say you're sorry for wasting his time.' The child obeyed, the door closed, and the policeman left. The child was in even graver danger now, left alone with an abuser who was determined to shut her mouth.

I was silent as the counsellor reported to me what the policeman had said, that for all the best motives we might have put the child at even greater risk. I realized we had to move at the child's pace, sensitively, to be sure that we did not make bad still worse.

But what the BBC's phone-line proved was that young people would ring for help. Children who nobody else knew were being abused would talk to counsellors about their pain. The day after the lines closed I rang my cousin, the *Childwatch* producer, Sarah Caplin. 'I've got a nightmare in my head,' I told her. 'If so many hundreds of children rang us while the lines were open, how many thousands more need help? Do you think it would be possible to open a children's helpline all the year round, and keep it open twenty-four hours a day?'

She thought about it, then rang me back. 'I think it's a good idea. We should call together the experts we have already contacted for *Childwatch*. Let's tell them the results of our survey, and ask if they would help us open a children's helpline.'

She and Ritchie Cogan drew up a guest-list for a day's conference. There were representatives from the NSPCC and the National Children's Home, from the Department for Education (which said, 'Don't children make all these stories up?') and from directors of Social Services. We sat around a huge table in a BBC conference room. We told the experts the results of our survey. Only a tiny fraction of our 3000 respondents had told us they had received any help from the child-protection agencies, the police or the social workers. Most of them said that in any case the help they did receive only made things worse for them.

Gloomy as the findings were, the professionals were unsurprised. From their own work they knew only too well the inadequacies of the law, and that most child-abusers go unpunished. We described the response to our helpline. We asked their advice. One by one round the table they told us that yes, children would use a helpline, but no, it would be impossible to set one up. It was simply

359

impractical. None of the other agencies could help.

But among the experts there were other, personal responses, too. Paul Griffiths from the NSPCC told us that whatever the difficulties, we must overcome them, because protecting children from pain was the priority. 'Child abuse,' he said, 'is an attack on a child's soul'. He became ChildLine's first director. Alan Holden, then a Director of Social Services, told us that if we were able to open a children's helpline, 'It must never become the means by which children suffer pain more comfortably'. In other words, the aim must be not simply to listen, but to protect. We must move the children from danger to safety. He became a ChildLine trustee.

At the end of the meeting Michele Elliott, who founded the children's charity Kidscape, told us: 'This has been a valuable discussion. But it's only too easy to mistake talk for action. What you need now is action'. We took her words to heart.

*　　　*　　　*

Sarah and Ritchie made an appointment for us to meet Sir George Jefferson, then the Chairman of British Telecom. Whether he saw us because I was the producer/presenter of *That's Life!*, and from time to time we had tweaked BT's nose on the programme, I can't say. Certainly he had many of his executive team sitting with him round his glossy table. For this crucial meeting I remember picking my smartest suit, grey Prince of Wales check with wide *Dallas* shoulders. I knew I had to look my best, instil confidence in him and his team.

Ritchie, Sarah and I had paced around a patch

360

of grass outside the office, planning what to ask. I started by telling Sir George about our survey. I quoted the woman who said she was never frightened of being raped or mugged on her way home in the dark because what was waiting for her there was so much worse. I talked about my own children's bedroom, a place of safety, a refuge for them from the rest of the world. I quoted the vivid descriptions in our survey, of children who waited with dread night after night for the footstep outside their bedroom door which meant the abuse was about to begin again. I described the huge response to our helpline, from children ringing to talk about their suffering.

'If we open a permanent helpline, a ChildLine,' I said, 'the telephone itself can become an instrument of child protection.'

Sir George was obviously moved: 'How can I help?' he asked me.

I had planned for the question. 'Please can we have free phone calls? The children must be able to ring from a safe phone, and that may mean a public callbox, and they probably won't have any money. We will have to pay for their calls.'

Sir George shook his head, and explained that the law did not allow him to discriminate in favour of one set of customers. If we had free phone calls, what about all the other helplines, the Samaritans for example? 'How else can I help?' he asked.

'We need a simple number,' I said. 'One that any child can remember. We thought about asking you for 111, like 999.'

Once again there were problems. If the call was free to the child, he explained, it would need the prefix 0800. And it would then need four digits. I sighed. One by one our plans seemed defeated. But a few days later a lugubrious telephone engineer arrived in our office and said, 'I see you've got one of our engineering test lines'. Sir George had given us 0800-1111.

'What else?' he asked.

I had reached the end of our planned wish-list, but God kicked me sharply in the brain. 'Could you give us free premises?' I heard myself asking brazenly.

Sir George smiled. 'Yes, I think we could help you there.'

They did, and they do. BT gave us our first office in Addle Hill in the City of London, in the shadow of St Paul's. We outgrew it almost at once. So then they donated us our headquarters in Islington. It has been of immense value to us, as our organization has grown. Without BT we could never have launched ChildLine, and we will always be grateful to Sir George, and his successor, Sir Iain Vallance.

Premises and a simple phone number were not enough, of course. ChildLine needed money. We had to find and pay our first director and team of counsellors. We had decided to employ trained social workers to answer the children, because we recognized that there would be a justified view among other child-protection agencies that, as television professionals, we knew nothing about helping abused children. But where could we find sufficient funds to open ChildLine, before the public knew it existed, and could send donations? In the nick of time God sent us another guardian angel, one I had already met when I was working on Ben Hardwick's story. Do you see what I mean about feeling guided?

After our first programme about Ben in 1984, we received a phone call from a very successful businessman, Ian Skipper. Not only is he wealthy, but he is compassionate and generous. I am proud to say I must be one of his most expensive friends. His wife, Penny, had watched Ben's story, and he rang our office to say, 'Anything that child needs he shall have, even if it means flying him to America for the transplant operation'. As it turned out, Ben had his operation on the National Health Service. But when Ben died Ian Skipper became one of the trustees of the Ben Hardwick Memorial Fund, helping to create the charity which paid for a paediatric unit at Addenbrooke's Hospital, and saved many children's lives.

That series of *That's Life!* had left us all shattered. We were physically exhausted, and the death of Ben, the little boy who meant so much to us, saddened us all. We invited Ian to the rather subdued party at the end of the series. To my astonishment, Ian invited my family and Shaun to stay in his home in Barbados for a brief holiday. I was thrilled. Desmond and I had just bought a cottage in the New Forest, but the builders were discovering rich seams of damp and dry rot, and it was clearly not going to be ready as a holiday home for months. We accepted Ian's invitation with gratitude, and Shaun and I joked that it might be a tin hut at the end of a rickety pier.

Shaun went out first. He rang me his first night in Barbados. 'You know that tin hut,' he said, 'it's made of marble and limed oak. Imagine a square pool in a marble courtyard, with baskets of green plants hanging low over the water. I'm sitting by

363

candlelight at a table decorated with orchids, overlooking a lush green garden, and beyond it the sea.'

'It sounds like Paradise,' I said.

'It looks like Paradise,' Shaun told me.

And for us it was. The memories of that holiday will stay with me all my life: the children running through warm showers of rain; the sunsets, scarlet and gold, as we swam together through soft waves. Desi and I could enjoy the laughter of the children, eat freshly baked chocolate-chip cookies, sit together in the jacuzzi.

Shaun and I spent day after day at the typewriter, putting together the book, *Ben, the Story of Ben Hardwick*, which became a bestseller and a major fund-raiser for Ben's charity. I tell you this just in case you hate Desmond and me for spending our whole holiday lotus-eating. But I admit we did spend most of it loving, laughing, being together and, yes, lotus-eating.

When we came back to England, Shaun and I decided to give Ian and Penny Skipper dinner, to thank them for their incredible gift to us. We chose the Waterside Inn at Bray, where the food and the atmosphere are equally delicious. Shaun couldn't decide whom to invite as his guest. In the end he took a girl he hardly knew, Camilla Sainsbury. It was the first time I had met her, and I was struck by her beauty. Camilla looks like a romantic Edwardian portrait by Sargent. She has masses of dark curly hair, dreamy blue eyes, pale skin, and is tall, elegant, and stylish. No wonder Shaun brought her to dinner.

At the meal I sat next to Ian Skipper and told him about our child-abuse survey. He was appalled at the scale of the suffering the survey had uncovered, at the pain adults could inflict on their own young. I told him that the telephone could release children from their prison of fearful silence. He asked what it would cost to underwrite the charity—'About half a million your first year, I suppose?' I nodded. 'Consider it yours,' he said.

We have cost him far more than that over the years, not just in money, but in time and anxiety as we got this difficult, dangerous charity off the ground. Ian stood by us, advised us and used his skill and ingenuity to support us. ChildLine will be forever grateful to him.

Meanwhile, on the other side of the table, I couldn't help noticing that Shaun and Camilla were getting on extremely well. The conversation became general, and the subject of capital punishment arose. Camilla, who is against it, argued passionately with Ian. I saw Shaun listening to her with admiration. Over the next few days, he rang me frequently: 'This is serious,' he said. And then: 'This is *very* serious'.

It was. At their wedding our daughter Rebecca was one of their bridesmaids, and Desmond read the lesson. I am their daughter Olivia's godmother. They have four delightful children. Shaun lived through an ordeal by fire when he was elected Conservative MP for Witney, and then crossed the floor to join New Labour. The press tore into him and his family, as I suppose he must have expected. But I know for him it was a matter of conscience, and he and his family have survived the brickbats. Shaun supported ChildLine's aims from the start, and he is also a ChildLine trustee. Camilla became one of our first fund-raisers. They continue to work quietly behind the scenes, helping innumerable different causes and individuals. Shaun and Camilla are among my closest friends, I love them both and owe them a debt of kindness I can never repay.

As the *Childwatch* date of transmission grew closer, we enlisted more supporters. I went with Ritchie and Sarah to meet Norman Fowler, then Secretary of State for Social Security, at the House of Commons. As I explained ChildLine's aims he looked across at his senior civil servant. 'I think we can support that, don't you, Rupert?' 'Yes, Minister,' said Rupert Hughes without great enthusiasm. Somehow Rupert was going to have to find extra money for this upstart charity from their already tight budget. But I discovered that Rupert was kindly, intellectual, and a great help to us over the next few years.

Some days after that meeting Sarah told me the Department of Social Security had said we must have a chairman for our Board of Trustees. 'You're elected,' she said. I was flattered, and unsure I had any of the necessary skills. But we agreed that my television role was helpful since I could use it to explain ChildLine's role to children who might need us, and to the public who might support us.

The Variety Club responded at once when we contacted them and generously donated a cheque for £25,000. So did the Department of Social Security. That meant we had enough money to recruit our first staff. Paul Griffiths, our first director, came from the NSPCC, and half a dozen social workers joined us as professional counsellors. We augmented them with another forty volunteers from already existing counselling

366

services. An art student designed our logo—a smiling telephone—free of charge. It is our logo still. Sarah invented our name, ChildLine. We were fortunate, many other charities have struggled to find a simple, identifiable name, and a recognizable symbol.

The composer B.A. Robertson donated to us a jingle so that children would remember our number, 0800 double-one double-one. The commercials director Jonathan Gershfield made an advertisement for the new charity, to run on the programme. On 30 October 1986, in the BBC's *Childwatch* programme, ChildLine was launched.

ChildLine would not exist without the BBC. When Lord Reith, eccentric, autocratic, created a broadcasting organization very much in his own image, he also inserted into its heart a powerful public-service ethic. The BBC wants to do good. It may not always succeed, but that is its purpose. Not to make money. Not to seize power. Not to promulgate propaganda. To be helpful, to be useful, and to work for the greater good. I hope that when the history of the eighties and nineties are written, someone in the mandarin hierarchy of the BBC's policy department will recognize that the creation of ChildLine was one of the BBC's most important achievements, directly attributable to the Corporation's public-service mission.

Of course we were lucky that in 1986 we producers were allowed considerable independence to interpret our mission. I have often wondered whether it would have been possible under John Birt, or if we would have breached too many of his rules or guidelines by launching a new independent charity on the BBC. After all, was it fair to the hundreds of other children's charities, that we should be given so much publicity, in the middle of prime time on BBC1? On that first day I appeared on nineteen different programmes talking about the launch of ChildLine. We were on the news bulletins, in the children's programmes and in all the newspapers. If that was a breach of the BBC's rules, I make no apologies. If children were to be told that this helpline was for them, if the most vulnerable children in our country were to know our number, and ring it, and be saved from appalling suffering, this was the right way to do it.

We were incredibly lucky to have Michael Grade's backing, and Will Wyatt as our head of department, both of them committed to our cause. When eventually the Board of Governors realized what we had done, Bill Cotton, another great ally, suggested I should appear before them and explain how ChildLine was set up. It was the first and only governors' meeting I had ever attended, and I was fascinated by the atmosphere. Alasdair Milne was still Director-General, but the antagonism between him and Duke Hussie, the Chairman, was palpable. Not long afterwards, Hussie forced Milne to resign.

At the governors' meeting, I was shocked to see that the most senior executives of the BBC were made to wait outside the meeting room like schoolboys waiting for the headmaster to decide their punishment. But I was only there to describe how and why ChildLine had been created, and the governors seemed satisfied. By then children were being counselled, the press was applauding us, and money was pouring in from the public. If we had broken any rules, nobody told me so.

I have been extremely lucky in my career to have

worked on many exciting programmes. But nothing, no general election, not the discovery of Sheena Easton, nor even the story of Ben Hardwick, compares with the impact of *Childwatch* and the launch of ChildLine. I am told now that our programme changed the public perception of child abuse. Before *Childwatch* most people thought incest only happened in East Anglia, or in Freudian fantasies. We provided evidence from thousands of viewers that abuse can happen in respectable houses up and down the country. Nobody really knows what goes on behind net curtains, unless the children are prepared to tell us and ask for help. But we must listen to their voices if we are to protect them effectively.

Childwatch had its critics, of course. Some people felt we had sensationalized the subject and exaggerated the danger. Marj Proops, the experienced and much loved agony aunt from the *Daily Mirror*, always believed we made it too difficult for men to cuddle their children, for fear of being suspected of abusing them. We were called by the MP Stuart Bell (the MP who exposed the Cleveland scandal) 'the most dangerous show on television' because he believed that we whipped up hysteria. The debate is important. No one is infallible, least of all a television journalist. I am sure I have made mistakes. But I have a letter in my files from someone who is no fan of mine. She wrote to me recently from Gloucester to say:

Thank you, Esther, for bringing the subject of child abuse out into the open. Back in the mid-eighties God used you to prod me in the right direction to get something done about a problem I had which was

369

not really my fault. I can see now God's hand on you at the start of my healing process.

Life is now so much better. The flashbacks have stopped; my relationship with my husband is—well— very nice thank you! And also my relationship with God is wonderful.

I am so grateful to you Esther for being a 'thorn in my flesh' all those years ago, (I would walk out of the room if you came on the telly). What God has given me in exchange for my torment is peace, acceptance as his daughter, and a freedom to walk forward and leave the past behind. I sincerely hope that I will be able to help others in similar circumstances.

Shortly after the *Childwatch* broadcast, I was standing in for Terry Wogan on his chat show while he went on holiday. As I walked towards his production office, a man held the door open for me. That's unusual in liberated ill-mannered television. A few days later he wrote me a memo:

When I was abused as a child I thought all the adults around me knew what was happening and were in a conspiracy of silence. Now I realize that they didn't know, didn't suspect, and more than that, with your helpline you have held your hand out to me and children like me. Now I know people care, it's changed my attitude to life.

He had felt imprisoned not just as a child but also as an adult. He couldn't share his memories with anyone at all.

I was at ChildLine on the day the programme was transmitted. A BT official took me up to the exchange and I watched the machinery roaring and shuddering under the impact of 50,000 calls. I took some of them. A great many came from adults, 'If only there had been a ChildLine for me when I was young. Where can I send you a donation?' But most, of course, were from children, describing for the first time the cruelty they had suffered for years.

I remember a child ringing from Glasgow, with an accent I could barely understand as she sobbed out her story. She was being brutally abused. Now ChildLine has a base in Glasgow so that children can be answered by counsellors who understand their background.

Another child rang, not because she was being sexually abused by her father—she had got used to that—but because he was about to take pornographic pictures of her six-year-old sister.

'Please tell me where you are,' I pleaded, 'so that we can help you.'

'No,' she said. 'I have two daddies, lovely Daddy and monster Daddy. If I tell you my name you'll come and take monster Daddy away, but then I'll lose lovely Daddy as well.'

That is the bitter dilemma of the abused child. She loves Daddy, but she hates what he does to her.

Sometimes it is better for the child if we do not involve the police or social services. Stopping the abuse without putting children through the ordeal of going to court may not be in the greater interests of justice, but it may be the most effective way of protecting the child.

I spoke to a ten-year-old boy for eighteen months before he told me why he was ringing ChildLine. The early phone calls were about his loneliness, his mother worked long hours. He told me about his dog, and how much he enjoyed football. Slowly he revealed to me that David, the male babysitter his mother liked and trusted, had been regularly sexually abusing him for years. I managed to persuade him to tell his mother. She was furiously angry with the man. But when I asked if she had reported David to the police, he said no. There was no medical evidence. I could see why she had decided not to risk taking the babysitter to court. It would have been the child's evidence against the man's. But the babysitter had a girlfriend with two sons—and it was clear that those little boys were at terrible risk.

Sexual abuse is an addiction. Paedophiles seek out and target children, groom them and intimidate them into silence. Only if children have the confidence to speak out can the abuser be brought to justice. But in 1986 our legal system was utterly insensitive to children's needs. Imagine being a child in court, surrounded by men in wigs and gowns, and having to describe, in public, while looking into the face of your tormentor, acts which you remember with shame and loathing.

One girl I interviewed for *Childwatch* wept as she described how her father's defence barrister had muddled and confused her, and then finally destroyed her by implying that she, at twelve years old, was sexually promiscuous. When he was acquitted, her father, who had repeatedly raped her at knife point, laughed in her face, and left the courtroom on her mother's arm. For the girl, the trial had been even more abusive, even more of an ordeal than the original abuse.

*　　　*　　　*

Shortly after ChildLine was launched, we were able to take the children's voices right into the heart of government. Margaret Thatcher, then Prime Minister, invited us to give a reception at 10 Downing Street. She issued a three-line whip to her ministers, and all the relevant ones at the Home Office and the Department of Social Security were there with their civil servants. So were millionaires who could help us financially, and stars and celebrities who could bring the message to the British public that, through the telephone, we could reach children who had nowhere else to turn.

I had never been inside Downing Street before. Mrs Thatcher took me through the splendid rooms before the guests arrived. She told me how at the time of Falklands she had walked up and down under the portraits of the other prime ministers watching her decision-making. Far from being intimidated by their example, she was determined to live up to them. She made me stand next to her in the receiving line welcoming the guests as they arrived. I had to pinch myself to believe that I was standing beside the Prime Minister.

When there was a lull in the stream of distinguished guests, she turned to me and asked, 'What are the long-term effects of child abuse?'

I told her what I had learned from reading our thousands of surveys: 'If everything we know about love and trust and loyalty we learn from our own parents,' I said, 'and if instead we only learn fear and pain and betrayal, it becomes very difficult for anyone to trust or build relationships as adults. So, often, they end up in prison, or in addiction units, or depressed with broken marriages.'

I saw her blue eyes had grown blank, and thought, 'Oh, no. I've bored millions of viewers over the years, now finally I've bored the Prime Minister.'

More guests arrived and we went back to shaking hands and welcoming them.

The time came for speeches. Mrs Thatcher stood on the small square embroidered footstool she kept for the purpose, and began her speech. She talked about Christmas, and the needs of children, mentioning her admiration for the work of the NSPCC. Then she began to talk about abuse. She said, 'If everything we know about love and trust and loyalty we learn from our own parents, and if instead we only learn fear and pain and betrayal . . .'

As she spoke, I had two reactions. Firstly, I admired her skill at taking an instant brief, although I hadn't for a moment realized that I had been briefing her. Secondly, I was very glad that I hadn't planned to say those words in my speech.

She finished, and I took her place on the footstool. I talked about the survey, and the voices of the children, about the injustice of the law as it stood, condemning so many children to suffer and so many paedophiles to go free. Desmond was standing next to Denis Thatcher, and heard him growl under his breath, 'Castration's too good for them'. Then I asked our third speaker, one of our volunteer fund-raisers, to speak. She stood on the footstool and began: 'My father was a policeman and a Mason,' she said, 'I tell you that so that you will understand that he was liked and admired by everyone in our community. But they never knew that for years he abused me . . .' and she stopped, silenced by tears.

There was a moment of absolute stillness in the room. Suddenly, under the bright chandeliers, amid all those affluent, powerful, confident people, the piercing cry of a desperate child was heard, a child it was now too late to save. She got down from the footstool and disappeared. I scrambled up in her place and said what I knew she had planned to tell them, that she was raising money to try and save today's children from the secret agony she had endured in the past.

I ended, and went to look for her. Somebody said she was in the Prime Minister's study. I found her there, sitting in a comfortable armchair. Mrs Thatcher was pouring her a glass of water and telling her, 'You can stay here as long as you want. Nobody will disturb you. And don't try to bottle things up, it's far better for you to cry if you need to'.

I was impressed. This was the tough, 'uncaring' woman so often caricatured as being unfeeling, obviously responding instinctively with compassion. But that wasn't quite the end of the story. That night's paper carried a banner headline on the front page, 'Abuse victim sobs in Downing Street'. Mrs Thatcher's efficient press machine had seen the value of the story.

Although her political views were different from mine (I have always been a floating voter, more interested in supporting those at the bottom of the heap than backing the winners at the top) I found Mrs Thatcher's performance that evening entirely impressive. That Downing Street reception helped put ChildLine on the map. Head and heart,

Margaret Thatcher was committed to child protection. In her day, children's issues were on the national agenda as they had not been before. Later she came to ChildLine's London office and said, 'They call this a helpline, I say it is a lifeline'. Then, away from the crowds and the cameras, she quietly took a personal cheque for ChildLine out of her handbag and gave it to me. I was told she did the same whenever she visited a hospital or a charity whose work she admired.

*   *   *

Childwatch and ChildLine campaigned for change. And there have been reforms. Now at least there are videolinks and screens, and children have the court procedure explained to them. But even today the law makes it almost impossible to convict abusers because our adversarial system is quite unsuited to achieving justice for children. Other countries manage to investigate crimes, and test children's evidence, without causing them so much additional pain. We should learn from them.

In 1986 Richard Johnson, who founded the Incest Crisis Line and had himself suffered horrific abuse, told me, 'The only evidence the court will believe is a child's dead body'. It sounded hopelessly cynical, but our survey confirmed his view. Many children fear they will lose everything if they dare to ask for help. Even Fred West's children decided to endure their pain, in order to stay with each other. Stephen West told me about his sister Heather, who was abused and later murdered by his father. 'When we realized what our father was doing to Heather,' he said, 'we all discussed whether to ring ChildLine. In the end we decided not to, because we'd lose each other, and we were all we had.'

Some day we must write the story of ChildLine's early years. They were tempestuous. Our first counsellors burned out under the impact of so many thousands of desperate children's calls. We had to create a system of training, supervision and debriefing. Listening to a sobbing child you cannot hold in your arms is like hearing a child screaming for help the other side of a busy road, yet being unable to cross the street to reach her.

How then can ChildLine help? The answer is by persuading the children they are precious, that they have the right to safety. The counsellors try to identify a trusted adult in their lives, mother, or granny, or a neighbour, someone the child can tell. If children need ChildLine to find someone for them—the police or a social worker—we do that, and carefully explain to the children what will happen next.

Our ChildLine children make excellent witnesses in court because by then we have convinced them they are not to blame for the abuse they have suffered. Abused children believe every other child is loved and safe, like the children they see in commercials, so it must be their own fault they are suffering. A paediatrician told me of a child she treated. His whole body was a mass of wounds from the flogging he had suffered. She asked him, 'David, why has this happened?' He answered, 'Because I'm bad'.

One of the most painful calls I ever took was from a girl in care in Northern Ireland. She told me that she had been sexually abused by her father, but that when she told a teacher, her mother had disowned her and said she could never see her brothers and sisters again.

'Who cares about you?' I asked her.

'Nobody,' she replied bleakly. 'You wouldn't like me either, if you knew me.'

I couldn't bear the loneliness in her voice, and the fact that her mother had rejected her reduced me to tears. I find the stories about cruelty by women the most agonizing to hear.

*　　　*　　　*

How do we know ChildLine really does help children? Because they tell us so. Sometimes simply putting their pain into words allows them to find a solution. The fact that our counsellors aren't shocked and don't blame them can give a child the confidence he or she needs. A teenager had been sexually abused by an uncle for years. She told me about it, and I asked her to ring me back after she saw him next. She did. I asked what had happened, and she said with satisfaction, 'I said I'd told you, I told him never to do it again, and I kicked him'. I jumped for joy, then warned her not to take any risks and endanger herself. It was an unorthodox solution, but very satisfying.

Not all our calls are about sexual abuse. I spoke to a girl who had run away from home and was on her way to Piccadilly. She'd run away before, and a man there had offered her a job in the sex trade, but a teenage girl with a baby had warned her not to take it, but to go home. She was in floods of tears, and it took time to discover the reason she was running away again. Then she revealed that she had been looking through a filing cabinet at home and had suddenly come across her own adoption papers.

'Now I understand why I am always alone in my baby pictures,' she said. 'But my parents never told me. They can't love me, they've lied to me all my life.'

'Perhaps their problem is that they love you too much,' I suggested, 'and can't face the fact that you aren't their biological daughter.'

I pointed out that all parents make mistakes, and children have to forgive them—mine have to forgive me frequently. I asked her about her birthdays, and Christmas. She laughed, and said 'Dad gave me an Elton John CD, although he can't stand Elton himself'. She told me that when she ran out of the house she had left the filing cabinet open, with the papers all over the desk. I suggested she should go home and tell her mother what she knew, so that they could talk about it together. We role-played, she practised telling me what she intended to say to her mother.

After forty-five minutes she sounded cheerful and optimistic. She told me she was going home. I don't know if she did, I have often wondered.

Some endings we do know about. In our earliest days I had a phone call from a journalist to tell me ChildLine had been commended in court. A boy had stopped on the way to school, talked to one of our counsellors, and been half an hour late for his first class. When the teacher asked him why, the boy, emboldened by our counsellor's reassurances, had said he had called us, and why. As a result, a man who had abused him and several other children had been convicted and imprisoned, and

379

the judge had said, 'Thank heavens children now have somewhere to ring for help'.

I have files of letters from children and their parents. One mother wrote to me to say:

I am writing to thank ChildLine from the bottom of my heart. Why? My two sons, aged nine and eleven, were victims of serious sexual abuse by a neighbour. My eleven-year-old twice tried to kill himself, cutting his wrists and taking an overdose. I knew something was wrong, of course, but didn't know what. We sought help from doctors, psychiatrists, anyone I thought might help. Then things got slightly better. One night my sons came to me and told me everything. I immediately told the police and the man was arrested. He was charged with 20 charges of gross indecency and buggery. He was sentenced to three years.

The thing is, after his suicide attempts our eleven-year-old started ringing ChildLine. It took a while but they persuaded him not to try and kill himself, but to tell me as soon as possible. I still encourage him to talk to ChildLine if he needs to. I am convinced if he hadn't rung in the first place I would only have one son today. God bless you, and all your efforts. Thank you for setting up this very essential helpline. Children need it.

I met that mother, with her son. I hugged him, and asked how often he had rung ChildLine before he managed to tell his mother about the abuse. He said, 'About fifty times'. I asked how long his first phone call had been. He said, 'Two hours'. He had gone to a phone box, when his mother had thought he was with his friends. The abuser was a neighbour, who assaulted him, his brother and several other boys in the village.

After the trial the other neighbours had sided with the abuser against the family who were new to the village, and the family had had to move. Even so, it is a reassuring story. Unlike so many of the children in our original survey, the boy had been believed by his mother and by the police. The abuser had been sent to jail. The abuse had stopped. The family allowed me to tell their story, which persuaded hundreds of other people to support our work. I took the family to ChildLine, to meet our team there. It was a very moving visit.

None of that happy ending would have been possible without the outstanding team who work for ChildLine. God moves in a mysterious way, they say. He seems to have aimed my family and my life towards the creation of ChildLine. My sister, Priscilla, took a degree in sociology, then trained as a social worker in Lambeth. One of her closest friends there, Hereward Harrison, was a social worker who has a disgraceful sense of humour and great insight into helping children. Hereward has been a lynch-pin in the ChildLine operation, first as Director of Children's Services, then as our Director of Policy, Research and Development.

Hereward and Priscilla were both trained by an outstanding social worker, Valerie Howarth, who later became Director of Social Services in Brent. A few weeks after Valerie joined Brent the body of a little girl, Jasmine Beckford, was discovered, murdered. Jasmine's case inflamed the nation, and Valerie became the scapegoat. Brent Council refused to allow Valerie to defend herself, but blamed her for every mistake. The fact was that Jasmine had been taken off the official at-risk register before Valerie arrived at Brent, so there was no way she could have intervened to protect her. That, however, made no difference. Valerie was pilloried, and in the end left social work to work in the charitable field.

Meanwhile, ChildLine had developed some serious management problems. It was hardly surprising, given that the counsellors were creating an entirely new way of helping children, under the impact of thousands of attempted calls which we simply did not have the resources to answer.

A management consultant came to analyze ChildLine's needs, and we started the search for a permanent Chief Executive. Priscilla reminded me about her old boss, Valerie. Priscilla was by now living in Australia and working with survivors of abuse there. She came to England when ChildLine opened its lines, and told me it was totally different from any of her previous work experiences.

'I've met many abused children,' she said, 'and when they are with you they very seldom look at you, or meet your eyes, or are able to tell you about their feelings or their experiences. They are overwhelmed with shame and fear. But the children who ring ChildLine are released by the telephone to speak freely. They feel safe, and tell you exactly what they have been through.'

It is very painful listening to sobbing children talking about their pain. No wonder our counsellors were burning out under the stress. Priscilla said, 'Valerie not only understands all the problems of trying to protect children, she is also an extremely competent manager'. I couldn't believe Valerie would be prepared to go back into the crucible. After all, her professional reputation had been almost destroyed by the Jasmine Beckford case.

However, Alan Holden, the Director of Social Services in Harrow, who became a ChildLine trustee, knew Valerie and also believed she might be exactly the Chief Executive we needed. He got in touch with her. She thought long and hard, and decided she would apply. She went through our interview process and gave an impressive performance. But two of our trustees were very concerned. If we appointed the 'Jasmine Beckford Director' to our brand new charity, they feared that the press might attack and destroy us. I asked my closest friend, Bryher Scudamore, for advice.

Bryher and I first met when she was a BBC Press officer. We liked each other instantly. (So, thank heavens, did our husbands. We took holidays together, made frightful puns together, and the weekend before Desmond died in September 2000, we spent happy days together in the south of France.) Bryher rose from being a researcher to becoming the Editor of *That's Life!*. From time to time she has dug me out of deep, muddy holes where I have been floundering.

Now she gave me invaluable advice. She looked up the official inquiry into Jasmine Beckford's death, which was conducted by the barrister Sir Louis Blom-Cooper. In his report he specifically said of Valerie that she was an excellent Director of Social Services, and that no blame for Jasmine's death should be attached to her. I asked Bryher to come with me to meet the doubtful trustees.

Bryher pointed to the relevant paragraph in the

383

inquiry report: 'Without that, I would agree, ChildLine would be in trouble. It would appear you are being reckless in appointing Valerie. But Louis Blom-Cooper's statement makes her role clear, and supports the appointment. If the press criticize you, read them what he says.'

Bryher was right. Only one newspaper attacked us for the appointment. The professionals working in Social Services knew Valerie's quality and also knew she had been blamed unfairly for Jasmine's death. They trusted her, and welcomed her appointment. In fact, she did a great deal to allay the blazing hostility in some parts of the social work press, based on what I came to call the 'WDTWTSI' syndrome—Who Does That Woman Think She Is?

Valerie brought calm to ChildLine's office. She created structures and processes so that the counsellors could work effectively. She put together a fund-raising department. She invented a strategy for growing the agency so that now we have eight bases round the country, in North and South Wales, Scotland, Northern Ireland, the Northeast, the Northwest, the Midlands and in London.

Now we are almost fifteen years old we have a thousand volunteer counsellors and have counselled well over a million children. We have saved children's lives and our evidence has brought paedophiles to justice. But we still can't answer every child who needs us. Our nightmare is the desperate child who plucks up the courage to run to a phone box, only to find our lines are all busy. We depend on the generosity of the public to pay for our phone calls. The more money they donate, the more children we can comfort and protect. We know that still more desperate children need our help, because we are the only place they can turn to. We believe that in the not too distant future we will be able to answer them all, with a little help from our friends.

Two years after we opened, our fund-raiser Camilla Sainsbury sent me an album. It was a remake of the Beatles record *Sergeant Pepper*, created by Roy Carr, who worked for the *New Musical Express*. Somehow Roy had cajoled and persuaded the top bands of the moment to record one track each. The album was to be sold in aid of ChildLine. When I listened to all the tracks, two particularly stood out—Billy Bragg's 'She's Leaving Home' and Wet Wet Wet's 'With a Little Help From My Friends'.

I asked someone on the *That's Life!* team to find a video of the Wet Wet Wet group. When I saw them I realized at once that they were stars, the lead singer, Marty Pellow, had terrific sex appeal. I suggested to the team we could feature the two songs on our show in successive weeks, and to introduce the Wet Wet Wet song we read our viewers a letter:

Dear Esther,
I am writing to thank you for having set up ChildLine. I know you must be busy helping other children and haven't really time for this letter so I'll try and make it short.
After being sexually abused for eleven years, starting at the age of six, I thought nobody cared for me. Sometimes I wondered if they knew I existed. At school I had to listen to my friends talking about their

new boyfriends and how much they loved each other. I used to hate it and was hardly ever there. When I left at sixteen I was pregnant. Everybody wondered whose it was. Only I knew it was my step-dad's child.

She described how she had miscarried, and lost the baby. The letter continued:

Then I rang ChildLine. The fact that someone cared was enough to make me realize something had to be done. I finally told my mum. She believed me, my stepdad admitted it and said he was sorry and it would never happen again and it hasn't. I have been out with a few boys and managed to sleep with one but it was awful and I don't want to go through with it ever again. I'm going to be lonely for the rest of my life. I've always been alone and so I suppose I should be used to it by now but I'm not. I think it's because I love kids and I'll probably never have my own. If I meet a boy I feel as though I've got to give him something but I've nothing left to give. He's taken away my pride, my dignity, self-respect, self-confidence and I still feel dirty and humiliated.

I probably sound ungrateful to you. At least I'm not being raped three or four times a week in my own home any more and when I think of that it always puts a smile on my face and that smile is keeping me alive.

Thanks for taking the time and trouble to read this. I hope a lot more young children use your ChildLine because that kind caring voice on the other end of the line is all it takes.

Thanks for everything, all my love, Julie.

The morning after the programme a group of

386

record company executives arrived in the *That's Life!* office. They explained that they had been sent by Wet Wet Wet, and that the band had watched the programme on Sunday night. They had been so moved by Julie's letter that they wanted their song and Billy Bragg's to be released as a double A-side single, in aid of ChildLine. The idea came from Tommy Cunningham, their drummer, and we leapt at it.

These projects are not usually easy to put together, but in this case, everything went extraordinarily smoothly. It was helped by the fact that the Wets are excellent musicians. They came into our studio and sang live to our audience.

That's Life! transmitted on Sunday night, and on Monday the song shot straight into the charts and stayed there. It was Wet Wet Wet's first number one, it remained number one for five weeks and raised £500,000 for ChildLine. That money, suitably for a Scottish band, enabled us to open ChildLine Scotland in Glasgow. It paid for literally thousands of children to be saved from intolerable suffering.

We invited Julie herself to our studio. She met the band and they gave her tickets to their concert. On their many sell-out tours they continued to collect money for ChildLine. I had a letter from a boy who told me that he was abused, but 'With a Little Help From My Friends' rang like an anthem in his head and gave him the courage to survive.

We had other good friends. Soon after we opened, Diana, Princess of Wales, sent us a personal donation. I had met her when I appeared (singing, dancing, best forgotten) in the Royal Variety Show. She was in what she later described

387

as her 'Fairy' stage. She was dressed in a long, floating, blue dress that intensified the blue of her eyes. She had diamonds in her hair and at her neck. The impact of her beauty hit me like a blow, I had never seen such a lovely young woman. No supermodel, no actress, nobody had her extraordinary charm. Well might she describe it as a 'Fairy' style—she certainly had a magic about her which spellbound everyone she met.

We invited her to open our ChildLine office in Islington. We knew the Princess would want to meet some of the children we had helped, and arranged for a child called Emma to present her with a bouquet. Emma had written to ChildLine and asked our counsellors to ring her at her school. When our counsellor phoned, a teacher went to fetch Emma from her class. On the way the teacher asked why she had written to us. Emma explained that she had been sexually abused by her father, and was terrified that she was pregnant.

The teacher told the police, as the law says a teacher must. The police interviewed Emma, then a social worker rang her mother. Her mum told me, 'My life was blown away by a phone call at four in the afternoon'. The police went to their home to arrest Emma's father. He was charged, convicted and sent to prison. Suddenly the family were on the breadline. Their neighbours knew the whole shameful story.

Princess Diana said to Emma, 'Are you glad you got in touch with ChildLine?'

Emma shook her head. 'No. It was my job to suffer.'

There is another way. In the United States they have pioneered what is called a 'diversion contract'.

388

When a father like Emma's admits his guilt, he is made to sign a full confession which would lead to instant conviction and imprisonment. But instead of going to jail he signs a contract committing himself to leaving the family home. However, he continues to work, and there is no shameful publicity for him and his family. The money he earns is used to pay for therapy for himself, and for the victims of his abuse, including his wife.

When and if the experts believe he and his victims are ready, he is allowed to meet them again, at first only in public places, but later at home. Eventually he may be reintroduced into the family. Then at last the abused children can have their dream. They can lose 'monster Daddy' but their 'lovely Daddy' is returned to them. Furthermore, the child who asks for help and protection does not then carry the guilt of destroying her family's life. It will no longer be her job to suffer.

Over the years I came to know Diana a little better. I remember watching her walk round ChildLine's office. When she turned, I saw her in profile and realized she was as thin as a knife blade. I gasped, 'How thin she is'. Her lady-in-waiting standing next to me instantly corrected me, 'but incredibly fit', as if I had accused Diana of being ill. And of course she was, although at that time I didn't suspect bulimia. I didn't even realize it when Diana came to our Glasgow office with a schedule that insisted she must have time to herself after lunch for undisturbed rest.

When she came to Scotland, I remember Diana asking about Christmas, whether we had a large number of calls then. 'It's such a tense and difficult time for a family,' she said, 'if a marriage is going wrong.' Judging from the intercepted phone call with James Gilbey, she knew that from personal experience.

I wrote to Diana in 1992 to invite her to open our new ChildLine office in Wales. A week later I was interviewed by the *Daily Mail*, and asked whom I would most like to take to lunch. I chose Prince Charles, because I share his love of The Goon Show, and thought he was getting an unfairly bad press at the time. On the front page they carried the line, 'Why Esther Rantzen would like to lunch with Prince Charles'.

A month later I received Diana's reply to ChildLine's invitation. Although we had offered her any date in the new year, Patrick Jephson wrote to say she was unable to accept. I was intrigued to see that he had altered the date of his letter by hand. Why? I looked back at the date the *Daily Mail* interview was published. Diana had dictated her refusal on the day that it appeared. Could she have seen it, been furious with me for praising Charles and decided to punish me? Patrick must have held on to the letter, and changed the date on it, so that I would not suspect the real reason. At that time the War of the Wales was not public knowledge.

After a while she forgave me. Diana launched our Tenth Birthday Appeal at the Savoy, tempting the rich and powerful to listen to ChildLine's plea for help when most of them would certainly not have spared us their time otherwise. She signed a copy of a ChildLine Christmas book just before she died. It was auctioned at our Ball, and I bought it myself. I have it still, and treasure it.

When I heard Diana had been killed in the

appalling car crash in Paris, I was stunned, as many people were. I felt deeply, personally bereaved. Not because we were close friends, but because she did so much good, transformed the lives of so many people. One was a child I knew, Bonnie Handel. When I met Bonnie she was dying of Aids. As a baby in the womb, Bonnie had failed to thrive. Her mother, Rebecca, had received an intrauterine blood transfusion at a time when Aids was unknown. The blood was infected. Bonnie caught the HIV infection while she was still in the womb, Rebecca caught it from her, and passed it to her husband. Only the older brother, Joshua, was uninfected.

Rebecca rang me to nominate both her children for a Heart of Gold award for their courage. At that time I was making *Hearts of Gold* for BBC1, the programme which honoured outstanding people for their unsung acts of kindness or courage. But Rebecca explained that it must be a secret award for her children. There was still so great a stigma the family had kept the illness secret. Their doctors were afraid that they might be fire-bombed or the children thrown out of school, as had happened in America.

I gave them their awards quietly, in a hospital in north London, then I went to visit the family. I went up to Bonnie's bedroom. Beside her bed was a signed photograph of the Princess in a handsome, heavy, silver frame. Bonnie showed me a two-page letter Diana had written by hand in her round, flowing handwriting, it was filled with sensitive affection.

The little girl, twelve years old and delicate as a leaf, was panting behind her oxygen mask, unable to sleep. I sat on Bonnie's bed and concocted a fantasy for her. I told her the bed was a boat, and we were rowing together on moonlit water, the oars splashing in a gentle rhythm, the clouds lit silver by the moon. We reached an island covered with bushes of white roses. Princess Diana was waiting for Bonnie as we landed, held out her hand to Bonnie, and took her for a walk under the stars.

Alas, my story was prophetic. When Diana died, her brother, Charles Spencer, buried her body on an island in a lake at his home at Althorp, and on it he planted dozens of white roses. Perhaps Bonnie's spirit was waiting for her there.

*   *   *

I was invited to the lunch given by Headway, the charity for head-injured people, in the Hilton Hotel, Park Lane, in December 1993. There were hundreds of reporters and photographers waiting outside. Diana herself, the guest of honour, seemed brittle. Her jokes as she walked round the reception were spiky. When she made her speech I understood why. It was the occasion when she announced she was giving up public life for a time. She said that although she had anticipated she would arouse great interest in her private life when she married Prince Charles, she had not realized how great that interest would become. She explained she needed time and space for herself and her family.

The speech, as always, was exquisitely delivered. She had a graceful simplicity of style which was either natural, or the result of professional coaching and practice. Either way, she stunned her audience. When she finished, the crowd in the dining room rose and gave her a standing ovation.

A few days later she was due to open a new centre for homeless young people for Centrepoint. They rang me in a panic. Now that Diana had officially retired from public life, would I please give the speech? Although Diana would be there, she felt she couldn't speak herself. I said yes.

On the day, the rain was pelting down. When Diana arrived, without a lady-in-waiting or a policeman to escort her, her hair was wet and she looked around for somewhere to prop her umbrella. The local mayor was an elderly woman who had brought her granddaughter as her official mayoress. They sat next to Diana in the front row, and as I made my speech I saw the six-year-old mayoress getting bored and restless. Diana gave her the royal handbag to explore. I watched as everything was pulled out and examined. All the cosmetics. The hairbrush. Then, to Diana's amusement, the little girl began to inspect the Princess's jewellery. The interplay between them was far more interesting than anything I had to say.

In spite of relinquishing her public duties, Diana continued to go where she felt she was needed in a private capacity. I saw her at another lunch, and told her that Bonnie was dying. I learned from Rebecca that Diana had instantly gone to the hospital with a bouquet of roses.

After Bonnie's death Diana invited Rebecca to lunch at Kensington Palace. When Rebecca died Diana sent a glorious bunch of roses, with a card paying tribute to a wonderful mother. These were all personal gifts, acts of kindness, creating memories for the whole family. Complicated mixture as she was—as everyone is—Diana gave of herself, and that gift made a difference to many vulnerable people's lives, at moments where others had turned aside.

Valerie and I were invited to Diana's funeral, representing ChildLine. I was in a section of the Abbey reserved for her charities. Her private secretary, Patrick Jephson, was sitting a few rows ahead of me. I saw him break down, overcome by tears when her coffin was carried in with its burden of white flowers. He, of course, knew her well. But people Diana never met felt the same anguished sense of loss.

I spoke to the crowds outside when I arrived at the Abbey because I was curious to know why they had come, why they waited so long, and where they had come from. I discovered they were from every part of the country. Many of them were clearly short of money and had brought their children with them. They had made the journey because they wanted to bear witness that Diana had touched their lives, too.

I knew how they felt. I had run into my own garden to pick some roses, since I knew she loved them, and took them to the Abbey to put them with the other grander flowers.

Her brother, Charles Spencer, made his speech at the service, blaming the world's press and paparazzi for hounding Diana to her death. In the silence at the end there was a sound like waves breaking. The crowd outside the Abbey had heard his words, profoundly agreed with him, and began to applaud. The sound came nearer, then we were all applauding, too. The people began the clapping, first the waiting crowds, then the charities who lost so much when she died, then slowly the noise rippled through the Abbey until the rows of the rich and powerful had to applaud as well. How could they stay aloof? It was an unforgettable moment.

After the service I walked with some workers from her other charities to Kensington Palace. The crowds were quiet, solemn, walking head down, reading the cards on the mountain of flowers, like any family after a funeral. Then we all went home.

Diana was no saint. But she had a unique gift. She could lift spirits, touch hearts, and for a moment make people forget the pain in their lives. She knew the power she had. Sometimes I have no doubt she belittled it herself, and made rude jokes about us behind our backs. I'm sure she could be hell to work for, and even greater hell to be married to. But charities like ChildLine miss her still. She was, as Tony Blair said, the 'people's princess', and she was literally irreplaceable.

A year after Diana died I was able to enlist another charistmatic woman to support ChildLine's work. I have always envied men their capacity to network. Pubs and clubs and golf courses give them an excuse to eat and drink and play, and make valuable contacts at the same time. In the autumn of 1998, I discovered that a hairdresser can perform the same function for women.

I was sitting under the dryer in Michael Van Clarke's salon, as I have twice a week during the last fifteen years of my working life. Under the lights of the studio my hair flattens into a limp mess without the lotions and potions they pour over my head. Looking across the basins I realized

Cherie Booth QC was also having her hair done. Did I respect her privacy? Not at all. I instantly introduced myself to her, and began to talk about the terrible injustice being done to abused children in our courts.

I quickly discovered that Cherie knew only too well from her own legal experience that children are denied justice. I invited her to ChildLine. She came, and was receptive and supportive to everything we showed her. Then we sat in Valerie Howarth's office and I said, 'Is there any way we can reach the backwoods lawyers, the ones who prop the system up because they either don't know or don't care that most abusers escape conviction at the moment? Would you consider chairing a conference about children and the law for ChildLine.'

She paused and thought for a moment. 'Yes, I'll certainly do that for you, but if we really want those lawyers to come, would it help if Hillary delivered the keynote speech?' We couldn't believe our ears. Would Hillary Clinton, the First Lady, really cross the Atlantic to come to a ChildLine conference? It seemed that she would, if Cherie invited her.

It was an extraordinary event. Besides two of the most illustrious women lawyers in the world, the Chairman of the Criminal Bar attended, so did the Director of Public Prosecutions, together with distinguished judges, lawyers and social workers, and experts flown in from all over the world who described how they handle things differently in foreign jurisdictions. In several countries children are not expected to give evidence in person at all, they are carefully protected from the frighteningly incomprehensible rituals of a trial. Nevertheless, their stories are still investigated thoroughly, perhaps more thoroughly than in our own courts which rely on the adversarial system.

We also invited a dozen mothers to our conference to tell their personal stories of injustice. They told of young children whose cases never went to court at all, of other children browbeaten by cross-examination, and of prosecutions dropped in spite of powerful corroborative evidence. My friend Donna came to the conference to describe how she and her husband had been appalled when they were told by lawyers the night before the trial began that they wanted to drop their case against 'Uncle Bob' because they thought it would be impossible to convict him. In fact, thanks to my friends' determination and the courage of their little daughter Polly, he was convicted and sent to prison. All the mothers' stories focused the debate on reality, piercing right through any complacency in the audience.

Cherie chaired the conference with her usual sensitivity and intelligence. Jack Straw, the Home Secretary, made a speech to launch the day's events. Hillary Clinton, arrived in the afternoon to deliver the keynote speech, as Cherie had told us she would. She was poised, elegant and direct. She impressed a very tough audience so greatly that they applauded her for well over five minutes. I whispered to her, 'That's a British standing ovation'. Had they been Americans, they would all have leaped to their feet.

We went back afterwards to Downing Street for a reception, where some of our most loyal supporters had the opportunity to meet and speak to Cherie and Hillary. We made a real impact on the lawyers who attended. I was later invited to address the criminal bar. One of the older lawyers shocked his colleagues by saying, 'It doesn't matter how much of a monster my client is, or what I have to do to break a child down, that is my job.' Depressing as that was to hear, it stimulated a worthwhile debate which continues in parliament and the media. All in all, a considerable achievement for the hair-network.

*   *   *

ChildLine's work goes on. Not long ago I was invited to the opening of a centre for homeless young people in the City of London. The Queen had agreed to cut the ribbon. I have a picture of us together, and have no idea why I was laughing so much when the camera clicked, nor why the Queen had such a broad smile. But I remember the day because, just before the Queen arrived, a young woman of about twenty jumped across the barrier, ran towards me and seized my hand in hers:

'Please thank everyone at ChildLine,' she said. 'Without them a couple of years ago I would have died. I had almost been killed in my home. I ran out to the nearest phone box, and rang ChildLine. The counsellors kept me talking while they fetched an ambulance. That's why I'm here today. Please, thank them for my life.'

She dazzled me. It was a great honour to meet the Queen that day, but for me, the real privilege was meeting that girl whose life was saved by ChildLine.

CHAPTER THIRTEEN

BUT WHAT ABOUT THE CHILDREN?

Two earthquakes shook my life in 1986. One was the creation of ChildLine; the other was Desmond's heart bypass operation.

The day after *Childwatch* transmitted I went into my office and said to my friends gathered there to prepare the next series of *That's Life!*, 'For the first time I've come across a subject which is more important to me than television itself. More than consumerism, more than transplantation or drug abuse, or any of the other subjects that have absorbed me during my career, child protection has seized my soul.'

My family, as I have explained, always had children at its heart, and made them our priority. My grandmother, with her love of children, and her enjoyment of their company, had set the tone for us all. I have always felt that when a child enters a room, it's as if the sun comes out, and I feel happier whenever a child is near me. The knowledge of the pain children are sometimes forced to suffer by ruthless and unscrupulous adults was like a sudden glimpse of hell. Fortunately, the viewers shared my view that this was a subject we should not be afraid to tackle, and they sent us more and more challenging stories to investigate. So, from that time on, *That's Life!* began to focus on ways of protecting children from misery and danger.

The summer of 1986, when we were preparing

the *Childwatch* programme, was hot and sunny. I travelled round the country interviewing people who had taken part in our survey. I remember a family of five sisters, all of whom had been abused by a family friend who worked as a first-aid officer in a zoo. I was horrified by the way paedophiles manage to worm their way into jobs which bring them into physical contact with children. I was also repelled to see how they can intimidate children into silence. The sisters had kept their secret even from each other. All this information was new to me, and over the months I had to deal with my own shock.

I remember Richard Johnson, the founder of Incest Crisis Line, explaining to me that each abused child is in fact three children:

'There is the victim of the abuse, the terrified child who can think of little else, who dreads every night, who feels guilty and defiled. There is the mask the child wears to survive—some children are bright and outgoing, and put all the efforts into their schoolwork because that's their only escape. Others channel it all into rebellion. Still others enclose it and become silent and shy at the back of the class. And finally there is the third child, the child he or she would have been if the abuse had never happened, and that's the child we all try to reach.'

At home our own children were not babies any more. Emily was eight, Rebecca six and Joshua four. By now our country cottage was habitable, and the family spent every weekend in the New Forest. I have always felt it to be a refuge and a healing place. As a city child, it was the only countryside I knew, and there is refreshment on hot summer days in the deep forest glades, where ponies graze, and pigs wallow in cool mud baths. Our cottage had lawns of rough meadow grass where the children could run and play.

One Sunday, as Desmond loaded our luggage into the car, he felt physically uncomfortable. I was in the television theatre in Shepherd's Bush, recording *That's Life!*, when he arrived in my dressing-room after the show and told me about his pain and breathlessness. I asked him to go to his doctor. He refused. I was his wife, after all, what did I know?

The next day he mentioned his discomfort to Janice, his assistant. She, more subtle than I, told him that David, her young strong husband was going for an 'executive check-up'. That sounded more appropriate for a man with a powerful sense of machismo. Desmond went round to his GP to ask for a test, and told him why. Two days later he was having a cardiac stress-test. A week after that he was booked into Charing Cross Hospital for an angiogram.

I dropped him at the hospital for the test, went into my office in Kensington House to work on *Childwatch*, then drove back to pick him up. Curse my autonomic system. Whenever someone I love is in danger, I pass out. It's a useless, infuriating habit. Not only does it make me helpless, but it also distracts attention. When I went into the hospital I saw Desmond still in his smart green surgical gown, sitting on a trolley, punching the buttons on his mobile phone. I sighed with relief. On the phone as usual, so not much could be wrong with him. He looked up, saw me and said, 'There you are, I was trying to phone you. They say I must have open

401

heart surgery tomorrow'. I fainted. I woke on the floor, with Desmond looking down at me with irritation. 'Esther,' he said, 'this is *my* moment.'

I drove home, packed his case, and took it back to him. As I ran into the house I saw a young woman sitting on the garden wall. She was a newspaper journalist. 'Can I have a quote, please, Esther, about Desmond's illness?' she said. News travels fast. I shook my head and kept on running.

With Desmond settled into his hospital bed, I lay alongside him, cuddling him. Tidy and practical as ever he went through all the things I needed to know if he died the next day. 'Oh, Lord,' he said, 'I never taught you to change a plug.' That was the least of our problems.

The bypass operation went well. I went to see Desmond in intensive care. He was in pain, but courageous as ever. I took him back to the New Forest to convalesce, and threw all the butter and dripping he loved so much out of the house. I bought jars of beans and lentils, trying to increase the fibre in our diet. The effect on our alimentary canals, however, was most antisocial—we sounded like two discordant trombones.

The spiritual effect on Desmond was more profound. He started to value each moment. Always before he had been pressured by deadlines, new ideas crowding through his mind at such speed that he worked fiendishly long hours. Work was his identity. He adored good journalism, and loved to practise it. Now he began to cultivate his soul. He wrote and broadcast three editions of 'Thought for the Day' for Radio 4. They were popular. He had sackloads of letters as a result.

He began seriously to study Judaism. He talked

402

to me about the memorial service he wanted me to create when the time came, and the grove of trees he wanted planted on the hill behind our cottage where he wanted his ashes to be strewn. I tried to reassure him, but Desmond was convinced that now he knew not when but how he would die, and planning for it was important to him. From that moment I, too, knew he was mortal. I stopped taking our life together for granted, but tried to savour each minute.

Of course we still had rows, we were a noisy pair, with strong views, and passionate tempers. But the rows were superficial. Our daughter Rebecca recently told me, 'You two shared everything, you discussed everything. Everything you enjoyed you did together. Everything that mattered you asked each other's advice about'. It was quite true. Our partnership was so complete we instinctively walked everywhere together hand in hand. He would ring me eight or ten times a day. I would wake him in the night to tell him what a wonderful lover, husband and father he was. I had to be sure he knew. I didn't know how long I'd have him with me.

He made a tremendous recovery, and within a couple of months had made a video for Wessex Heartbeat explaining the operation to other coronary patients, and then was off around the world filming his 'Visit' documentaries.

Work crowded in on me, too. The campaigning work on *That's Life!* continued, much of it featuring children. I had been invited to present some awards in a Kingston hospital. A consultant anaesthetist told me about a heartbreaking experience he had just had, telling a mother her two-year-old toddler had died. The mother and child had been out for a drive together, and the child had stood up in the back of the car, while they were crawling at five miles an hour in a traffic jam. The mother had braked, the child had fallen forward on to the handbrake and cracked her skull.

'You would never put precious china loose on the back seat,' the doctor told me. 'Why don't people belt their children safely into their seats?'

I was as guilty as anyone. Desmond, who understood the danger, always insisted our children were belted in when he drove them, but I was much less meticulous. *That's Life!* filmed me arriving at school, all three children unbelted in the back seat. To prove how wrong I was, we showed blurry inadequate film from America of children's bodies flying through the windscreen under the impact of an accident at twenty-five miles an hour.

The day after the programme was transmitted Peter Bottomley, Minister for Transport, arrived in our office and said, 'What can I do to help your campaign?' We asked him to provide us with clear, explicit film showing what happens in a car smash when children are loose in the car. He did, and the film was shown over and over again. Our campaign, researched by Patsy Newey (who was later to become Editor of my talk show on BBC2), prompted a change in the law. Now children must be belted in, for their own safety.

A mother wrote to say her child had been badly hurt in a playground, having fallen a couple of feet from the steps of a slide on to a concrete surface. We tried to find statistics of playground accidents, but there were none. Nobody knew how often children injured themselves in playgrounds, nor how serious those accidents were. But instantly after our programme the letters began to arrive, demonstrating just how dangerous concrete and tarmac can be. We discovered safer surfaces which could replace them, rubber tiles on which you can drop a plate without breaking it, wood chips that soften a fall.

This campaign, researched by Richard Woolfe, was effective not because it changed the law, but because our viewers decided to take action themselves. Parents all over the country began to insist that the old concrete and tarmac should be removed. Parent-teacher associations dug up dangerous surfaces and paid for new safe surfaces to be installed. Unhappily, many councils failed to follow their example. As I write, local authorities around the country are saving money by closing playgrounds and chaining up equipment, rather than installing safe surfaces. In a country where children's needs are so often forgotten or neglected, we desperately need a Minister for Children to protect their interests.

In 1987 I put forward the idea of 'Children of Courage' which became part of the BBC's major charitable appeal, *Children in Need.* It was the most popular segment of the evening, not just in audience terms (fourteen million viewers at its height), but also because it inspired the most donations. I loved presenting it. I have already described one memorable moment when a girl looked intensely at me as I was in mid-flow live on the air and said, 'Esther, do you know you've got a big lump of spinach stuck in your teeth?' What could I do? 'Please take it out for me,' I said. She did, inspected it, said 'Yuck' and threw it away.

We showed so many amazing children over the years it is difficult to pick out individuals. I remember the children who battled uncomplainingly against illness, or disability: Julie Hunt, for instance, who could skate, water-ski and turn cartwheels in the studio in spite of the fact that her leg had been turned back to front to enable her to walk. Oliver Broderick, who raised so much money for other children, in spite of his own exhausting dialysis. Lee Cummins, who having lost a leg to cancer, played football nevertheless, and left me a wickedly funny doll to remind me of him when he tragically died.

There were others equally impressive, who put their own lives at risk to save others. Caroline Tucker was badly burned when she went back through the flames of her own burning house to try and rescue her little sister. Matthew and Katie Evans, aged thirteen and eleven, outwitted two robbers who had broken into their house and imprisoned the rest of the family. Matthew Lee saved the life of his father, who had been injured and lost in the mountains, by going ahead by himself to find help. These and so many more prompted our viewers to say to me, 'I'll never complain again', having seen the children's courage and resilience.

Why is such a fascinating and inspiring show no longer being made? Perhaps because a 'disability lobby' mounted a persistent attack upon it. The lobbyists were a group of politicized self-appointed spokesmen, who claimed to represent the disabled community. No disabled people I spoke to, however, felt any kinship with them. They achieved the publicity they craved by giving me an award for being 'patronizing' when I interviewed the children. I asked them for specific examples. They searched the programmes at my request, but failed to come up with any. Their militancy, however, killed the programme, and not only cost the viewers and the children themselves a great deal of pleasure, but cost *Children in Need* one of its most effective and popular segments.

What a shame. I'd love to know what positive result the lobbyists ever achieved with their attitudinizing. Certainly, when my own daughter was in a wheelchair, she never had the slightest support or help from them.

*   *   *

Fuelled by more and more cases that came to *That's Life!* and ChildLine we continued our campaigns to reform the child-protection laws. We were careful to protect the children's identities, and only told their stories if they wished us to. But sometimes the law had let them down so badly, publicity was the only weapon left to them.

One day in 1989 a letter landed on my desk and I walked round it like an unexploded bomb. I let it lie there for three weeks. It was from a boy, Martin, who had written to me at ChildLine. Hereward Harrison, the Director of Children's Services, forwarded it to me with a note. 'Esther,' he said, 'we must do something about this.' From time to time I would ring Hereward and assure him I was doing something. I was thinking about it.

Martin wrote about the school he attended in Newbury. It was called Crookham Court. His brother went there, too. Martin said that he had just discovered that his brother had been sexually abused by one of the teachers there, Anthony Edmunds. Martin himself had also been abused by the owner of the school, a seventy-four-year-old multi-millionaire called Philip Cadman. If true, it was a hideous situation. How could we investigate such a closed world without distressing the children and their parents?

I showed the letter to Richard Woolfe. We pondered it together. I rang John Birt and asked him whether he would support our investigation, or regard it as trial by television, and therefore out of bounds. He said we should go ahead.

The first step, obviously, was to talk to the two boys and their parents. They were angry and appalled at what had happened to them. They described the school to us. Cadman had deliberately set out to attract vulnerable children. He targeted the sons of service families, whose parents would be scattered around the world, and he brought his fees down so low that they would be covered by the grants supplied by the Ministry of Defence. Most boarding schools were too expensive for ordinary service families to be able to afford. Crookham Court was the exception. He also targeted children with special needs, dyslexia, for example. That, too, would mean a child was less confident and therefore less likely to ask for help.

Martin's family told us that one child had complained of abuse at the school in the past, and the police had been called in, but they could find no corroborative evidence, so Cadman was left stronger than ever. The police could not go in again without concrete evidence, otherwise they would be accused of harassment. The social workers couldn't go in at all, they had no legal responsibility for the welfare of children at private boarding schools. That changed as a direct result of the Crookham Court case.

After my three weeks of fearful paralysis, with coaxing and support from Hereward and Valerie at ChildLine, Richard and I started our research. We learned that the school had been given an extremely poor report by the Department for Education inspectors. Then, through talking to the boys, Richard discovered that sexual abuse was part of the culture of the school. The boys talked about it, made jokes about it with each other. But that in itself was not evidence. How could we persuade the boys to trust us enough to tell us the truth?

One morning, knowing that Cadman was away at a meeting, we asked the Headmaster of the school to invite ChildLine to address the boys. He agreed. Hereward, Richard and I made the journey together. The boys assembled in the hall. They were clearly embarrassed, knowing and yet not knowing why we were there. I told them about ChildLine's work, and about the many different reasons children rang for help. Then I approached the most sensitive subject, sexual abuse.

'Children find it very difficult to ask for help,' I explained, 'because they often feel ashamed or guilty, as if it's their fault. But abuse is never a child's fault. The adult is always to blame. It's as if you had fallen into an enormous cowpat.'

I always tried to make my language suitable for the children I was talking to, and if my comparison was funny or vulgar, I admit it helped me when they laughed. I wanted them to feel that an abused child was not a freak, that the crime was extremely nasty, but not too foul to put into words.

'If you fell into a cowpat the size of a mountain,' I said, 'and you came out covered with muck, you'd think you were disgusting, smelly, revolting. But then you'd have a bath, and all that nastiness would be washed away down the plughole, and there you'd be, pink and sweet-smelling again. The abused children I've met find that actually talking about what happened is just like that bath, it makes them feel clean and whole again. It's the abuse that's nasty, not the person it's happened to.'

The embarrassed giggles had stopped. As I spoke there was complete silence, none of the boys met my eyes. At the end Hereward handed out ChildLine leaflets. The boys took them from him eagerly and leaped away, healthy young animals again, all their boisterousness and energy restored. I later discovered they had pinned our leaflets up all over Cadman's flat in the school building. When I walked round the grounds the children ran to surround me, asking questions about *That's Life!*. A teacher took a picture he later sent me, with the caption, 'One of the happiest days at Crookham Court'.

Richard patiently collated a list of the children who might have suffered abuse at the school, and contacted their parents. It took great tact and delicacy. We didn't want to frighten them unnecessarily. They had to give us permission to take their son out of the school to interview him. The previous police investigation had proved that no child would disclose abuse while he was still inside the school, because the culture of abuse imprisoned them. They felt they would be letting their parents down if they told the truth about the school their parents had chosen for them. Many abused children keep silent in order to protect their parents.

Another teacher, Bill Printer, was soon revealed to be behaving very suspiciously, intimidating children and keeping them for hours in his room. He had left a previous school under a cloud. I spoke to the headmaster of that first school, and he told me he had let Printer leave quietly, even though a boy had tape-recorded him asking for sexual favours in return for money, because Printer promised only to work in girls' schools in the future. It was common practice then for schools to agree to let teachers go without reporting them to the police, because they dreaded a scandal which might destroy the school's reputation. That practice, I hope, has now ceased.

One of the staff at the school had a son—I will call him Peter—who was at grave risk. I offered to let him stay in our home with our family. Later, during the trial, this was thrown in my face. The defence said I had done it as a 'sweetener'—a bribe to make him invent the allegations of abuse. The fact that when boys came out of the school to talk to Richard, we put them up in the Hilton Hotel, was also attacked. I had to explain to the jury that this was not the glamorous Park Lane Hotel, but a humbler branch in Shepherd's Bush.

As we interviewed the boys and discovered more incidents of abuse the parents became very distressed. I remember trying to find a quiet room in Lime Grove Studios where one mother and I could talk, and the only place I could find was a storeroom full of cardboard boxes. There we sat,

411

while she wept and told me she herself had been abused as a child, and she couldn't bear the idea that she had unwittingly condemned her son to the same torment. I tried to reassure her that it was not her fault, that she had done her best to provide a good school for him, that all the blame should lie with Philip Cadman himself.

Our researcher, Richard Woolfe, had married a lovely, long-suffering young woman, Hilary. Now she was expecting their first baby. How she tolerated his long working hours and the phone calls I bombarded him with day and night I will never know. At a very delicate moment in the Cadman investigation, Hilary went into labour and Richard took her to hospital. I rang him several times there, apologizing each time. Then, as Hilary went into the second stage of labour, Richard rang me to say he was turning his mobile phone off.

I waited an hour or so, then couldn't stand the suspense any longer. I rang the labour ward, 'Can you tell me how Mrs Woolfe is doing? Has she had her baby yet?' The nurse asked who was calling, and then asked me to hold on. I later learned that she had gone down the ward to where Hilary was pushing conscientiously and said with excitement, 'Esther Rantzen's on the phone!' What Hilary said is unprintable. The nurse came back and told me the baby was not quite there yet. It turned out to be a marvellous little girl, Elise, and Hilary did forgive me, in time.

The programme was very carefully checked by the BBC's lawyers. Barrister Michael Bloch (now a ChildLine trustee) went through each boy's statement. The day after the *That's Life!* programme was broadcast I took a phone call from

412

a furious parent. One of the teachers we had named, Anthony Edmunds, had left the school; and we were told that he had left teaching and had joined a firm of solicitors. The mother who rang us said that he was back in teaching, and was an excellent teacher—charismatic—the only one her son really liked. Paedophiles learn how to attract and 'groom' the children they target. They also go out of their way to make sure the parents like them, too. They need to reach the stage of absolute trust and be treated as a friend of the family so that they can be alone with a child. That way it becomes almost impossible for a child to ask for help, because the paedophile convinces him that nobody would ever believe his story.

Although we handed all our research over to the police, and pleaded with them to act as quickly as possible, it took weeks for them to decide to arrest the teachers we named, Cadman, Printer and Edmunds. 'I'm sure Cadman is still abusing children,' I said. The police were incredulous. 'He'll never do that, now he's been rumbled.' But he did. After all, he had got away with abuse for years.

After our programme a man came forward and told us that when Cadman was a housemaster in another school, twenty-five years before, he had done the same to him. For Cadman it was clearly a compulsive addiction.

At last the police moved. When they arrested Edmunds, the charismatic teacher, he made a phone call to his mother, telling her to 'destroy the diaries'. The police overheard, went to his home and found diaries which detailed 111 assaults on children, together with the sums of money he had paid each one. He pleaded guilty. The others, Cadman and Printer, pleaded not guilty. Richard and I were subpoenaed to give evidence.

When Ian Skipper read the headlines as the case began, and saw that I was being accused of bribing the boys, he decided I needed support. As much to protect ChildLine as me, he hired Michael Mansfield, the illustrious barrister. I was amused to meet him. He swept into his chambers and ran his fingers through his hair with a flourish. It was like being with a famous actor. He explained to me the court process. He told me he was not allowed to coach me in any way, but asked me about ChildLine, and argued with me about the efficacy of counselling abused children.

I became aware that I could, after all, answer questions clearly and cogently under pressure. But I also realized that I was terrified at the prospect. And yet I was not unused to speaking in public, and did not myself face the prospect of talking about my sex life to total strangers in open court. How much more terrified, then, the children who were giving evidence must have been, and they didn't have the benefit of Michael Mansfield to guide them.

The trial was in Reading. Keith Samuel, the BBC's most senior Press Officer attended every day that Richard and I gave evidence, and his support was very valuable. Ian Skipper had booked Michael Mansfield for the first day I was in the witness box, and although he was silent, his presence disconcerted the other barristers most gratifyingly.

As the moment came for me to be called, my stomach turned to water. I ran to the lavatory.

414

Then I came back to the room where my team were waiting, and paced round the table. After a while Richard could stand it no longer and said, 'Esther, you've tucked your skirt into your knickers'. I jumped, turned round and caught a glimpse of my own black suspenders. I imagined walking the length of the courtroom in that condition, and standing in front of the accused. Not that the paedophiles would have cared.

I was two days in the witness box. At one stage the barrister asked why I seemed to think it was so difficult for children to reveal that they had been sexually abused. I tried to explain it to the jury:

'I am a middle-aged married woman,' I said. 'And yet if you asked me to tell you in detail what my husband and I did in bed, I would be embarrassed and humiliated. We are both adults, we love each other, and what we do together is quite legal. I can only imagine what it must be like to be a child, and try and describe an act which I know is criminal and which fills me with disgust and shame to remember.'

I came home and reran every word of my evidence through my mind. I told Desmond I thought I had failed the boys. If the jury believed the defence argument, that I had persuaded them to make up their allegations, either because I was obsessed and saw abuse everywhere, or because I wanted to increase the ratings for *That's Life!*, Cadman would get away with it once more. He could go back to his school utterly beyond the reach of the law. Nobody would be able to accuse him again. He would abuse more generations of schoolboys—would be invulnerable, unassailable.

When I fell asleep late that Friday night I

dreamt I was trying to attract God's attention. He was wearing a long black legal gown, and was obviously busy, sorting out a famine in Ethiopia, I think. I nagged and nagged Him with my worries about the trial, that my evidence had been weak, that Cadman and Printer would be acquitted and the boys would have to go back to the school, until He could bear it no more:

'Don't be ridiculous,' He said. 'They'll both be sent down.'

I woke with His voice in my head, and a sudden bright light in the bedroom. Sunlight was streaming between the curtains. I rang Bryher:

'I think I've just spoken to God,' I said, 'and He's told me not to be ridiculous, they'll both be sent down.'

'Great,' she said. 'That means I can go shopping with no worries.'

And she did.

I rang Richard and told him the same news.

'Ah,' he said.

From his tone it was obvious he thought I had gone quite mad.

However, God, as is His wont, turned out to be quite right. Both Cadman and Printer were sent down. So was Edmunds. Years later I met the judge at the trial, Sir Maurice Drake. I was struck by a thought. 'Did you ever dream that I had pestered you with questions during that trial?' I asked.

'No,' he said.

'But suppose I had. Would you have said I was ridiculous to doubt the strength of the evidence? Would you have told me that they'd both be convicted?'

'I wouldn't have been allowed to speak to you at

all,' he said. 'But, yes, I knew they'd be convicted on the evidence.'

'And would you have used the phrase "they'll be sent down?"' I persisted.

'That is the phrase I would have used, yes,' he told me.

So take your choice. Perhaps God spoke to me. Perhaps I telepathically beamed into Sir Maurice Drake in his sleep. Or maybe it was just my own subconscious. I make no judgements, but I remember that conversation very clearly, and it certainly eased my anxiety that weekend.

The day the jury retired to deliver their verdict was the day of the annual cricket match between the *That's Life!* team and our village in the New Forest. I was in an excruciating dilemma. As President of one team, and Vice-President of the other, I was required to bowl the first ball, but I was longing to stay in the court in Reading instead. I decided to try and dash between one and the other, but as it happened, the jury came to their verdict far earlier than anyone anticipated.

As I sat beside the cricket pitch my mobile phone rang. All action on the cricket pitch stopped. I stood and listened. The fielders, all of them members of the *That's Life!* production team, turned and watched me. I began to jump with joy, and they started to run towards me. We met in the middle and hugged each other, then I leaped into my car and raced back to Reading. My thought was for those brave children who had given evidence—one of them so small he could barely see over the edge of the witness box. Their ordeal in court had been worthwhile. The abusers, thanks to the courage of those children, had been caught and

417

convicted.

There were other results, too. Now every boarding school must have a confidential phone box so that the pupils can talk privately if they need to. David Mellor called me into his Social Services Department when he was seeing the Children Act through parliament, and listened while I explained that social workers had not been able to intervene in Crookham Court because they had no legal responsibility for the welfare of children at private boarding schools. He added a clause to the Act allowing them to be responsible.

Martin (the boy whose letter had revealed the crimes in Crookham Court) and his brother came to ChildLine when the Princess of Wales visited us, and they presented her with a bouquet. And I was grossly libelled by a Sunday newspaper.

It was an odd case. Brian Radford, a journalist who lived near Crookham Court School and worked for a Sunday tabloid newspaper, decided to attack our investigation. His editor, Richard Stott, backed him all the way. Mr Stott published a banner headline, 'Esther and the Sex Pervert Teacher' and the article implied that I had put children at risk by failing to expose another teacher at the school who we knew had horrible sado-masochistic literature in his briefcase. In fact, we had researched the teacher, but had failed to find any child who disclosed any abuse by him, they all spoke of him in glowing terms. So we reported the discovery of the sado-masochistic literature to the police and left the ensuing investigation to them.

When, in page after page of the newspaper, I read Brian Radford's allegations against me, I was horrified, not just on my own behalf, but also on

418

ChildLine's. It was incredibly damaging. I decided I had to sue the paper for libel. I went to see George Carman for a preliminary conference. He cross-examined me meticulously. I was fascinated to see that he measured every answer I gave by the way he predicted a jury would react. When I had finished, he gave me three pieces of advice. Firstly, he said that I would win. Secondly, that it would be the most harrowing period of my life. Thirdly, that nobody could predict what the damages would be.

Carman was right on all three counts. At the trial, I was represented by the brilliant team of Richard Hartley and Geoffrey Shaw. It was indeed a harrowing experience. Each night I would wake at two in the morning, my mind churning over the evidence of the previous day. I would sit on our bathroom floor, making endless notes. Desmond was angelically tolerant, and gave excellent evidence during the trial. I was intrigued that two women friends of mine, both successful in their careers, refused to give evidence for me because, as they frankly told me, they didn't dare alienate the press.

In the end I won, and the jury awarded me damages of £250,000. All that money would have gone to ChildLine, because I wanted no part of it. But the newspaper instantly appealed against the damages, and won. The Appeal Court reduced the amount to £110,000. Still enough, you might think. But having lost the appeal I had to pay the costs of it. They, together with the untaxed costs of the first action, came to well over my damages.

I wrote to my lawyers, asking them if they could reduce their bills and they did. That meant I could at least give £25,000 to ChildLine. The BBC had agreed to support my action—I could have asked them to cover the costs so that all my damages, all £110,000, could go to ChildLine. But I didn't. The BBC is funded by licence-payers who might have wondered why they should pay the costs of my libel action. On the other hand, that huge sum of money could have paid for so many children's phone calls to ChildLine. Perhaps I was crazy not to let the BBC pay.

*   *   *

By 1994, I had been well educated into the horrors of child abuse. I had met many survivors, listened to children, talked to paedophiles, wrestled with the law. We collated many of the letters we received from viewers describing their experiences of going to court, and sent them to the Pigot Committee, which was set up by the Home Office, and which recommended reforming our legal system. If I thought I knew everything about abuse, I was wrong. Fate, or God, or sheer bad luck, decreed that two of my favourite child friends were sexually abused, one of them in the swimming pool of our New Forest cottage.

Desmond and I were on our way to London from a posh day out. I was sitting uncomfortably in my smart suit, my silly hat discarded on the back seat as we drove home, when the carphone rang. A close and dear friend, Donna, was in tears. She said, 'Polly has been sexually abused'.

My heart stopped. Polly was seven, a lovely child with long dark hair and big dark eyes. Who could possibly have abused her?

Our friend told us, 'It's a neighbour, an old man

420

called Robert Gillings. He lives next door. He and his wife have always been friendly. In fact, they came to the hospital with presents when our two daughters were born, and always offered to babysit if I needed to go shopping or we were going out to dinner. Sometimes the Gillings even had the girls to stay overnight.'

'How did you find out?' I asked.

'When you lent us your cottage for a holiday, we invited the Gillings to tea. Polly was in the pool when she suddenly shouted, "Please, Mummy, stop Uncle Bob doing that". I looked and he had his hands under her swimsuit. I went completely cold. I told Polly to get out of the pool. I waited until the Gillings had left, then asked Polly if he'd done it before and she said yes.'

I steeled myself to tell my friend the truth, as I saw it.

'The fact that he was so relaxed, so confident that he could do it to her when you were standing nearby probably means that he has done it many times before. And he may have done it to Jill as well.'

Jill was her second daughter, two years younger than Polly.

'The crucial thing is that you try to absorb your own shock, try not to pass it on to the children. Of course, let them see how angry you are with Uncle Bob, and how much you care about them, but don't let them suspect how badly you are hurt, or they may try and protect you by not telling you the worst. Have you told social services?'

'Yes, I rang them, and said I'd phone them back when I had spoken to the children.'

'Don't ring them back for a day or two,' I

advised her, breaking all the rules. But I had heard too often that social workers try to prevent children confiding in their mothers, for fear of 'contaminating the evidence'. Can you imagine how hurtful that is, to both child and mother? 'Over the next few days you need to map the problem, discover just how serious it is. Find moments when you can talk to both girls. Ask them what he did to them. Let them tell you without showing them how shocked you are.'

It was tough for Donna and her husband, even tougher for her children, and I was amazed how furious it made me. I rang Valerie Howarth at ChildLme and confided in her:

'It makes me so angry,' I said, 'to think what that monster did to those lovely children.'

By now, Donna had discovered that Polly had physically attacked Uncle Bob, punching him, her fists flying, to try and stop him abusing her little sister aged five. And when she asked how long he had been abusing them both, Polly said as far back as she could remember. He would take them out into the garden, or up into the bedroom where he could be alone with them and out of sight.

Donna then told me of the many days when Polly had wept on the way to school, and she had wondered if she was frightened because she was being bullied. In fact, the little girl was terrified of being taken to kind Uncle Bob's house after school, and what he would do to her there.

When I met the two little girls again, I used a technique I had often used before when talking to abused children. Please bear with me, because I must confess that on these occasions my language is dreadful, and I use the worst kind of schoolboy slang. I use it deliberately to deflate the picture in our minds of the all-powerful monstrous abuser— to turn him into a piece of rubbish, and to make the children laugh.

I said to Polly and Jill, 'You know what Uncle Bob is?' They shook their heads, eyes wide with painful memories. 'Uncle Bob is an old shit-bag,' I said, watching their faces.

They looked at me with disbelief. What was a respectable middle-aged woman doing, using language like that? Then a smile broke over their faces. I went further. 'He's a nasty, smelly, old shit-bag.' I picked up a cushion, threw it on the floor and punched it. 'So there, Uncle Bob, how dare you do that to my friends.' I jumped heavily on the cushion. It wasn't good for the furnishings, but it was doing wonderful things for my immortal soul. 'You are a stupid, nasty, old shit-bag, Uncle Bob.' The girls giggled with delight.

I once had a letter from a boy who had been sexually abused by a local evangelist. The boy had been given a carved plaque from his social worker inscribed 'To the bravest boy I know'. She had brought him to meet me, because the evangelist, thanks to evidence from one of his favourite converts, had just been acquitted of abusing the child. The convert had also abused the child. Indeed, they had taken pleasure in assaulting the child together.

I hugged the boy and told him his social worker was right, he had been incredibly brave. I explained that a trial has its own rules, and sometimes they are not fair, especially to children. We went through all the people in his life who knew he had told the truth, his own family, the police, the social services. I watched him visibly grow in confidence. My letter from him said, 'I don't have nightmares about the shit-bag any more. My social worker says I can call him that, because you did'. I certainly did.

Once she thought the girls had told her everything, Donna rang social services again, and they took video statements from the two children. The girls were medically examined, and it broke Donna's heart again when she was told that Uncle Bob had damaged Polly so seriously he had left scars.

Through Valerie and Hereward at ChildLine both little girls were referred to Great Ormond Street Hospital for assessment. The team in the hospital taped interviews with the children which revealed that the abuse had been even more serious than anyone had realized. One evening Donna met me, deeply troubled. The police had warned her that if Polly revealed more abuse at the trial than she had described during their first official interview, the discrepancy would be used by the defence to discredit the little girl.

This is yet another example of the flaws in our legal system. No allowance is made for the way children disclose abuse, bit by bit, as they gather the strength to describe the horror they have endured.

More difficulties were to follow. The Crown Prosecution Service decided that Donna's younger daughter was not old enough to withstand cross-examination, therefore Bob Gillings could not be charged with any offences against her. The jury would never be told of the agonizing moment when Polly had rushed at him, her fists flying, trying to protect her little sister from him. Then to our horror someone in the police force leaked the story to the *Sun* newspaper. The headlines were all over the front page, that a man had been charged with sexually abusing a child in my swimming pool.

At first I was furious. Then Donna rang me again. The *Sun* had printed a picture of Bob Gillings. A woman had seen the newspaper, telephoned her daughter and apologized to her. Twenty-four years previously her daughter had also been abused by Uncle Bob and had told her mother, who hadn't believed her. Now she did. The family went to the police, and they took a statement from the girl, now a young woman. As with Polly and Jill, Uncle Bob had taken her into his garden to abuse her; and had used the same kind of little presents to try and buy her silence.

For one wonderful moment we thought at least the jury would hear that. But the judge decided the jury could not be told. The offences were too long ago, he said. So seven-year-old Polly was deprived of the corroboration that I believe the jury had the right to hear. Some lawyers are scathing about a jury's ability to reach the right verdict. But I believe juries make mistakes when they are prevented from knowing crucial facts by our archaic and irrational legal system.

The night before the trial, the legal team met Donna and her husband. Was it to support and encourage them? Not at all. It was to try and persuade them to agree that the trial should be abandoned and the case dropped. Why? Because, relying as they were on the evidence of one seven-year-old child, they were convinced they would never obtain a conviction.

My friend and her husband, Bill, stood firm. Bill,

an ardent Christian, believed they must do what was right. Donna was determined that, whatever the cost, Uncle Bob must answer for his crimes. In the face of their determination the Crown Prosecution Service agreed to continue with the case. I have received dozens of letters over the years from families, bitterly disappointed that their cases have been dropped at the last moment, without explanation. It nearly happened to my friend Donna and her family.

Uncle Bob was defended by a woman barrister. I once caused high indignation by suggesting that women are often retained by rapists and abusers on the grounds that if a jury sees that a woman is prepared to defend him, he can't be all that bad.

Uncle Bob's counsel told Polly eleven times that she was lying. Polly held firm. She was giving her evidence over the video link, with nobody she knew alongside her. But God or Fate was kind. She could see, by means of a video camera, the barrister who was asking questions. She could also see, sitting behind the lawyer, her own grandparents smiling their encouragement. So each time she was accused of lying, she replied quite calmly that she was telling the truth, that she had been told she must always tell the truth.

Luckily, Uncle Bob had been foolish enough to abuse her in the pool in front of her mother, so Donna could give evidence which backed up her daughter's story. Still he denied everything.

I was in court to listen to Uncle Bob's elderly wife giving evidence on his behalf, portraying Polly as a liar and sexually precocious, which she certainly was not, and describing the layout of her home and garden in such a way as to imply the

426

abuse could not have taken place without being observed by other people. The sweet old lady in a cardigan looked demure and infinitely trustworthy. No wonder Donna had left the girls day after day, night after night with the couple, never suspecting what was happening to them in that respectable home.

The jury, however, believed Polly, and convicted Uncle Bob. He was sentenced to eighteen months in prison, and served nine. Of course, that was only for abusing Polly. For justice to be served, he should have been tried for his crimes against three children, not one.

I often wonder why our lawyers continue to practise in a system that they must know allows dangerous criminals to walk free. Yes, we must protect the innocent, but surely that should include innocent children who remain dangerously unprotected with the law in its current mess. It is still the truth that the vast majority of child-abusers are walking free on our streets.

But at least things have improved since we first launched *Childwatch* and ChildLine. At least Polly was believed when she cried for help. At least she was able to give her evidence via the video link, without Uncle Bob intimidating her. And when I asked her how great an ordeal the trial had been, she proved once again the strength and courage some children possess. She said, 'It was scary, but it was worth it. By telling people what Uncle Bob did to me, I was able to protect other children'.

*   *   *

Some children face pressure which is so intense

that in the end it breaks down their strength and their courage, even their will to live. In 1992 I was forcibly reminded that bullying can create that kind of pressure. At the time the generally accepted view of bullying was that it was a natural part of growing up, one that we all have to learn to withstand. I was standing by my desk in the *That's Life!* office when my phone rang. I picked it up, and a woman, Susan Bamber, started to speak to me with such urgency and desperation that I instinctively stood to listen to her. She told me that she had just found the body of her seventeen-year-old daughter, Katharine, hanging in their garage. Katharine had left a suicide note which made it plain that the cause of her death was the bullying she had endured at school. Her mother was not in tears, she sounded as if she had cried the tears dry.

'I want you to start a campaign on your programme,' she told me. 'It mustn't just be an item that comes and goes and is forgotten. This evil is going on in every classroom in the country. You must make people realize the damage it does, and the lives it costs.'

I could only say yes. Katharine had died, it was now up to us to try to make a memorial for her, a campaign to save other lives. We researched her story. Katharine had not been the victim of punches or kicks, there were no bruises on her body or broken bones. It was a more subtle, more malevolent process. She had been sent to Coventry. Other girls had pretended to make friends with her, had agreed to meet her, at a time and a place, and then failed to turn up.

From her photograph Katharine was obviously a lovely girl. She was also intelligent and sensitive, and perhaps it was that sensitivity which provoked the cruelty in the other girls. For all my affection for children I do recognize that sometimes they can be quite savage to each other. Katharine had talked to her parents when the bullying first happened, and they thought it had been dealt with. When it started up again Katharine decided to shield them from the truth. She bottled up her distress until she could stand it no longer, then she killed herself.

People reacted to Katharine's story in different ways. An independent anti-bullying helpline was set up. We pressured the Department for Education into taking action, and it decreed that every school should develop an anti-bullying policy. We consulted a range of experts and they suggested schools should run anonymous questionnaires on a regular basis, checking with their own pupils how widespread bullying was at any one moment.

There are several different techniques for dealing with bullying, for example, the 'No Blame' approach, or the 'Bully Court'. We discussed and illustrated them on the programme. Nothing we said affected Katharine's own school, which steadfastly refused to speak to us, and the local authority flatly denied that bullying was to blame for her death. They even held a press conference to say so, without telling Katharine's family or us. We were tipped off by a local journalist just in time, and Katharine's father was able to attend, taking with him a copy of her suicide note.

One morning a local London radio station invited me to take part in its breakfast programme to discuss bullying. It was a bright morning in early summer. Desmond grumbled at me as I tiptoed around the bedroom far too early, getting dressed.

He always complained that he never woke me when he had to leave at dawn, whereas I tiptoed about like an elephant.

'Why do you have to do this?' he muttered into his pillow, as I went to the radio van parked at the end of the garden. What a good question that turned out to be.

The interviewer was an 'award-winning' Australian, new to Britain, and new to me. I had never heard of him. I put on my headphones and heard him introducing the topic of bullying from a studio in central London. He asked me one anodyne question and then went into the attack: 'Miss Rantzen, you are simply exploiting people's emotions to prop up your own flagging ratings. You're like a ring-master in a circus.'

I explained that the Bamber family had contacted us because they wanted Katharine's story told. I said *That's Life!* had never been afraid of emotional subjects, I reminded him of the story of Ben Hardwick, for instance, or our campaign against child abuse. He had no idea what I was talking about, and accused me once again of using the Bamber family tragedy for my own glory. I had had enough of him. I looked out of the window at Hampstead Heath, the long grass shining in the sunlight, and I laughed.

'Why are you laughing, Miss Rantzen? Don't you take this subject seriously? I'm sure our listeners do.'

I stopped laughing and apologized: 'I'm sorry. I was just thinking what a waste of time this discussion is. I hoped we would be talking about bullying, not about my motives or my programme. I'm sure there are children and their families

430

listening to your show right now who are suffering, as Katharine Bamber suffered, and who are desperate to find ways to stop the bullying. Why don't we try to help them? Of course this is a serious subject. I wouldn't have got up this early on a beautiful summer day if I didn't think it was serious. But now can we please talk about the problem, and the best ways of protecting children?'

He wouldn't let me. At the end he said goodbye to me, turned my microphone off, and said to his listeners, 'Ah well, fools rush in'.

The engineer apologized to me as I climbed out of the van, and when I got to my office I found our fax was filling up with angry letters from listeners who were irritated by his attitude. Angela Rippon, who had her own programme on the same station, told me their switchboard was jammed with complaints. Richard Littlejohn, who ran a phone-in after the breakfast show, had so many calls about the interview that he had to declare his own show an 'Esther Rantzen-free zone' to try and persuade his listeners to change the subject.

Bullying, thanks to Katharine Bamber's story, is no longer a trivial subject. But we are no nearer to resolving it. Last year it was the most common problem that children rang ChildLine about. There were 22,000 calls from desperately worried children. Bullying doesn't only happen inside schools, but also on the streets. Children are being robbed of their lunch money; are being driven out of school entirely, into truancy and absenteeism. Bullies can become violent adults. Their victims can become unconfident adults, friendless and frightened all their lives. The simple truth that ChildLine has discovered is that bullying doesn't

431

stop of its own accord, it must be stopped by parents and teachers, and, if necessary, by the police. Otherwise we will continue to lose valuable young lives, like the lovely seventeen-year-old Katharine Bamber.

I have mentioned my belief that we need a Minister for Children. Recently a group of the major children's charities combined to press all political parties to put this idea into their manifestos for the next election. At the moment children are sliced thinly between government departments. The Department of Education regards children as products to be informed and trained. The Home Office regards them as a series of problems—criminals, drug addicts and so on. Social Services deal with them when all else fails, fostering them, putting them into care, funding child-protection agencies. All these ministries do their best, but each only deals with one aspect of the child. Who is looking after the whole child?

I have criticized aspects of our legal system which make it almost impossible to obtain justice for abused children, particularly if they are very young. The law has been described as an 'abuser's charter', because the adversarial system is utterly unsuited to dealing with children, either as victims of crime, or perpetrators. Europe was quite right to criticize the way our courts handled the Bulger case. The murder of toddler Jamie Bulger shocked the nation and the world because the murderers themselves were children. But what on earth were we doing bringing two ten-year-old boys to their trial in a closed van with booing crowds surrounding them? How could they be expected to understand what was going on around them in the courtroom? I know the crime was absolutely appalling. But these were still children.

As a mother, and as Chairman of ChildLine, I have come to believe that the inquisitorial system used in many other countries is far more appropriate to children. The ritual of two battling barristers was designed to intimidate adults into telling the truth. It terrifies children into silence, or drives them to say anything they think will stop the questioning.

The barrister in my friend's case believed she was treating Polly kindly and considerately, and yet she accused her of lying eleven times. And little Jill was never heard at all.

When is the legal profession going to wake up to the fact that they are colluding every day with major injustices in our trials? I did make this plea in a meeting of the criminal bar; and one man told me, 'It doesn't matter how much of a monster my client is, or what I have to do to break a child down, I must do it. That is my job.'

In that case, change the job.

But remember, too, that the unhappiness of our children in the twenty-first century extends well beyond our legal system. We have created a lonely, uncomfortable world for them—and the result is that there are more and more young suicides and mental health charities are increasingly worried about the amount of illness in the very young.

I believe this is because we have forgotten how to provide for our children's most basic requirements. Children need two loving parents. They need security, and space to play, so that they can develop their own skills. But their needs are always bottom of our list of priorities. When we build new housing estates and shopping malls, the planners take care of our cars, design roads, and garages and parking lots. But where are the clubs for young people, the open, safe play spaces? We are bulldozing existing playgrounds, turning them into car-parks, and schools all over the country are selling off their playing fields to make way for housing estates. Is it any wonder, in inner-city estates where even a game of football is forbidden, that children become vandals, or arsonists?

I wonder how many people have time these days to put children first? The old extended family has been shattered long ago. Granny may live hundreds of miles away. Mum and Dad may be divorced. Even if they are still together, both parents probably go out to work, and work very long hours.

A boy rang ChildLine and told me about a very serious problem. He was so deeply unhappy, I said he ought to tell his mother. He said he couldn't, that she was so tired when she got home at night that he couldn't talk to her. I suggested he might try at the weekend. He said she worked in a shop which was open all day on Saturday and Sunday. They literally had no time to talk—and she had no idea how much he was suffering.

How many parents in these frantic times have the time to notice if a child is quiet and withdrawn? We are all struggling to get the work done, make a living for the family. Most parents care deeply about their children and want to help them, but will they pick up the warning signs that a son is being bullied, or a daughter is being abused?

As a working mother myself, I worried that I couldn't have the long conversations with my children that my own mother had with me. I was

434

reassured by other working mothers who told me the quantity of time doesn't matter, it's the quality that counts. But now I'm not sure I believe that.

Clearly, there is no point in trying to turn the clock back, and insisting that all mothers must stay at home. But, given that it is in the interests of women and the economy that mothers should go out to work, that night shifts are common, and Sunday is just another working day, the question is: who is looking out for the interests of the child?

I believe that just as a Minister for Disabled People helped to focus attention on the needs of the disabled community, so a Minister for Children is vitally necessary now. Children are our future, their safety and happiness should come first in our lives. We need to recognize the danger of neglecting them, and focus our attention on the needs of our children, before it's too late.

CHAPTER FOURTEEN

THE AXE FALLS

While *That's Life!* ran for six months every year, from January to July, I found it exciting and mentally refreshing to make different kinds of shows in the second half of the year. I most enjoyed making documentaries, and in 1976, Bryan Cowgill, then the Controller of BBC1 (the man who created the huge popularity of *That's Life!* by moving it from late on Saturday night to 9.30 on Sunday night), came up with an idea for me.

An American reporter, George Plimpton, had made a very entertaining series of documentaries by learning various different skills—as a footballer, for instance. Bryan decided I could do the same for British audiences, and his first thought was that I should train as an astronaut.

When Desmond came back from his meeting and told me the news, I looked glum. As always, he said, 'If you don't like an idea, don't dump it, replace it'.

I went up to the canteen with a producer friend, Tim Slessor, and shared the problem with him.

He said, 'The trouble is, if you tried the astronaut training you'd never survive because you're not fit enough. But if you were an amateur athlete, you would. Why don't you suggest a series using talented amateurs, and give them the challenge of their lives?'

I went back to my desk and worked out a format. We could introduce each gifted amateur to the top professionals in a chosen field and give them the chance of their dreams. A cook could create a banquet. A dressmaker could make a dress for a top fashion show. A kid with a good voice could make a record.

The documentary series *The Big Time* was born.

As ever, I was lucky during the next three years to work with outstanding researchers and directors. I was also lucky that my professional life had brought me into contact with some fascinating characters who had stuck in my memory.

For the cook, I contacted Gwen Troake, the Devon farmer's wife who had won the 'Cook of the Realm' competition when I was one of the judges for *Nationwide*. As the dressmaker, I recruited Ada Johnston from Dalbeattie in Kirkcudbrightshire. She was the wife of the convenor of Dalbeattie Civic Week—you may recall that was my first appearance as a 'celebrity'. Ada had dazzled me then by changing at least three times a day into spectacular outfits, each with perfectly matching hat, bag and shoes, and all her dresses and suits had been made at home on her sewing-machine. In addition, she was an extrovert with a superb sense of humour.

For our jockey, Desmond suggested we should look for a woman. 'Put her in a professional race,' he said, 'and pick a jump-jockey. That's much more exciting.'

When Desmond was a boy growing up in the Cotswolds he had taught riding, and loved hunting and point-to-points. He knew what he was talking about.

The *Big Time* films were a joy to make. Gwen Troake's confrontation with television chef Fanny

Cradock made television history. Gwen was a wonderful cook. It was her pleasure to add a good dollop of Devon cream to her dishes, 'to cool it down', and her voice had the same soft, creamy texture. We had arranged for her to invent the menu for the Foyle's Literary Lunch at the Dorchester in honour of Sir Edward Heath. She chose dishes she knew were popular with guests at her own lavish farmhouse lunches in Devon: duck with a bramble sauce, followed by a delectable coffee pudding.

I went to the Lime Grove studios to meet Fanny Cradock, then at the height of her career as a TV cook, to see if she could advise Gwen how to serve her pudding. Fanny's view was that Gwen should devise something far more sophisticated for Sir Edward—she suggested little pastry boats surrounded by spun sugar to evoke his yacht, *Morning Cloud*. She agreed to appear in our film provided we arranged for her to have lunch first with Eugene Kauffler, the chef de cuisine at the Dorchester in his private dining-room. He wasn't thrilled at the idea, but he agreed.

I was perpetually on a diet in those days, so I wasn't thrilled either when Fanny peered at every dish she was offered and said in her raspy baritone, 'Eugene, that looks magnificent, but I couldn't eat a crumb of it'. Somebody had to eat the stuff, otherwise Eugene might have been offended. So I did, spooning heaps of rich mixture on to my plate and trying to chew each mouthful a million times to use up the calories. Not for the first time I discovered that didn't work.

At the end of lunch Ian Sharp, the director, joined us to discover where he should place the camera team. I looked inquiringly at Fanny.

'I'm not going to touch any food,' she said very firmly.

That was a surprise to me. At our meeting she had described exactly the ingredients for her little boats, and I had brought them all to the kitchen. I reminded her, and showed her the list I had written at her dictation. She took it from me with a flourish, tore it up and handed it grandly back.

The grandness was catching. I handed the list to Ian, and he stuffed it into the pocket of his jeans. Then I realized I had written my questions on the back of the paper, and rather less grandly had to ask for it back and tried to piece it together. Meanwhile, Fanny was in full flow.

'You have not paid me anything like enough for a cookery demonstration. My minimum fee for *Nationwide* is two hundred and fifty guineas.'

I bargained with her. 'Could we show the food we've brought, arrange it next to you?'

'Why?' she asked, as intimidating as Lady Bracknell in high dudgeon.

'Because how else will the viewers know that "couverture" for instance is cooking chocolate?'

'My viewers will know because I've been telling them so for twenty-five years.'

Eventually she agreed to sit next to the pile of ingredients she had recommended, but by this time Ian had black smoke coming out of his ears. He told me later that she was so intolerably rude, he thought I should just have packed up and gone. But my job was to get the scene on film, and that's what we did.

Fanny agreed to be filmed in the pudding section of the cavernous Dorchester kitchen, and off she went to have her radio mike arranged on her. In her absence the crew needed to know if her husband Johnny was going to be part of the scene. He had been silent all through lunch, amiable but vague. Fanny returned merry and bright, obviously all the better for having roughed us up. I asked if she wanted us to lay a place for Johnny while we tasted Gwen's coffee pudding.

'What are you paying him?' she asked.

'Nothing,' I said.

'Then no,' she said. So Johnny disappeared to the other end of the kitchen.

Fanny sat down next to Gwen, who by now was looking at her the way a nut looks at a descending sledgehammer. Fanny smiled sweetly at our cameraman, Dave Whitson, from whose ears black smoke was also starting to spiral. Fanny didn't notice, but gestured towards her waist, 'No tighter than here, darling, please'.

She meant she wanted him to stay in a kindly wide shot, as opposed to a cruel close-up. Dave leant round the lens and bowed sweetly to her. I could have told her Dave was at his most dangerous when he was sweetest, but I didn't.

The ensuing scene became a television classic. Fanny had been so furious with us that she genuinely thought she was being kind and caring with Gwen. The viewers, however, thought she was a bat from hell. She asked Gwen what the main course was to be. 'Duck with bramble sauce,' said Gwen. Fanny raised her eyebrows, which she had already pencilled into towering arches. 'What,' she enquired, 'is a bramble?' She knew perfectly well it was a blackberry, she just asked it to prove to Gwen that a humble bramble has no place in *haute cuisine.*

But that was just the opening move, the *hors d'oeuvre*, so to speak. She moved to the pudding, and here again, to continue the culinary metaphor, she didn't mince her words.

'I thought we could give Mr Heath my famous coffee pudding,' said Gwen.

Fanny pursed her lips so they puckered like a drawstring, and pretended to vomit. Dave zoomed his lens in to her mouth for each grimace. Gwen was downcast. She tried to defend her pudding. Fanny retched again, Dave zoomed in once more, devastatingly.

Back in the cutting room we tried to shorten the scene, and failed. In the end it played on screen exactly as it had happened, and the viewers rose in protest. Their letters filled the columns of *Radio Times* and the newspapers, and Fanny did not, to my knowledge, appear on television again.

I had had no intention of doing her career such damage. Even now I feel slightly guilty. But we had to show the scene. It was an integral part of the documentary, and there was no escaping Fanny, any more than you could produce *Macbeth* without Lady Macbeth. What's more, those blessed pastry boats in their spun sugar all fell to pieces when the waiters tried to serve them. Coffee pudding would have been far better.

The jockey's film was completely different. We found a courageous, attractive woman, Joan Barrow, who had a great deal of amateur experience point-to-pointing, and had always dreamt of competing in a professional race. She trained for us in the Cotswolds, in David 'The Duke' Nicholson's stables.

441

Ian Sharp and I had met The Duke when we were preparing the film, and I returned forlornly to the office. The Duke was famous for never using two words when a grunt would do. His longest sentence to me was 'Don't get kicked', good advice when his elegant, neurotic racehorses were trotting past me on their way to the gallops, but otherwise none too explicit.

'We may not get much dialogue, so I think this had better be a visual film,' I said to Ian, who needed no encouragement.

We were filming in the most glorious summer. There is no lovelier country than England in the sunshine, and no lovelier part of England than the Cotswolds. Ian filmed Joan as, to strengthen her legs, she rode up and down the hills on a bicycle with no saddle. When they set the fields alight to burn the stubble, he filmed Joan riding through hazy smoke on the back of her great white carthorse. It was a beautiful, evocative film, and won a documentary award from the Royal Television Society.

On the day of her race, Joan's hard work had its reward, she won it by twelve lengths. But Ian, his crew and I were so busy we didn't have a penny on her.

My biggest lost chance to become a multi-millionaire was during the *Big Time* film about a pop singer, when we discovered Sheena Easton. By this time John Pitman had joined the series as reporter, and with characteristic skill he made a wonderful job of it. I was the series producer. I always knew this particular programme would be a challenge. Young people all over the country would watch, thinking they could sing at least as well as the person we picked. We had negotiated a plum prize, a contract to make two records. I said to our researcher, Linda McMullen:

'We've got to be very careful to make sure whoever we find is really outstandingly talented'.

I had promised the record company to bring them three or four possible candidates to choose from, and we agreed, because they were the fashion of the moment, to try to find a new black group. Linda duly found us a dozen possibles, including several black groups. They auditioned for John Pitman, Patricia Houlihan, our director, and me. At the end I turned sadly to Linda and said, 'I'm awfully sorry, but I don't think we've found what we need'. She went off around the country again; and we set up another audition, with another dozen hopefuls.

On the day, Linda was looking smug, but said nothing. We were in the basement of Television Centre, in Wood Lane, west London. It was a windowless, airless dressing-room, extremely dreary but at least it had a piano. Phil Philips, a skilled accompanist (and the composer of Jimmy Young's signature tune on Radio 2) was our rehearsal pianist. He wore the audition pianist's usual expression of dogged resignation as act followed act. The last candidate arrived, a short, dark, Scottish girl. I raised my eyebrows at Linda. This was not a black group. She clearly knew that, but remained cheerful.

The Scottish girl introduced herself, Sheena Easton. She was, she told us, a drama student. She sang occasionally at dentists' dinner-dances. We asked if she had any other performing experience. She told us she had played Snow White in a school production. 'The dwarves were all taller than I was. When I bit the poisoned apple and the curtain fell on the first act, they all leaned over me and said, "Gie us your apple!". They were so much bigger than me I had to hand it over'.

We laughed, but my heart sank. She was extraordinarily pretty. She told her story with natural punch and wit. There was no way she'd be able to sing as well.

She went to the piano and started with scales. I looked at Phil, he nodded at me. Sheena sang two perfect octaves. Then she sang 'Feelings' to us. It's not an easy song. She sang it brilliantly. By the end of the audition I could see why Linda had looked so smug. I thanked Phil and went back to the office. There I said to Linda, 'Are you going to resign or am I? If you or I became her manager, ten per cent of that will be worth a fortune'.

Neither of us resigned. Sheena is now one of the richest women in the world.

As a precaution, before we took Sheena to the record company, I rang Bill Cotton, who was by now the Controller of BBC1. I explained our problem. 'We have negotiated with a record company to make two records, but we've found someone who is so extraordinary, so very talented, that I don't want her to be tied to the contract if it's not in her interests.'

I wanted Sheena to be free to take up any offers after the show. I didn't want her to criticize us in the future for binding her to a contract that held her back. Bill told me to check the contract with my own agent, Richard Armitage, who understood the music business as well as anyone. He did, and said it was fair. So on the appointed day we went to the record company.

I later discovered that the executives there had met that morning in a desperate bid to try and find a way of turning us down. I had warned them that instead of bringing several candidates for them to choose from, we would only be bringing one. I further admitted that she was not a black group. They knew we were factual programmemakers, and concluded that we would know nothing about show business. But we were arriving with a crew to film the audition. How could they say no to us on film without appearing rude to the poor little Scottish girl we were bringing to meet them?

We arrived in the sound studio, set up our cameras, and Sheena started to sing. She chose 'Feelings' once again, and sold it to them with every ounce of emotion in her. At the end the executives were silent. Then one of them looked at the others. 'I see no problem there,' he said. Sheena had convinced them instantly, just as she had convinced us.

They found a song for her, 'Modern Girl', and we introduced her to a number of different experts, including Lulu and her agent, Marion London. Marion became notorious for telling Sheena that she would never succeed unless she changed her image. But Marion was right, and Sheena listened carefully to her. When we first met Sheena she resembled Dana, the Irish singer. She deliberately hardened that image, to become her own person.

We filmed her recording the song. She nearly got into the charts, but just missed. She didn't quite manage the top thirty, so she didn't appear on the prestigious Top of the Pops. For the documentary it was a disappointing moment. But Sheena's moment was to come.

As soon as our film was broadcast, fans besieged the record shops asking for 'Modern Girl'. But it was nowhere to be had, not even for ready money. The record company had withdrawn it when it failed to make the charts, and had instead put her second record, 'Morning Train', into the shops. The fans bought it, sending it instantly into the charts. When the company saw the demand, it rushed out her first record, and that went into the charts as well. Bill Cotton told me that no other singer since Ruby Murray had had two records in the top ten at the same time.

Among the viewers of *The Big Time* was Cubby Broccoli, the producer of the James Bond films. He was about to select the singer for his latest film, *For Your Eyes Only*. Just after our broadcast he went to America to discuss whether to pick world-famous singers, such as Olivia Newton John. Then he said to the film company executives, 'You'll think I'm mad, but I've just seen a documentary about a little Scottish girl I'd love to use'.

From their expressions they clearly did think he was mad, but they asked her name.

'Sheena Easton,' he said.

What he didn't know was that her record had just been released in America and had gone straight to number one in their charts. He had his way. Sheena recorded the Bond theme song, and is still the only singer to be seen in vision in the titles.

Many years later I interviewed Sheena and she told me *The Big Time* had set her out on the yellow brick road to the magical world she had dreamed of, singing alone in her bedroom, in her council house in Scotland. For a time she had been labelled in Britain as the girl from *The Big Time*, or the girl 'discovered by Esther Rantzen', and she must have become heartily sick of it.

Now she is her own woman. She has recorded with Prince, has her own show in Las Vegas, and is enormously wealthy. But successful as her records are, I still believe nobody has heard just how good her voice really is, since that *Big Time* audition day in 1978 when Phil Philips played for her in the basement of Television Centre.

*   *   *

While I was spending the first half of each year investigating and exposing crooks on *That's Life!* it made the perfect contrast for me to spend the second half of the year celebrating talent, or acts of unknown heroism. So, in 1988, when I knew Michael Grade was looking for a new Saturday night show for BBC1, I sent him a one-page format that I called *Hearts of Gold*. The inspiration for it had come from three different sources.

Firstly, it sprang from a poignant story we told on *That's Life!*. *A* man called Nicholas Winton had rung us. Just before the Second World War broke out he had organized a train to take Jewish children out of Prague to escape the Nazis. Some of the children had given him their few prized possessions, documents to identify themselves and their families. He had kept these safely in an album for forty years.

Now he wanted to trace the children whose families had long ago perished in the concentration camps, to return these fragments of their past to them. He knew how much these scraps of paper

447

would mean to them.

We pored over them in the office. They made deeply moving reading.

We put together a plan. Katinka, our researcher, would try to find these children, adults now, of course, and invite them into the studio, without telling Mr Winton what we were doing.

We recorded *That's Life!* in the Television Theatre, Shepherd's Bush, and found enough of Mr Winton's children to fill the whole of the ground floor. I told the story on the air, and we showed our viewers some of the documents in the album. I explained that Mr Winton wanted to return them to their owners, and asked them to contact us if they recognized any of the names or faces in the photographs.

Then I said to Mr Winton, as he sat in the front row of the theatre listening to me, 'There is a woman sitting next to you who wants to say something to you'. A middle-aged woman took his hand and said, 'I want to thank you for my life'. Then the woman sitting on his other side put her arm round him and embraced him. Then I asked all those who owed their lives to him to stand, and row upon row stood to do him honour. The camera cut back to me. For the first and only time in the history of *That's Life!* I sat for a moment in silence, then turned in my chair and left the stage. My eyes were filled with tears, I couldn't speak. The heroism of this quiet man had taken my breath away.

There were two other inspirational moments that led me to the invention of *Hearts of Gold*. One was Russell Harty's memorial service. He had died at fifty-four, hounded by critics who derided his style, and lambasted him for his private life. Following his death, the church in Piccadilly was filled with distinguished and famous friends. I watched them arrive, and hoped that somewhere, somehow, Russell was watching, too. Then Alan Bennett delivered the address, a piece of writing so affectionate and yet so filled with controlled rage at the way Russell had been made to suffer, that in the end the congregation gave him a standing ovation. I went home thinking that all too often the British, reticent nation as we are, pay fulsome tribute to people only after their death, when it's too late.

I was also invited by Radio 4 to chair a phone-in for them, an unofficial honours list. Ordinary people rang in to celebrate other ordinary people for acts of personal kindness and courage. It made a wonderful programme, an antidote to all the bad news that filled the media then, as it does now.

All these threads wove together in my mind, and I suggested to Michael Grade that we could invent our own honour, the Heart of Gold award, and present it to unsung heroes. The point of the programme was not that the BBC would nominate them but that those who knew them best, their own friends and colleagues, should do so. He accepted the idea, and it ran for seven years. After a while we on the team claimed that we could recognize the typical 'heart of gold face', an open smile, clear eyes, an undefended personality, somebody who always put others first.

To demonstrate that not everyone has a heart of gold, we went onto the streets to conduct what we called our 'Good Samaritan Survey'. I wore various disguises to test the passers-by. In one film I was a

449

cleaning lady who dropped an elaborate flower display, to see who would stop and help me put it together again. In another I was the bride in a wedding where the best man turned up at the last moment drunk and disorderly.

Sebastian Scott, a clever young man, less than half my age, was our series producer. When I suggested I should be disguised as the bride, fond of me as he was, he could not conceal his horror. I suppose it's every young man's nightmare that a bride should lift her veil to reveal a forest of elderly wrinkles. In Jewish weddings the bridegroom meets the bride just before the ceremony and lifts her veil, just to check. After all, Jacob married the wrong sister—the old, ugly one!

In the event, a passing trombonist saw the 'drunk' best man collapsed outside the church and agreed to take his place. When eventually I unveiled myself, he laughed and kissed me. But then he was only the best man, after all.

For these films we had to hide our cameras and microphones, and usually that was no problem. But when we filmed in Liverpool we hid them in a skip, and then watched helplessly as the passers-by picked through the skip, found our expensive pieces of recording equipment, stuffed them into their pockets and ran off with them. Outside Bonham's auction room I dressed as a parking warden, and watched Charles Spencer, Princess Diana's brother, stop and help our actress by carrying a piece of furniture for her. He was a charming Good Samaritan, and quite calm when I marched up to him. He recognized me at once.

My teeth were always difficult to disguise. I was forbidden to smile, and we went to great lengths to

450

try to cover them. For one programme I was dressed in purdah, in black robes and a face mask. I hated it. It felt like a denial of a woman's right to exist. For another I dressed in the enveloping black-and-white robes of a nun, which I loved. The traditional uniform made a positive statement of a spiritual commitment. It was also a far more effective disguise. As I walked down the pavement I passed my own dentist. I said, 'Bless you, my son'. Even he didn't recognize me. He smiled, thanked me and walked on.

Hearts of Gold was a delight to work on. What could beat watching tributes being paid to such outstanding people. Some of them were doctors, charity workers or carers. Others were just people who rose to a challenge, saved lives in an emergency, and then disappeared back into the crowd.

A peculiar aspect to the programme was the number of 'hearts of stone' that we discovered alongside the hearts of gold. Time and again, while we were researching a story, someone would drip poison into our ear. 'Don't give your award to him, he hasn't really achieved anything.' Or: 'Don't give it to her, she's stolen the credit, but she's really done nothing'.

Invariably our researchers discovered that the 'hearts of stone' were motivated by jealousy. Once a volunteer working for a charity was so incensed that we were going to honour the founder that she gave the secret away, in the hope that when it had leaked out we would cancel the programme. We did indeed cancel it, although we found a different way to honour the founder in a subsequent show. An intrinsic part of the programme was the fact that we never told our subjects in advance that they were to be honoured. Most of them were so modest they would have denied they deserved it anyway. So we had to trick them, in the nicest possible way, to lure them to the studio.

One of the most elaborate plans we invented was for a child called Amanda Thompson. Amanda had cancer, and had to undergo intense chemotherapy and bone-marrow transplants. She was completely bald as a result of the drugs she had taken but she refused to wear a wig. In spite of her illness and all her arduous treatment, she had managed to raise a good deal of money for the Malcolm Sargent Cancer Fund for Children. This fund had paid for her to go on the only holiday she had had during her illness, and she was determined to pay them back.

Amanda was, and is, a very talented musician. She studied the piano at the prestigious Chetham's School, Manchester. In every free moment she used to take her keyboard out to local shopping malls and play there, raising money for the fund. We decided to try to help her by creating a record in aid of her charity.

I rang Richard Harvey, the composer, to ask his advice. He suggested that Gounod's *Ave Maria* is a lovely melody, which Amanda could easily play. Then we contacted the opera singer Lesley Garrett and told her Amanda's story. She instantly agreed to join our conspiracy. Next we pretended to Amanda that there was to be a concert in aid of the Malcolm Sargent Cancer Fund in London. We asked if she would be prepared to accompany Lesley Garrett in the concert. Amanda agreed, so we asked her to come to a studio to rehearse.

452

She did not realize that her meeting with Lesley Garrett took place in a recording studio belonging to Richard Harvey. What she believed was only a rehearsal was, in fact, the recording of the CD. Lesley sang *Ave Maria* with Amanda playing the piano. After she and Lesley left, other musicians arrived to add their harmony. I was hiding behind the scenes, and when Richard played me his final arrangement, with Lesley's glorious soprano soaring over Amanda's sensitive accompaniment, I was thrilled.

The day Amanda arrived for what she believed would be the concert was, in fact, the recording of *Hearts of Gold*. We went to extraordinary lengths to disguise our television studio as a concert hall. Behind the scenes our designer enjoyed himself each week creating fake sports centres and radio studios, and, in this case, concert-hall dressing-rooms.

Our set was built on a revolve, so on cue the doors slid back and Amanda saw our audience for the first time. She was astounded when we presented her with the CD in the studio. She played and Lesley sang live on the show. Their *Ave Maria* went straight into the charts, and they both appeared on *Top of the Pops*. Lesley, sumptuous and glamorous, Amanda, completely bald, playing steadfastly as ever. Both were making a statement—Lesley that lovely music need not be inaccessible; Amanda, that there is no need to be ashamed of having cancer. And, thanks to everyone who concocted our conspiracy, Amanda made well over £100,000 for the Malcolm Sargent Cancer Fund. As I write, she is well, and continuing her studies.

Hearts of Gold ran until 1995, and, in fact, outlived *That's Life!*. As an experienced producer I knew the time must come some day for *That's Life!* to fall out of favour. I was astonished it lasted for twenty-one years. In 1994 the axe fell. *That's Life!* was killed by Alan Yentob, then Controller of BBC1. Did I feel bitter or angry? Not for a moment. That was his job. No programme has a divine right to transmit. Alan felt it had served its purpose, and it was time to move on.

There had been press rumours of its impending demise for a couple of years. Our ratings had dropped from the towering heights when nobody could assail us, to a more vulnerable seven or eight million. We were still the most popular consumer programme, but no longer dominated the BBC charts. Why had we lost viewers?

I believe there were several reasons. The previous Controller of BBC1, Jonathan Powell, had moved us to Saturday night, which turned out to be a mistake. And by then television technology had moved so far that many viewers now had their own camcorders. They should have been telling their own stories, rather than having their experiences presented for them by our reporters.

Perhaps, too, although I hate to admit it, I needed a break. When yet another catastrophic holiday or dangerous car story came along, I heard myself saying in production meetings, 'The last time we told a story like this—' But for our young team it was the first time they had heard it. It was fresh to them, but familiar to me. So why didn't I make the decision myself, quit and leave the audience wanting more?

I have asked myself that question, and realized that would have felt like desertion. How could I abandon the people who were still writing to me by the thousand, asking me for help? How could I let go? Like many another Jewish mother, I couldn't. When my beloved sister, Priscilla, got married, my mother ran after the car she and her new groom drove away in, and they were nervous she might catch up with them and climb in. It's hereditary. When I sensed the bosses were whirling their axes over our heads, I could no more have deserted *That's Life!* than I could my own children in similar danger.

When the decision had been taken, one boss did suggest that I should tell the press it had been my choice. I looked at him as if he were speaking to me in Old High German. 'But when they ask me why, how on earth could I explain it?' I said. There are of course a million tried and tested formats. I could have said, 'I need to spend more time with my family,' or 'I have exciting new offers I want to try out'. But the press would have known I was lying, and so would I.

I did ask Alan Yentob one favour when he killed *That's Life!*. I said I would rather go out with a bang than a whimper, and told him the title that I had been preparing for some years should the occasion arise, *That's Life All Over*. He agreed. In fact, he did better than that. He conspired with the producer of our last programme, Richard Woolfe, to extend it by ten minutes from the sixty minutes I expected, to accommodate a last-minute surprise.

The programme gambolled lightly over some of

455

the high spots of the last two decades, the moments with Annie Mizen, with Ben Hardwick, the talking dogs and ping-pong playing pussies, the campaigns, and then I turned to camera for the last time to announce that the brass band, who played our signature tune, was with us in the studio to play us out.

As I turned I saw David Frost shouting to me. He was walking down the stairs through the audience. My mind went completely blank. I let out a guttural cry, as if I had been kicked in the stomach. Although I love surprises, they always leave me winded and speechless. He led me on to the stage, where all the reporters, my friends, were waiting. He gave me a book filled with some of the most poignant letters from viewers we had received when they knew we were coming off the air, people who had found the programme useful in their own lives, and wrote to tell me so. And then he pointed towards a huge screen. Unknown to me they had put a special farewell film together.

First Terry Wogan paid tribute to the programme, calling it 'Twenty-one years of glorious television and fantastic work for the British public'. And then, mischievously, he said, 'You've probably forgotten all those years ago when I applied to be one of your boys and you turned me down'.

Anne Diamond, who did so much to save babies' lives with her own campaign about cot death, talked about the show's contribution to children's safety and children's rights.

The Viscount Tonypandy, the outstanding Speaker of the House of Commons, said, 'I am proud to know you, and grateful for the service that you have given'.

That was nothing to the pride I feel at having known him.

Finally, unbelievably, the Prime Minister himself, John Major, paid his own tribute to the show for having inspired the creation of ChildLine. 'In building up ChildLine,' he said, 'Esther has used her public personality for private good. So, Esther, on behalf of all those that ChildLine has helped over the years, let me say thank you, and wish you every success in the future.'

It was overwhelming. I think I could have kept my emotions under control, but for one other interviewee. My team, who understood me well, had tracked down Matthew Whittaker. I had last met him when he was thin as a thread, battling terminal illness in Addenbrooke's Hospital. Suddenly his face appeared on the screen, reminding me of that moment.

'I was eleven years old at the time,' he said, 'and dying of liver disease. The doctors said there was nothing they could do for me. But five weeks after you told Ben's story, of his needing a transplant, I had my transplant. I've been doing fine ever since. And I am fine now. I am studying at college for my A-levels. I'd just like to thank you, Esther, not for me but for all the other children and adults who have had transplants, for the way you drew attention to the desperate shortage of organs needed for transplantation.'

It was too much for me. Tears poured down my face. David brought me to my senses by making me describe how I felt. I stumbled through the jumble in my mind. I tried to explain that the real credit was due to the brave people who had written to us and allowed us to tell their stories. And all those other people who had watched the programme and decided to help. Then I said, 'And I'm thinking, is my mascara falling all over my face?' He reassured me, Adrian appeared with champagne, the band played, and the series was over.

The critics who liked us least found the whole occasion typically nauseating, 'Who does she think she is?' they asked scornfully, 'Mother Teresa?'

No boys and girls, I don't. But my friends and colleagues were determined to give the show the celebration farewell party they thought it deserved. Nobody consulted me, so I just lay back and enjoyed it.

Then it was time to move on. Of course I felt a sense of loss. I loved the direct contact *That's Life!* had with our viewers, the letters we received, the people we met, who trusted the programme. They made me feel useful, and valued. I know the programme had its faults and its detractors, but it did entertain many millions of viewers, allowed us all to enjoy the eccentricities of our extraordinary nation, and, through its campaigning work, changed life just a little for the better.

Nothing has replaced it. There are other workmanlike consumer shows, most of which aim themselves firmly at the moneyed middle-classes, protecting them from shopping scams and rotten holidays. They do a good job. But there is still a gap in the schedules for a show with a wider brief, a mass-audience show to help viewers who can't afford to go for advice from expensive lawyers or accountants. If you doubt me, have a look at the following list, covering just a few of the subjects we talked about over the years, which I have taken from memory.

We regularly tackled shoddy goods and services, and partly as a result of our effort the law was tightened to protect consumers. We used hidden cameras to film door-to-door salesmen making false claims and forging signatures on contracts. As a direct result, parliament brought in a cooling-off period in hire purchase agreements to frustrate dishonest salesmen, and allow their customers time to think again.

We ran campaigns against animal cruelty. For example, we exposed puppy farms and successfully outlawed veal crates in which calves were fed iron-deficient diets and prevented from moving. Our campaign for child seat belts changed the law. Our publicity helped in the banning of Skoal Bandits, vicious little sacks of tobacco which cause cancer of the jaw, were lobbied for in parliament by Neil Hamilton, and were about to be launched on to the British market. We exposed the danger of sugary fruit drinks being fed to babies in their bottles, which rot their teeth.

We returned over and over again to the neglect of mentally ill people, who were turned out on to the streets when the old psychiatric hospitals closed. We secretly filmed in mixed hospital wards, which put patients in danger, and in which they lose all dignity. We exposed time-share swindles, loan sharks, door-to-door salesmen who pretend to be physically disabled, fake offers of home-work for the poorest and most disabled, which are simply unscrupulous ways of costing them money.

We tackled many safety campaigns, including the importance of cycle helmets and riding hats, the danger of tranquilliser addiction, the life-saving importance of smoke alarms. And we brought major new inventions to public attention for the first time.

That's Life! was the first programme to demonstrate that DNA testing can show whether a child is really related to his mother. We were told about a boy whose mother had been given asylum in Britain, but the immigration authorities thought he was unrelated to her and that she was just trying to get him into the country illegally. We had him tested, and he was indeed her son.

We showed for the first time the dramatic effect that a cochlear implant can have on some deaf people, allowing them to hear again. Then there were the landmark campaigns I have already mentioned in previous chapters about transplantation, safe playgrounds, child abuse and so on.

Week by week the programme improved people's knowledge of their rights in a real, measurable, practical way, and because it was entertaining it reached many millions of viewers with this information. I hope that one day someone will create a new show to fill the gap. If anyone does yearn for the old format, you have only to travel to the continent of Europe to find it. *That's Life!* continues to transmit there. It is the BBC's most successful format, and has made more than two million pounds for the Corporation in format rights alone. And before you jump to conclusions, not one penny of that money comes to me.

We could never have made the programme without skilled and dedicated researchers. But for all their best efforts, sometimes, as all journalists do, we made mistakes. There were libel actions, some of which failed, a few of which succeeded.

Throughout the years our investigative team did their best to uncover and report the truth. There were, however, hoaxes—times when we deliberately deceived our audience. The programmes which transmitted on April the First always contained one mischievous April Fool spoof.

The first was in 1979. We had already featured a great many films about talented dogs by then. Understandably, our film director, Nick Handel, was feeling hounded. Then an actress contacted us and said she had a lifelike Old English sheepdog costume. We met her in our film-cutting room, not daring to ask her to come to our office, in case she was seen and our secret leaked out. Our director, Nick Handel, watched her climb into a suit covered with woolly black-and-white hair. We worked out the plot of our film.

Chris Serle was to be the reporter. A friend of Nick's, who had a solemn dead-pan face, played the dog's owner. We hired an actor to play a policeman, and Nick took the crew to a private road he knew near London. First of all Chris interviewed Nick's friend about his incredibly talented dog, who had somehow been trained to drive. We showed the car being driven by the dog, and the reactions of astonished passers-by, including a cyclist who caught sight of the dog and wobbled off the road. We showed the car's pedals, specially adapted so the dog could reach them.

We then showed the moment when the car was flagged down by a traffic policeman, who asked the dog-owner for his driving licence. The dog took fright, and accelerated away, leaving the policeman standing on the pavement, yelling at him to come

461

back. Chris, sitting in the back seat, protested. The dog's owner turned to him, smiling and said, 'Don't worry, who can he ever tell?'

When we broadcast our film, the BBC switchboard jammed. Viewers rang in fury. How could we support such a dangerous practice as teaching a dog to drive? How could we encourage the dog to break the law? We had to put out a special press release explaining that the film was transmitted on April the First.

The next time, in 1984, we filmed at the London Zoo, showing a strange new animal from Tibet called the Lirpa Loof. The name should have been a give-away—so should the animal's habits, kindly explained to our viewers by Dr David Bellamy. It left purple droppings. Odder still, it imitated anyone who watched it. We hid our cameras and saw tourists pointing at the Lirpa, who pointed back. The zoo told us that charabancs arrived all the following week with visitors avid to see the Lirpa. Alas, it was there no longer.

Our final spoof, broadcast on April the First 1990, exposed a dangerous ointment called Dorian Cream. Our producer, Richard Woolfe, dreamed it up with me. Dorian was a cream which removed the wrinkles from women's faces, but transferred them on to their backsides. Gavin Campbell interviewed a couple whose marriage had been wrecked by the wife's wrinkly behind. Edwina Currie told us on film that it was a scandal, and she would draw it to the Prime Minister's attention.

We showed a large tanker drawing up at the zoo to collect Dorian Cream's principal active ingredient, rhinoceros spit. (I don't think rhinoceroses can spit, the horn gets in the way. So

Tom Brisley, our film director, spent many happy hours in the dubbing theatre, putting disgusting spitting noises over film of a rhinoceros grazing on an African savanna.)

A few months later I read in a tabloid gossip column that Michael Jackson now uses a special skin cream made from rhinoceros spit. If he does, I'd love to know where he finds it.

*   *   *

When *That's Life!* ended, I feared that one of my small pleasures—the invention of these daft practical jokes—would end, too. But I was immediately asked by Michael Jackson, then Controller of BBC2, to present a talk show for him, *Esther*, which continues to this day. And I was grateful when Patsy Newey, the Editor of the talk show, who had worked on *That's Life!* for years, kindly allowed me to continue the tradition of April Fool programmes.

The first of these was at the expense of an Essex boy who had already taken part in one of our talk shows, bragging about the wicked way he had with women. He was due for his come-uppance. We put him on the set, allowed him to brag again, and then introduced an actress who revealed that he had loved her for a night, then deserted her. He looked mystified, but his memory was fallible enough for him to be convinced by her tears and reproaches. I pointed my finger accusingly at him, our sound supervisor played the record of a baby crying, and I wheeled a pram on to the set, out of which I unfurled a banner saying 'April Fool'. He was delighted.

The talk show was, and still is, an exciting challenge for me. I'm never sure what is going to happen in the studio, and I always learn something new. People sometimes suggest that it must be intrusive or exploitative for our guests to be asked to describe their innermost feelings in front of an audience. In my experience it can be the reverse, both supportive and therapeutic.

One of our guests described what happened when she awoke from a coma, to find she had forgotten everything and everybody in her life. She had to relearn how to walk, and talk. She was meeting her husband, her children, her whole family as if for the first time. We had invited another woman to the studio because she had the same experience. They looked at each other with amazement. One of them told me, 'Up to this moment I felt as if I was a Martian on the wrong planet'. It had never occurred to her that anyone else would understand what she had been through. They stayed in touch with each other for many months after the programme.

The same happened when we interviewed mothers whose children had been stolen from them. One had her newborn baby taken from a cot in hospital. Another had her toddler abducted while she was on holiday. As they talked to each other, nobody else in our studio existed for them. It was as if the two mothers were connected by a tingling current of electricity.

I realized this could become the basis for a new programme which could consist of conversations between people who had each been through an extraordinary experience, who believed they were unique, and lonely in their uniqueness, but who

464

found one other person who shared it with them. I believed their conversation could make a marvellous new programme, and I was determined to offer it. I did, but the consequences almost wrecked my faith in the medium I have loved so long. But that was a while away.

Patsy Newey and her team pushed at the barriers of the talk show, exploring difficult and dangerous subjects. Not dangerous as American talk show hosts would understand it—we had no fisticuffs in the studio, no assassinations either. We did something far more dangerous. We made a programme about stammering (can you imagine a talk show filled with stammerers? Forget jokes about overrunning, we ran perfectly to time, and the show was nominated for a BAFTA award).

We made shows about deafness, about men's health and women's gambling. And however difficult the subject our audiences steadily grew. We made shows about history and mathematics and astronomy. We asked if there was historical evidence for the stories in the Bible. To our delight our audiences loved them. Once again, Huw Wheldon's principle held true, 'Always assume maximum intelligence but minimum information in your viewers'.

It was a privilege and a treat to interview outstanding people, some unknown, others famous and popular. I talked to stars from Dame Thora Hird to Sir Norman Wisdom, and from Rolf Harris to Dame Edna Everage. I interviewed popular heroes like Sir Richard Branson and Terry Waite. I even spoke to Michael Winner, in a programme about rudeness, though he insisted that nobody should be allowed to sit next to him on the podium, and was so appalled when I revealed that fact to our audience that, later in a newspaper article, he called me an 'old bag'. Would I invite him back? Certainly. Would he accept? I think not.

From time to time we were able to create our own stars on the show. On a trip to Leeds to launch an appeal for ChildLine's northeast base, I heard a school inspector speak at a lunch. You might not imagine a school inspector would be the most riveting speaker. But Gervase Phinn held the vast dining-room, a tough audience of lawyers and bankers, spellbound with his stories of the children he had met during his career. Gervase is a natural performer, but more than that, he loves and understands children. He has collected their thoughts, their drawings, their entertaining sayings, and puts them into context for his audience. I, too, was spellbound.

When I came back to London, I described him to Patsy Newey, the Editor of the talk show, rashly suggesting 'I think we should devote a whole programme to him, with no other speakers. Will you meet him?' Patsy had lunch with him, and agreed.

At that time I was also talking to Penguin about a ChildLine Christmas book. The Penguin Editor, Luigi Bonomi and I met. I spent most of our meeting describing Gervase to him.

We made two shows with Gervase, and after each one the BBC's duty log was jammed with viewers asking for it to be repeated as soon as possible.

Penguin have now brought out two books by Gervase. The second was serialized on Radio 4 and spent months on the bestseller lists. Luigi has become my literary agent. And ChildLine's northeast appeal was a resounding success. The base in Leeds is up and running, and comforts desperate children every day. So that was a story with many happy endings.

*   *   *

Presenting the talk show has been as surprising and exciting as riding the sudden climbs and drops on a rollercoaster. I never know what someone will choose to reveal on the air, and how our studio audience will react. In a programme about 'Betrayal' I spoke to a tiny little man sitting between the two sisters. One was his first wife, whom he had betrayed to marry the other. They were very much bigger than he was, so unexpectedly he became the toast of the show, the audience roaring for him, 'Bertie, Bertie!'

There have been moving and illuminating moments, too. I talked to Leah Betts' younger brother. She had been only eighteen when she died from taking Ecstasy, and I discovered that her brother blamed himself for her death, even though she had been killed by the drug she took. He felt he should have been able to stop her. As he spoke, other children in our studio revealed that they felt equally guilty about the deaths of their own brothers and sisters. The programme demonstrated how deeply this guilt can run in a child—it can be felt even more intensely than parents who are struggling with their own grief, sometimes realize.

*   *   *

On the talk show I met many families whose lives had been touched by tragedy; and, throughout my career, I have interviewed parents whose children were gravely ill, or seriously disabled. In 1995 I was to discover the difference between work and personal real-life tragedies. By then we had settled into our home in Hampstead. It's a big, happy house on the edge of the Heath. We had two shaggy mongrel dogs, father (Marmite) and daughter (Milly). Milly in her turn produced a litter of puppies. From the outside we must have looked an idyllically happy and successful family. Emily had taken her GCSE exams triumphantly, and was garlanded with A's and A-stars. So much so, that Joshua said to me plaintively, 'Couldn't she have done just a little less well?' But there was a flaw in all this happiness. Sometimes when I looked at Emily I felt there was some kind of doom hanging over her—a sword of Damocles waiting to drop.

Occasionally, Desmond and I used to discuss our worries. In 1992 when Emily was fourteen she'd contracted glandular fever. At first she seemed to recover, but then she relapsed. Indeed, from that time she never seemed entirely well. She missed a great deal of school so she taught herself the GCSE syllabus by copying out her friends' notes.

I didn't realize that, because she felt so ill and tired so much of the time, she would go to the school gym and work out for hours, desperately trying to build up her strength. It had the reverse effect.

One evening, when I was walking upstairs behind her, I noticed how slowly she climbed up, dragging one heavy foot up after the other with obvious difficulty and pain. She told me later that she would sit at the foot of school staircases and see them stretching up like mountain peaks in front of her. She would go to the library and cry, or fall asleep.

After Christmas in 1995 Joshua came back from a week's skiing with a sore throat. Emily caught it from him. Her throat became acutely painful, and she developed constant headaches. I would see her balance her chin on her hand as she sat at our kitchen table, her eyelids drooping as she fell asleep. I began to fear there was something very seriously wrong. Could it be MS? Or a brain tumour? I took her to our GP. He diagnosed chronic fatigue syndrome, usually known by its popular name, ME.

How lucky I was to have a family doctor who recognized and accepted this widely derided illness, still then known as 'yuppy flu'. He told us he had other patients with ME, and he knew a consultant neurologist, Professor Lesley Findley, who was prepared to treat them. That took some courage on Findley's part.

Later I met another GP who confided in me that he had the illness, but never dared admit it to his partners for fear of their reaction.

The problem is that doctors have never yet found a micro-organism on which to blame the disease. Therefore many take the view that it is a psychiatric illness. That has had dire consequences for some, especially for children. Parents have also been accused of causing their children's illness by abusing them. Children have been taken into care, imprisoned in hospital units against their will and their parents' wishes. I dread to think what would have happened if Emily had been referred to one of those doctors.

I got to know a family whose life was shattered by the treatment they received. The boy, Chris, had been made a ward of court, because the local paediatrician and social workers decided his ME was caused by his life at home. He was taken to the psychiatric unit of their local hospital, where he became worse. His parents took him home, the medical team fought them in court. His father became so desperate he fled the country with his son.

Returning alone to Britain, the father was thrown into prison for contempt of court. He had no choice but to bring his son back into Britain, and Chris was put into a locked psychiatric unit in Great Ormond Street Hospital.

At this point Chris and his parents appealed to ChildLine for help. One of our counsellors rang the hospital, but was told that he was not allowed to speak to Chris, that phone calls with Chris would be counterproductive to the treatment he was receiving. Chris sent me letters, desperately unhappy and frightened. I contacted Claire Francis, President of Action for ME. Together we raised enough money to pay for Chris to be treated privately. We found a solicitor to represent him. Eventually he was allowed home. He is still gravely ill. Stress and unhappiness, it is widely accepted, make the symptoms of ME very much worse.

Fortunately, our family was spared the extra agony of being blamed for causing Emily's illness. It was painful enough for us to watch her deteriorate. She managed one term of her A-level syllabus. Then she left school. After a while she could no longer climb the stairs at all. Then she

470

took to a wheelchair because she could no longer walk. Finally she was in bed all day. The light was so painful that curtains were not enough to screen it out. I had to put heavy drapes over the windows.

She, who loved books, could no longer read, and lay still, listening to tapes of the books she would have loved to explore herself. Her body was not just fatigued, it was numb. 'I'm not in my back, or my legs,' she would tell me, her voice barely audible. Her face was ashen. Her feet were so icy cold she had to wear thick bedsocks, whatever the outside temperature.

When I took her hand there was no response in it, the fingers just curled lifelessly. She managed one bath every evening, by candlelight, and I used to talk to her then, gently, optimistically. Then I would help her back into her bed, and massage her limbs, trying to bring back some kind of pleasant feeling. It did no good. Dr Findley decided he must take her into hospital.

There has been an official report into ME which recognizes it as an organic illness, but states that treatment in hospital is not necessary for ME patients. That sounds to me like an opinion based on economics rather than patient care. Certainly for Emily it made a difference. Dr Findley and his team created a regime for her. The curtains would be open five minutes the first week, then ten minutes the second. She would try to walk one step each day for the first week, then two the next. She would sit in a chair for ten minutes, then fifteen. She would write three words a day, then four. It was baby steps, but the steps were in the right direction, just.

When she came out of hospital after six weeks,

she still lay in her wheelchair, curled up as limply as a rag doll. She persevered with the programme. It was a ferocious battle, but she was determined not to be beaten.

From time to time during this period I would meet Alan Yentob, the Controller who killed *That's Life!*. At the time he had suggested that I should try to create another show for him, but never came up with a specific idea. In spite of the success of the talk show on BBC2, which had good ratings and was twice nominated for BAFTA awards, I missed the campaigning television I had made for so long, and I told him so.

In 1996 he commissioned Patsy and me to make *The Rantzen Report* for BBC1. Unfortunately, he only gave us six weeks to make it, with no pilot and very little money. We had to make two programmes a night, a difficult task when these were intended to be tough journalistic exercises. We came up with three subjects, and collected together a team to make them. The first one—capitalizing on 6,000 letters I had received since Emily's illness became public—was about ME.

The programme ran into instant trouble. We invited ME sufferers into the studio, but they warned us that it is such an unpredictable illness, they might be too ill to attend. So our researchers overbooked their guests. On the day nearly all of them arrived in the studio, but there was not enough room for everyone. They were understandably furious.

In the front row of the studio was the medical correspondent of *The Times*, Tom Stuttaford. He believes, or believed, that ME is a psychiatric disorder, closely allied to depression. That view

472

provoked even greater fury among the sufferers in the studio. It's not hard to understand why. When you are not feeling at all depressed, but you are unable to walk, or tolerate bright light, or go to work, or out with friends, a doctor saying you are suffering from depression must be infuriating. Tom was outnumbered, and shouted down, and he answered back with a column in the newspaper.

The programme was broadcast in the height of summer—the 'silly season'. It is a time when the politicians are on holiday, when there are no legal cases, and the newspapers traditionally turn to television as a source of news. For a heady week or so, our ME programme became their target. In all the sound and fury there were, sadly, many aspects of the programme which were completely ignored.

We had showed a child who had been punished for her illness by nurses who took her clocks away, refused to feed her, and left her on the floor when she fell out of bed, not because they were cruel, but because they genuinely believed that if she wanted to move, she could move. They even dropped her in a pool, thinking she would swim to save her own life. She didn't.

We had showed a doctor who claimed to be able to cure ME with a black box. We recorded him saying that I wanted Emily to remain ill, which was why I had turned down alternative remedies. In fact, it was Emily who refused all the so-called cures we were sent, the aloe vera, the cold baths, the dousing, the feng shui. She felt, and feels, that since there was no evidence they could work, it would be foolish to waste time and money on them. She is enviably logical.

In other words, we showed the damage that can

be done to ME patients and has been done to them by treatments that don't work but are costly or injurious.

I also spoke during the programme to Mrs Proctor about her son Ian. He had been taken into care by doctors who believed he was being abused at home. The Proctors fought a fierce legal battle to get him home, and they won. We showed him walking down a beach near his home, now completely recovered from his illness.

'Always remember, Esther,' Mrs Proctor told me, 'no matter how bad things are, there is light at the end of the tunnel.'

I remembered her words, and clung on to them over the next months. Personally and professionally, things were about to get very bad indeed.

CHAPTER FIFTEEN

SEPTEMBER SONG

The third *Rantzen Report* was about advocacy. In it we put the argument that everyone in residential care, be it a child, an old person, a disabled person, or a patient in hospital, should have the right to have their problems or complaints taken up by an independent representative who could act as their 'advocate'. Families are often disregarded as being too close to the situation—too emotionally involved. And they themselves often fear that taking a complaint forward may only make matters worse for a vulnerable relative.

What a child in care or an old person in a nursing home needs is someone accessible, with clout, not part of the system, who will listen when things go wrong. The advocate need not be an official, or a lawyer. We gave an example in our programme of an old person whose advocate was almost as old as she was, and visited her regularly. The problems need not be major ones. We gave another example of a child with cerebral palsy who simply wanted to be allowed to put her own coat on without help, rather than being shoe-horned into it. But we did have more serious examples.

A concerned mother, Janet Parker, had come to see us. She told us that her son, Ian, was profoundly disabled. He was 'locked in' by severe brain damage caused by illness when he was a baby, and could not express his wishes in speech. He was being looked after in a hospital in south London called the BHHI (the British Home and Hospital for Incurables—an old-fashioned name with obviously unpleasant connotations, which is why it is usually known by its initials).

Janet told us she was unhappy with the way her son was being looked after there. She felt the staff regarded him as being too disabled to be included in many of the activities, and that he was therefore being left without stimulation for much of the time. She had tried to put that point to Matron Kelly, but as Ian's mother felt she was not being heard. So she came to us.

We did two things. We went into the hospital on the day it was holding a fête which was open to the public, to film Ian; and we invited Mrs Kelly, the Matron, to the studio to join in our debate. She refused, indeed she would not talk to us at all. Instead, the hospital lawyers sent us a letter, the salient points from which we used in our programme, including the fact that, although it provided appropriate treatment for less disabled people, the BHHI was not a suitable hospital for profoundly brain-damaged patients.

The week the programme was broadcast I went to the Edinburgh Television Festival. The Festival is fun, a hotbed of gossip, and there are workshops and controversial speeches throughout the weekend, on all the talking points of the moment. My close friend Bryher and I love to go there together, taking in some of the late-night comedy from the Fringe of the festival, and enjoying a weekend in one of the most beautiful cities in the world.

On the Saturday we went to one of the hotel bars, where Peter Bazalgette was having a drink. I knew him well from his days as a researcher on *That's Life!*. Now he is one of the most creative and successful independent producers. He waved a copy of a newspaper at me, 'What is the *Sunday Telegraph* going to say about you?', he demanded. I had no idea. Nobody from the paper had contacted me at all. I looked at the headline he was pointing at, next to a hideous picture of me, it said it was going to reveal how I 'twist the facts'.

Keith Samuel, the BBC's most senior information officer, who was looking over my shoulder, offered to ring the paper to see if they would tell me what they were going to say about me, and if I would be allowed to comment. We were told brusquely that it was too late, the story was in print, and that if I didn't like it, I would have to write a letter to the paper the next week.

Bryher rang my hotel room the next morning. 'It's the most full-scale and personal attack I've ever read,' she said. She brought the paper to me, and I read it with disbelief. It was written by someone I had never heard of, John Ware, who was described as a distinguished *Panorama* reporter. He had devoted acres of print to me. The burden of the article was that we were quite wrong about the BHHI, which looked after its patients lovingly, and frankly the BBC should not allow inadequate journalists like us to make such programmes.

The violence of the attack was, as Bryher had said, quite alarming. Why did this John Ware feel so strongly? The article implied that it was because a friend of his, another *Panorama* reporter, Ian Smith, was a patient in the same hospital. He had had a tragic skiing accident and had suffered such severe brain damage he was being nursed in the

477

BHHI. John Ware described how he had read to Ian Smith there.

All the television journalists were at the Edinburgh Festival looking for stories and this one fell into their laps like manna. I tried to respond to their questions, but I was mystified, and our team of researchers and producers were, of course, back in London. I didn't realize until I flew back to London myself that Patsy Newey, the Executive Producer of the *Rantzen Report*, had received a phone call from Jan, Ian Smith's closest friend, as soon as the article appeared.

Jan had said she deeply disagreed with John Ware's article. She had tried to act as Ian's advocate in the hospital, but found it very difficult to be heard. Far from being satisfied with the treatment Ian was receiving at the BHHI, she was extremely concerned. We checked with Ian Smith's brother and mother. They both agreed with Jan, and were astonished and indignant to read the article. So that can't have been why John Ware had decided to defend the BHHI and attack me.

Jan explained one possible reason. She told us that although John Ware was married, he was going out with Wendy Robbins, a television presenter. Wendy's mother, Anita Robbins, worked as the Volunteer Co-ordinator—a senior executive at the BHHI.

There is a very important journalistic principle that you must declare your interests. When I presented the programme about ME I was careful to disclose right at the beginning that my own daughter Emily was a sufferer. If that meant some of the audience thought I was less than objective, so be it, but I had to declare it. I have since learned that John Ware prides himself on his research and his meticulous attention to detail in the programmes he makes. I find it very strange, therefore, that in his article he forgot to mention his personal connection with the hospital we had criticized.

The row went on. There are, as you will imagine, rules in the BBC about writing for publication. John Ware had not submitted his article to anyone in advance. I can understand why. As the newspaper was calling for my head on the block he would hardly have wished to warn anyone ahead of time. The BBC conducted an investigation after which he was reprimanded. I asked the Press Council to investigate. They decided they could not rule on the content of the article because John Ware was writing as a freelance, but the newspaper, they said, should have contacted me for a response before publishing.

The BHHI wrote to the Broadcasting Standards Commission (BSC) and asked them to investigate. The BBC asked me to attend the hearing. I desperately wanted to, but by the time the hearing happened I was laid low by a devastating bug I had caught while filming for a *Holiday* programme in Africa, and was confined to my bed.

In the event, the BSC decided we had made some mistakes in minor details in the programme—for instance, wrongly saying that the windows of Ian Parker's ward overlooked the fête. But far more importantly they came to the extraordinary decision that they could not make any judgement about the medical issues we raised—which were of course the point of the programme. Further, they upheld Mrs Kelly's complaint, and said that we had invaded the hospital's privacy by filming there. And yet we had filmed on a day when the BHHI was open to the public, and we had filmed Ian Parker with the permission of his mother.

As I have previously argued, if such a ruling were to be taken seriously it would make important investigations into closed institutions impossible. *That's Life!*, for example, would not have been able to show the indignity of mixed wards; and John Willis, twenty years ago, could not have revealed the cruel treatment in a notorious psychiatric hospital. Far from having the right to privacy, I believe every institution—from prisons to hospitals and residential homes—should have an obligation to be open and accountable.

There are, however, several happy outcomes to this story. John Ware and Wendy Robbins have a baby girl together. And I have had a letter recently from Janet Parker saying that because of our programme her son Ian has been moved from the BHHI to a more suitable hospital. There he has put on three stone in weight, and has a far more varied life, filled with activities, including outings to the local pub. Janet says that his case has acted as a legal precedent so that other patients who have been unhappy in their hospitals or nursing homes have been given the right to ask for more suitable accommodation. But still, sadly, we have not won the right to advocacy for patients who cannot speak for themselves.

Ian Parker's story is not unique. It is an immense problem for us to recognize that some patients who cannot speak, and cannot control their own facial expressions or their body's movements, may still have a lively intelligence. I first became aware of this when Toby Baylis, a further education lecturer, wrote to *That's Life!*. He had suddenly been struck down by an illness which had damaged his brain so severely that some of his doctors believed he was mentally and physically a cabbage. He heard them saying so as they discussed him across his bed. There was no way he could contradict them or argue. He could barely lift a hand, and couldn't smile or speak at all. Only his wife suspected the truth. She visited him regularly, and she could read his eyes. She always believed his mind had been left intact by his appalling illness, and that his brain was as sharp and intelligent as ever.

One summer he was transferred to another hospital for a few weeks during the holiday period. The letter accompanying him from the previous hospital said he had 'no mental ability', but the new consultant didn't agree. He suggested to Toby's wife that she should try to find a very light keyboard and let him try that.

The result was dramatic. Slowly, painfully, he moved his fingers over the keys and began to communicate. It took him three weeks to tell his story. He described his 'silent screams'. He urged his doctors to recognize that 'behind this dribbling whispering wreck of a man burns an intelligence worthy of restoration'. His letter to us was poetic in its strength and intelligence. Finding a means of communication was, he said, 'for me a voice at last. Let there be light, saith the Lord!'

I fear there are other patients in hospital wards round the country hearing themselves described as 'vegetables'. I can only hope that neurological tests will soon become sufficiently subtle and precise to detect a brain which is alive, intelligent, and monstrously frustrated by the inability to communicate.

*   *   *

The John Ware row came at a terrible time at home. The constant phone calls, the letters and memos that had to be composed at all times of day and night inevitably brought great stress into our house. Emily was gravely ill. The anxiety communicated itself to her and made her worse. A journalist came to talk to me about the controversy, and asked me about Emily. As I explained that she was lying all day in her bed in a darkened bedroom, my eyes filled with tears I could not hide.

By the summer of 1997 I was working hard. In addition to the daily BBC2 talk shows, I had been commissioned to make a documentary series for BBC1 about prostitutes. Then the Editor of the *Holiday* programmes rang and suggested I should make a film about my most memorable holiday. I could retrace my steps for the programme. I realized that would be an opportunity to take my younger daughter, Rebecca, back to Zimbabwe. Seven years before, I had been invited to go there to give a speech to a women's federation. We had had many adventures, including getting badly lost in the bush during a tropical rainstorm at night, and feeding orphan baby rhinos. I couldn't resist it, I said yes, I would love to go back there again with Rebecca.

The Zimbabwe trip was an exciting adventure. Rebecca and I found the orphan rhinos, now as large as tractors. We went on a walking safari, ducking behind bushes as we followed herds of elephants that could at any moment have turned and trampled us. We spent a few nights in a camp, living rough in little tents, with only a drooping strand of barbed wire to protect us from the animals that roamed through it every night.

One night a hyena broke in. We heard it clattering around the open kitchen looking for scraps. I lay sleepless, my heart thundering in my ears, listening to it. In the morning we found a metal sugar bowl crushed by its powerful jaws. Rebecca has the bowl still.

Our guide told us how he, as a boy, had gone on safari with his father. They had lit a fire, and slept either side of it, without even a tent to protect them. As the sun rose they woke, and saw in the ashes of the fire the perfect imprint of a lion's body. It had lain all night between them, enjoying the warmth of the cinders. Imagine waking up in the night to find a lion lying beside you. He told us the story by the flickering firelight of our own bonfire, and we shivered.

As it turned out, I was in danger in that camp, but not from lions or hyenas.

At mealtimes our guide urged us to drink the water. 'It comes from a very clean bore-hole,' he told us. Rebecca ignored him, and stuck with the cans of fizzy drink. Idiotically I drank glasses of water with each meal. Why? I admit it may well have been machismo on my part. I suppose I wanted to prove I could take on tougher assignments than street interviews with Annie in the North End Road.

When Desmond heard, he was furious with me:

483

'No real traveller would do that,' he said, and painstakingly explained to me that David Attenborough, and Alan Whicker, who are world-travellers, are always immensely careful not to drink the water. I, an ignorant stay-at-home, drank glasses filled from the bore-hole. The effect was to last more than two years.

I knew something was wrong the moment I returned home. This felt quite different from the tummy trouble I had often caught when travelling in exotic places before. But I had no time to investigate. I had to go away on location immediately, to interview the prostitutes who were the subject of my next series. The first, a beautiful woman called Talia, was one of the most fascinating and articulate interviewees I have ever met. Our conversation lasted three hours. I tried to tame my stomach by taking the stop-up pills which had always worked well in the past. Talia told me about her abusive childhood, showed me her working wardrobe, and described how she dealt with her clients.

At the end of the day, when I went back to my hotel, I realized I couldn't see. Not that my eyes weren't working, but that my brain refused to make sense of the images. I dragged myself to my room and fell on to the bed. I could just about ring Desmond. I described to him how I felt. He put it down to exhaustion, and lack of food. I had been unable to eat lunch. He, Jewish husband as he was, prescribed chicken soup for me. I ordered it, but when it arrived I couldn't touch it. I slept instead.

The next day I went back to London and visited a doctor. He told me I was suffering from stress. That would have been logical, except that I have always enjoyed stress, and use it as a kind of fuel. The doctor told me to rest. So, obediently, when I had finished the filming, I went to our cottage in the New Forest and rested. But although I was able to sleep and relax in my favourite refuge, I seemed to get worse and worse. I felt weak, I could hardly walk across the garden.

The talk show team came down to see me and discuss subjects for the next series. After twenty minutes I felt dizzy, and had to excuse myself and lie down. Looking back it seems quite ridiculous that I didn't realize I was ill. But I had always taken my body, my health and my energy for granted. That's dangerous. I was about to learn my lesson.

Gradually over the weeks new symptoms began to emerge. I became sleepless. My stomach gurgled and erupted, and felt bloated, with a high, unfamiliar ache. I went to a specialist. Seeing a middle-aged woman in front of him, he performed the classic tests upon me. I had cameras where no camera had been before. Extrovert as I may be, I didn't enjoy it. I lost a stone in weight. When I saw my own reflection I didn't recognize it. My skin was pale grey. I looked like a poster for some starving old people's charity. I lay in bed all day. My appetite had left me entirely. I existed on slivers of boiled chicken and plain boiled rice. Then I met a widely travelled doctor. He listened to me and said, 'Giardia'.

I do hope you never have to learn first-hand what *Giardia lamblia* are. They are as tiny as bacteria, but are in fact single-cell parasites. When they are clever they adapt to their host so that you can live a fairly normal life, although they do sap your strength and cause unpleasant symptoms.

They are notorious for being extremely difficult to trap and photograph under a microscope, because they hide very artfully, and are often confused with other conditions such as coeliac disease. When they are rampaging, as mine were, they knock you over, causing nausea, depression, fatigue, and all the other nasty symptoms I've described. They are water-borne. Hence the advice of seasoned travellers like my husband—on no account to drink the water.

It took six doctors to get me the diagnosis, and then the pills that eventually seized the *giardia* by the throat (not that a single cell has a throat, but by heaven I wish it had). Should you ever be overrun as I was, the drug that did the trick for me was Tinidazole. I also recommend the internet, which explains the various treatments for giardiasis, and tells you which are the most effective. Doctors may dispute this advice, and I am aware that you can't believe everything you read on the internet, but the experience of dozens of other patients across the world does make very valuable reading.

*   *   *

Throughout my illness the production team of the *Esther* talk show were incredibly patient. Patsy had to find replacements for me at the very last moment, and extremely good they were. One of them was Jill Dando—who was savagely murdered on her own doorstep. She met her fiancé, Alan Farthing, in my studio when she was presenting the programme. I only met Jill once, but like all her fans I found her enchanting. I wish I could claim to have played Cupid, but tragically it was not to be.

486

As soon as I possibly could I came back to work. The team were magnificently supportive. I remember ringing Desi from my dressing-room, describing my symptoms with self-pity and saying, 'I don't think I can make the programme'.

'Yes, you can,' he said. 'Push through the pain.'

Desmond was the most courageous man I ever met, so I tried to follow his advice and example. Slowly I got better, and the giardiasis retreated. It didn't cheer me up much that in my first studio debate there was one guest who told me he suffered from giardiasis for ten years, and another for fifteen. No wonder experts say no matter how clean the bore-hole, don't touch the water.

*   *   *

The series ended, and in the summer of 1998, the family headed back to the New Forest each weekend. My birthday arrived. The garden gleamed in the early morning sunshine, filled with blossom and butterflies. I seized a white chiffon hat, shaped like a meringue, threw off my nightdress, put on the hat and danced otherwise naked on the grass. Desmond tut-tutted, then ran to fetch his camera.

Why did I do it? Partly to amuse him, partly to prove there was life in the old girl yet, but mainly because it felt so good. Those are the reasons that all too many middle-aged women commit improprieties. Good for us, I say.

Desmond gave the unexposed film of my overexposed body to his assistant, Sue Santaub, hoping she would find somewhere in a distant suburb to print them. She took them round the corner to our local Snappy Snaps, who leered at her when she came to collect them and said, 'Esther enjoyed her birthday then?' Not that I minded. I had other things on my mind.

*   *   *

For a couple of months I had been unhappy about Desmond's health. He was suffering from chest pain, and sounding breathless. I urged him to go to a specialist. He did, and was told he was fit. So we drove down the motorway to the cottage. Desmond was still feeling unwell when we arrived, and went early to bed.

I woke at four in the morning to find Rebecca in the bedroom. She told me Desmond had gone to the bathroom, and she heard him there, crying out in agony. I went to find him. I have never seen a man in such pain. I ran to ring for an ambulance. Desmond roared at me not to. He said the pain would pass. I paid no attention. The ambulance arrived in fifteen minutes. They loaded him into it, Rebecca driving behind us in her Mini. I could see her through the back window, frowning with intense concentration as she tried to match our speed. It was lucky the road was completely empty.

We went into the Accident and Emergency Department of Southampton General Hospital. I heard Desmond explaining to the consultant that it was just pancreatitis, from which he had suffered before. She listened patiently. Then she said, 'Desmond, I can see from our graphs that you are having a heart attack, and we are trying to control it'. For the first time I saw my husband speechless.

They took him to the coronary ward, where a

group of young doctors surrounded him. They decided to administer a clot-busting drug. One of the young men started to tell me the possible side-effects. I didn't want to hear them. I told him to go ahead with the treatment. Rebecca steadily supported me. The cold, bleak, dawn hours wore on. Bright white hospital lights in the corridor burned into my brain. But by the time morning came, Desmond was responding well to the drugs. His consultant arrived, and they decided to put a stent in the blocked artery. They explained that a stent was like a little roll of chicken wire, keeping the walls of the artery apart so that the blood could flow through.

Gradually Desmond improved enough to be moved to another ward, where he was linked up to equipment supplied by the charity Wessex Heartbeat. That gave him huge satisfaction. He was one of their patrons and had raised money to buy the equipment.

After a few days the doctors let him come back to our cottage. It was crammed with flowers, bunches overflowing in the fireplace, and on every table and windowsill. I watched him reading the cards, forcing himself onwards, 'Pushing through the pain' as he had urged me. My heart filled. While he was wandering around our May garden, admiring the tulips and forget-me-nots, I rang our synagogue.

'Is it possible,' I asked, 'now that Desmond has converted to Judaism, for us to have a proper religious wedding ceremony in the synagogue?'

Our senior rabbi, David Goldberg, was reassuring. 'Yes, of course, it is'. Desmond came in and, overhearing the conversation, responded indignantly: 'What are you arranging, without consulting me?' he asked.

I explained that nothing was arranged, I was just asking the questions. He would not be mollified, until he saw tears in my eyes, and then, at once, he calmed down.

'I nearly lost you,' I said. 'I want everyone to know—our friends and family—how precious you are to me.'

He smiled, and we held each other.

Once more I tried to go back to work. But my heart was with Desmond. Battered by the *giardia*, which still lurked in my system and returned regularly to plague me, my head swam as I walked into the studio. I finished the first show, then collapsed in my dressing-room. There was a doctor in the audience who came to see me there. I told her what had happened. She said, 'Go home. There are some kinds of pain you must not ignore. You almost lost your husband. You must both look after yourselves.' I took her advice.

Desmond and I walked round our garden hand in hand. I told him my dream, that we would both retire and travel round the country together. I pointed out that he knew it far better than I, and he loved driving. I have never seen Hadrian's wall, or Portmeirion. He laughed at me, but I knew we would have such fun together. We always did, chattering away, buying souvenirs to remind us of special days, as Cyril had taught us so long ago. Gradually we both gained strength—I gaining mine from his recovery.

*   *   *

A few weeks later I was getting dressed, listening as I always did to Radio 4, when I heard something that first turned me cold, then hot with anger. With growing incredulity I realized what I was hearing. It was a programme I had invented myself. A few months earlier, a talented young radio producer, Sara, had interviewed me with my mother and at the end of the recording she had asked me for ideas. There was a new controller for Radio 4, she said, and he wanted fresh new programmes.

I told her of the idea I had, inspired by my television talk show. I explained it would consist of two people who shared a rare experience, each of whom believed that they were unique, but who suddenly found they had everything in common with each other. I described the two women who had completely lost their memories—and the two whose children had been stolen from them.

The young producer was very interested, and promised to put my concept forward. She then wrote me a letter saying that the controller might think it more suitable for a different time slot. Thank heavens she wrote, otherwise nothing would have been on paper. I was naive, but then I had worked for the BBC for thirty years. I had no reason not to trust the Corporation. When I realized that I was listening to the programme I had invented, I waited to hear the credit at the end of the programme. It came. It was now called *Between Ourselves* and was produced by Sara, the producer I had spoken to, the very same talented woman who had written to me about it.

What had happened? I understand that Sara has always readily admitted it was my idea. So presumably someone somewhere higher up had decided they liked the idea, but wanted someone else to present it. Had they said so to me I would have agreed with alacrity. I am a producer, and love my ideas being turned into programmes. All I asked was a credit, and a small fee per programme to prove it was my idea. They agreed to credit me, but only on the first and the last programmes in the series. They offered a fee, but on two conditions. They wanted all the rights, even if it went to television, and I must keep the contract secret. I didn't like those clauses. So, as I write, the matter is still unresolved.

Why do I care so much? Because I'm proud of the idea. And I am proud of the programmes. They are just what I hoped they would be—revealing and illuminating. My concept has produced excellent conversation. And also because I hate to feel that the BBC, for whom I have worked so happily for so many years, has treated me shabbily. It's like catching a well-loved granny stealing ten pence out of your money-box.

So I have decided it must be a mistake. Not mean or malicious. Just a clerical error. The BBC does occasionally make them. Some of them are delicious. My most recent contract negotiation is a case in point.

When the time came to renew my contract, the bosses discussed the minimum fee they could pay me, and the maximum. They laid it all out in a pretty diagram. They recognized that there were risk factors in the negotiation because, for instance, they had doubled the length of the programme without raising my fee. And, they said, I had a new agent, who might want to show her strength.

How do I know all this? Because the confidential

memo that the Head of Contracts sent was copied round the BBC. He e-mailed the controller of the channel, the daytime commissioners, my head of department, and Claire Skinner.

I stood it for three weeks, then rang them: 'Who is Claire Skinner?' I asked.

'A finance clerk,' they said.

'No, she's not,' I said, 'she's my P. A.'

Every detail of their proposed negotiation had been carefully copied by them to my P.A.

It did no harm. I giggled for three weeks, so did Claire. Then I settled for the top offer, without haggling, and my agent, Jan Kennedy, settled for the fee with some sadness but great dignity. So if the BBC could make that mistake, perhaps putting my idea on the air without telling me, crediting me, or paying me, was a simple clerical error as well. I do hope so. And I hope they put it right.

*   *   *

In 1998, for the first time, I started to work for ITV, making a Sunday morning programme called *That's Esther.* It was designed as a social action programme, dealing with campaigns, with disability issues, and interviewing celebrities about their favourite charities. I enjoyed presenting the show alongside two gifted young women.

Heather Mills is an extraordinary character. She used to be labelled the 'one-legged model' having been the victim of a road accident. Now she is labelled 'Paul McCartney's girlfriend'. Neither label does her justice. She is determined, difficult, creative, and has set up her own charity, the Heather Mills Health Trust. She works tirelessly for other amputees, especially children, whom she helps by demonstrating how in her own life she has refused to allow her disability to hold her back. She skis, she models, her interests are too wide to be boxed into our programme, and she is in demand all over the world as a motivational speaker. So she left us, but I am delighted to have worked with her.

Lara Masters is also outstanding, both in her own personal achievements and as a campaigner. She has a spinal disability which means she has to use a wheelchair, but that does not affect her optimism nor the fact that she is extremely sexy and attractive. Although it is a gruelling ordeal for her to travel across the country to film her reports, her determination forces her on. She loves working in television, and the camera loves her. She wants to act, and recently starred in a controversial film made for the cinema, designed specifically to change attitudes to disabled people. I am proud to work alongside her, impertinent as she often is to me, in spite of my age and wisdom.

*   *   *

Once Desmond had got used to the idea of marrying me again, he embraced the idea. We picked the date of our wedding anniversary, December 2, and booked the same place for our reception, Searcy's, where we had held our first one twenty-one years before. The first time, eight months pregnant, I had worn an enormous blue chiffon tent. This time I decided to splash out with the dress I chose, after all you're only a bride twice, and I went to Princess Diana's favourite designer, Catherine Walker.

Catherine was tough with me. When I wanted something long and flowing she refused. She insisted that I show my only good feature, my legs. I bought a hat from Philip Somerville, a huge honey-and-cream concoction covered with roses. Things were going well.

As I drove back on Friday from the last fitting for my dress, the phone rang in my car. It was Desmond. 'I've just been for a test,' he said. 'They said I may have to have another operation. The stent has blocked.'

I don't know how we got through that weekend. The medical team filled Desmond with drugs to stop his blood clotting further in the blocked artery. He went in for more tests on Monday. I didn't need to be told the results. I had seen his breathlessness and tiredness increase week by week, and by now I could read the signs. We went into hospital together on Tuesday. His cardiologist, Rodney Foale, came in to talk to him. Desmond wasn't listening to the alternatives. He would not for one moment consider life as a permanent invalid.

'Do the operation,' he said.

'Who would be the surgeon?' I asked.

'Did you have someone in mind?' Rodney asked.

I had spent the night with my favourite book, the *Good Doctor Guide*, by Catherine Vassallo. It's a consumer guide to doctors.

'Rex Stanbridge,' I said.

'Just who I had in mind,' said Rodney.

Then he took me out of earshot into a very cramped washroom.

'Does Desmond know the risks?' he asked.

'He's made his decision,' I said. 'He is the most

courageous man I know, he has survived dangers and adventures that should have killed him a hundred times. He understands the risks. He is prepared to face them.'

*   *   *

On the day that Desmond was operated on, I offered to make the scheduled talk shows. Patsy and Anne Morrison, my head of department, scolded me and refused to let me. So I waited at home. The phone calls from the surgeon took an age to come. The operation lasted far longer than I expected. Later, far later, I learned there had been a multi-organ failure—his liver, kidney and lungs. Desmond had almost died. But he wasn't ready to go yet. On the day we should have married I arrived in his room in a Catherine Walker going-away dress, with a Philip Somerville hat, all in the brightest scarlet. I wasn't ready to let him go either.

Three days after the operation Will Wyatt, the Chief Executive of BBC Broadcast, organized a party to celebrate my thirty years on BBC television. It was a glamorous dinner in the Council Chamber, with many of my friends and colleagues. Will, the BBC's wittiest speechmaker, was on great form. He told anecdotes about me which I suppose I must believe. He said that when I was honoured with an OBE, I arrived at the next *That's Life!* production meeting and told the team that nothing would change, I would expect to be treated exactly as before. While I was saying this, I took a tinsel tiara out of my handbag, and jammed it on to my head.

He said that when Chris Choi, now a

distinguished ITN reporter, joined our team as a researcher, during his first briefing I started to rub my leg in a worried way. I was wearing trousers, but I had discovered a very big lump on one calf. I reached inside the trouser leg and, by my ankle, found the toe of a black stocking. I handed the toe to Chris and asked him to pull. Slowly, the stocking emerged, followed by a suspender belt and another stocking. I'm afraid that anecdote was true, too. I was only grateful at the time that the stockings and suspender belt had not been followed by a pair of knickers.

When it was my turn to speak, I looked round the table and all I could see was my husband, pale, transparent at the edges, but having a wonderful party, radiating, as someone said recently, love and laughter. Once again, just when I didn't want it to happen, I choked with tears—this time with tears of love and thankfulness.

We had been due to go on honeymoon to the Bahamas just after Christmas with the whole family. Even though we had cancelled our wedding, we decided to have the honeymoon. We looked a strange straggling caravan of a family at the airport, with Desmond and Emily both in wheelchairs. Michael and Shakira Caine came over to talk to us and sympathize, which gained me huge street credibility in my children's eyes. Not much impresses them, but that did.

A photographer from *Hello!* magazine joined us on holiday and took some of the best photographs I have ever seen of the family together. Desmond was relaxed, Emily looked gorgeous, her health steadily improving, Rebecca and Joshua looking glamorous, too. Never having been at all glamorous myself, I find it extraordinary that my children should have turned out so well. Desmond must have had gorgeous genes.

We rearranged the wedding for May 20. I went to the synagogue beforehand to discuss the music, and explain why I wanted to surprise Desmond with 'September Song' while the marriage certificate was being signed. I told the musical director how he used to sing it to me, 'and the days dwindle down, to a precious few—these golden days I'll spend with you'. Once again my tears embarrassed me.

As tradition dictated, I spent the night before the wedding away from my husband-to-be. Less conventionally, I had my daughter Rebecca with me, since she was to be our bridesmaid. Emily, alas, was still too ill to come to the wedding. As Rebecca and I got dressed in the luxurious Lanesborough Hotel, I was amazed how nervous I was. Rabbi Goldberg gave Desmond a few drops of Rescue remedy before we started, obviously worried about his heart.

I was dizzy with fear. Why? I was about to marry the man I adored, and had lived with for thirty years. But for me this was a frighteningly serious moment. It was a spiritual commitment, a public gesture in front of my community of friends and family, in the centre of my Jewish faith. I saw the canopy, the chupah, waiting for me just as I had seen it waiting for a hundred brides, and my feet faltered.

Desmond, of course, was solid as a rock. I had chosen his favourite music, a Klezmer band, like the musicians in the film *Fiddler on the Roof*, and a wonderful singer, Jane Emanuel, to sing the religious music in the ceremony, and then 'September Song'. Rabbi Goldberg gave a superb sermon, pointing out Desmond's religious Orthodoxy to the great delight of the Jews in the congregation, and the baffled amusement of the non-Jews. What fun we had.

*   *   *

For our honeymoon we decided to spend a few days together at our cottage. Giardiasis had put me off travelling far. Even when I go to the Isle of Wight these days I take a bottle of mineral water with me. I told Desmond I would cook for him on our wedding night. He looked dubious. I explained that I thought the meal should consist of beluga caviare. So all I would need to cook would be hot toast, hard-boiled egg yolk, and finely chopped onions.

Desmond bought a tin of beluga. When it arrived he thought it looked rather small for two, so he bought another. The bill for two tins would have covered a night in a very smart hotel, but we preferred it our way.

Over the years we have changed our cottage garden to suit the family as they grew. When we first bought it, the wide lawns had been perfect for games of French cricket. As the children grew older I began to dream of streams and ponds. Our garden designer, Sarah Eberle, listened to my dreams and made them concrete. Or rather, instead of concrete she filled plastic liners with golden boulders and reeds and irises. They looked natural and beautiful until the ponds grew lumps of disgusting green algae. I went to our local water garden centre and described the problem. The owner said, 'I'll send our manager to look at it this evening. She lives round your way'.

As evening fell a green truck arrived in our drive. Someone got out, pulled on a pair of waders, then lifted a basket of lilies and tramped up the garden to the pond. She strode into the middle of the water and started to heave out hanks of slime. 'This is very satisfying,' she told me, with a lilt of a Hampshire accent.

I stared at her. So did Roy, our gardener, eighty years old and one of my best friends. There, standing in the middle of my pond in front of us, was the most ravishing woman I had ever seen. She had flowing red-gold hair, wide blue eyes, and a straight nose that a Greek sculptor would love to immortalize. She had not a trace of make-up, and clearly no vanity either. When I got to know her better she told me she was making a 'little television programme. It's fun because we all get on so well'.

Then I saw her picture in the newspaper and congratulated her. 'Wait till you see what the *Radio Times* has done to me,' she said. 'It's embarrassing. I'm going to try and buy up all the copies.'

I did see the *Radio Times*. It was hard to miss. She was all over the cover, wearing nothing but flowers and trailing ivy, doing a very exact impression of Botticelli's 'Venus'. She, of course, is Charlie Dimmock, now the toast of the nation, whether they garden or not.

On the evening of our wedding Charlie arrived at the cottage with a bottle of champagne and we all drank it together. Then Desmond and I sat in the evening glow by our pond, piling dollops of caviare onto hot toast. Although I say it as shouldn't, I cooked it well. We talked together about our future. Up to then we had always been a pair of workaholics, but now I told Desmond I was concerned that we spent so little time together. Our happiest times were when we were simply pottering about at the weekends, or on holiday. We always found so much to talk about and amuse each other. We learned from each other. We explored the countryside together. But these moments were far too brief, stolen from an over-stuffed life. So much of every year was spent in studios or on location.

I tried to persuade Desmond that over the next year we should cut back on our work. But I couldn't convince him. He had been earning his own living since he was fifteen. There was nothing he enjoyed more than putting his travel kit together—visas, first aid, alarm clock, family photographs, and setting off on an adventurous location. And there was a vital film yet to make.

After he left the BBC and became an independent producer, Desmond created more than ninety films for *The Visit* series. These included profiles of Ray Barnett, who collected orphans from African countries ravaged by war and famine, and turned them into choirs which fund-raise all over the world, paying for their keep and education. And Pat Kerr, the British Airways stewardess who created an orphanage in Bangladesh.

Desmond made the first 'docusoap', a series of films called *The Marriage*, which followed an attractive lusty Welsh couple who were about to get married. The series reached audiences of twelve

501

million, and although the critics had doubts that the marriage would succeed, they were quite wrong. The couple are not only extremely happy, they have four delightful children.

The most memorable of all Desmond's films told the story over twenty years of the Boy David, David Jackson, the Peruvian boy whose face was almost entirely destroyed by disease. David's face was rebuilt by surgeon, Ian Jackson, who with his wife, Marjorie, adopted David. In the autumn of 1999 Desmond, with Alex McCall and the rest of his team, were to make one last chapter, as David went back to Peru to see his own birthplace.

So we carried on as we had always done, pounding the television conveyor belt. I made my studio talk shows for the BBC, and my campaigning programmes for ITV. Desmond made his film with David, and a documentary about the Millennium Wheel.

The children were working equally hard. By now Rebecca, having achieved straight A's for all her A-levels, was studying English at Somerville College, Oxford. I tried not to burst too obviously with pride. Joshua was taking his A-levels, with an extraordinary spread of subjects, English, Physics, Maths and Chemistry. Emily had enrolled in a college in Kensington to take business studies, and was determinedly independent, living in a hostel during the week.

Despite all this activity, I knew that Desmond believed he didn't have much time left with us. And as I watched his tiredness grow and his strength fail, I shared his anxiety. Each night as we curled in each other's arms, I would ask him, 'Do you know how much you are loved? What a wonderful husband and father you are? How admired you are for your talent?' He would grunt contentedly. But I also knew the fear in his heart, and mine. Would that agonizing pain strike him again tonight? And in the small hours, when we are all at our most vulnerable, he would whisper to me, 'I can't go through that again'. I would hug him and pray that he wouldn't have to.

*   *   *

Our last six months together were filled with lovely moments to remember. We spent New Year's Eve at the foot of the Millennium Wheel, watching the fireworks burst in an explosive fiery haze over the river. In March I plotted with the *This Is Your Life* team to surprise Desmond. We succeeded, but typically he surprised us, too. Most subjects of the programme are so overwhelmed with shock and pleasure that they say little or nothing themselves. Desmond was irrepressible.

When Charlie Dimmock talked about the water garden she had helped to create for us, he said, 'Water feature? She's turned it into the Grand Canyon'. When Michael Aspel described how he had been blinded by a gangster and had to be operated on by a surgeon in Switzerland, Desmond said, 'Yes, I was in hospital in Berne. But Berne's so boring it really doesn't matter if you've lost your sight'. Sadly most of his wickedness had to be cut from the programme, but the producers let me have a copy of the unedited version, a rare privilege. For Desmond the high spot of the programme was seeing Emily walk towards him, unaided and without her wheelchair, to embrace

503

him.

The summer was a series of treats. I celebrated my sixtieth birthday with several parties—one on a boat, another in our cottage. We had our family and friends about us, and Desmond made loving speeches to me that made me blush. We spent a weekend in New York. We did all the right things together. We went to see *Kiss Me Kate*, a superb production which showed why for years American musicals ruled the world. We took a rickshaw to the Stage Delicatessen, which served us chopped liver and salt-beef sandwiches which made our jaws drop. They looked as high as the Empire State building.

We took the QE2 back across the Atlantic, Desmond lecturing about his life as a journalist. Then he interviewed me, and I him, interspersing our questions with marital rudeness which the audience loved. If only the BBC rules had allowed it, we would have been a great double act. On the ship he met an old friend, Harry Evans, the finest newspaper editor of our generation, and they made plans together to make a film from Harry's most recent book about America.

The first weekend in September we spent with our friends Paul and Bryher in the south of France, in St Paul de Vence, a medieval village in the mountains behind Nice. Desmond and I stood on a balcony overlooking the sweep of the valley, holding hands. We vowed that we would come back together every year at that time. If we couldn't return together we promised that we would come back alone, and drink a toast to our missing partner. If that sounds morbid or gloomy, we didn't feel it. I have pictures of Desmond that show his eyes shining with happiness. We had never loved each other more, or had happier days and nights together.

On the Monday we were back at work. I was writing this book, and struggling to meet my deadline, as usual, so I stayed in the cottage. Desmond, who had a meeting of the BAFTA Council, went to London. He cared deeply about his work on the Council, and was convinced that it was crucial to defend the ever-eroding standards in the new television age, when skill and craft were being lost to the new philosophy of 'pile 'em high, sell 'em cheap'. Desmond always loved the craft of making good programmes. He chose the finest craftsmen to work with—cameramen, soundmen, editors—all of whom equally loved working with such an appreciative producer.

On Tuesday afternoon I drove up to London. As I approached Shepherd's Bush my phone rang. Sue Santaub, Desmond's PA, was bravely controlling her anxiety as she told me that he had collapsed at lunch with a suspected heart attack. I drove straight to the hospital, St Mary's Paddington, where his cardiac team were waiting for him to arrive by ambulance. Rodney Foale, his cardiologist, had assured Sue that the latest bypass was so strong, it couldn't have given way. He was right, it hadn't. But Desmond himself knew exactly what had happened.

As I arrived at the Accident and Emergency unit I heard him telling the consultant that something had ripped inside his chest. In fact, it was a major blood vessel.

There was no way to repair it. A doctor came to tell me. Terror struck me like a bolt of lightning.

How could I go and see Desmond with that knowledge in me? I couldn't bear to frighten him. By now Emily had arrived, and with her help I collected myself and went to his bedside. He was in great pain. I insisted to the doctors that he should be given enough pain relief to make him comfortable. They said the drugs would depress his breathing. I looked at them in consternation. What possible harm could that do now? They gave him the morphine he needed, and his mind cleared at once.

His children gathered round him so that he could say goodbye to them. His oldest daughter, Cassandra, was now back in England with her husband and her baby daughter, Rosie. Emily, Rebecca and Joshua had rushed to his bedside from various parts of the country, and I saw them gazing at him, memorizing his face. He looked at them and said, 'My lovelies'.

For ten sweet minutes he lay with his arms about me, before the medical team pulled us apart to perform yet more tests. I wondered then why these were necessary, and I wonder that still. Later in the evening, Desmond took off his oxygen mask, kissed me and said, 'I adore you'. I told him how much I adored him, too. At another time he looked far into the distance ahead of him and said, 'There *is* a bright white light'. The nurse thought he meant the light in the ceiling. I knew he was seeing something else.

As the night wore on I rushed home with Emily to collect our Jewish prayer books. A doctor rang me there to say his heart had arrested, but they had resuscitated him. We drove back to find him breathing lightly but regularly, his eyes closed. We read from the prayer books, and recited the Shema, the prayer which is the core of Judaism, and which Desmond carried in his wallet wherever he went. Then I put my arms around him and sang the two songs he loved most, 'She Moved Through the Fair,' and 'September Song'. My voice broke as I sang to him. But as I ended, the nurse standing behind us said, 'Look, he's smiling', and he was.

And so Desmond died. It was peaceful, gradual, not like a bitter battle, but a gentle retreat. As life left him he hardly changed. We held his hands until we knew we had to let go. Then I took his wedding ring and put it on my hand, where it is now. The children took tiny locks of his hair, and the next day Sue's husband Mel very carefully put them into silver lockets. I looked through his wallet, and, next to the Shema, found a love letter I had written to him twenty years ago. I carry one of his in my wallet, too.

By an extraordinary chance, Desmond died on September 6. So, too, in 1992, did my father. They were the two strong men in my life, the men I loved, and who moulded me. My father's death had been from heart failure. Like Desmond he had no deterioration, at ninety he was fit and vigorous, mentally and physically. They were always friends in life. I hope they are playing chess contentedly together in heaven.

The morning Desmond died Cassie and I spoke to Adam and Claire, Desmond's twins who live in Australia, and they instantly made arrangements to fly to England for the funeral. The Press Association asked me for a statement. I told them we felt as if the sunshine had left our lives. Desmond must have heard me. On the day of the

507

funeral the sun shone as bright and warm as a summer's day.

I had asked for two dozen long-stemmed red roses to be placed on his coffin, the kind of roses he used to give me every Valentine's Day and wedding anniversary. A shaft of sunlight blazed through one window and lit the roses as they lay there. Rabbi Goldberg once again delivered a perfect sermon, affectionate, admiring, and witty. Desmond would have loved it.

So we all struggled to keep our lives together without the funny, loving man who had protected and energized us all. I could hear his voice in my head, urging us to 'push through the pain'. All six of his children responded with the strength and courage they have inherited from him. Emily, Rebecca and Joshua stood about me like a shield. They never let me be alone, even sleep alone in those early days.

When I went to address the Samaritans' Conference in York, Joshua kept me company. To my astonishment the 1200 Samaritan volunteers gave me a standing ovation, but then it was an assembly of some of the most compassionate people in the country, trained to befriend and support others in pain.

From the moment the news bulletins carried Desmond's death, we were deluged with sympathetic letters and bushels of flowers. I do hope Desmond realized how greatly he was loved. There were letters from the Prime Minister, Tony Blair, and Cherie Booth, from Prince Edward and the Director-General, from John Birt and Michael Grade. Letter after letter described spontaneous acts of kindness and generosity by a man who could not see need or sadness without instantly providing the necessary help. Time and again they told me that working with Desmond was the happiest period of their working lives.

I also had letters from countless people who had figured in his programmes over the years, saying that he had treated them with dignity and respect, and that the films he made had left them better than he had found them. How many other programme-makers, the smash and grab merchants, the clever boys who mock and exploit their subjects, could have tributes like these?

Desmond had been due to receive an honorary doctorate from South Bank University on November 2. He had gloated horribly about it, claiming it was a far better degree than mine. Imagine my guilt when the university wrote to me after his death expressing their sympathy, and saying that they would confer the degree on me instead.

The day of the ceremony was stormy and overcast. I told Gerald Bernbaum, the Vice-Chancellor, that I feared Desmond in heaven would be furious, so we should beware of thunderbolts. At that very moment there was a huge thunderclap, followed by four more. We picked our way through the heavy rain to Southwark Cathedral, where the ceremony was to take place. There I realized that I was to be presented with two honorary doctorates, one for Desmond, the other for me.

As I stood in the appointed spot, listening to the eulogy about him, another shaft of sunlight suddenly gleamed through one of the cathedral windows, and I was bathed in light. Sue, his PA, sitting in the front row, and I both knew who was responsible. Desmond had forgiven me for collecting his degree.

*   *   *

The most difficult production of my life, far harder and more taxing than any television programme, was Desmond's memorial service. But it was only difficult emotionally. Practically, Desmond had left very clear instructions, which I followed obediently. He wanted 'September Song' of course, so I asked Dame Cleo Laine to sing it with her husband, John Dankworth.

As Cleo sang in her gorgeous autumnal voice. 'These golden days, I'll spend with you,' I covered my eyes to hide my tears. They had indeed been golden, those last days we spent together. Desmond had told me he wanted me to sing 'She Moved Through the Fair', but, having sung it to him as he left me, I knew I would not be able to sing it without breaking down. Not only that, but my voice has dropped two octaves since the day twenty years ago when I sang it to him on Bantry Bay.

Luckily, my niece, my sister Priscilla's daughter Kate, has a lovely soprano voice. She flew over with Priscilla from Australia, and sang it perfectly. The Reverend Dr Colin Morris (once Head of Religious Broadcasting at the BBC, who worked next door to Desmond and was awestruck by his vocabulary), gave the address, describing my husband as a man who radiated love and laughter. David (Boy David) Jackson flew from America to pay tribute to the man he cared deeply for because he knew Desmond 'loved me as I am, for what I am'.

The music, the poetry and the laughter embellished the serious heart of the service, which was Desmond's faith in God. Not that his was a conventional faith. As a Jew he had insisted that his service should be held in the Church of St Martin-in-the-Fields. It was unusual. But thanks to the sensitivity of the vicar, the minister and the rabbi, it made perfect ecumenical sense.

Children played a great part in the memorial service, as was appropriate for a man who loved children and fought all his life to protect them from pain. His own children acted as the narrators and paid tribute to him. Two young choristers from Salisbury Cathedral sang Lloyd Webber's wonderful *Pie Jesu*.

And the climax of the service was a joyous performance by the African Children's Choir, about whom, as I have said, Desmond had made a captivating film. The choir was founded by Ray Barnett, who described in his introduction how the children had instantly adopted 'Uncle Desmond' when he filmed them.

Ray taught me one of the most valuable lessons in my life, when I first met him. I had asked him how he could continue his work rescuing orphans and creating a new life for them when so many more were starving or being killed all over Africa. Surely the problem was just too big for anyone to solve? Ray nodded. 'But then you must remember the starfish story,' he said. And told it to me.

A man who was walking along a seashore, rounded a bend and saw the next beach was covered with thousands of starfish. A freak wave

511

had swept them up on to the sand, and they were lying there, dying under the hot sun. In the distance he could see another man, a ragged, sunburnt figure, moving between the sand dunes and the edge of the sea. He was curious. He walked up the beach until he reached the man and saw that he was carrying starfish one by one from the burning sand, and dropping them back into the water. He couldn't resist asking him why.

'There are thousands on the beach here,' he said. 'What's the point? You can't really make any difference.'

'You're probably right,' the man said. 'But look.' He dropped one into the water. 'I made a difference to this one. And,' he picked up another and dropped it into the sea, 'I made a difference to that one, too.'

*   *   *

What of the future? I am on the brink of an entirely new life, without Desmond, my friend and lover, the inspiration for my work. My mirror makes me face the fact every day that I am a sixty-year-old woman, working in a highly competitive medium where youth is prized above all. Should I give in gracefully? Must I sell the house which is filled with the memories of our happiness together, and move into a retirement bungalow by the sea?

Recently for my ITV show I interviewed two pensioners. One was Joan Collins. At sixty-seven her face was without a line or a blemish. Her hair was a mass of billowing dark curls. She wore a cream trouser suit, with a sparkling butterfly on her lapel. I asked if she was thinking of retiring. She looked at me as if I was mad and retorted sharply, 'No, are you?'

The other was a footballing granny from Middlesbrough, Mary Maughan, aged ninety-two. She was wearing the scarlet football strip of her team, 'The Argylle Bombers'. Her face was tanned and weather-beaten, she had white feathery hair and a broad grin.

At the end of the programme Joan and Mary, the two grannies, sat down beside me and talked together. The recording ended, and Joan started to leave the studio, swaying her hips with a *Dynasty* swagger. Ninety-two year old Mary looked after her and said, 'Oh, I do hope I'm as pretty as that when I'm her age'. Joan, without turning, said, 'Good one'.

I have so many marvellous moments to look back on in my life, but why look back when you can look forward? Those two pensioners have shown me the way. I do hope I can be as stylish, as witty, and above all as gutsy as they are, when I'm their age.

Desmond has asked me to plant a grove of trees in his memory on the hill above our cottage. I have planted winter prunus, to flower in the bleakest coldest months in winter; scarlet holly for Christmas; woody azaleas for their fragrant spring flowers; and red oak for its autumn colour.

They are only saplings now, but in time they'll grow. We'll put a seat up on the hill under their branches. We'll take a picnic for our family and friends, perhaps a little caviare and champagne. I'll cook the toast. And we'll drink to Desmond's memory. There's time for a few more golden days yet.